TimeOut
London

LONDON'S
BEST
BARS

timeout.com

**FIND A HUNDRED PEOPLE
IN A ROOM THAT FITS FIFTY
AND YOU'LL FIND**

FINDKOPPARBERG.COM

Contents

London's Best Bars	5
About the Listings	7
Where to Go for...	9

Cocktails & Spirits	19
Hotel Bars	39
Wine Bars	47
Classic Pubs	59
Beer Specialists	107
Gastropubs & Brasseries	127
Rooms with a View	159
Good Mixers	171
Gay Bars	199
Clubs & Music Venues	203

A-Z Index	222
Advertisers' Index	228
Area Index	229
Maps	235

Published by

Time Out Guides Limited
Universal House
251 Tottenham Court Road
London W1T 7AB
Tel +44 (0)20 7813 3000
Fax +44 (0)20 7813 6001
email guides@timeout.com
www.timeout.com

Editorial

Editor John Shandy Watson
Written by Peterjon Cresswell and Will Fulford-Jones,
with additional reviews by Simone Baird, William Crow,
Guy Dimond, Euan Ferguson, Kate Hutchinson,
Ben McFarland, Susan Low, Charmaine Mok,
Francis Percival and Jamie Warburton
Researchers William Crow, Jamie Warburton
Proofreader Ismay Atkins

Managing Director Peter Fiennes
Editorial Director Sarah Guy
Series Editor Cath Phillips
Business Manager Daniel Allen
Editorial Manager Holly Pick
Assistant Management Accountants Margaret Wright,
Clare Turner

Design

Art Director Scott Moore
Art Editor Pinelope Kourmouzoglou
Senior Designer Kei Ishimaru
Guides Commercial Designer Jodi Sher

Picture Desk

Picture Editor Jael Marschner
Acting Deputy Picture Editor Liz Leahy
Picture Desk Assistant/Researcher Ben Rowe

Advertising

New Business & Commercial Director Mark Phillips
Magazine & UK Guides Commercial Director
St John Betteridge
Account Managers Jessica Baldwin, Michelle Daburn,
Ben Holt
Copy Controller Alison Bourke

Marketing

Guides Marketing Manager Colette Whitehouse
Group Commercial Art Director Anthony Huggins

Production

Group Production Manager Brendan McKeown
Production Controller Katie Mulhern

Time Out Group

Chairman & Founder Tony Elliott
Chief Executive Officer David King
Chief Operating Officer Aksel Van der Wal
Group Financial Director Paul Rakkar
Group General Manager/Director Nichola Coulthard
Time Out Communications Ltd MD David Pepper
Time Out International Ltd MD Cathy Runciman
Time Out Magazine Ltd Publisher/MD Mark Elliott
Group Commercial Director Graeme Tottle
Group IT Director Simon Chappell
Group Marketing Director Andrew Booth

Thanks to Claire Boobbyer, Guy Dimond, Mina Holland, Anna Norman and Khoo Hui Shan.

Maps John Scott, john@jsgraphics.co.uk.

Cover photography by Rob Lawson. **Drink styling** by Alex Kammerling.

Photography pages 7, 14 (bottom), 29, 32, 44, 49, 89, 125, 129 (top right, bottom left), 147 (top), 197 (left), 153, 166, 212, 214, 217, 218 Jonathan Perugia; pages 9, 34 (bottom), 38, 69, 79, 109, 133, 154, 157 Michael Franke; pages 10, 26, 36, 43, 46, 54, 123, 173, 174 (bottom), 193 Britta Jaschinksi; pages 12, 34 (top), 129 (top left, bottom right), 197 (right) Ming Tang-Evans; page 16 (bottom) Alys Tomlinson; pages 22, 103, 202 Heloise Bergman; pages 23, 122, 194 Thomas Skovsende; pages 30, 58, 136, 139, 140, 165 Tricia de Courcy Ling; pages 41 (right), 181 Hayley Harrison; pages 53, 63, 72, 78, 97, 100, 110, 114, 143, 147, 149, 150, 161, 162, 169 Rob Greig; pages 68, 84 (left), 145, 164 Nick Ballon; page 71 Nina Kelly; pages 81, 84 (right), 90, 92, 146 Nerida Howard; page 83 www.simonleigh.com; page 87 Ed Marshall; page 93 Vizualeyez Ltd; pages 95, 190 Gemma Day; page 101 Christina Theisen; page 104 Oliver Knight; page 116 Will Robson-Scott; page 146 Moe Kafer; page 168 Kate Beatty; pages 178, 206, 220 Rogan MacDonald; page 189 Anthony Webb; page 205 David Axelbank; page 207 Craig Dean.

The following images were supplied by the featured establishments: pages 18 (top), 24, 41 (left), 121, 182, 213.

Printed by Wyndenham Peterborough Ltd, Storey's Bar Road, Peterborough, Cambridgeshire PE1 5YS.

Distribution by Comag Specialist (01895 433 800).

ISBN 978-1-905042-61-6
ISSN 2047-0932

London's
Best Bars

Welcome to the Time Out guide to *London's Best Bars*, a comprehensive round-up of the 500 finest places to drink in the city. You'll find a huge variety of venues within these pages, from old-fashioned pubs to cutting-edge cocktail bars. The only rule for inclusion is that the pubs and bars featured here are among the best in their particular field.

London's Best Bars is divided into ten themed sections, which are detailed in brief below. Of course, many venues fit comfortably into more than one category: hotel bars that serve great cocktails; gastropubs with excellent beers; classic pubs with impressive wine lists; and so on. To take this into account, we've included each venue in the category that we think suits it best, but have also added a set of additional recommendations that directs you to other worthwhile venues that are featured in full elsewhere in the book.

Within each themed section, the bars are divided by area: central London, north London, north-east and so on. At the back of the book, you'll find a full A-Z of venues featured in the book, along with a separate neighbourhood index so you can easily find all the venues in your particular part of town.

Cocktails & Spirits
The 40 venues in this section deal in everything from traditional martinis to elaborate molecular concoctions.

Hotel Bars
Nothing says London luxury like a cocktail-fuelled retreat in one of the city's hotel bars. These are our favourites.

Wine Bars
The rise in popularity of wine in London has been reflected in the recent rise in the number and quality of wine bars, with new ventures joining old favourites all over town.

Classic Pubs
It's hard to define a classic pub, but we usually know one when we see one. The category is a broad church, home to everything from dimly lit neighbourhood taprooms to airy, spruced-up taverns in the middle of town.

Beer Specialists
Most of the 50 or so venues in this section specialise in real ale, but others cast their net wider: head here for details of where to find the finest brews from Belgium, the Czech Republic and the USA.

Gastropubs & Brasseries
You can simply drink in all these venues – but they've really been included here because they also serve excellent food.

Rooms with a View
From rooftop cocktail bars to cosy pubs on the edge of the Thames, all the venues in this section offer splendid aspects from window or terrace.

Good Mixers
The most elusive chapter title in the book, we admit – and also the most varied section. The bars here are great all-rounders that do several things well: cocktail bars with decent food, sturdy pubs with DJs and other similar ventures.

Gay Bars
An introduction to the capital's gay scene and the venues to head out to first.

Clubs & Music Venues
Everything from traditional jazz haunts out west to the bleeding-edge DJ bars and bar-clubs that are making the east the most exciting part of London for a night out.

The OWL & PUSSYCAT

....

34 Redchurch Street
Shoreditch London E2 7DP
020 3487 0088
owlandpussycatshoreditch.com

Pub - Restaurant - Garden

The **Defectors Weld**
Free House

–

170 Uxbridge Rd London W12 8AA
020 8749 000 | defectors-weld.com

The FELLOW
Pub & Dining Room

the **Lock Tavern**
Free House

wi-fi
garden
terrace
fine ales
noted roasts
free entry

24 York Way London N1 9AA
Reservations: 020 7833 4395
thefellow.co.uk

35 Chalk Farm Road London NW1 8AJ
020 7482 7163 | lock-tavern.co.uk

About the Listings

Opening hours

We've listed opening hours for all 500 venues in this book, as well as the hours during which food is served. 'Food served' can mean anything from a three-course meal to a cheese sandwich. When the opening times and food-service times are run together ('Open/food served'), you can expect food to be offered until shortly before closing time.

Admission charges

Many venues, especially late-opening bars in central London and clubs all over the city, charge admission after a certain time and/or on selected nights of the week. We've listed these details where possible, but drinkers should note that prices do vary and are often at the discretion of door staff who aren't above exploiting potential customers by boosting their prices on busy nights.

Babies & children

Children between the ages of 14 and 17 are allowed entry to pubs and bars, but can only consume soft drinks while on the premises. Under-14s are only allowed into gardens, separate family rooms and restaurant areas of pubs and wine bars unless the venue in question has a special children's certificate, in which case kids of all ages are allowed full access if they're accompanied by an adult. Note, though,

that some venues limit the hours during which children are welcomed; we've included these times in our listings.

Disabled access

We've given details of all venues that contain a disabled-adapted toilet. Readers should generally assume that this means the venue itself is disabled-accessible, but it's usually wise to call ahead and check in advance.

The best of the best

All 500 venues in this book are worthy of a visit, but we've pulled out some of the highlights in the front of the book. For details, see pp9-18.

The small print

During the lifetime of this guide, some of the venues in it will change hands, change name, change their decor or simply close their doors. If you're making a special trip, it may be worth calling the venue or checking its website (if it has one) before setting out.

Reviews in this guide are based on the experiences and opinions of Time Out's reviewers. All venues are visited anonymously and Time Out pays the bill. No payment or incentive of any kind has secured or influenced a review, and no venue has been included because its owner has advertised in the guide.

THE
BLUES
KITCHE

BLUES, BOURBON & GOOD TIM

Where to Go for...

Sunday roasts

Antelope p148
Tooting gets a gastropub, and a very good one it is too.

Cadogan Arms p151
There's fine and hearty fare at this reliable gastropub from the Martin brothers' stable.

Charles Lamb p138
Traditional Sunday-lunch food given a gentle gastropub update.

Princess Victoria p155
Slap-up Sunday lunches are served in the handsome dining room of this old Victorian gin palace.

Royal Oak p147
Old-fashioned pub grub at its finest.

Princess Victoria

Themed bars

Blue Bar p41
It's blue. Very, very blue.

Book Club p186
As the name suggests, expect a live, literary bent to proceedings at this Shoreditch bar. There's a ping pong table downstairs if it all gets a little too highbrow for you, as well as live music and DJs.

Café Kick p175
Exmouth Market's old reliable hangout is still going strong. Remember: no spinning...

Trader Vic's p46
You haven't been drunk in London until you've wound up at this ridiculous subterranean tiki bar, nursing a Suffering Bastard. (It's a cocktail.)

Windsor Castle p77
God save the Queen!

Jukeboxes

Boogaloo p209
Rock classics rub elbows with the young pretenders on the jukebox at this music-themed pub in Highgate.

Bradley's Spanish Bar p175
Lee Marvin's soporific 'Wand'rin Star' never sounds quite as good as it does after a skinful of Cruzcampo at this Hanway Street legend.

Prince George p84
The part-edgy, part-cheery tunes here are programmed by the Duke Spirit's Liela Moss, whose dad owns this Hackney stalwart.

Where to Go for...

Social p181
The DJ line-ups here are great, but it's almost worth avoiding them for a chance to play the jukebox.
Three Kings of Clerkenwell p77
Vintage vinyl, lovingly curated on the jukebox in the upstairs room of this splendid, charismatic boozer.

Outdoor drinking
Avalon p90
Like the front terrace? You've seen nothing yet. How about the pretty side garden? Just wait. At the back is not just the best pub garden in Balham, but one of the best in London.
Boundary Rooftop p163
Look down on the Shoreditch scene (who doesn't?) from the top of Terence Conran's multi-faceted establishment.
Junction Tavern p141
If the benches in the large outdoor space at this Tufnell Park gastropub are all gone, the airy conservatory is a very civilised place in which to grab lunch.
Scolt Head p84
It might be small, but the verdant garden at this De Beauvoir beauty fills its triangular space admirably with mature trees and plants and a pleasing array of furniture.
White Horse p124
This Parsons Green favourite really saddles up in the summer with an enormous outdoor patio, a brilliant barbecue and a well-heeled local crowd.

Unusual entertainment
Balham Bowls Club p192
Surely the only public bar in London with a full-sized snooker table.
Bedford p91
Real ale and line-dancing classes: together at last.
Bistrotheque Napoleon Bar p186
Cabaret nights are a mainstay at this much-loved Bethnal Green bar.
Dog & Bell p117
One of the few bar billiards tables left in London.
Nags Head p73
We've always said that London's pubs could do with more antique what-the-butler-saw slot machines.
Off Broadway p185
Knit and cross-stitch every Wednesday at the Fabrications club.

Café Kick. See p9.

Where to Go for...

White Horse. *See p10.*

Early opening

El Vino p53
Drown your financial sorrows with an early glass of wine in the City.

Fox & Anchor p68
Add a pint to your hearty, meaty breakfast at this Smithfield stalwart.

Market Porter p120
Start the day with one of a dozen ales in the shadow of Borough Market.

Families

Botanist on the Green p158
The perfect pitstop after a botanical tour of Kew Gardens, complete with ice-cream and drawing kits.

Brown Dog p151
A back garden, plenty of pictures of pooches on the walls, a child-friendly menu and other entertainments for youngsters (and dogs) make this Barnes local ideal for families.

Clissold Arms p139
A Muswell Hill stalwart that recognises a parental demographic when it sees one. Consequently, there's plenty of room in the dining area for families to spread out and the menu caters intelligently for both grown-up and childish tastes.

Herne Tavern p147
Another reliable local that welcomes families with open arms. The slightly shabby back garden is perfect for games of hide and seek and has even played host to sports days and a petting zoo in the past (check the website for events).

Lansdowne p141
A Chalk Farm gastropub that draws in families, kite-flyers and dog walkers from Primrose Hill. The pizza menu usually goes down well with children even if there isn't a specific menu for the little ones.

Where to Go for...

Dog & Bell. See p10.

Authentic international

Bar Estrela p192
European football (with Portuguese commentary) blaring out of the TV, Super Bocks and *pastel de nata* custard tarts make this bar a star player in London's Little Portugal.
Bar Pepito p49
This authentic Andalusían sherry *bodega* crams in punters to taste its small but perfectly formed sherry list.
Capote y Toros p51
This colourful newcomer brings a taste of Spain to South Kensington. There's good food and unusual wines, but it's the sherry list – 48 varieties – that really stands out.
De Hems p179
Drink countless Low Country beers and scoff *bitterballen* bar snacks in the bar that was once

the centre for the Dutch Resistance during World War II.
Off Broadway p185
Probably the closest you are likely to get to New York's East Village without actually going there. Low-key, dimly it and, quite contrarily, *on* Broadway Market.
Prague p189
A strangely spooky and veritably Bohemian creative vibe permeates what would otherwise be just another Shoreditch theme bar. The excellent Budvar Dark on tap is another good reason to visit.
Tiroler Hut p198
OK, it's not that authentic – but this Hungarian-themed basement bar is great fun, and it does serve Unicum, Hungary's herbal digestif liqueur.

Fox & Anchor. See p12.

Where to Go for...

Winter warmers

Earl Spencer p151
A classy old boozer-cum-gastropub (on a humdrum Southfields street) serving a decent array of wines and a variety of ales for supping by an open fire.

Grand Union p169
You can be fireside here all year round – there's an open fire and sofas to hunker down in on long winter evenings, and weekend barbecues on the canalside terrace come summer.

Holly Bush p106
The perfect place to warm up with a fireside pint after a bracing winter walk on Hampstead Heath. There are board games too.

Holly Bush

Clissold Arms. *See p12.*

Lord Clyde p81
Fight your way through the faithful local Islington crowd, order a pint of Harveys Sussex Best and grab the big armchair in front of the roaring hearth.

Three Kings of Clerkenwell p77
Warm your cockles at this delightful, unorthodox and friendly pub and the chances are that you'll also catch some decent music from either the jukebox or a DJ.

Something for everyone

Anthologist p172, Folly p178
Two huge new operations, both in the City and both run by Drake & Morgan, encompassing cocktail bars, restaurants, a wine shop, a deli and even a florist.

Where to Go for...

Anthologist. See p16.

which are available in around 50 pubs across town.

Fuller's London Pride
If Fuller's London Porter were more widely available, it would get the nod instead. But Pride remains the city's most reliable pint.

Meantime London Pale Ale
The best of the beers from Alastair Hook's pioneering brewery. Sample it at the source: at the Greenwich Union (*see p119*) or at his latest venture, the Old Brewery (*see p120*).

Redemption Pale Ale
Brewed in the wilds of Tottenham; a somewhat difficult to find but very toothsome pint.

Sambrook's Wandle
Duncan Sambrook's easy-drinking ale, brewed in Wandsworth, is increasingly visible across town.

Wenlock & Essex p183
This Islington newcomer is part local boozer, part burlesque bar. Great beer, cocktails, food and a separate mini-club, Satan's Circus.

London beers

Brodie's Sunshine
Jamie and Lizzie Brodie brew a bewildering number of beers in their Leyton brewpub William IV (*see p115*), and this summery ale is one of the best.

Camden Town Brewery
Jasper Cuppaidge's microbrewery, established in 2010, produces four main beers (Camden Hells Lager, Camden Pale Ale, Camden Wheat Beer and Camden Bitter),

Cocktails & Spirits

Central	20
North	32
East	34
South East	37
South	37
South West	37
West	37

Cocktails & Spirits

Nothing seems so hip at the moment as speakeasy-type bars – witness the recent openings of the **Experimental Cocktail Club, Nightjar, Purl** (and its Dickensian sister bar **Worship Street Whistling Shop**) – but you can't very well pose in one with a can of Red Stripe in your hand. So it's no surprise that the increased popularity of cocktails in London shows no sign of abating. Indeed, all kinds of watering holes now offer some sort of mixed-drink menu: the crowd filling the dancefloor at that ever-buzzing DJ bar may be fuelled by caipirinhas and sazeracs; the waiters at that unassuming restaurant may hand you a cocktail list with your food menu; and, if you ask nicely, even that once-shabby local boozer may be able to rustle up a passable bloody mary. But the bars in this section, along with many in the Hotel Bars chapter and a handful of other enterprises, constitute the cream of the cocktail crop.

The wider availability of cocktails in London has, however, had its drawbacks. A cocktail list is often seen as a short cut to sophistication, and it's easy to be drawn in by flowery descriptions of read-better-than-they-taste recipes, the mismatching of their ingredients made the more insulting by sky-high prices. Stick with the venues in this chapter, though, and you'll be fine, whether supping on an old-school concoction at **Mark's Bar**, a new-school mix at **Loungelover** or one of the perfectly pitched reinventions that make up much of the menu at Islington's **69 Colebrooke Row**.

Central

1 Lombard Street

1 Lombard Street, EC3V 9AA (7929 6611, www.1lombardstreet.com). Bank tube/DLR. **Open** 11am-midnight Mon-Fri. **Food served** 5.30-10pm Mon-Fri. **City**
A class act, this – as classy as its adjoining Michelin-starred restaurant. The main space of a converted corner bank is bookended by a circular cocktail bar. Be in little doubt about the mixing skills and quality materials on show here. You can order your vodka martini with countless types of vodka, all of them pretty serious: Grey Goose, Snow Leopard, Snow Queen, Belvedere, Smirnoff, Absolut Level and Wyborowa Single Estate, among others. Your bellini, meanwhile, may be mixed with lychee juice, white peach or blackberry purée. There are 50 wines (most of them French), including a score by the glass. Snacks include twice-fried potato skins and manchego cheese with olives, but the food in both the restaurant and the brasserie is worth further investigation.

Disabled: lift, toilet. Function room (40 capacity). **Map p245 Q6.**

Albannach

66 Trafalgar Square, WC2N 5DS (7930 0066, www.albannach.co.uk). Charing Cross tube/rail. **Open** noon-1am Mon-Sat; noon-7pm Sun. **Food served** noon-11pm Mon-Sat; noon-6.30pm Sun. **Trafalgar Square**
Albannach flies the flag of Scotland as deep in enemy territory as you can get: right on Trafalgar Square. The decor is sleek and modish, but the house speciality is welded to tradition: the drinks list here is all about the whiskies. A map on the menu details the origins of the Highland and Island malts, the likes of a 16-year-old, sherry-matured, cask-strength Bowmore (£13), Bruichladdich 15-year-old (£9) and Bunnahabhain 1968 Auld Acquaintance (£65). The menu isn't capped at Scots varieties: there are also Irish and Japanese whiskies, along with bourbons. The cocktails (around £8) aren't solely reliant on the Gaelic grain, but you may as well investigate a Smoky Martini (Tanqueray

or Smirnoff Black with a spoonful of Laphroaig 10-year-old) or Albannach Stag (Pampero Special rum, fresh berries, angostura bitters, lime, ginger ale). Salmon and haggis feature prominently among the decent if pricey food offerings. *Disabled: toilet. Dress: smart casual. Function rooms (150 capacity). Tables outdoors (5, terrace). Wireless internet.* **Map p241 K7.**

Baltic
74 Blackfriars Road, SE1 8HA (7928 1111, www.balticrestaurant.co.uk). Southwark tube. **Open/food served** noon-11pm Mon-Sat; noon-10.30pm Sun. **Waterloo**
With a small square of front terrace, a modern bar and a grand, sunken restaurant, this little piece of Poland has been a worthwhile stop on Waterloo bar crawls for many a year. It's mainly a cocktail bar, known for its extraordinary range of flavoured *wódkas*: they create their own peppercorn, mint, dill, caramel, ginger, cherry, lemon and redcurrant varieties, the last the base for the Porzeczka (shaken with Wyborowa Pure and grapefruit juice). 'Super luxury vodka martinis' are made with the likes of U'Luvka, Chopin, Wyborowa Exquisite, Belvedere Pure and Potocki Polish Rye. An equally Polish menu includes stuffed pierogi pasta parcels, blini with smoked salmon and *barszcz* beetroot soup. *Babies & children admitted. Booking advisable. Function rooms (70 capacity). Tables outdoors (5, terrace). Wireless internet.* **Map p250 N8.**

Boisdale
13-15 Eccleston Street, SW1W 9LX (7730 6922, www.boisdale.co.uk). Victoria tube/rail. **Open/food served** noon-1am Mon-Fri; 6pm-1am Sat. **Admission** £5 before 10pm, then £12. **Victoria**
The drinks menu at this part-sophisticated, part-kitsch Scottish-themed enterprise – tartan *everywhere* – is less of a list and more of an encyclopaedia. The histories of various whisky regions are outlined within its pages, which also contain individual tasting notes worthy of the most pedantic oenophile. The nose of a 15-year-old Glen Garioch (£12) offers hints of 'Parma violets and heather', while a rare single-cask Ardbeg from Islay 'is rich with layers of dense oily phenols, tropical and green fruits, with a distinctive medical streak running through it'. For £245 a shot, you'd expect nothing less. The food's good, but those just here for a drink may prefer to take theirs with a Cuban smoke on the heated, covered Cigar Terrace. The admission fees are billed as an 'optional jazz charge', but the music's often of a high enough standard that it's a price worth paying. There's more of the same at the Boisdale's City branch (Swedeland Court, 202 Bishopsgate, EC2M 4NR, 7283 1763) and enormous new Canary Wharf setup (Cabot Place, E14 4QT, 7715 5818). *Dress: smart casual. Entertainment (jazz 9.30pm Mon; 10pm Tue-Sat). Function room (34 capacity).* **Map p249 H10.**

Crazy Bear. *See p22.*

Cinnamon Club

Old Westminster Library, 30-32 Great Smith Street, SW1P 3BU (7222 2555, www.cinnamonclub.com). St James's Park or Westminster tube. **Open** *Library bar* 11am-11.45pm Mon-Sat. *Club bar* 4-11.45pm Mon-Sat. **Food served** noon-2.30pm, 6-10.45pm Mon-Sat. **Westminster**
This classy two-floor operation, an imposing space that easily reveals its past as a public library, is divided between a top-notch Indian restaurant, a trendy evenings-only DJ basement and a study-like cocktail bar by the lobby. They take their cocktails seriously enough to stage mixing classes every month. But if you're packing plastic (it's not cheap), you can simply pay others to mix for you from an inviting menu that takes in such signature drinks as a Curry Up! (Plymouth dry and sloe gins, lemon, curry nectar) and a James Dean (Appleton V/X and Matusalem 15-year-old rums, Jerry Thomas bitters, own-made green tea, pear and cinnamon syrup). A substantial wine list adds appeal, as does impeccable service. Your fellow drinkers will be wealthy but not ostentatiously so. *Babies & children admitted. Booking advisable. Disabled: toilet. Dress: smart casual. Function room (35-90 capacity). Wireless internet.* **Map p249 K10.**

Floridita. *See p24.*

Cottons

70 Exmouth Market, EC1R 4QP (7833 3332, www.cottons-restaurant.co.uk). Farringdon tube/rail or bus 19, 38, 341. **Open** noon-11.30pm daily. **Food served** noon-10.30pm Mon-Thur, Sun; noon-11pm Fri, Sat.
Clerkenwell
You could easily miss the unassuming entrance to Cottons, but as you leave Rosebery Avenue behind, you'll soon be transported in spirit to the West Indies. As you enter, you'll be greeted by the large lounge bar, stocked high with 250 varieties of rum. Naturally, they feature heavily on the list of mixed drinks advertised as 'cocktails from the island': potent yet refreshing daiquiris; a Reggae Rum Punch, with Wray & Nephew Overproof rum (63% ABV), pineapple, orange and lime juice; and a terrifying-sounding Killer Doppi, blending four types of rum with apricot liqueur, blue curaçao, orange, pineapple and lime juice. Served in the adjacent dining area, food is smartened-up Jamaican fare (fiery jerk beef fillets, deep-fried tilapia); downstairs is the Rhum Jungle, where DJs play at weekends. The Camden original (55 Chalk Farm Road, 7485 8388) offers a similar vibe. *Babies & children admitted (until 6pm). Booking advisable. Tables outdoors (7, pavement). Wireless internet.* **Map p242 N4.**

Crazy Bear

26-28 Whitfield Street, W1T 2RG (7631 0088, www.crazybeargroup.co.uk). Goodge Street tube. **Open** noon-midnight Mon-Wed; noon-1am Thur-Sat; noon-11.30pm Sun. **Food served** noon-2.45pm, 6-10.30pm daily. **Fitzrovia**
Perfectly groomed hostesses greet arrivals to this basement den. The atmosphere is lively and, better still, the cocktails are superb: try a Lychee Mojito, which fuses Havana Club Añejo Blanco, lime juice, lychees and mint, or a martini made with Hendrick's gin and cucumber garnish. Still, it's best to make sure your wallet is full: Crazy Bear charges luxury-hotel prices but misses out the free luxury-hotel nibbles, and ordering two rounds of drinks with small-plate eats (dim sum, spring rolls and the like) can make for an expensive hour. The bar's heavily mirrored toilets can be difficult to find, but don't worry: male staff and customers are quite used to ladies accidentally opening the wrong door. *Babies & children admitted (restaurant). Booking advisable.* **Map p240 K5.**

Detroit

35 Earlham Street, WC2H 9LD (7240 2662, www.detroit-bar.com). Covent Garden or Leicester Square tube. **Open** 5pm-midnight Mon-Sat. **Covent Garden**

Paying homage to the near-bankrupt American city in name alone, this long-established urban cocktail destination near Seven Dials is part Prague metro in appearance (dig those retro reversed-out spots!) and part cool dive, although it's not for the claustrophobic. Lovers and intimate friends whisper or cackle in alcoves, while sassy staff serve contemporary drinks from a long bar. Mixes range considerably in price and strength. The 16 standards show a fruity touch – the King Kong with four rums and four tropical juices; the Royal Garden with gin, pea-shoot and nettle purée, and lemon verbena foam – while the super-premium list includes an Earlham Street made with rum, absinthe and strawberries. Cusqueña, Viru and Asahi are among the beers, standard-priced goujons, skewers and focaccie among the bites. *Entertainment (DJs 8pm Fri, Sat). Tables outdoors (2, pavement).* **Map p241 L6.**

Dollar

2 Exmouth Market, EC1R 4PX (7278 0077, www.dollargrills.com). Farringdon tube/rail. **Open** noon-midnight Tue; noon-12.30am Wed; noon-5pm, 6pm-1.30am Thur; noon-2am Fri; noon-3am Sat. **Food served** noon-5pm, 6-11pm Tue-Sat. **Clerkenwell**

By day a restaurant, and after dark a cocktail bar – hence the 'Grills & Martinis' sign – Dollar provides a slightly tacky slice of Americana. At lunch, you'll find wage slaves firing into hulking great steaks and burgers served by a somewhat grumpy waitstaff, with mixed drinks coming into their own once the working day is over. More unusual ingredients in the house cocktails (£8.50) include melted white chocolate in the Swiss White Chocolate, and martinis of fresh rhubarb or watermelon. A recherché selection of bottled beers features Anchor Steam, Blue Moon, Bath Ales Barnstormer and Belgian Deus. Most wines are in the £30 range, a Chablis Domaine de Charmoy setting you back £42. On this night, though, with the right crowd in the basement martini bar, Dollar is just about worth the price. *Entertainment (DJs 9pm Fri, Sat). Function room (12 capacity). Tables outdoors (5, pavement).* **Map p242 N4.**

El Camion

25-27 Brewer Street, W1F 0RR (7734 7711, www.elcamion.co.uk). Piccadilly Circus tube. **Open** 6pm-3am Mon-Sat. **Food served** noon-11pm Mon-Sat; noon-10.30pm Sun. **Soho** El Camion is Mexican-themed but, unlike the kitsch Baja Californian restaurant above – where you can corral generous burritos, tortas

Hakkasan. *See p26.*

and tacos – it's more a discerning basement drinking den where Día de los Muertos (Day of the Dead) iconography sits above a series of snugs. The drinks are overseen by maestro mixologist Dick Bradsell, there's swift and smiling table service, and it's open late. With 38 different bottles covering blanco (white), reposado ('rested') and añejo ('aged'), it's a temple to tequila. You can sip the better ones neat, but it'd be remiss to ignore the marvellous margaritas, of which Tommy's Margarita is the pick. Mezcal is also well represented, alongside several rum daiquiris and cachaça-driven batidas; bottled Mexican beers include Pacifico Clara, Bohemia and Negra Modelo. *Booking advisable Thur-Sat. Entertainment DJs 10pm daily). Tables outdoors (2, pavement).* **Map p241 K6.**

Experimental Cocktail Club
13A Gerrard Street, W1D 5PS (7434 3559, www.chinatownecc.com). Leicester Square tube. **Open/food served** 6pm-3am Mon-Sat; 5pm-midnight Sun. **Chinatown**
Quite fancy, a little French and fairly flipping phenomenal, the London outpost of Paris's ECC is a stylish (sort of) speakeasy. The main, first-floor bar is classic, slightly colonial and cosy – blending brickwork, plush fabrics and a touch of the Orient. Later on, you can cut some absurdly retro rug in the equally impressive and intimate bar upstairs. The cocktails aren't cheap but they're extremely decent indeed – these lads know their liquids. A less-bitter twist on the negroni uses lavender-infused gin; the Rag Time is a heady collective of Rittenhouse 100 rye, Peychaud's bitters, Aperol and absinthe. Rare vintage gins and vodkas, served in classic cocktails for £150, offer a bling imbibing experience. While the wine list is strong, beer is a baffling blind spot; food is French and simple – boards of bread, cheese and charcuterie. **Map p241 K7.**

Floridita
100 Wardour Street, W1F 0TN (7314 4000, www.floriditalondon.com). Tottenham Court Road tube. **Open/food served** 5.30pm-2am Tue-Thur; 5.30pm-3am Fri, Sat. **Admission** £10 after 9pm Fri, Sat. **Soho**
The classy, late-opening Floridita, comprising a contemporary restaurant at street level and cocktail bar downstairs, offers Cuban-themed live entertainment and authentic mixed drinks based on the Havana landmark of the same name. The drinks menu's 'Ten of the Best' list honours personalities who frequented El Floridita (the house-style martini with Akvinta

Hawksmoor. *See p27.*

The Blind Tiger

PROHIBITED BEVERAGES & ILLICIT DINING

SW8 London 0207 498 0974

Reservations@blindtigerlondon.co.uk

www.blindtigerlondon.co.uk

THE LOST ANGEL

BAR, RESTAURANT & BOOZER

339 Battersea Park Road SW11 4LS

0207 622 2112   info@lostangel.co.uk

www.lostangel.co.uk

LOST
SOCIETY

LATE NIGHT BAR & RESTAURANT

697 Wandsworth Road SW8 3JF

0207 652 6526 info@lostsociety.co.uk

www.lostsociety.co.uk

CITIZEN SMITH

DRINKERY & EATING HOUSE

160 Putney High Street SW15 1RS

0208 780 2235 info@citizensmithar.co.uk

www.citizensmithbar.co.uk

Worship Street Whistling Shop.
See p35.

vodka or Tanqueray gin commemorates Marlene Dietrich; the Hemingway Special mixes Havana Club Anejo 3 with a touch of maraschino). Rum cocktails are paramount: Myers, Appleton and Havana Club are put to good use in the Planter's Punch, Jamaican Swizzle and Cuba Libre, while the five house daiquiris might be the best you'll sample in London. High-quality food (Cuban lobster, suckling pig, chorizo hamburgers) and cigars keep the theme and complete the picture. *Babies & children admitted. Booking advisable. Disabled: toilet. Entertainment (DJs & musicians 7.30pm Tue-Sat). Function rooms (60-80 capacity). Wireless internet.* Map p241 K6.

Giant Robot

45-47 Clerkenwell Road, EC1M 5RS (7065 6810, www.gntrbt.com). Farringdon tube/rail. **Open** 10am-midnight Mon-Wed; 10am-2am Thur-Sat; 10am-10pm Sun. **Food served** 10am-11pm Mon-Wed; 10am-1am Thur-Sat; 10am-5pm Sun. **Clerkenwell**
The building that formerly held Match EC1 was revamped in 2010 by Match supremo Jonathan Downey, and in pretty fine style. Lined with brick walls and a handsome tin ceiling, Giant Robot pulls off the neat and unusual trick of feeling both industrial and cosy, and the split-personality nature of the decor extends to the food and drinks. During the day, it's a café-diner

offering coffees, snacks and Italo-American food favourites such as spaghetti with meatballs and salt beef. In the evenings, you can dine or just drink from a fine, American-themed cocktail list (the manhattan stars Rittenhouse rye, a Brooklyn cocktail comes with Woodford Reserve). And the later it gets, the more the drinks come to the fore. A welcome and successful reinvention. *Babies & children admitted (until 8pm). Disabled: toilet. Function room (160 capacity). Tables outdoors (7, pavement). Wireless internet.* Map p242 O4.

Hakkasan

8 Hanway Place, W1T 1HD (7907 1888, w3.hakkasan.com). Tottenham Court Road tube. **Open** noon-12.30am Mon-Wed; noon-1.30am Thur-Sat; noon-midnight Sun. **Food served** noon-3pm, 6-11.30pm Mon-Wed; noon-3pm, 6-12.30am Thur-Sat; noon-4pm, 6-11.30pm Sun. **Fitzrovia**
This long, thin strip of a bar behind the Chinese screens of Hakkasan's exalted dining room gets astonishingly crowded, and with good reason: it hasn't lost an ounce of glamour since opening in 2001, and the cocktails are still superb. Made with Hendrick's gin and Belvedere vodka as well as Akashi-tai saké, the saketini is a thrilling diversion, while bloody mary fans will be tickled by the Sushi Bartender's Breakfast. Beer (Yebisu from Japan) and wines by the glass (from

countries as diverse as Turkey and Uruguay) add interest, and then there's the bar food: dim sum platters, crispy duck rolls, sesame prawn toast and the like, all cooked to the restaurant's sky-high standards. Don't be put off by the door staff, the dark descent to the basement or the bevy of hostesses asking about your booking: it's worth the perseverance. *Babies & children admitted. Booking advisable. Disabled: toilet. Entertainment (DJs 9pm daily). Function room (65 capacity).* **Map p240 K5.**

Hawksmoor

157 Commercial Street, E1 6BJ (7247 7392, www.thehawksmoor.com). Liverpool Street tube/rail. **Open** noon-midnight Mon-Fri; 11am-midnight Sat; 11am-4pm Sun. **Food served** noon-3pm, 6-10.30pm Mon-Fri; noon-4pm, 6-10.30pm Sat; noon-4pm Sun. **City**
How much of Hawksmoor is given over to drinkers depends on how busy the restaurant is. On quieter nights, you may be able to snag a table; otherwise, you'll have to hope there's room at the corner bar. If there's so little space for drinkers, why include it in this guide? Simple: the cocktails are among the best in town. Bartender Nick Strangeway may have moved to Mark's Bar in Soho, but his influence is still visible on a menu that nods in the direction of pre-FDR America with a lengthy list of variations on the mint julep, an array of 'expat classics' enjoyed by travelling Yanks during Prohibition, and an assortment of other arcane recipes, some of which date back the better part of 150 years. But while the education provided by the descriptions of each drink on the menu is welcome, the drinks sell themselves without them, especially given the reasonable prices (most around £7.50). *Babies & children admitted. Disabled: toilet. Wireless internet.* **Map p244 R5.**

Jetlag

125 Cleveland Street, W1T 6QB (3370 5838, www.jetlagbar.com). Goodge Street, Great Portland Street or Warren Street tube. **Open** 11am-11.30pm Mon-Thur; 11am-midnight Fri; noon-midnight Sat; noon-10.30pm Sun. **Food served** 11am-9pm Mon-Fri, Sun; noon-midnight Sat. **Fitzrovia**
Here, the travel joke wears thin but everyone seems to be enjoying it so much that it hardly matters. Served by an amiable antipodean, cocktails are themed from a travel agent's atlas, so you can visit New Zealand with a Feijoa Fizz (42 Below vodka, kiwi and feijoa), Thailand with a Lady Boy (lemongrass-infused vodka, star aniseed and blackcurrant) and, ha ha, Scotland with a Big Yin (Hendrick's gin, cucumber and

raspberry); they work out cheaper if you get an 'Around the World' ticket (£25 for six cocktails). Beers are similarly global: Oranjeboom and Asahi on draught; Tasmanian James Bay, Catalan Estrella and Little Creatures from Perth by the bottle. Food is either 'flip' (international street snacks, yakitori, coxinhas and so on) or 'flop' (beach eats such as souvlaki, Jalisco prawns and burgers). It all takes place on two levels done up in light wood and contemporary decor. *Babies & children admitted. Booking advisable. Function room (100 capacity). Tables outdoors (4, pavement). Wireless internet.* **Map p240 J4.**

London Cocktail Club

61 Goodge Street, W1T 1TL (7580 1960, www.londoncocktailclub.co.uk). Goodge Street tube. **Open/food served** 4.30pm-midnight Mon-Sat. **Fitzrovia**
With swallow-themed wallpaper, knobs on the gents' door and knockers on the ladies', this basement bar is kind of kitsch and, accompanied by a soundtrack of guilty pleasures, kind of cheesy. A bit of a tight squeeze when busy with an up-for-it after-work crowd, the L-shaped bar area is overseen by a team of established and experienced bartenders whose drinks are made quickly and competently with no small amount of smiley showboating. The drinks list contains both contemporary and classic London cocktails alongside some gin drinks and a section dedicated to gastro-mixology – cocktails inspired by the kitchen. The retro food menu is big on British and a touch tongue-in-cheek, with pick 'n' mix, penny chews and screwballs featuring beside pork scratchings, sharing platters and pudding cocktails. *Booking advisable (Thur-Sat). Dress: smart casual. Function room (40 capacity). Wireless internet.* **Map p240 J5.**

Mahiki

1 Dover Street, W1S 4LD (7493 9529, www.mahiki.com). Green Park tube. **Open** 5.30pm-3.30am Mon-Fri; 7.30pm-3.30am Sat. **Food served** 5.30-11pm Mon-Sat. **Admission** £10 after 9.30pm Mon-Wed; £15 after 9.30pm Thur-Sat. **Mayfair**
Don't try to take this mock-Polynesian palace seriously. You can't. It's silly, it's tacky, it attracts moneyed airheads – and it's bags of fun, made likeable by an international team of bar staff well versed in the twin arts of mixing drinks and dealing with too-trashed idiots. Given the just-off-Piccadilly setting and the candlelit-Hawaiiana surrounds, prices for early-evening drinks aren't too brutal: less than a tenner for a Honolulu Honey (with Chairman's Reserve

rum from St Lucia) or a Dark & Stormy (also rum-based, this time with Gosling's Black Seal). Go later, though, and you'll need to factor in a hefty admission fee (up to £15), which may make shared drinks the way to go. Try the three-person Bikini Blast (with El Jimador tequila), the four-person Zombie (with various rums and absinthe), or the eight-person Mystery Drink (it's a mystery!).
Entertainment (DJs 10pm Mon-Sat).
Map p241 J7.

Mark's Bar
66-70 Brewer Street, W1F 9UP (7292 3518, www.marksbar.co.uk). Piccadilly Circus tube.
Open/food served noon-1am Mon-Sat; 11am-11pm Sun. **Soho**
Opened in 2009, together with the Mark Hix-operated restaurant on the ground floor, this is a destination in its own right. It's a subterranean speakeasy with plenty of style – low zinc bar, tin ceiling panels, comfortable Chesterfields, bar billiards table – but with precious little attitude. Former Hawksmoor bartender Nick Strangeway celebrates the seasons on his fascinating, history-minded cocktail list; highlights include the Hanky Panky (Beefeater, Fernet Branca and red vermouth), created in the 1930s for Charles Hawtrey by a Savoy bartender, and the Scoff-Law Cocktail, a rye-whisky-based drink from the same period. There are plenty of appetising alternatives on the 150-strong wine list and the enlightened beer menu, with pale ales, bitters, stouts and Hix's own porter all served in gleaming tankards. The conditions of the licence mean drinkers have to order some food, either selections from the restaurant menu or lovely bar snacks (pork crackling, fennel sausage, posh fish fingers).
Babies & children admitted (until 5pm). Disabled: toilet. Wireless internet.
Map p241 J7.

Milk & Honey
61 Poland Street, W1F 7NU (7065 6841, www.mlkhny.com). Oxford Circus tube.
Open *Non-members* 6-11pm Mon-Sat (2hrs max, last admission 9pm). *Members* 6pm-3am Mon-Sat. **Soho**
You could walk past the door of this Soho speakeasy every day and never know it was there, and that's just how the owners like it. For the busiest times of the week, Milk & Honey is open only to members (£250 a year, plus a £50 joining fee), but mere mortals can book a table until 11pm early in the week; it's well worth the effort. The Prohibition ideal is carried through to the vaguely art deco interior (dimly lit, adding to the air of secrecy), the jazz and ragtime

soundtrack, and the perfectly executed classic cocktails. Granted, the atmosphere isn't at its most kinetic at, say, 7pm on a Tuesday, but the excellent cocktails more than make up for it. Everywhere you look, the emphasis is on quality, from the daily squeezed juices and twice-frozen ice to the stock of premium spirits. It's almost enough to make you want to join – and membership will also get you in late to nearby sister bar, the Player (8 Broadwick Street, 7065 6841, www.thplyr.com).
Booking essential for non-members. Function rooms (50 capacity). **Map p241 J6.**

Purl
50 Blandford Street, W1U 7HX (7935 0835, www.purl-london.com). Bond Street tube.
Open 5-11.30pm Mon-Thur; 5pm-midnight Fri, Sat. **Marylebone**
A lovable place that aims to recreate the atmosphere of a New York speakeasy, Purl's decor is simple but endearingly eclectic. The bar occupies the basement of a Georgian house and features low vaulted ceilings and lots of individual seating areas. The list of original cocktail creations is divided between molecular mixology and a confident mastery of classicism. Among the former, an Absinthe Sazerac, served in a silver egg cup, blends cognac, sugar and bitters with absinthe bubbled on top; meanwhile, a Silver Fizz, a variant on the gorgeous Ramos gin fizz using gin, lemon, sugar syrup, egg white and fizzy water, is made with precise two-stage shaking to guarantee the right texture: this is as good a cocktail as you'll find anywhere.
Map p238 G5.

QV Bar
26-29 Dean Street, W1D 3LL (7437 9585, www.quovadissoho.co.uk). Tottenham Court Road tube. **Open** noon-midnight Mon-Sat.
Food served noon-11pm Mon-Sat. **Soho**
The small ground-floor bar below Quo Vadis used to be a holding area for the dining room, but it's been rebranded as the QV Bar to make it a destination in itself. The tan leather seats are sumptuous, every surface is polished, and the service is impeccable. It feels comfortable and luxurious, and it's filled with the sort of people who turn left upon boarding planes. The brief cocktail list (mostly £8.50) includes the Aviation (gin and lemon juice in a conical glass, aromatic with violet and cherry bitters, and a booze-soaked cherry) and the Floradora (gin with crushed raspberries, topped with ginger ale) – and jolly good they are too. There's also a decent selection of wines by the glass. The bar menu's brief, the dishes (burger and chips, grilled quail) mostly small and pricey.

Purl

Babies & children admitted. Function rooms (12-24 capacity). Tables outdoors (7, terrace). Wireless internet. **Map p241 K6.**

Ruby Lounge

33 Caledonian Road, N1 9BU (7837 9558, www.ruby.uk.com). King's Cross tube/rail. **Open** 4-11pm Mon-Wed; 4pm-midnight Thur; 4pm-2am Fri, Sat; 3-9pm Sun. **King's Cross**
An odd spot, this: an oasis of sleek bar culture in a quite dreadful estuary of King's Cross that's characterised by labourers' pubs, unappealing B&Bs and careworn takeaways. But once you've found a little table around the pentagonal island bar within a handsome interior, you could be in Notting Hill, the location of sister venue Ruby & Sequoia (*see p197*). The Ruby Lounge is pitched at a young, salaried clientele; the ten Ruby Favourite cocktails are priced fairly, with four hours of two-fer glugging on all cocktails every night of the working week. There are fresh blueberries in the blueberry margarita, to say nothing of the passionfruit and vintage rum in the Lilikoi; equal attention is paid to the glassware. DJs play at weekends. *Entertainment (DJs 6pm Thur; 9pm Fri, Sat; jazz 8pm alternate Thur). Tables outdoors (3, pavement).*

Salt Whisky Bar & Dining Room

82 Seymour Street, W2 2JE (7402 1155, www.saltbar.com). Marble Arch tube. **Open** 11am-1am Mon-Sat; 11am-12.30am Sun. **Food served** 11am-12.30am Mon-Sat; 11am-11pm Sun. **Marylebone**
Although it's now Indian (and has a food menu to match), Salt still offers as wide a choice of whiskies as you'll find anywhere in London. Amid the hardwood and natural slate of the solitary bar-room – a classy, dark, square-shaped interior at odds with the gaudy brightness of Edgware Road – Salt feels like a sanctuary for discerning followers of the grain; many customers are Asian or Middle-Eastern in origin. The whisky directory lists 200 available by glass or bottle, categorised by provenance and accompanied by individual tasting notes. Standouts among the Scottish malts include a limited-edition Port Ellen 25-year-old from Islay, a Glenfiddich 1973 Vintage Reserve and a dauntingly priced Dalmore 1973 Haut Marbuzet Finish; there are also 20 American, ten Irish, one Welsh and three Japanese varieties. Cocktails are inevitably whisky-based, but you'll also find novelties such as a pomegranate caipirinha. *Dress: smart casual. Entertainment (DJs 8.30pm Thur-Sat). Function room (75 capacity). Tables outdoors (12, pavement).* **Map p238 F6.**

Shochu Lounge

Basement, Roka, 37 Charlotte Street, W1T 1RR (7580 9666, www.shochulounge.com). Goodge Street or Tottenham Court Road

Mahiki. *See p27.*

Shochu Lounge

tube. **Open** 5.30pm-midnight Mon-Sat; 5.30-11pm Sun. **Food served** 5.30-11.30pm Mon-Sat; 5.30-10.30pm Sun. **Fitzrovia** Beneath landmark Japanese restaurant Roka, the buzzing, chic Shochu Lounge deals chiefly in drinks built around the vodka-like distilled spirit from which it takes its name. Often overlooked in favour of saké, its more widespread counterpart, shochu is here used in healthy tonics and cocktails. The former include *ki lazubeli shu* ('helps improve memory') and jasmine flower *shu* ('for coughs and sore eyes'); among the latter are the Nightingale (*shisho shu*, lime, elderflower and orange bitters) and the Hallo Kitty house punch (shochu, raspberry, rose, lemon and sparkling water). There's more: 15 vodkas (Kauffmann, Slwucha, Uluvka, Potocki), for instance, served alone or in cocktails. All drinks are expertly mixed at the rustic bar counter, and served with style. Food? The full Roka menu is available. *Dress: smart casual. Entertainment (DJs 9pm Thur-Sat).* **Map p240 J5.**

Zuma

5 Raphael Street, SW7 1DL (7584 1010, www.zumarestaurant.com). Knightsbridge tube. **Open** noon-11pm Mon-Fri; 12.30-11pm Sat; noon-10pm Sun. **Food served** noon-2.15pm, 6-10.45pm Mon-Thur; noon-2.45pm, 6-10.45pm Fri; 12.30-3.15pm, 6-10.45pm Sat; 12.30-3.15pm, 6-10.15pm Sun. **Knightsbridge** This contemporary Japanese *izakaya* attracts a loyal, moneyed clientele. The 40-deep saké

selection is as attractive as any in town – there's even Azure Ginjoshu Tosatsuru, sourced from a spring at the bottom of the North Pacific – but it's the cocktails that keep the chattering shoppers coming back. Three sparkling *kaze* types include the house spritzer (Ume-shu plum wine, prosecco, orange and angostura bitters), while four long (*mizu*) and six short (*tsuchi*) varieties include Ega-nya, made with Whitley Neill gin, shisho and mint leaves, aloe vera, fresh lemon and lime. Martinis and daiquiris show another touch of south-east Asia, with Thai-spiced mango used with abandon. Kirin Ichiban and Asahi Super Dry and Black comprise the beers, but note that while the snacks are cheaper than the dishes served to diners at the restaurant tables (drinkers are confined to the bar area), 'cheaper' should not be taken to mean 'cheap'. *Babies & children admitted. Disabled: toilet. Function rooms (14 capacity). Tables outdoors (4, garden).*

Also recommended...

190 Queensgate (Hotel Bars, *p40*); **5th View** (Rooms with a View, *p160*); **Anthologist** (Good Mixers, *p172*); **Artesian** (Hotel Bars, *p40*); **Bar Polski** (Good Mixers, *p172*); **Barrio Central** (Good Mixers, *p173*); **Beaufort Bar at the Savoy** (Hotel Bars, *p40*); **Blue Bar** (Hotel Bars, *p41*); **Bourne & Hollingsworth** (Good Mixers, *p175*); **Cellar Door** (Good Mixers, *p175*); **Circus** (Clubs & Music Venues, *p205*);

Loungelover. *See p35.*

Claridge's Bar (Hotel Bars, *p42*); Coburg Bar (Hotel Bars, *p42*); Connaught Bar (Hotel Bars, *p43*); Dukes Bar (Hotel Bars, *p43*); Folly (Good Mixers, *p178*); Freud (Good Mixers, *p178*); Galvin at Windows (Hotel Bars, *p43*); Hunter 486 (Hotel Bars, *p44*); Kanaloa (Good Mixers, *p179*); Lexington (Clubs & Music Venues, *p206*); Library (Hotel Bars, *p44*); Lobby Bar (Hotel Bars, *p45*); Mandarin Bar (Hotel Bars, *p45*); Mustard Bar & Lounge (Good Mixers, *p180*); Oxo Tower Bar (Rooms with a View, *p160*); Pearl Bar & Restaurant (Hotel Bars, *p45*); Skylon (Rooms with a View, *p161*); Skylounge (Rooms with a View, *p161*); Trader Vic's (Hotel Bars, *p46*); Zetter Townhouse (Hotel Bars, *p46*).

North

25 Canonbury Lane

25 Canonbury Lane, N1 2AS (7226 0955, www.25canonburylane.com). Highbury & Islington tube/rail. **Open** 5pm-midnight Mon-Thur, Sun; 4pm-2am Fri, Sat. **Food served** 6-10pm Mon-Sat; 6-9pm Sun. **Islington**
Regulars enjoy the intimacy of neat, petite 25 Canonbury Lane – the main room is just bigger than the average corner newsagent's – and the fact that the friendly staff can fix a proper cocktail. With a nod to the bar's name, the house

cocktails include the 25 Virgins (rum, mango, lime and ginger beer), alongside classics such as mojitos and negronis; alternatively, find your spot on the squishy brown sofa or counter barstool and call up something more exotic, such as a Canonbury Gardens (gin, elderflower, lime, apple and cranberry). Wines number nine of each colour by the glass; alternatives include the more mundane likes of Beck's Vier and Staropramen on tap, or Budvar, Anchor Steam and Little Creatures by the bottle. The concise list of 'English tapas' includes scotch eggs and Stoke Newington smoked salmon.
Babies & children admitted (until 7pm). Wireless internet. **Map p255 O26.**

69 Colebrooke Row

69 Colebrooke Row, N1 8AA (07540 528593 mobile, www.69colebrookerow.com). Angel tube. **Open** 5pm-midnight Mon-Wed, Sun; 5pm-1am Thur; 5pm-2am Fri, Sat. **Islington**
Tucked away off the Islington Green end of Essex Road, 69 Colebrooke Row bears an impressive pedigree. Opened in mid 2009, it's the brainchild of Tony Conigliaro, familiar from his work at the likes of Isola, Roka and Shochu Lounge, and Camille Hobby-Limon, who runs the nearby Charles Lamb pub. With just a handful of tables supplemented by a few stools at the bar, it may be smaller than your front room, but the understated, intimate space proves a fine environment in which to enjoy the pristine

cocktails (liquorice whisky sours, raspberry and rosehip bellinis, gimlets with own-made rhubarb cordial, depending on the season), mixed with quiet ceremony by an elegantly bow-tied Conigliaro. Still, for all the excellence of the drinks, it's the little touches (impeccably attired staff, handwritten bills, tall glasses of water poured from a cocktail shaker) that elevate this lovely enterprise from the pack.
Booking advisable. Entertainment (pianist 8pm Thur). Wireless internet. **Map p255 O2.**

Gilgamesh
Stables Market, Chalk Farm Road, NW1 8AH (7482 5757, www.gilgameshbar.com). Camden Town tube. **Open** 6-11.30pm Mon-Thur; noon-11.30pm Fri-Sun. **Food served** noon-midnight daily. **Camden**
Reached by escalator between some ornate walls carved with ancient world-style motifs, Gilgamesh feels part Mesopotamian epic, part Cecil B DeMille. The miles-over-the-top interior – bronzed walls, pillars inlaid with polished stones – is extremely, wilfully ridiculous, but it's hard not to admire the absurdity. Drinks are also themed along Babylonian lines: the Sun God Anu is celebrated in martini form with Absolut Peach, Bombay gin, peach and cucumber; the Sumerian city of Shuruppak is honoured with 42 Below vodka, apricot, peach, watermelon, berries and pineapple. Even the mocktails are named after the Tigris and Euphrates, and involve a whole mess of cranberry, lychee, pink grapefruit and rose petal. The only beer is Tiger, from Singapore – surely somebody could have dug up a bottle of ancient Sumerian Ninkasi?
Babies & children admitted. Booking advisable. Dress: smart casual. Entertainment (DJs 10pm Fri, Sat). Function room (400 capacity). **Map p254 H26.**

Also recommended...
Blues Kitchen (Clubs & Music Venues, *p209*).

East

Callooh Callay
65 Rivington Street, EC2A 3AY (7739 4781, www.calloohcallaybar.com). Old Street tube/rail or Shoreditch High Street rail. **Open/food served** 6pm-midnight Mon-Wed, Sun; 6pm-1am Thur-Sat. **Shoreditch**
This admirable, relatively recent addition to the Shoreditch bar scene is characterised by its funky, cosmopolitan feel and touch of class. Taking inspiration from Lewis Carroll, it's an evening-only cocktail bar, and an imaginative

69 Colebrooke Row. *See p32.*

one at that: the seasonal drinks menu features such original mixes as an Ale of Two Cities (half-pint of 42 Below Feijoa, Punt e Mes, nettle cordial and malt syrup) and an Anise & Nephew (Wray & Nephew rum, Velvet Falernum, Pernod). In the main bar room of low, purple seating, these drinks are served from a long bar counter by savvy staff featured in the childhood photos above. And then there's the handsome back-room Jubjub Members Bar, hidden behind a heavy wardrobe door (not a looking glass, but a nice touch regardless) and more atmospheric than the front space (refreshingly, membership is based on appreciation of drinks rather than money). DJs spin at weekends. *Booking advisable Fri, Sat. Disabled: toilet. Entertainment (DJs 8pm Fri, Sat). Function rooms (20-60 capacity). Wireless internet.* **Map p244 R4.**

Loungelover

1 Whitby Street, E1 6JU (7012 1234, www.loungelover.co.uk). Liverpool Street tube/rail or Shoreditch High Street rail. **Open** 6pm-midnight Mon-Thur, Sun; 5.30pm-1am Fri; 6pm-1am Sat. **Food served** 6-11.30pm Mon-Thur, Sun; 6pm-midnight Fri, Sat. **Shoreditch**
First, the cocktails. Often brilliant, they involve deft mixes such as Citadelle raspberry vodka with white cranberry and grape juice (Love Letter, £8); Ketel One vodka shaken with lemon, wasabi, ginger and cucumber (Zatoichi, £9); and fig liqueur and lemon oil with prosecco (Loungelover, £9). Second, the pricing policy. An initial 'discretionary' 12.5% service charge is later followed by a Mexican stand-off over the card-swipe as you're invited to negotiate its tricky buttons and either add even more gratuity or stick at 12.5%, all under the anticipative glare of your black-uniformed waiter. To be fair, you will have been shown to your table and served at it (bar space being at a premium), but this hardly warrants an additional tip. Food comprises sushi and hot Japanese snacks, while the decor is a jarring mish-mash of baroque, kitsch and exotic; at any rate, it's perhaps not the 'seamless marriage of old and new' suggested by the management, also responsible for Les Trois Garçons restaurant around the corner. *Booking advisable. Disabled: toilet. Dress: smart casual.* **Map p244 R4.**

Nightjar

129 City Road, EC1V 1JB (7253 4101, www.barnightjar.com). Old Street tube/rail. **Open/food served** 6pm-1am Tue, Wed, Sun; 6pm-3am Thur-Sat. **Shoreditch**

With its inconspicuous entrance and its subterranean setting, Nightjar is a stylised stab at a Shoreditch speakeasy: a late-opening cocktail bar and music venue that leads with live jazz, swing and cabaret, and debonair drinking. First and foremost, the cocktails here are excellent and original: liquid legacies from cocktail's golden era and pre-Prohibition drinks incorporating homemade infusions, and liqueurs and bitters. Brought to your table by (maybe overly) meticulous staff and accompanied by an array of canapés, they both look and taste the business. The BBC, made with calvados and Becherovka cordial, is served with 'absinthe smoke', while misty 'dry ice' vapours add allure to the Fog Cutter, an alcoholic orgy of rum, sherry, gin and Cognac. With its trio of open-plan areas big on brass, black leather booths and dark wood, it's a dapper, dusky place to drink. *Booking advisable Fri, Sat. Disabled: toilet. Entertainment (live music 9pm Wed, Thur, Sat).* **Map p244 Q3.**

Worship Street Whistling Shop

63 Worship Street, EC2A 2DU (7247 0015, www.whistlingshop.com). Old Street tube/rail. **Open** noon-1pm Mon-Thur; noon-2am Fri, Sat. **Food served** noon-10pm Mon-Sat. **Shoreditch**
Fluid Movement's second subterranean bar opened in May 2011. But whereas its sister bar Purl pays homage to Prohibition, this latest venture venerates all things Victorian. The U-shaped space feels like a Dickensian drinking den with its gas lamps and Chesterfield sofas – even the staff wear period clobber – though there are bits (including the music) that feel more 1980s than 19th century. Overseen by acclaimed drink-maker Ryan Chetiyawardana, the cocktail list is a revival of Victorian recipes using modern molecular mixology techniques alongside the bar's bespoke alcoholic inventions. In a laboratory located in the dining area, they've devised spirits using the Champagne method, and created liqueurs steeped with herbs and spices. The Black Cat's Martini, for instance, is made by distilling cream in gin at low pressure and withdrawing the distillate. Barrels behind the bar hold infused cask-aged spirits: 'Gin and Pep' is Tanqueray 10 gin and crème de menthe aged in new oak. In the 'dram shop', an honesty bar comes stocked with an array of gins. For the unspirited, there's Kernel Porter and Meantime Stout, plus a trio of reds and whites. Evening food, meanwhile, is a collection of pies, oysters, potted shrimps and sharing platters; lunch is a more substantial affair. The line between

Nightjar. *See p35.*

authentic and a little bit silly blurs somewhat, but the drinks and staff here are terrific.
Babies & children admitted (until 7pm).
Booking advisable Mon-Sat. Function room (10 capacity). Wireless internet. **Map p244 Q4.**

Also recommended...
Redchurch (Good Mixers, *p190*).

South East

Hide Bar
39-45 Bermondsey Street, SE1 3XF (7403 6655, www.thehidebar.com). London Bridge tube/rail. **Open** 5pm-midnight Tue; 5pm-1am Wed, Thur; 5pm-2am Fri, Sat; 3-11pm Sun. **Food served** 5.30-10pm Tue-Sat; 4-10pm Sun. **Bermondsey**
The Hide Bar has ridden out the credit crunch with aplomb, filling to the gills from Thursdays onward with nine-to-fivers happy to be sinking quality mixed drinks near a transport hub. Most cocktails are priced in the £6.50 to £7 range, including house specials such as the Passionate Englishman (Hendrick's gin stirred with passion fruit purée), the Bermondsey Martini (Jensen's gin and Noilly Prat) and the American in London (Knob Creek bourbon infused with Earl Grey tea, peach liqueur, Peychaud's bitters and sweet vermouth). Seventy-odd other options are available, drawn from a selection of spirits that would put most bars in London to shame (and all sold by the glass to boot). Wines are equally well sourced: you won't find Mezcala tinto (a Bordeaux-style Mexican blend) in too many places. There are a few mains but the platters are more intriguing – the Southbank pairs soft-shell crabs, stuffed baby squid and gravadlax with mango, mint and tomato salsa.
Babies & children admitted (until 7pm). Booking advisable. Disabled: toilet. Function room (30 capacity). Wireless internet. **Map p250 Q9.**

South

Also recommended...
Lost Angel (Good Mixers, *p193*);
Lost Society (Good Mixers, *p193*).

South West

Also recommended...
Citizen Smith (Beer Specialists, *p124*).

West

Lonsdale
48 Lonsdale Road, W11 2DE (7727 4080, www.thelonsdale.co.uk). Ladbroke Grove or Notting Hill Gate tube. **Open** 6pm-midnight Mon-Thur; 6pm-1am Fri, Sat. **Food served** 6-11pm Mon-Sat.
Bayswater
It's been a fair few years since Dick Bradsell was behind the counter here, but his legacy lives on in the shape of the fine modern cocktails: the Rose Petal martini (Bombay Sapphire with Lanique rose liqueur, lychee juice and Peychaud bitters), for example, or the Elderflower Fizz (elderflower cordial, lemon juice, champagne). The 'London contemporary classics' offer the best in British mixes from recent times, such as Jason Fendick's Quiet Storm (Ketel One, guava, lychee and pineapple juices, coconut cream and lime); there are also classics from bygone eras, among them the Bloodhound (Plymouth gin, Noilly Prat, raspberries and maraschino cherries). Mixing and service are fittingly old-school, and the environment – a sun-catching front terrace, a long bar counter and wide, candlelit main seating area at the back – is a pleasing one.
Disabled: toilet. Entertainment (DJs 9pm Fri, Sat). Function room (75-80 capacity). Tables outdoors (5, terrace). **Map p247 A6.**

Montgomery Place
31 Kensington Park Road, W11 2EU (7792 3921, www.montgomeryplace.co.uk). Ladbroke Grove tube. **Open** 5pm-midnight Mon-Fri; Sun; 2pm-1am Sat. **Food served** 5-11pm daily. **Bayswater**
Montgomery Place keeps a low profile, its dark exterior embellished by a couple of tables outside in summer. Inside, the prime table just by the window is usually taken, as are the places at the bar; for intimacy, head, instead, to the more spacious back area. Declaring that the bar takes its inspiration 'from the roaring era of Hemingway... and the rebirth of cool', the venue's thick, juicy menu contains plenty of variety: the extra-dry Montgomery Style martini blends ice-cold Tanqueray with a suspicion of Noilly Prat; the mint julep is built around Woodforde Reserve; and the Old Cuban is a combination of a mojito and a champagne cocktail. Look out, too, for in-house mixes such as the Silver Pine (Havana Club, Campari, grapefruit, agave nectar and passion-fruit syrup), created at the bar's now-closed sister operation Dusk in Battersea.
Babies & children admitted (afternoon Sat). Tables outdoors (2, pavement). **Map p247 Z6.**

Lonsdale. See p37.

Portobello Star

*171 Portobello Road, W11 2DY (7229
8016, www.portobellostarbar.co.uk).
Ladbroke Grove tube.* **Open** 11am-11pm
Mon-Thur; 11am-12.30am Fri; 10am-
12.30am Sat; 11am-11.30pm Sun.
Notting Hill
Gentrification has sunk its claws into this once-
scruffy boozer, for years one of the holdouts
along the Portobello Road. Fronted by a couple
of pavement tables but no real sign, Portobello
Star 'take two' is a long, thin room; the only
relief from the plain walls is provided by the
sturdy bar along one side and a lovely radio-
themed mural. It's a handsome space, more
appealing than it seems at first glance, but
the real draws are the likeable bartenders'
powerful, convincing renditions of cocktails
both traditional (a richly flavourful mint julep
with Woodford Reserve, a margarita modified
by agave) and modern (Dick Bradsell's
Bramble). You may have to shout to make
yourself heard when the DJs crank it up a little
– the music policy bounces from generic indie
to more danceable tunes – but the lively crowd
of Notting Hillbillies don't mind a bit.
*Disabled: toilet. Entertainment (DJs 9pm Fri,
Sat). Function room (30 capacity). Tables
outdoors (2, pavement). Wireless internet.*
Map p247 Z6.

Saf

*Whole Foods Market, W8 5SE (7368 4555,
www.wholefoodsmarket.com). High Street
Kensington tube.* **Open** 10am-11pm Mon-Sat;
10am-6pm Sun. **Food served** 10am-10.30pm
Mon-Sat; 10am-5.30pm Sun. **Kensington**
The first floor of the UK's best organic
supermarket is devoted to a mall-style food
court. It has the usual pizza, burger and sushi
joints – organic, of course – but, since 2010,
it's also had a branch of Saf, the Shoreditch raw
vegan café-restaurant with a surprisingly good
cocktail bar. This west London outpost has none
of the cool of its Shoreditch counterpart, but it
makes a nice change from the massed wine bars
and ale houses of Kensington. The bar's USP
is organic ingredients – even the spirits, which
should help get your chakras open while the
alcohol's killing off your brain cells. The short
list of cocktails are well made, and staff are
friendly. A word of warning: don't ask a London
cab driver to take you to 'Saf Kensington',
or you'll likely end up in South Kensington.
*Babies & children admitted. Booking
advisable Fri-Sun. Disabled: toilet.
Wireless internet.*

Westbourne House

*65 Westbourne Grove, W2 4UJ (7229 2233,
www.westbournehouse.net). Bayswater or
Royal Oak tube.* **Open** 11am-11.30pm Mon-
Thur; 11am-midnight Fri; 9am-midnight
Sat; 9am-10.30pm Sun. **Food served** 11am-
3pm, 5-11pm Mon-Fri; 9am-11.30pm Sat;
9am-10pm Sun. **Bayswater**
On a quiet strip west of Bayswater, Westbourne
House offers professional drinks to professional
people. Drinks history is revered: half of the
menu is a timeline of libations, from the mid
18th-century gimlet and mint julep, through
the Americano Cocktail invented by Gaspare
Campari 100 years later and the turn-of-the-
century daiquiri (here with Havana Club three-
year-old rum), to the much more recent Earl
Grey MarTeaNi and their own Bobby De Niro
(Bombay Dry gin, apricot, lemon and jam).
Mixing and service at the zinc-topped bar
counter match the ambition of the menu;
candles, and a fire in winter, provide ambience.
There are outdoor tables in summer.
*Babies & children admitted (until 5pm).
Function rooms (up to 45 capacity). Tables
outdoors (7, pavement). Wireless internet.*
Map p247 B6.

Also recommended...

Lodge Tavern (Good Mixers, *p196*);
Ruby & Sequoia (Good Mixers, *p197*);
Trailer Happiness (Good Mixers, *p198*).

Hotel Bars

Central   **40**

Hotel Bars

Most of the bars listed within this section are housed in extremely upscale hotels, where one night in a standard double room costs about as much as the weekly rent on a two- or even three-bedroom flat. It probably goes without saying that the price of drinks is no less eye-watering. You're unlikely to find a bottle of beer for less than a fiver or a cocktail for under a tenner at any of these venues; indeed, we'd be surprised if the gaudy, garish **Rivoli at the Ritz** isn't the most expensive place to drink in the country.

Pricey though the drinks may be, these bars offer an entrée to some glamorous places – you don't need to stay at these hotels in order to drink in them. Wondering what a £220 million makeover looks like? Swan into the **Beaufort Bar at the Savoy** and find out. Yes, you may need to smarten up: if the bars in this chapter operate a dress code, we've mentioned it, though you'd probably do well to look sharp even if they don't. You may also need to book a table in advance. But otherwise, the only obstacle to enjoying a cocktail in one of these lounges is financial.

Still, for special-occasion evenings, it's hard to find anywhere better than these unashamedly upmarket operations. The decor will be handsome; the cocktails will be exquisite, whether traditional martinis (**Dukes Bar** at Dukes Hotel) or modern concoctions (**Artesian** at the Langham); and the service will be note-perfect. This is one area of the London drinking scene where you really will get what you pay for.

Central

190 Queensgate
Gore Hotel, 190 Queensgate, SW7 5EX (7584 6601, www.gorehotel.com). Gloucester Road or South Kensington tube. **Open** noon-1.30am daily. **Food served** noon-11.30pm daily. **South Kensington**
In a library-like atmosphere of dark wood and low lighting, the bar staff at the Gore Hotel in South Kensington go about their business of providing varied, classy cocktails to a likewise varied, classy crowd. The menu's 'signature' selection includes the Londoner, with gin, fresh rhubarb, Aperol, lime juice and sugar, while the Royal Mojito tops up the standard mojito's rum (Premium Mount Gay XO, in this case) with champagne, and the French 190 updates the classic French 75 with grapefruit. Beaumont des Crayères is the bubbly of choice; the wines and beers display a Spanish touch, but the Iberian management could surely do rather better than the desultory tapas on offer. On a happier note, there are 30 varieties of vodka, including Snow Leopard and Grey Goose, and the service is excellent. The clientele here is occasionally starry and always rich. *Function room (150 capacity). Wireless internet.*

Artesian
Langham Hotel, 1C Portland Place, W1B 1JA (7636 1000, www.artesian-bar.co.uk). Oxford Circus tube. **Open/food served** noon-midnight daily. **Marylebone**
David Collins' redesign of this handsome room in the Langham Hotel updated the pillars, marble fittings and high ceilings with a considered yet glamorous touch. The result has visual impact, blending grand Victorian decadence (a marble bar, soaring inset mirrors, embroidered napkins) with modern details (purple snakeskin-effect leather seats, a carved pagoda-style back bar, faultless service). Cocktail highlights include the heady Artesian Punch (Poire William, pineapple, citrus and three rums); indeed, rum is a speciality of the house, with a list running to 60 varieties, from Gosling's Black Seal (£9) to Havana Club Maximo (£300). A cut above. *Babies & children admitted (until 6pm). Disabled: toilet (hotel). Games (dominoes). Wireless internet.* **Map p238 H5.**

Beaufort Bar at the Savoy
The Savoy, 100 Strand, WC2R 0EW (7836 4343, www.the-savoy.com). Charing Cross tube/rail or Embankment tube. **Open** 5.30pm-1am Mon-Sat. **Strand**

Following a £220m revamp, the Savoy's devotion to debonair drinking now stretches beyond the iconic American Bar. The Beaufort might be less famous but it's definitely the looker of the pair, and combines a wow-factor interior with good service and top-quality (if pricey) drinks. Art deco opulence abounds, £38,000 of gold leaf adorns the alcoves and ornate cornicing, and the black velvet furnishings are suitably plush The broad range of bubbly leans heavily towards Louis Roederer, starting at around £16 a glass; beers (£6) include Meantime Pale Ale and Guinness. While the Beaufort doesn't boast the wealth of cocktails available at the American Bar, the seven-strong list is worth exploring: the Sugar Strut is a terrific twist on a rum old fashioned that blends Bacardi 8 Year Old with Guinness Foreign Syrup; the Gilded Cage (vodka, fresh passionfruit and chartreuse) comes served in a birdcage. Be warned, though: at both bars, you may need to queue to get in.
Disabled: toilet (hotel). Dress: smart casual. Entertainment (cabaret 8pm daily). Wireless internet. **Map p241 L7.**

Blue Bar

The Berkeley, Wilton Place, SW1X 7RL (7235 6000, www.the-berkeley.co.uk). Hyde Park Corner tube. **Open/food served** 4pm-1am Mon-Sat; 4-11pm Sun. **Knightsbridge**

The name isn't just a caprice: this David Collins-designed bar really is as blue as a Billie Holiday album. The sky-blue armchairs, the deep-blue ornate plasterwork and the navy-blue leather-bound menus combine with discreet lighting to striking effect. It's a see-and-be-seen place, but staff treat all-comers like royalty, and the cocktails are a masterclass in sophistication. Not everyone can afford to scale the frightening heights of the bar list, worth perusing just to confirm that there is such a thing as a £4,210 bottle of champagne or a £925 shot of whisky (Macallan 55-year-old). Leave those to the A-list, and just enjoy the elegance and luxury of one of the finest hotel bars in the city.
Disabled: toilet (hotel). Dress: smart casual.

Brasserie Max

Covent Garden Hotel, 10 Monmouth Street, WC2H 9HB (7806 1000, www.coventgarden hotel.co.uk). Covent Garden tube. **Open/food served** 7am-11pm Mon-Fri; 8am-11pm Sat; 8am-10.30pm Sun. **Covent Garden**

Beneath a row of flags topping the stern, stylish Covent Garden Hotel, this bar-restaurant offers a lovely environment in which to sip drinks and munch on snacks – but at a price. The tone is set by an ice bucket of Krug on the bar counter; however, the fine cocktails, old-school martinis and updated classics such as the Covent

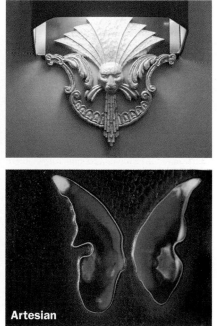

Artesian

Garden Mojito (with blood-orange purée), may be a better bet. The wine list is good but, like everything else here, it's not cheap. Platters (£25!) come in Asian, Mediterranean, dumpling and mini-burger varieties. Waiters squeeze their way between the half-moon chairs from the zinc bar in a bid to create a brasserie atmosphere. *Babies & children admitted. Disabled: lift. Function rooms (50 capacity). Entertainment (dinner & film 8pm Sat). Tables outdoors (7, pavement). Wireless internet.* **Map p240 L6.**

Brumus Bar

Haymarket Hotel, 1 Suffolk Place, SW1Y 4BP (7470 4000, www.firmdale.com). Piccadilly Circus tube. **Open** 7am-midnight Mon-Sat; 8am-11pm Sun. **Food served** 7am-11.15pm Mon-Sat; 8am-10.30pm Sun. **Piccadilly**
Everything screams for attention at the Haymarket Hotel's bright, almost brash bar, though the kaleidoscope of pink and red, patterned with geometrics on the bar stools and florals on the sofas, may not be to everyone's taste. The upscale class of the hotel, part of Tim and Kit Kemp's Firmdale group, brings in a relaxed crowd. The cocktail menu steers a course through standards and new creations: a Haymarket Cosmo (£11), for instance, adds limoncello, mint and crushed ice to the expected vodka and cranberry. The fine staff balance friendliness and professionalism. *Babies & children admitted (until 6pm). Disabled: toilet. Function rooms (50 capacity). Tables outdoors (5, pavement). Wireless internet.* **Map p241 K7.**

Claridge's Bar

Claridge's, 49 Brook Street, W1K 4HR (7629 8860, www.claridges.co.uk). Bond Street tube. **Open/food served** noon-1am Mon-Sat; noon-midnight Sun. **Mayfair**
Claridge's remains one of London's best hotels. The downside: everyone knows it, and its beautiful bar (designed by David Collins) can be a little oversubscribed. On a quiet night, there are few finer spaces in which to enjoy a cocktail, whether traditional or 21st-century. Walk in when it's busy, though, and you'll have to fight for space with Taras gossiping about their PR clients over a bottle of sauv, big-night-up-west partiers getting warmed up with a glass of bubbly, and a scattering of ostentatiously rich Eurotrash. Still, the staff treat everyone with respect and always mix their cocktails with care. And if the crowds prove too much, the hotel's Fumoir bar, a cigar-lover's paradise until the smoking ban, is an elegant escape hatch. *Dress: smart casual. Wireless internet.* **Map p239 H6.**

Blue Bar. *See p41.*

Coburg Bar

The Connaught, Carlos Place, W1K 2AL (7499 7070, www.the-connaught.co.uk). Bond Street or Green Park tube. **Open** 11am-11pm Mon, Sun; 11am-1am Tue-Sat. **Food served** 11am-11pm daily. **Mayfair**
There's no velvet rope barring your way to the Connaught's destination bar, and no door-nazi attitude: you can just walk straight on in. And once you've done so, the service will be faultless. The room oozes sophistication, with modern touches (grey velvet wing-backed chairs, black-glass tables) that enhance the historic character of the space. The drinks list charts the evolution of the cocktail, with each drink – the greatest hits of the last two centuries, more or less – well worth the expense. The wine list is exemplary, if pricey, with an emphasis on fine French marques. Tip-top nibbles are free of charge; better, a tiny skewer of iced fruit on a silver dish appears with each cocktail as a palate-cleanser. Luxurious, elegant and discreet, the Coburg Bar is everything a good hotel bar should be. *Disabled: toilet. Wireless internet.* **Map p239 H7.**

Connaught Bar

The Connaught, Carlos Place, W1K 2AL (7499 7070, www.the-connaught.co.uk). Bond Street or Green Park tube. **Open** 4pm-1am Mon-Sat. **Mayfair**

The Connaught's other bar is both cosy and elegant, with unobtrusive lighting, pastel walls and a conspiratorial duskiness that settles through the rooms as the evening goes on. After a liquid amuse-bouche, a dainty flute of pineapple juice with mint and berry-infused gin, the drinks have a lot to live up to, but they should meet most expectations. The house martini is worth ordering simply for the tableside theatre: a waiter will pour gin and vermouth from a crystal tumbler into a frozen glass in front of you, then invite you to select a dash of infused bitters from an apothecary-style array. Service is always charming, and the complimentary nibbles are exemplary. *Disabled: toilet (hotel). Function room (200 capacity). Wireless internet.* **Map p239 H7.**

Dukes Bar

Dukes Hotel, 35 St James's Place, SW1A 1NY (7491 4840, www.campbellgrayhotels. com). Green Park tube. **Open** 2pm-midnight Mon-Thur, Sun; noon-midnight Fri, Sat. **St James's**

With its engravings and fringed chairs, the tiny, comfortable bar at this exclusive hotel looks like an upper-class Georgian sitting room, but few butlers could manage martinis of this calibre. If the art looks simple, that's because it is: the quiet waiters simply flick dry vermouth into an iced glass, fill it with gin or vodka (various premium options, all priced accordingly) and then drop in a sliver of lemon peel. Whether the secret is the elegant wooden tray, the vermouth flask that resembles a vinegar bottle in a cheap chippie or the staff's mannered method of delivery, sipping a drink amid the murmur of the grown-up clientele while munching nuts and Puglian olives is one of the most soothing, elegant drinking experiences in the city. *Dress: smart casual. Tables outdoors (4, garden). Wireless internet.* **Map p249 J8.**

Galvin at Windows

London Hilton on Park Lane, 28th floor, 22 Park Lane, W1K 1BE (7208 4021, www. galvinatwindows.com). Hyde Park Corner tube. **Open** 11am-1am Mon-Wed; 11am-3am Thur, Fri; 3pm-3am Sat; 11am-10.30pm Sun. **Food served** 11am-12.30am Mon-Wed; 6pm-12.30am Thur-Sat. **Mayfair**

Your rewards for sussing out the Byzantine lift-button system and negotiating the compulsory coat-check are breathtaking panoramic views, from both the bar (to the left) and restaurant (to the right). The expansive bar area comprises olive-green divans and high-backed armless chairs; the tone is amplified by champagne buckets next to each table. The cocktails exude

Connaught Bar

an exotic Latin-Med touch: the Croatian Lover (Akvinta vodka, Grand Marnier and grapefruit juice) is among the list of six Galvin's Specials, while the Capri C'est Fini (Absolut Citron, Absolut Mandarin, lime and mint) sits in the Love & Lust section. Nothing's cheap, but you're paying for the views, the nuts and the Gioconda smile with which every order is delivered.
Disabled: toilet (hotel). Dress: smart casual. Wireless internet. **Map p239 G8.**

Hunter 486

Arch London, 50 Great Cumberland Place, W1H 7FD (7724 0486, www.thearchlondon. com). Marble Arch tube. **Open/food served** 6.30am-10.30pm daily. **Marylebone**
Its name taken from the pre-war telephone code for Marylebone – hence the phone dial logo on the beer mats – HUNter 486 is a relaxed but upscale lobby bar and restaurant in the boutique Arch Hotel. Drinking and dining areas merge amid high-sided, half-moon seating areas, but the bar counter is a squeeze. Cocktails, conceived by the Gorgeous Group, include pisco sours created with 1615 Peruvian brandy, and the Leopard's Punch, with Snow Leopard vodka, Hungarian apricot pálinka schnapps, fresh raspberries and a splash of prosecco. A HUNtini involves Van Wees Three Corners dry gin and Manzanilla dry sherry, while the Earl Grey MarTEAni has Tanqueray infused with the namesake tea, lemon juice, sugar and egg white. A 40-strong choice of wines runs all the way up to a Château Margaux 1er Cru 1998 (£475), while the Musetti 202 coffee has been specially blended for the bar.
Babies & children admitted. Booking advisable Fri, Sat. Disabled: lift. Dress: smart casual. Wireless internet. **Map p238 F6.**

Library

The Lanesborough, 1 Lanesborough Place, Hyde Park Corner, SW1X 7TA (7259 5599, www.lanesborough.com). Hyde Park Corner tube. **Open** 11am-1am Mon-Sat; noon-10.30pm Sun. **Food served** noon-midnight Mon-Sat; noon-10.30pm Sun. **Belgravia**
Across the road from Hyde Park and carefully muffled against the noise of Hyde Park Corner sits the Lanesborough, a former hospital that now offers a rather more luxurious kind of sleepover. Master bartender Salvatore Calabrese left some years ago, which may account for a slight slippage in cocktail quality: on our last visit, the Lanesborough, a combination of champagne, limoncello, aperol and fresh orange juice, tasted more like a simple Buck's Fizz. But the upholstery is still comfortable, the rosewood and mahogany bookshelves remain gracious, and the service continues to be gently attentive. And if you're clever enough to arrive mid-afternoon, you'll be offered proper canapés as well as Bombay mix and olives.
Disabled: toilet. Entertainment (pianist 6.30pm Mon-Sat). Function rooms (180 capacity). Wireless internet.

Lobby Bar

Lobby Bar

*One Aldwych, WC2B 4RH (7300 1070,
www.onealdwych.com). Covent Garden or
Temple tube.* **Open** 8am-midnight Mon-Sat;
8am-11pm Sun. **Food served** noon-5pm, 5.30-
11pm Mon-Sat; noon-5pm, 5.30-10.30pm Sun.
Aldwych
Although the unflattering flight-attendant-style
uniforms of the staff might suggest otherwise,
the luxurious One Aldwych seems intent on
proving that hotel lobby bars don't have
to resemble airport lounges. It's hard not to be
wowed by the soaring space, with its triffid-
sized flower arrangements, elegant pillars and
ceiling-height windows; but the majesty of the
room is lent intimacy by high-backed armchairs,
comfortable sofas and shimmering candles.
Staff at the sleek black bar dispense a selection
of expertly mixed cocktails – starting at £11.50,
or £12.50 for champagne varieties – from a
seasonal list that might include a warming
Winter Essence (Calvados Boulard, bay leaves,
cinnamon and own-made prune syrup). On our
last visit, we were served house champagne
instead of the requested Louis Roederer,
but service is otherwise slick and friendly.
*Babies & children admitted. Disabled: toilet.
Function room (10 capacity). Wireless internet.*
Map p243 M7.

Mandarin Bar

*Mandarin Oriental Hyde Park,
66 Knightsbridge, SW1X 7LA (7235 2000,
www.mandarinoriental.com). Knightsbridge
tube.* **Open/food served** 10.30am-1.30am
Mon-Sat; 10.30am-11.30pm Sun. **Knightsbridge**
Step out of the Knightsbridge chaos into the
Mandarin Oriental's cool marble surrounds and
you might initially expect to be greeted with a
proper British colonial drinking experience, all
obsequious waiters and opium-tinted drinks.
But, for better or for worse, the Mandarin Bar
smacks more of the 1980s: the staff mix drinks
behind a glowing frosted glass panel, the floor
is as shiny as a banker's pearl cufflink, and the
size of the cocktails bespeaks an era that
recession forgot. They're not bad, either: a bit
sweet (five spoonfuls is a lot of sugar, even for
a caipirinha) but well balanced, and they really
are huge. There's no obligatory service charge,
which, given that the staff are splendid and the
crisps are replenished at five-minute intervals,
is pleasing. When casting your eyes around the
place, look out for the glass corridor containing
the restaurant's supply of wines. They're
conditions to make a sommelier weep, but those
of us who can't afford the contents can at least
enjoy a good look at what we're missing.
Disabled: toilet (hotel). Dress code: smart casual.

Pearl Bar & Restaurant

*Chancery Court Hotel, 252 High Holborn,
WC1V 7EN (7829 7000, www.pearl-
restaurant.com). Holborn tube.* **Open**
11am-11pm Mon-Fri; 6-11pm Sat. **Holborn**
After having passed the flunkies gesturing
to chauffeured guests as they pull into this
upscale Marriott outpost, you're faced with a
choice: to the right, the CC Bar; to the left, Pearl,
part French restaurant and part cocktail bar.
A corridor contains five seating areas divided
by strands of illuminated beads, each with an
oval table and a thick drinks menu; the light
wood and fawn colour scheme is echoed by
half a dozen stools along the bar. The cocktails
are inventive, well-mixed and pre-crunch
pricey: fresh fruit, exotic mixers, high-end base
fuels. Seven 'bartenders' choices' (£13.75)
include a Bumble Bee, made with honey and
vanilla vodkas, Disaronno and fresh mint;
the list of 'Pearl specialities' (£11.50) includes
Oriental Fusion, made with Luksusowa vodka,
chilli pepper syrup and lychee liqueur. Not
cheap, then; but if you're in an affair and/or
on expenses, Pearl is money well spent.
*Babies & children admitted (until 7pm).
Disabled: toilet. Dress: smart casual.
Entertainment (pianist 7pm Wed-Sat).*
Map p242 M5.

Polo Bar

*Westbury Hotel, New Bond Street, W1S 2YF
(7629 7755, www.westburymayfair.co.uk).
Bond Street or Oxford Circus tube.* **Open** 9am-
1am Mon-Fri; 11am-1am Sat; noon-midnight
Sun. **Food served** 10.30am-midnight Mon-
Fri; 11am-midnight Sat; noon-midnight Sun.
Mayfair
'Art deco lite' might best describe the look of
the Westbury Hotel's Polo Bar: the bar is
marble-topped, the tables are inlaid wood, and
the pillars chunky and square. Yet perhaps
because it's such a long, large room (there'll be
no eavesdropping here), the place doesn't blare
its design at you, allowing the drinks to take
precedence. Or, at least, they could if they
weren't a little lacklustre: the Ketel One martini
doesn't kick you in the head quite as it should,
although it does contain a very fine oversized
olive; and the bellini lacked the scent of
summer and that unctuous mix of peach and
alcohol that makes the imbiber feel like a
drunken wasp. Not a destination bar, then, but
its location makes it a useful escape hatch for
weary shoppers fresh from Regent, Oxford and
New Bond Streets.
*Babies & children admitted (until 6pm).
Disabled: toilet (hotel). Dress: smart casual.
Wireless internet.* **Map p241 J7.**

Rivoli at the Ritz

Ritz Hotel, 150 Piccadilly, W1J 9BR (7493 8181, www.theritzlondon.com). Green Park tube. **Open** 11.30am-1am Mon-Sat; noon-11.30pm Sun. **Food served** noon-10pm daily. **Piccadilly**

The Ritz's dress-code requirement is outlined by the hotel's liveried flunkies – box hats, birds' feathers and all – who address many guests by title and surname as they pass through the lobby. The stratospherically over-the-top decor in the Rivoli bar harks back to the golden era of cocktails between the wars, although it's far more garish than it needs to be. The prices here will only appear sensible if money is of no consequence: among the nine house speciality cocktails are the Cesar Ritz (£120), made with Courvoisier L'Esprit, Ruinart Blanc de Blancs champagne and angostura bitters; and, a comparative snip at just £17, the Ritz Whiskers (Four Roses small-batch bourbon, Ketel One vanilla vodka and amaretto). Champagne cocktails, martinis, long drinks and after-dinner cocktails are priced in similarly if-you-have-to-ask-you-can't-afford-it fashion. *Babies & children admitted (lounge area). Disabled: toilet (hotel). Dress: jacket & tie, no jeans or trainers.* **Map p241 J8.**

Beaufort Bar at the Savoy.
See p40.

Trader Vic's

London Hilton on Park Lane, 22 Park Lane, W1K 4BE (7208 4113, www.tradervics.com). Hyde Park Corner tube. **Open/food served** noon-1am Mon-Wed, Sun; noon-3am Thur, Fri; 5pm-3am Sat. **Mayfair**

This warren of Samoan-themed, carved-wood campery in the bowels of the Hilton has been here since 1963. There's even a cocktail in honour of its arrival: the London Sour, made with scotch, orange, lemon and 'a whisper of almonds'. On the cover of the menu, bare-breasted native lassies engage in Tahitian revelry while a sailor type soaks in rum. As the 50-strong list within urges, 'Pirates, buccaneers and beachcombers never bandy their drinking.' Thus, Trader Vic's Grog, a 'potent blend' of dark rum, pineapple and passion fruit, or the Suffering Bastard, a 'forthright blend' of rums and lime from the Shepheard Hotel in Cairo. Many of these flamboyant concoctions are served in agreeably daft vessels: it's almost worth ordering the Samoan Fog Cutter just for a close-up look at its absurd, vase-like glass. For better or worse, a London institution. *Babies & children admitted (restaurant). Disabled: toilet (hotel). Entertainment (bands 10.30pm Mon-Sat). Function room (70 capacity).* **Map p239 G8.**

Zetter Townhouse

49-50 St John's Square, EC1V 4JJ (7324 4545, www.thezettertownhouse.com). Farringdon tube/rail. **Open** 10am-midnight Mon-Thur, Sun; 10am-1am Fri, Sat. **Food served** noon-5pm, 6-10.30pm daily. **Clerkenwell**

Spread across the ground floor of a Georgian townhouse across from the original Zetter hotel, this quirky cocktail lounge is a collaboration with the founders of Islington's 69 Colebrooke Row. Head barman Tony Conigliaro is an expert alchemist, renowned for his leftfield libations created with an array of bespoke bitters and innovative infusions. The switched-on staff are happy to talk you through the experimental yet refreshingly uncomplicated 13-strong cocktail menu (£8.50), which includes the Flintlock (Beefeater gin, gunpowder tea tincture, sugar, Fernet Branca, and dandelion and burdock bitters) and Les Fleurs du Mal (rose vodka, lemon juice and a hint of La Fontaine absinthe). The decor is an eccentrically British affair akin to a stately home, teeming with curiosities alongside an apothecary-style bar, but with its soothing French accordion music it feels cosy and comfortable. There's afternoon tea as well. *Babies & children admitted. Booking advisable. Disabled: lift, toilet. Function room (20-40 capacity). Wirelesss internet.* **Map p242 O4.**

Wine Bars

Central	48
North	55
North East	55
South East	55
South West	56
West	57

Wine Bars

In spite of the recession, increasing adventurousness on the part of bar owners and entrepreneurs across the capital has left London with a broader and more appealing range of wine bars than it's ever boasted before. It reflects a growing interest in – and knowledge of – wine around the country, a trend capitalised on by outfits such as **28°-50° Wine Workshop & Kitchen**, which encourages a finer appreciation of wine and, like many of the bars in this section, places an equal emphasis on food.

The most successful venues are those giving their customers transparent value. Most notably, the *enoteca* model, which sees bars offering customers the choice of drinking on the premises or taking away their purchases, has proved triumphant. Outstanding examples include **Vinoteca**, with a new branch in Marylebone, **Green & Blue** in East Dulwich, the **Kensington Wine Rooms**, and London's two excellent department-store wine bars, Fortnum & Mason's **1707** and Selfridges' **Wonder Bar**. The blurring of distinctions between on and off sales is also reflected in the wine-retailing operations at restaurants such as **St John**.

However, perhaps the biggest development of recent years has been the growth of the 'natural' wine bar. The natural wine movement can be broadly defined as a commitment to non-interventionist vinification, with sulphur dioxide as the only permitted additive and then only at bottling and in small amounts; the growers work sustainably in the vineyards and many produce organic or biodynamic wines. Makers of natural wines are hugely fashionable in France – Paris teems with bars dedicated to their wines – and London has started to catch on, with venues such as **Terroirs** and newcomer **Bar Battu** at the head of the pack.

Central

1707

Fortnum & Mason, 181 Piccadilly, lower ground floor, W1J 9FA (7734 8040, www. fortnumandmason.com). Piccadilly Circus tube. **Open** noon-10pm Mon-Sat; noon-5pm Sun. **Food served** noon-9.30pm Mon-Sat; noon-4pm Sun. **Piccadilly**

Although it's named after the year in which Fortnum & Mason, its parent operation, was founded, 1707 looks to the future. The decorative lines are clean and modern, unpolished wooden slats line the walls, and the wine list goes beyond the traditional choices. The store has collaborated with some top-flight producers (Verget, Torbreck, Cherillon) for its own-label wines, but the real fun comes if you're willing to pay £10 corkage on the retail price of wines stocked by the shop's wine department. There's predictable strength in traditional areas of France, including a superior champagne list that features the full range from cult producer Jacques Selosse, but also a fine selection of Austrian and Portuguese bottles; as well as the individual bottles and glasses, wine flights are available. The food spotlights produce available in the adjacent food hall, but tends to be average. *Babies & children admitted. Booking advisable. Disabled: toilet. Dress: smart casual. Entertainment (guitarist 6pm Mon-Sat).* **Map p241 J7.**

28°-50° Wine Workshop & Kitchen

140 Fetter Lane, EC4A 1BT (7242 8877, www.2850.co.uk). Farringdon tube/rail. **Open** noon-midnight Mon-Fri. **Food served** noon-2.30pm, 6-9.30pm Mon-Fri. **City**

This venture, named after the latitudes between which wine is produced, is a dark, concentrated basement for serious contemplation of wine and food matching. It's a real joy to be able to sample three or four distinctive, high-quality wines and come out blinking into the daylight still sober (wines are sold in almost homeopathic measures of 75ml, or 150ml). The list includes 15 each of reds and whites, from Barossa Valley shiraz

2007 brut, for example, served in a flute) and a few sherries. Food is on-trend in size – there are small plates of tapas/cicchetti drawing on French, Italian and Spanish influences, plus charcuterie plates and a few pan-Euro 'main plates'. With its modish, New York-style make-over (bare brick walls, functional furniture, industrial-chic lights hung low over tables), Bar Battu is simply a very nice place to drink some seldom seen, well-chosen wines and thoughtful food helped along by City-slick service.
Babies & children admitted. Booking advisable. Disabled: toilet. Function rooms (50 capacity). Wireless internet. **Map p245 P6.**

Bar Pepito
Varnishers Yard, Regent Quarter, N1 9NL (7841 7331, www.camino.uk.com/pepito). King's Cross tube/rail. **Open** 5pm-midnight Mon-Fri; 6pm-midnight Sat. **Food served** 5-11pm Mon-Fri; 6-11pm Sat. **King's Cross**
Tucked away in a courtyard accessible via an alley at the foot of Pentonville Road, this rustic, Andalucian-themed bar is dedicated to sherry. With room for only four or five tables, all shaped from sherry casks, it's a tiny place – so small, in fact, that the toilet is across the road at Camino (run by the same folks; *see p175*) – but no less appealing for its lack of size. The 15 sherries span all styles: fino, which is dry, delicate and pale; manzanilla, comparatively brusque and briny; the sweeter, fruitier styles made with the pedro ximénez grape; and so on. You can sample the breadth of flavours by buying a sherry flight for around £8. The tapas-style cold-food menu features cured meats, olives, regional cheeses, pickled anchovies and figs coated in dark chocolate. The candelabra and bare-brick walls make it cosy, if squeezed; thankfully, there's room outside in summer.

Barrica
62 Goodge Street, W1T 4NE (7436 9448, www.barrica.co.uk). Goodge Street or Tottenham Court Road tube. **Open** noon-midnight Mon-Fri; 1pm-midnight Sat. **Food served** noon-11pm Mon-Fri; 1-11pm Sat. **Fitzrovia**
Vinos, finos and manzanillas are the order of the day at this slavishly conceived Noho version of a Spanish sherry bar. Boss Tim Luther previously worked in the wine trade, and is clearly an oenophile who knows his onions. More than a dozen types of sherry are (for the most part) available by the 100ml or 375ml measure; a standard Tio Pepe is an eminently affordable £3.50. All types are clearly and intelligently described, with suggestions of food to complement them – yes, there is a full selection

to Corsican vermentino, on the ever-changing list. The food menu is just as enthusiastically prepared, with ingredients of a high quality, served at City prices: fillets of pan-fried red mullet come with a bouillabaisse-like sauce of clams; a plate of charcuterie, Spanish and Italian, gives a range of flavours and textures as varied as the wines. The service is fastidious.
Babies & children admitted. Booking advisable. Function rooms (6-12 capacity). **Map p243 N6.**

Bar Battu
48 Gresham Street, EC2V 7AY (7036 6100, www.barbattu.com). Bank tube/DLR. **Open** 11.30am-11pm Mon-Fri. **Food served** noon-10pm Mon-Fri. **City**
'Natural' wines are still something of a rarity, and it's more unusual still to see a whole carte devoted to them. Many are available by the glass or carafe, and an enthusiastic sommelier is on hand to guide drinkers as to how 'natural' methods affect cloudiness, body and how expressive the character is. There are also upscale French ciders (Eric Bordelet's elegant

of tapas and, yes, they are indeed authentic. White wines are categorised by grape – albarino, godello – and reds by flavour. Serious and far wealthier Hispanophiles can pick out a UK rarity, such as a Llicorella pedro ximénez (£37) from Catalonia. Note, too, the Basque spirit pacharán, sloe-flavoured and capable of delivering serious hangovers. Hanging hams lend that Iberian touch.
Babies & children admitted. Booking advisable. Tables outdoors (2, terrace). Wireless internet. **Map p240 J5.**

Bedford & Strand

1A Bedford Street, WC2E 9HH (7836 3033, www.bedford-strand.com). Covent Garden tube or Charing Cross tube/rail. **Open** noon-midnight Mon-Sat. **Food served** noon-10.30pm Mon-Sat. **Covent Garden**
In an area otherwise dominated by tourist traps, Bedford & Strand is popular with local workers, who stream to the basement bar for after-hours drinks. Named, American-style, after its two cross streets, the bar also has a New York feel to its wine list. The headline page of the list offers around two dozen selections available by the glass, carafe or bottle, split into five price-defined sections: 'Reliable', 'Honest', 'Decent', 'Good' and 'Staff Picks'. The rest of the list is available by the bottle only, with the exception of a few sherries and champagnes. There's a balance of New and Old Worlds, along with some curiosities (Brazilian wine, for instance). Pricing isn't aggressive, but it pays to trade up. A glazed

St Pancras Grand Champagne Bar.
See p54.

partition separates the bar from the white-tableclothed dining area, where bistro staples are on offer. A separate deli counter serves finger foods and charcuterie.
Booking advisable. Wireless internet. **Map p241 L7.**

Bleeding Heart Tavern

Bleeding Heart Yard, 19 Greville Street, EC1N 8SJ (7404 0333, www.bleedingheart.co.uk). Farringdon tube/rail. **Open** 7am-11pm Mon-Fri. **Food served** 7-10.30am, noon-10pm Mon-Fri. **Clerkenwell**
The current incarnation of this historic tavern may be more refined than its 18th-century forebears (you're unlikely to get 'drunk for a penny, dead drunk for two pence'), but Bleeding Heart is well aware of its heritage: the relaxed atmosphere is more pub than wine bar. However, owner Robert Wilson, who also runs the restaurant next door, has a real wine geek's enthusiasm, and the extensive list covers every major wine-producing area in some depth. Wilson has a stake in the Trinity Hill winery in Hawkes Bay, and his own wines feature prominently on the list. However, the real strength lies in the far more expensive reds: the Homage syrah is one of New Zealand's greatest. In the basement, the Tavern Dining Room offers a choice of straightforward roasts and grills, together with such comfort food as fish pie.
Babies & children admitted. Function room (120 capacity). Tables outdoors (16, terrace). **Map p242 N5.**

Cellar Gascon. See p52.

Café des Amis
11-14 Hanover Place, WC2E 9JP (7379 3444, www.cafedesamis.co.uk). Covent Garden tube. **Open** 11.30am-1am Mon-Sat. **Food served** 11.30am-11pm Mon-Sat.
Covent Garden
A useful bolt-hole if you don't fancy the Opera House bars, this Covent Garden veteran is determinedly French in outlook. Done out with mini-chandeliers, dark alcoves and prints of prima ballerinas, the studiously inoffensive basement bar fills up quickly at peak times; a late licence allows for more protracted post-show drinking. Wines are split between France and *vins étrangers*, with an emphasis on the former, especially among the reds. Although the menu descriptions are an exercise in risible pseudo-winespeak, the quality is sound and there are around eight of each colour by the glass. Bar food is standard brasserie fare: starters of steak tartare, omelettes, own-made terrine, along with some large salads and mains such as rib-eye steak and moules marinière. *Babies & children admitted (until 5pm). Booking advisable Wed-Sat. Function room (100 capacity). Tables outdoors (12, terrace).* **Map p241 L6**.

Capote y Toros
157 Old Brompton Road, SW5 0LJ (7373 0567, www.cambiodetercio.co.uk). Gloucester Road or South Kensington tube. **Open/food served** 6-11pm Tue-Sat.
South Kensington
Like its sister restaurants (Cambio de Tercio and Tendido Cero) that together create a sherry-and-tapas triangle on Old Brompton Road, Capote y Toros is done out in vibrant colours. The deep pink and ultra-orange echo the bullfighters' capes in the framed portrayals of bullfighting that fill an entire wall in this small, shop-front sherry and jamón bar. The same sense of bravado carries over to the bill of fare. The wine list explores the great names (Rioja, Ribera del Duero) and lesser-known regions of Spain. The main attraction here, though, is not the wines, but the sherries. You can taste them in all their multifaceted glory, the 48 varieties available by the glass, ranging from bone-dry, pale-straw-coloured finos and manzanillas to unctuously rich, raisiny sweet pedro ximénez. The menu is a mini gastro-tour of Spain's great and good, so you can order Andalucian-style chilled gazpacho soup, or Galician-style boiled octopus dusted with paprika, as well as dishes cooked using various styles of sherry. *Babies & children admitted (until 9pm). Function room (60 capacity).* **Map p248 A4**.

Bow Wine Vaults
10 Bow Churchyard, EC4M 9DQ (7248 1121, www.bowwinevaults.com). Mansion House tube or Bank tube/DLR. **Open** 11am-11pm Mon-Fri. **Food served** 11.30am-3.30pm Mon-Fri. **City**
Part-wine bar, part-restaurant, this City staple aims for simplicity. Done out in plain walls and clean woods, the bar area is as straightforward as any pub, albeit a little brighter; there are restaurants adjacent and below. Five wines of each colour are available by the glass, including a Chilean chardonnay and a French chablis; the 50-odd varieties by the bottle run from a sauvignon blanc from the Van Zylshof Estate in South Africa to rarer reds from the likes of Italy's Guerrieri Rizzardi; most bottles are priced in the £20 to £30 range. The wine-bar menu features uncomplicated comfort-cooking: sirloin steak sandwich, Welsh rarebit with a cheese and ale topping, and so on. *Tables outdoors (15, pavement).* **Map p245 P6**.

Cellar Gascon

59 West Smithfield, EC1A 9DS (7600 7561, www.cellargascon.com). Barbican tube or Farringdon tube/rail. **Open** noon-midnight Mon-Fri. **Food served** noon-11.30pm Mon-Fri. **Clerkenwell**

The wine-bar arm of Vincent Labeyrie and Pascal Aussignac's Smithfield temple to the gastronomy of their native Gascony has a clubby feel. Certainly, the well-dressed City workers who come here to enjoy the excellent selection of wines should feel at home amid the leather banquettes and subdued lighting. The food comes in tapas-sized portions; as at Club Gascon, the restaurant next door, foie gras is king. The region's reds are dark and brooding, but there's an admirable selection of sweet wines to match the foie gras; the lush Domaine de Causse Marines' Grain de Folie Douce, a Gaillac Doux, displays hints of apricot and quince. Service is skilled. A little more choice by the glass would be nice, but overall, this is an outstanding operation. (For off-sales, investigate the similarly noteworthy Comptoir Gascon across the market; 61-63 Charterhouse Street, EC1M 6HJ, 7608 0851.)

Babies & children admitted. Booking advisable. Tables outdoors (3, pavement). **Map p242 N4.**

Cork & Bottle

44-46 Cranbourn Street, WC2H 7AN (7734 7807, www.thecorkandbottle.co.uk). Leicester Square tube. **Open/food served** 11am-11.30pm Mon-Sat; noon-10.30pm Sun. **Leicester Square**

Blink and you might miss this unexpected spot, founded by New Zealander Don Hewitson in 1971 and now a lively holdout against the grim pizza joints and the high-street chains that surround it. Mumm is on display as you head down to the basement, which gets packed with pre-theatre diners munching burgers. The simple menu is paired with a diverse global wine list; names to watch out for might include Peter Barry from South Australia's Clare Valley or the Grant Burge shiraz from the nearby Miamba valley, contrasted with cellared Bordeaux (from chateaux Kirwan and Citran). The only real grumble is the glassware: better stemware would do more justice to this attractive list.

Babies & children admitted. **Map p241 K7.**

Ebury Wine Bar & Restaurant

139 Ebury Street, SW1W 9QU (7730 5447, www.eburywinebar.co.uk). Sloane Square tube or Victoria tube/rail. **Open** noon-11pm Mon-Sat; noon-10pm Sun. **Food served** noon-10.15pm Mon-Sat; noon-9.15pm Sun. **Victoria**

A Belgravia fixture for more than 40 years, the Ebury is an appealing synthesis of new and old. A small front bar caters to those who want to pop in for a quick drink from the eclectic wine list, which offers a good 30 choices by the glass. New and Old Worlds receive roughly equal billing; from the Rheingau region of Germany, Johannisberger Erntebringer riesling kabinett 2009 is packed with unpretentious charm. There's dark wood panelling and a garish trompe l'œil fresco in the rear dining room, where the menu nods to grand French tradition (pork fillet with prunes and brandy) while also taking in casual Mediterranean flavours (sea bass with roasted aubergine and chickpea compote) and simple grills. *Babies & children admitted. Booking advisable.* **Map p249 H10**.

El Vino
47 Fleet Street, EC4Y 1BJ (7353 6786, www.elvino.co.uk). Chancery Lane or Temple tube. **Open** 8.30am-9pm Mon; 8.30am-10pm Tue-Fri. **Food served** 8.30am-8pm Mon; 8.30am-9pm Tue-Fri. **City**
The television with the sound turned down, the red-and-white sign outside boasting wines from 'Spain, Portugal, France, Germany', the knowledgeable, softly spoken staff – everything about this wine bar ('est. 1879') is discreet and old-school. A library hush reigns within the dark-wood surrounds, as a professional, middle-aged and mainly male clientele – no journos these days, chiz chiz – quaff well-chosen wines from a 200-strong list that features many lesser-known producers: a 2008 Viu Manent cabernet sauvignon, for example. The enterprise also operates as a wine shop and runs a delivery service. Lunch includes the traditional likes of hot open sandwiches and ploughman's with five cheese choices, but also more exotic tapas: courgette and pine nut bruschetta, devilled whitebait and battered calamari. *Booking advisable. Function room (65 capacity). Tables outdoors (4, courtyard).* **Map p243 N6**.

Gordon's Wine Bar
47 Villiers Street, WC2N 6NE (7930 1408, www.gordonswinebar.com). Embankment tube or Charing Cross tube/rail. **Open** 11am-11pm Mon-Sat; noon-10pm Sun. **Food served** noon-10pm Mon-Sat; noon-9pm Sun. **Strand**
Gordon's was established in its present form in 1890, but the exposed brickwork, flickering candlelight and tobacco-stained fixtures and fittings in the low basement vaults make it feel older still. Like the crowds, which are younger and livelier than you might expect, the wine list

Bar Battu. *See p49*.

is surprisingly modern, hopping readily from the classic regions of France to South America and beyond. But the real eye-catchers are the fortified wines drawn directly from casks behind the bar: ports, sherries and Madeiras that fit nicely with the resolutely uncomplicated buffet-style food (pies, salads, cheeseboards) and tapas in the evening. When the subterranean rooms are crammed, which is often, it can get distinctly warm in the semi-darkness, but a drink or two here remains a classic London experience. And in summer, you can repair to the terrace alongside the Embankment Gardens for barbecued food with a cheeky Australian. *Babies & children admitted. Tables outdoors (20, terrace).* **Map p241 L7.**

St Pancras Grand Champagne Bar

St Pancras International Station, Pancras Road, NW1 2QP (7870 9900, www.searcys.co.uk/ st-pancras-grand). King's Cross tube/rail or St Pancras International rail. **Open** 9am-11pm Mon-Fri, Sun; 8am-11pm Sat. **Food served** 9am-10.30pm Mon-Fri, Sun; 8am-10.30pm Sat. **King's Cross**

The operators' claim that this is 'Europe's longest champagne bar' is a little misleading. While the tables stretch a fair distance along the length of the Eurostar terminal, the bar itself is a squat little thing. Still, sipping champagne beneath William Henry Barlow's Victorian roof is a lovely experience, not unlike drinking in a vast secular cathedral. Searcy's has installed a professional operation with witty references to Anglo-French endeavour: selections from the champagne list, which features every significant Grand Marque and includes around 15 by the glass, are served in English-made Dartington flutes. It's possible to spend £880 on a bottle of 1996 Krug Clos de Mesnil; more affordable temptations include Tsarine Cuvée Premium Brut NV (£10.50 a glass or £61 a bottle). The short menu focuses on British ingredients. *Babies & children admitted. Disabled toilet (station). Dress: smart casual. Wireless internet.*

Terroirs

5 William IV Street, WC2N 4DW (7036 0660, www.terroirswinebar.com). Charing Cross tube/rail. **Open/food served** noon-11pm Mon-Sat. **Strand**

One of the most likeable London arrivals of recent years, this bright, handsome wine bar and restaurant takes food and drink seriously yet without pretension. The speciality is 'natural' wines, made with organic and biodynamically grown grape varieties or without added sulphur, sugar or acid. The unstuffy list is dominated by

28°-50° Wine Workshop & Kitchen. *See p48.*

French regions, augmented by a short Italian section and a 'token Spanish' red and white; the excellent staff are more than able to point you in the right direction if you ask for advice. The food, too, is terrific: a tapas-style selection of French bar snacks, charcuterie and seafood, plus *plats du jour* of the pot-roasted quail or brandade de morue variety. It's bigger than it looks, spread over the ground floor, the lower ground floor and a surprisingly airy, pleasant basement, but you'll still probably need to book – it's a popular place, and with very good reason. *Babies & children admitted. Booking advisable. Tables outdoors (3, pavement).* **Map p241 L7.**

Vinoteca

15 Seymour Place, W1H 5BD (7724 7288, www.vinoteca.co.uk). Marble Arch tube. **Open** noon-11pm Mon-Sat; noon-5pm Sun. **Food served** noon-3pm, 6-10pm Mon-Sat; noon-5pm Sun. **Marylebone**

The original Vinoteca in Farringdon is full-to-heaving most nights, so it's no surprise they have kept their winning formula for this second branch: it's a wine shop as well as a restaurant, the visual focus being the full-wall display of wine bottles. There aren't many places in the capital where you can order a glass of müller-thurgau from Slovakia or Arbois Traminer from Jura – or you can choose something equally pleasing from the 285-strong list to take home (at shop retail prices); the enthusiastic staff are happy to make recommendations. Each of the dishes on the modish, frequently changing Modern European menu (smoked mackerel salad, parmesan pancake filled with wild mushrooms) comes with a suggested wine by the glass. The food doesn't play second fiddle to the wine here, though. Even if you're just here for drinks, you'll need to nibble something (licence laws) but small bar snacks (£2-£4) are available. *Babies & children admitted. Booking (lunch only) advisable. Function room (40 capacity). Tables outdoors (4, pavement).* **Map p238 F6.**

Wonder Bar
Selfridges, 400 Oxford Street, W1A 1AB (7318 2476, www.selfridges.com). Bond Street or Marble Arch tube. **Open/food served** 9.30am-9.30pm Mon-Sat; 11.30am-6pm Sun. **Marylebone**
When the Wonder Bar opened a couple of years ago, occupying a red and blond wood space on a mezzanine above Selfridges' wine department, the concept seemed very attractive. The new Enomatic machines would serve as 'wine jukeboxes': customers would be able to help themselves to small measures from up to 52 different wines, with the tiny 25ml pour bringing extremely expensive wines into the reach of ordinary mortals. The intervention of trading-standards officials put paid to the novelty, with the bar subsequently limited by law to a minimum serving of 125ml; there's hope that the law will be changed, though the government may have other priorities. Even so, the choice of wines remains good, with a nice mix of favourites and new, challenging flavours. *Babies & children admitted.* **Map p239 G6.**

Also recommended...
Anthologist (Good Mixers, *p172*); **Camino** (Good Mixers, *p175*); **Cinnamon Club** (Cocktails & Spirits, *p22*); **Coach & Horses** (Gastropubs & Brasseries, *p130*); **Coburg Bar** (Hotel Bars, *p42*); **Duke of Wellington** (Gastropubs & Brasseries, *p130*); **Fellow** (Good Mixers, *p177*); **Hawksmoor** (Cocktails & Spirits, *p27*); **Honey Pot** (Gastropubs & Brasseries, *p133*); **Mark's Bar** (Cocktails & Spirits, *p28*); **Only Running Footman** (Gastropubs & Brasseries, *p133*); **Opera Tavern** (Gastropubs & Brasseries, *p134*); **St John** (Gastropubs & Brasseries, *p135*); **Seven Stars** (Gastropubs & Brasseries, *p136*); **Somers Town Coffee House** (Gastropubs & Brasseries, *p136*); **Temperance** (Gastropubs & Brasseries, *p136*); **Vertigo 42** (Rooms with a View, *p163*); **White Swan Pub & Dining Room** (Gastropubs & Brasseries, *p137*).

North
Also recommended...
Drapers Arms (Gastropubs & Brasseries, *p139*).

North East
Also recommended...
Prince Arthur (Gastropubs & Brasseries, *p144*).

South East
Boot & Flogger
10-20 Redcross Way, SE1 1TA (7407 1184). Borough tube. **Open** 11am-8pm Mon-Fri. **Food served** 11am-7pm Mon-Fri. **Borough**
'JHn. Davy Free Vintner' reads the sign on the wall of an empty Borough side street, above an 071 number. It may as well read 'Southwark 1184' for all the modernity present within. 'Hello, Sir,' calls out Peter Common from behind a hatch as you enter, admiring the beautiful wood-panelled interior and occasional finely upholstered chair amid the wooden ones. A bowl of water biscuits awaits on the counter, where the promise of rare sirloin and cured ox tongue cold cuts is chalked up alongside game pie and fresh Newlyn crab meat, white only. The wine selection is concise: affordable house French red or white among a dozen by the glass; another dozen half-bottles; and a premium list of limited-availability reds and magnums of claret. A sign says that the Boot & Flogger offers 'port, sherry and Madeira direct from the wood'; but alas, the glasses (around £4.50) are no longer filled from the cask. Among the decorative pictures is a notice calling for men to join the Light Brigade; indeed, this is the kind of place officers would have gathered before the fateful journey to the Crimea. *Function rooms (50 capacity). Tables outdoors (10, courtyard).* **Map p250 P8.**

Green & Blue
36-38 Lordship Lane, SE22 8HJ (8693 9250, www.greenandbluewines.com). East Dulwich rail. **Open/food served** 9am-11pm Mon-Wed; 9am-midnight Thur-Sat; 11am-8pm Sun. **Dulwich**
Green & Blue is perhaps the purest example of the new generation of wine shop/bar/cafés. One room has a small deli counter and shelves of wine for retail; the other has an equally small bar and the majority of the seating. The wine list isn't huge, but there's a lot to love: owner Kate Thal has done an excellent job combining

big-name superstars with some oddities and new discoveries such as Emile Heredia's Domaine de Montrieux, Pétillant Naturel 'Boisson Rouge', a joyously sparkling Loire red. The food is an exercise in good sourcing, with panini, salads, and some platters of cheese and cured meats. In a neat inversion of the usual corkage fee, for £3 you can bring your own food, and staff will provide plates and cutlery. Every high street could do with a place like this.
Babies & children admitted (until 7pm). Booking advisable. Disabled: toilet. Wireless internet.

Vivat Bacchus
4 Hays Lane, SE1 2HB (7234 0891, www.vivatbacchus.co.uk). London Bridge tube/rail. **Open** 7am-midnight Mon-Fri; 5pm-midnight Sat. **Food served** 7-11am, noon-10.30pm Mon-Fri; 5-10.30pm Sat.
London Bridge
In a bland modern development off Tooley Street, this branch of the South African-owned mini-group sticks to a winning formula, with a basement restaurant complementing the deli counters upstairs. Although there's wine-themed decoration in the form of posters and crates, the climate-controlled cheese and wine rooms provide the most attractive element of the design. The list pays attention to all the classic French regions (Champagne is particularly well represented, although mark-ups are brutal), but it's difficult to avoid drifting back to the outstanding selection of South African wines. From a good choice by the glass, Ken Forrester's FMC 2007 chenin blanc from Stellenbosch is one of the country's best whites, matching clever use of oak with lovely ripeness.
Babies & children admitted. Booking advisable. Disabled: toilet. Entertainment (jazz 8pm Sat). Tables outdoors (22, terrace). Wireless internet.

Wine Wharf
Stoney Street, Borough Market, SE1 9AD (7940 8335, www.winewharf.com). London Bridge tube/rail. **Open** 4-11.30pm Mon, Tue; noon-11.30pm Wed-Sat. **Food served** 5.30-10pm Mon, Tue; noon-3pm, 5.30-10.30pm Wed-Sat. **Borough**

Priceless Tip
MasterCard If wine gets better with age, then what about wine bars? Head to the vaulted stone cellars of Gordon's Wine Bar (*see p53*) to sample the atmosphere of London's oldest vintage (est. 1890).

Vinopolis's Wine Wharf inhabits a reclaimed Victorian warehouse located just by Borough Market, all exposed brickwork, high-ceilinged industrial chic and big leather sofas spread over two storeys (half of the upper one being given over to diners). You could drink very well here from the 300-bin list that stretches to a 1953 d'Yquem (a mere £916.50 a bottle) and some serious prestige cuvée champagnes. However, with over half the wines available by the glass, this is a great opportunity to experiment. The wine list is organised by country and price rather than region or style, which can make navigation somewhat difficult, but the staff generally know their stuff. Bar bites and sharing platters are available, together with more substantial dishes in the restaurant upstairs. Wine-phobes may find more appealing drinks a stone's throw away at beer-themed sister operation Brew Wharf.
Babies & children admitted (until 8pm). Booking advisable Thur, Fri. Disabled: toilet. **Map p250 P8.**

Also recommended...
Hide Bar (Cocktails & Spirits, *p37*).

South West

Amuse Bouche
51 Parsons Green Lane, SW6 4JA (7371 8517, www.abcb.co.uk). Parsons Green tube. **Open** 4-11pm Mon, Sun; 4pm-midnight Tue-Thur; 4pm-12.30am Fri, Sat. **Food served** 4-10.30pm daily. **Parsons Green**
Dedicated to the democratisation of champagne (although the residents of Parsons Green hardly qualify as the great unwashed), Amuse Bouche has hit on a winning formula: a list of 40 or so champagnes – including at least eight available by the glass – that are served in relaxed, modern surroundings. The prices are admirably restrained, but with such specialisation it would be good to see some of the exciting champagnes being produced by the new wave of growers, rather than the big brands to which Amuse Bouche sticks so resolutely. Food is restricted to tapas-style nibbles on a global theme (wun tuns, mini fish 'n' chips, plates of cured meats); the champagnes are supplemented by a small selection of non-sparkling wines. On warm weekend evenings, the windows open on to the street and the champagne cocktails flow happily.
Babies & children admitted (until 6.30pm). Booking advisable Thur-Sat. Function room (50-70 capacity). Tables outdoors (3, garden). Wireless internet.

Vinoteca. *See p54.*

Putney Station

*94-98 Upper Richmond Road, SW15 2SP
(8780 0242, www.brinkleys.com). East Putney
tube.* **Open** 5pm-midnight Mon-Thur; 5pm-1am Fri; 11am-1am Sat; 11am-5pm Sun.
Food served 5-11pm Mon-Fri; 11am-11pm
Sat; 11am-5pm Sun. **Putney**

This outpost of the Brinkley's group is a vision
of 1980s styling, all big plate-glass windows,
venetian blinds and pot plants. It's very much
a neighbourhood joint, with a food menu
consisting of daily-changing specials with a
Modern European focus, but it's one with an
unusually well-constructed wine list, which has
a revolutionary pricing policy that does away
with conventional restaurant mark-ups and
sticks closer to shop prices. No one country or
region dominates the 60-bottle list, which takes
in a spread of vintages from France, Italy, Spain,
Australia, New Zealand, South Africa, South
America and beyond. Bottles start around £8
and run to about £40; given the extremely
decent prices, it's easy to forgive the limited
choice of wine by the glass.
*Babies & children admitted. Tables outdoors
(4, pavement; 10, garden). Wireless internet.*

West

Albertine

*1 Wood Lane, W12 7DP (8743 9593).
Shepherd's Bush Market tube.* **Open**
10am-11pm Mon-Wed; 11am-midnight
Thur, Fri; 6.30-11pm Sat. **Food served**
| 11am-10.30pm Mon-Fri; 6.30-10.30pm Sat.
Shepherd's Bush

Just down the road from BBC Television
Centre, Albertine's small bar has something of
the student union about it, with closely packed,
battered wooden furniture and a blackboard
for wine and food specials. The bottles are
displayed on shelves for off-sales at take-home
prices, but you can also drink here from the
global list of over 130 wines, with plenty of
options by the glass. There are some real gems:
you might find an Ataraxia chardonnay from
the Western Cape rubbing shoulders with a
dense, velvety Cahors malbec blend from the
Lot valley. Food ranges from bar nibbles to
homely mains (fish pie, sausages with mash);
a better bet might be to match a glass or a
bottle of something comparatively sweet with
selections from the extensive cheeseboard.
*Function room (40 capacity).
Wireless internet.*

Finborough Wine Café

*Finborough Road, SW10 9ED (7373 0745,
www.finboroughwinecafe.co.uk). West Brompton
tube/rail.* **Open** 8am-11pm Mon-Sat; 10am-11pm Sun. **Food served** 8am-10pm Mon-Sat;
10am-10pm Sun. **Earl's Court**

This all-day café, wine bar and shop all rolled
into one offers a haven for oenophiles. The
ground-floor bar has a real fire, leather sofas
and welcoming young staff, while downstairs
you'll find the wine-tasting tables, as well as
the wine cellar. The wine list is stylistically and
geographically diverse: around 50 wines are
stocked at any one time, ranging from the odd
cliché (Cloudy Bay sauvignon blanc, a Chateau
Musar from Lebanon) through good-value
options (Alsatian whites, a Sicilian red) to
recognised classics (Kiwi pinot noirs, a red
burgundy). The real appeal of Finborough is
not just the wines but the opportunity to learn
about them: for £8, you can taste 12 wines of
your choice. Knowledgeable staff attend
throughout, making a real effort to engage
every level of wine appreciator. During the day,
coffees, Jing teas and pastries are available, and
the bar menu keeps it very simple with cheese
or meat boards and breads.
*Babies & children admitted. Booking advisable.
Disabled: toilet. Function room (200 capacity).
Wireless internet.*

Julie's Wine Bar

*135 Portland Road, W11 4LW (7727 7985,
www.juliesrestaurant.com). Holland Park tube.*
Open/food served 9am-11pm daily.
Holland Park
Overlooking a petite, pedestrianised square
tucked away in a peaceful corner of Holland
Park, the landmark Julie's attracts the same kind
of customers for whom Julie Hodgess opened
the place in 1969: successful creatives, most with
their own children and grandchildren (note the
groundbreaking Sunday crèche, which runs
until 4pm), who chat over well-chosen wines in
the various cosy rooms and on the roof terrace
that make up the two-level bar and restaurant.
The near 40-strong wine list features Julie's own
Bordeaux Maison Sichel (£22), plus quality
labels such as a Sancerre Gérard Morin 2007
Loire and a Chablis 1er Cru Domaine des
Montmains 2007 JM Brocard, handily available
in a half-bottle measure. A dozen come by two
sizes of glass, most notably a Marqués de Riscal
Reserva Rioja 2006 and a Sauvignon Esprit de
Serame 2009. There's also Breton cider from Val
de Rance, standard cocktails (around a tenner)
and pricey bottles of Budvar, Cobra and Stella.
Still, you're not here for the beer, are you?
*Babies & children admitted. Booking advisable.
Function room (50 capacity). Tables outdoors
(10, pavement).* **Map p247 Z7.**

Finborough Wine Cafe. *See p57.*

Kensington Wine Rooms

*127-129 Kensington Church Street, W8 7LP
(7727 8142, www.greatwinesbytheglass.com).
Notting Hill Gate tube.* **Open** noon-midnight
daily. **Food served** noon-11pm daily.
Kensington
Thor Gudmunsson and Richard Okroj's stylish,
delightful wine bar offers around a hundred
well-chosen bottles, together with five Enomatic
wine machines serving 40 varieties by the glass
(they're proud of the latter, too, as their chosen
URL makes abundantly clear). Superior hams
hang over the sleek metal bar; burgundy
colours and dark wood add warmth to the
seating area. Through the arches is a spacious
dining room with open brickwork where you
can choose from a short menu of mostly
Mediterranean dishes, though there's also the
likes of tempura-style fish with skin-on, hand-
cut chips and, only at weekends, brunch food
such as eggs benedict. There's a compatible
wine recommendation for each dish on the
menu. Check online for details of the regular
wine classes held here.
*Babies & children admitted. Booking advisable
Wed-Sat. Wireless internet.*

Negozio Classica

*283 Westbourne Grove, W11 2QA (7034
0005, www.negozioclassica.co.uk). Ladbroke
Grove or Notting Hill Gate tube.* **Open/food
served** 3pm-midnight Mon-Thur; 11am-
midnight Fri, Sun; 9am-midnight Sat.
Westbourne Grove
When Portobello Market is in full swing on
a Saturday lunchtime, the people-watching at
Negozio Classica is tremendous. However,
be sure to keep an eye on the impressive wine
list; Tuscany and Piedmont are the mainstays,
alongside interesting selections from Sicily and
Slovenia. Most producers are stocked in multiple
bottlings (for consumption on site or to take
away), so it's possible to sample relatively
inexpensive wines from iconic names; wines
from Dolcetto and Barbera, from the leading
Barolo wine-makers, are among the bargains.
The bar's interior display could have been
arranged by the Italian tourist board, with
regional specialities and dry goods unsubtly
interspersed amid the shelves of wine, but the
quality of stock is excellent. Food includes
cheeses, cured meats and classic antipasti.
*Booking advisable. Tables outdoors
(3, pavement).* **Map p247 Z6.**

Also recommended...

Princess Victoria (Gastropubs
& Brasseries; *p155*); **Warrington**
(Gastropubs & Brasseries, *p156*).

Classic Pubs

Central	60
North	78
North East	83
East	85
South East	86
South	90
South West	94
West	97
North West	105
Outer London	106

Classic Pubs

It's counter-intuitive, we realise, but the definition of a classic pub has changed a lot over the past couple of decades. In the 1980s, when bar furniture began to be made from wood rather than metal and continental lager overtook British ale as the office drone's after-work drink of choice, the phrase was closer to a term of abuse than a term of affection, applied to forlorn-looking, frosted-window boozatoria with sticky carpets, flat beer and a clientele for whom middle age was a distant memory.

Some of those places remain. Indeed, a few cherishable examples of the breed are buried in this book. But these days, the phrase 'classic pub' conjures up something more immediately appealing. The wood might have been buffed up a little, the carpets may have been replaced with bare floorboards, the real ales will have returned to the once-dormant handpumps, the choice of wine ought to extend beyond red from a box and Liebfraumilch from a bottle, and the kitchen should offer comfort food (pies, sausages) parachuted in by the central office of the pubco that quietly oversees proceedings. The result is often a kind of ersatz authenticity, an attempt to recreate a past that the pub probably never enjoyed in the first place.

And yet there's still room for plenty of character and eccentricity within the classic pub. In this chapter, the largest in the book, you'll find delights of every stripe: centuries-old, centrally located, tourist-friendly pubs and quiet, isolated, backstreet locals; beautifully maintained Victorian taverns and just-remodelled 20th-century taprooms; pubs with kitchens and pubs with dartboards; landlords offering piano singalongs, life-drawing lessons, beer festivals and pilates classes. The only characteristic linking the venues in this section is a come-one-come-all ambience and a vague sense that the past isn't something about which to be embarrassed. The future, though, is anyone's guess...

Central

Admiral Codrington
17 Mossop Street, SW3 2LY (7581 0005, www.theadmiralcodrington.co.uk). South Kensington tube. **Open** 11.30am-midnight Mon-Thur; 11.30am-1am Fri, Sat; noon-10.30pm Sun. **Food served** noon-2.30pm Mon-Fri; noon-3.30pm Sat; noon-4pm Sun.
South Kensington
Hiding behind the unappetising nickname of the Cod, this neighbourhood pub has been scrubbed up to meet the 21st century, with cream walls, spot lighting and varnished pine furniture ticking most of the modern-boozer boxes. Pictures of carefree cricketers and jolly huntsmen hint at the Admiral Codrington's former Sloane Ranger reputation, but these days, it's better known for the unpretentious pub food on offer in the adjacent restaurant: as well as steak tartare, there are such fishy dishes as salmon and haddock fishcakes, seared scallops and – yes! – cod. If the draught ales aren't to your taste, the 30-strong wine list can be enjoyed by diners and drinkers alike, with bottles from around £15. The unusually well heated courtyard is relished by smokers in the winter months.
Babies & children admitted. Function room (60 capacity). Games (backgammon). Tables outdoors (6, garden). **Map p248 D3**.

Angel
61-62 St Giles High Street, WC2H 8LE (7240 2876). Tottenham Court Road tube. **Open** noon-11pm Mon-Sat; noon-10.30pm Sun.
Food served noon-8pm daily. **Bloomsbury**
At the time of writing a major overhaul was changing the shape of this venerable pub behind Centre Point. Upstairs, two dining rooms provide comfort to city-centre workers, shoppers and musos from nearby Denmark Street as they

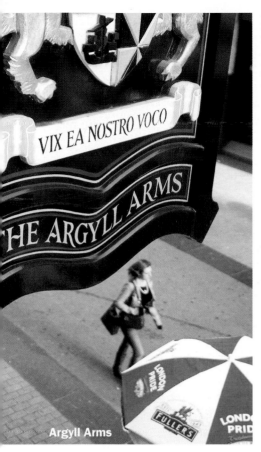

Argyll Arms

Favoured at various times by both Charles Dickens and DH Lawrence, this splendid pub is packed tight on summer evenings, the front terrace and wide main bar area filled with professional blokes chugging Adnams Broadside while their female equivalents put bottles of sancerre on expenses. Solicitors can – indeed, do – celebrate a successful case with a bottle of Châteauneuf-du-Pape. But despite the stereotypes, the Anglesea has always had more aura than the average South Kensington hostelry. Perhaps it's the erotic painting of Fifi, the ghost that roams its cellar; perhaps it's the link with the Great Train Robbery, allegedly planned here. On quieter winter lunchtimes, it's the ideal place for a quality foreign lager (Kirin, Bitburger) and a heart-to-heart over a plate of squid linguine at one of the bottle-green banquettes overlooked by random portraits. *Babies & children admitted. Function room (36 capacity). Tables outdoors (12, pavement). Wireless internet.* **Map p248 B4.**

Argyll Arms
18 Argyll Street, W1F 7TP (7734 6117). Oxford Circus tube. **Open** 10am-11pm Mon-Sat; 10am-10.30pm Sun. **Food served** 10am-10pm daily. **Soho**
Robert Sawyer created this ornate Victorian pub in the dying days of the 19th century, and he'd still be proud of his Grade II-listed, Nicholson's-run monument to mahogany and etched glass by one of the West End's busiest pedestrian intersections. Within, the unhurried sipping and supping of quality ales might recall a quiet rural pub but for the rapid turnover of the international clientele, all happy to have found a real London pub with a broad range of beers and an array of suitably eccentric little spaces in which to drink them. Expect to find Sharp's Doom Bar and Timothy Taylor Landlord, joined by the varied likes of White Horse Village Idiot, Brains Milkwood and Downtown Honey Blonde from California; ask for the beer menu if you can't see the taps for the crush at the bar. Traditional dinners (toad in the hole, meat pies) keep locals and tourists happy; there's table service at the equally elegant Palladium Bar upstairs. *Babies & children admitted. Function room (50 capacity). Tables outdoors (5, pavement).* **Map p240 J6.**

lay into affordable servings of roast beef and Yorkshire pudding, and fish and chips. Comfort is what this tavern, then the Bowl, provided condemned men in Elizabethan times as they gulped their last drink on their way to the gallows. Sam Smith's ale in all its varieties is now served in pint glasses in three spaces at street level: the main one with a fireplace; the darts room lined with theatre posters; and an intimate one behind for uninterrupted chat. A small courtyard comes into its own in summer. *Games (darts). Tables outdoors (6, garden).* **Map p240 K6.**

Anglesea Arms
15 Selwood Terrace, SW7 3QG (7373 7960, www.capitalpubcompany.com). South Kensington tube. **Open** 11am-11pm Mon-Sat; noon-10.30pm Sun. **Food served** noon-3pm, 6-10pm Mon-Fri; noon-5pm, 6-10pm Sat; noon-5pm, 6-9.30pm Sun. **South Kensington**

Audley
41-43 Mount Street, W1K 2RX (7499 1843). Bond Street or Green Park tube. **Open** 11am-11pm Mon-Sat; noon-10.30pm Sun. **Food served** 11am-10pm Mon-Sat; noon-9pm Sun. **Mayfair**

Black Friar

The local family history outlined on the exterior of this beautifully renovated public house dates from 1127, and it's fair to say that any one of the landed Audley gentry down the centuries would have been proud of the appearance of this ornate Victorian establishment. Personable, black-shirted girls of Mediterranean origin run the long main bar, lined with an impressive array of handpumps: Deuchars IPA, Wells Bombardier, Young's Gold, St Austell Tribute, Fuller's London Pride and Greene King Suffolk Swift might be among the ale choices. The expansive, carved-wood and gilt interior is filled mostly by regulars, with this portion of Mayfair sitting a little off the tourist trail; perhaps inspired by the succulent meaty smells, many choose to line their stomachs with solid pub grub (steaks, burgers and the like).
Babies & children admitted (until 6pm). Disabled: toilet. Function room (100 capacity). Games (pool). Tables outdoors (6, pavement). **Map p239 G7.**

Bell

29 Bush Lane, EC4R 0AN (7929 7772). Cannon Street tube/rail. **Open** 11am-10pm Mon-Fri. **Food served** noon-3pm Mon-Fri. **City**
Tucked down a sloping street beside Cannon Street station, next door to a bookie's shop, the Bell offers a taste of Macmillan-era London – there's even a framed portrait of Sid James on one wall. They also promote and sell Courage beer, one of several ale options (Sharp's Cornish Coaster, Harveys Sussex Best, St Austell Tribute, Hooky Bitter) that encourage a blokey crowd to gather in an intimate, wooden, low-ceilinged interior. A kitchen serves hot food five times a week – this is the 'home of the Bell burger' – but most punters come here to talk over the cricket scores before catching the train back home to the suburbs. Wine choices, chalked up by a museum-piece back bar, include unnamed sauvignons, chardonnays and pinot grigios at City prices.
Babies & children admitted (lunchtime only). Wireless internet. **Map p245 P7.**

Black Friar

174 Queen Victoria Street, EC4V 4EG (7236 5474, www.nicholsonspubs.co.uk). Blackfriars rail (& tube from late 2011) or Mansion House tube. **Open** 10am-11pm Mon-Thur, Sat; 10am-11.30pm Fri; noon-10pm Sun. **Food served** 10am-10pm Mon-Sat; noon-10.30pm Sun. **City**
Built in 1875 on the site of a medieval Dominican friary, the Black Friar had its interior completely remodelled in the Arts and Crafts style. Now a Nicholson's, its bright panes, intricate friezes

and carved slogans ('Industry is Ale', 'Haste is Slow') still make a work of art out of the main saloon, adjoined by a prosaic one linked by a marble-topped bar. Outside, a large terrace faces traffic approaching Blackfriars Bridge, and a tick-box blackboard by the doorway gives notice of the considerable choice of guest ales – Sharp's Doom Bar, Kelham Best, St Austell, Bateman Victory – that complements the tap Erdinger and Peroni. Wines start at £11.95 a bottle and include a Chablis Bouchard, while food runs from bar bites to Sunday roasts of beef topside. *Babies & children admitted (until 9pm). Tables outdoors (10, pavement).* **Map p243 O6.**

Blue Posts

28 Rupert Street, W1D 6DJ (7437 1415). Leicester Square or Piccadilly Circus tube. **Open** 11am-11.30pm Mon-Thur; 11am-midnight Fri, Sat; noon-10.30pm Sun. **Food served** noon-8pm Mon-Sat; 1-5pm Sun. **Chinatown**

One of Soho's unsung and superior destinations, this lovely little corner pub flanking a narrow alleyway in the heart of the gay quarter attracts a real cross-section. Older types might drop by for the Sunday afternoon jazz sessions or the weekly quiz, while regular DJs bring in a different crowd. Events take place in a cosy room

French House. *See p69.*

upstairs, while down below, Timothy Taylor Landlord, Hoegaarden, Leffe and Magners cider are served. The bar staff's predecessor of a century ago, Fred D Harris, is honoured on the wall, as is the late, legendary Terry, whom many Sohoites may remember from the Dive Bar days. Food includes signature salt-beef sandwiches and sundry pies, minces and omelettes. *Babies & children admitted (until 6pm). Entertainment (jazz 4-7pm, 8-10.30pm Sun). Function room (30 capacity). Tables outdoors (2, pavement).* **Map p241 K7.**

Carpenters Arms

68-70 Whitfield Street, W1T 4EY (7580 3186). Goodge Street tube. **Open** noon-11pm Mon-Wed; noon-11.30pm Thur; noon-midnight Fri, Sat; noon-10.30pm Sun. **Food served** noon-10pm daily. **Fitzrovia**

Run by the same management team as the nearby Crown & Sceptre (*see p67*) and sharing many elements of the drinks and food selection, the Carpenters nonetheless seems to appeal to a younger, more studenty crowd. There are fish-finger sandwiches, for a start, from a menu covered in denim; Red Stripe among the draught beers alongside decent ales (including Sharp's reliable Doom Bar); and quirky decorative touches (such as Erica's notable cleavage on a dinner plate) around a mock sitting room. If all this is a little 'seen it and done it', then make a beeline for the Belle Bar upstairs or the roof terrace – though come here after any working day and the media crowd will be occupying this entire corner of pavement, busy networking. *Babies & children admitted (until 6pm). Disabled: toilet. Function room (50-70 capacity). Games (board games). Tables outdoors (4, roof terrace; 12, pavement).* **Map p240 J4.**

Cask & Glass

39-41 Palace Street, SW1E 5HN (7834 7630, www.shepherd-neame.co.uk). Victoria tube/rail. **Open** 11am-11pm Mon-Fri; noon-8pm Sat. **Food served** noon-2.30pm Mon-Fri. **Victoria**

Shepherd Neame's quaint Cask & Glass sits incongruously behind a new office development that now dominates Victoria Street. Outside, overflowing hanging baskets decorate a cottage-like exterior embellished with any number of best-bar award plaques; inside, a sign promises 'Pale & Stock Ales Guaranteed Malt and Hops Only'. Sure enough, pumps of Spitfire, Kent's Best and Master Brew line the little bar, in which there's just enough room for a counter, half-a-dozen tables, a wall of framed caricatures and loyal, chatty regulars who choose to come after work even though it'll be standing room only.

QUINNS

GAELIC GAMES & SKY SPORTS SHOWN ON 3 SEPARATE SCREENS

65 Kentish Town Road
(2 minutes from Camden tube station ⊖)

☎ 020 7267 8240

Opening Times

Mon, Tue & Wed
11am-12am

Thur, Fri & Sat
11am-2am

Sunday
12pm -12am

RESTAURANT MENU

The reason? Probably not the wines (from £3.30 a glass) or the snacks and sandwiches. It's the warm feel of a no-faff, no-fruit-machine pub in an area where all outside is gleaming commerce and the fevered rush to and through the station. *Tables outdoors (3, pavement).* **Map p249 J9.**

Castle

26 Furnival Street, EC4A 1JS (7405 5470). Chancery Lane tube. **Open** 11am-11pm Mon-Fri. **Food served** noon-3pm, 5-10.30pm Mon-Fri. **City**
This black-fronted, pie-slice of a pub is an unlikely place to find such a range of sought-after, high-quality ales. In truth, it's not a very sympathetic environment: the room is a little characterless and the music is usually too loud. But the staff do their best and the drinks are decent: you can expect an array of unusual ales, which seem to rotate on a barrel-by-barrel basis. Large taps advertising Peroni and Erdinger Weissbier add variety for drinkers, as do bottled Corona, Beck's and Budweiser, alongside around a dozen wines of each colour. The food here is another important feature: doorstep sandwiches stuffed with roast pork; bangers and mash; and burgers. A big fan by the bar counter gives relief in summer; fat candles in glasses provide atmosphere in winter. *Function room (40 capacity). Games (darts).* **Map p243 N6.**

Cittie of Yorke

22 High Holborn, WC1V 6BN (7242 7670). Chancery Lane tube. **Open** noon-11pm Mon-Sat. **Food served** noon-2.30pm, 6-9.30pm Mon-Sat. **City**
The copper sign swinging over pedestrians on High Holborn speaks of 'beer brewed at Yorkshire's oldest brewery'; the sign just out from a mock-Tudor façade above reads 'established on the site of a public house in 1430'. So far, so faux, but the interior is authentically dingy, wobbly and warren-like, the kind of place in which to film a period drama. The main room is lined with conspiratorial dark wood alcoves, with old barrels over the long bar and framed portraits from *Vanity Fair* c.1870. Bright labels advertising beers and ales from the Sam Smith's stable bring some colour to the brown tableau, a counter of taps (Alpine Lager, Pure Brewed Lager, Old Brewery Bitter) abutted by a food display (steak and ale pie, beef suet pudding). A cellar bar embellished with mounted caricatures and a smaller bar by the main door both offer intimacy. *Babies & children admitted (until 5pm).* **Map p242 M5.**

Coach & Horses

29 Greek Street, W1D 5DH (7437 5920). Leicester Square or Piccadilly Circus tube. **Open** 11am-11pm Mon-Thur; 11am-midnight Fri, Sat; noon-10.30pm Sun. **Food served** noon-3pm Mon, Tue; noon-3pm, 5-10pm Wed-Fri; noon-10pm Sat. **Soho**
One day, there will be a review of this Soho landmark without mentioning its legendary, long-gone landlord Norman Balon - but not just yet. The grouch who presided over the Coach's louche years, when equally legendary columnist Jeffrey Bernard and fellow wisecracking, literary sourpusses were regulars, still looms large. 'The West End's most famous pub' now features 'Norman's Coach & Horses pub piano singalong' twice a week and the Private Eye dining room upstairs, named after the satirical stalwart whose editorial team met here. Quality food is another recent reinvention: minute steak with garlic butter, or Scottish smoked salmon with sour cream and soda bread, with walnuts dipped in chocolate to follow. It's a 'fresh food' pub, so all pâtés, sausages, biscuits and soda bread are made on site, the butter is hand-churned farmhouse and there are squat candles on each table within the venerable, wooden interior. Moreover, the range of drinks on draught – Orchard Pig, Meantime Helles, Hobgoblin, Cotswold cider – befits a 'gastropub'. Not that gastro would have meant anything in Norman's day. 'Gastro? You're f****** barred!' *Babies & children admitted (until 9pm). Entertainment (piano singalong 7-11pm Wed, Sat; dinner & cabaret 7pm Fri). Function room (36-50 capacity). Wireless internet.* **Map p241 K6.**

Cross Keys

31 Endell Street, WC2H 9EB (7836 5185). Covent Garden tube. **Open** 11am-11pm Mon-Sat; noon-10.30pm Sun. **Food served** noon-2.30pm Mon-Fri; noon-3pm Sat, Sun. **Covent Garden**
A pavement smoking-and-drinking seating area consisting of planks of wood placed on beer barrels doesn't promise much. However, a peek inside the flower-fringed open window reveals that this is an agreeable little place, a cosy, ages-old pub decked out in ancient copper utensils, London street signs and remarkable pop memorabilia. The clientele is working-nearby regulars for the most part; you can spot the occasional tourist as they gawp through the dimness to marvel at a poster for the Beatles' Royal Command Performance of 1963, along with a napkin that was once used by Elvis and a newspaper article about the landlord's £500 bid to buy it. Ales might include Bombardier

Duke. *See p68.*

and selections from the Brodie's brewery in Leyton; the food (doorstep sandwiches and the like) doesn't deviate from the old-fashioned path. *Function room (40 capacity). Tables outdoors (3, pavement).* **Map p241 L6.**

Crown & Sceptre

26-27 Foley Street, W1W 6DY (7307 9971, www.thecrownandsceptrew1.co.uk). Goodge Street, Oxford Circus or Tottenham Court Road tube. **Open** noon-11pm Mon-Sat; noon-10.30pm Sun. **Food served** noon-10pm Mon-Sat; noon-9pm Sun. **Fitzrovia**
If you had to find the perfect example of the conversion from sad corner pub to gastro drinkerie, this would come pretty damn close. Still pub-like in appearance – a prominent pentagonal bar counter is the focus of a large saloon space beneath a high, brown stucco ceiling – the cannily run Crown & Sceptre offers choice in serious measure. Beer taps include Blue Moon, Brooklyn, Kirin, Paulaner, Kozel, Purity UBU, New World Brown Ale, Sambrook's Wandle, Sharp's Doom Bar, Thornbridge Ashford, Bateman's Victory and Estrella. Boards list some 30 wines, all by the glass and bottle, from Casa Juanita Malbec Mendoza to Spy Valley Riesling. Food, best enjoyed in the homely adjoining dining corner or at tables outside, is equally well-sourced, the daily-changing menu perhaps featuring the likes of Cotswold lamb steak with red lentils, chilli and peppers, or salmon and smoked trout fishcakes. *Babies & children admitted (until 5pm). Disabled: toilet. Tables outdoors (2, pavement).* **Map p240 J5.**

Crown & Two Chairmen

31-32 Dean Street, W1D 3SB (7437 8192, www.thecrownandtwochairmenw1.co.uk). Tottenham Court Road tube. **Open** noon-11.30pm Mon-Thur; noon-midnight Fri, Sat; noon-10.30pm Sun. **Food served** noon-10pm Mon-Sat; noon-9pm Sun. **Soho**
Although it's changed a little in recent years, brought up to date after years as an old-school holdout, the darkly handsome Crown & Two Chairmen remains a Soho crowd-pleaser. There's real ale, plenty of lager and cider on tap, and substantial, high-end pub grub. Bar stools at the windows allow singletons to entertain themselves with central Soho street life, while a low-lit slouchy area of tattered red leather banquettes and red-beaded lampshades at the back gets the vote of courting couples. Quirky details – such as a 'Beer tastes better in a plastic glass' sign for those wanting to drink outside – add appeal for the chatty, friendly mix of slumming-it business types

Dog & Duck

and self-consciously bohemian media workers who make up most of the pub's clientele. *Babies & children admitted (until 5pm).* **Map p241 K6.**

Dog & Duck

18 Bateman Street, W1D 3AJ (7494 0697). Tottenham Court Road tube. **Open** 10am-11pm Mon-Thur; 10am-11.30pm Fri, Sat; noon-10.30pm Sun. **Food served** 10am-10pm Mon-Sat; noon-9pm Sun. **Soho**
A Soho landmark for generations, the Dog & Duck is known chiefly for its literary heritage and for its ever-changing ale selection. Some of the beers will be familiar, the likes of Sharp's Doom Bar, Fuller's London Pride and Timothy Taylor Landlord, but others are more unusual: the selection might take in rare but worthwhile brews from Brains in Wales or the Cairngorm Brewery in Aviemore. Fish 'n' chips are the highlight of the food menu; it's that sort of place. Surroundings are authentically vintage: etched mirrors, carved mahogany and so forth. The George Orwell room upstairs (the writer sometimes drank here) usually offers more space, although some punters prefer to spill out on to the pavement. *Babies & children admitted. Function room (25-40 capacity).* **Map p241 K6.**

Duke

*7 Roger Street, WC1N 2PB (7242 7230,
www.dukepub.co.uk). Chancery Lane, Holborn
or Russell Square tube.* **Open** *noon-11pm
Mon-Sat; noon-10.30pm Sun.* **Food served**
noon-10pm Mon-Sat; noon-9.30pm Sun.
Bloomsbury

The Duke is a little slice of London from
between the wars: heavy-framed mirrors, long-
leafed plants, a black Bakelite phone and
amusing deco details (pale green glass in the
shape of a whipped ice-cream, a nymph
cavorting under a lamp). The main bar has
scuffed linoleum, wooden booths and, as if
a warbly 'When You're Smiling' and Billie
Holiday on the stereo weren't front-parlour
enough, a red-painted piano. A couple of real
ales are offered – our pint was topped up
without our having to ask, despite there being
a rush on at the bar – as well as Staropramen
and plenty of whiskies. The secluded location
keeps the few street-side tables tranquil, and
a tea light-strewn dining room has an
unambitious menu (chargrilled sea bass, pork
cutlet, sausage of the week). Otherwise,
reasonable beer sustains a nicely mixed crowd
of student girls in vintage garb and well-fed
architects belted tightly into their suit trousers.
*Babies & children admitted. Function room
(50 capacity). Tables outdoors (3, pavement).*
Map p242 M4.

Fox & Anchor

*115 Charterhouse Street, EC1M 6AA (7250
1300, www.foxandanchor.com). Barbican tube
or Farringdon tube/rail.* **Open** *7am-11pm
Mon-Thur; 7am-1am Fri; 8.30am-1am Sat;
8.30am-10pm Sun.* **Food served** *7-11am,
noon-9.45pm Mon-Fri; 8.30-11am, noon-9.45pm
Sat; 8.30-11am, noon-4pm, 6-9pm Sun.*
Clerkenwell

Pristine mosaic tiling and etched glass scream
'sensitive refurbishment' from the moment you
arrive at this stalwart. Inside, the dark wood
bar is lined with pewter tankards (don't expect
to be given one if you want to drink outside);
to the back is the Fox's Den, a series of intimate
booths used for both drinking and dining. Local
sourcing is a priority and a pleasure here:
in addition to the pub's own-label ale, the cask
beers might include offerings from Suffolk's
Nethergate brewery or Purity's Mad Goose from
Warwickshire. The bar food is outstanding,
uncomplicated British cuisine rendered in
perfect and generous portions; the bar snacks
range from pork scratchings, pickled eggs
and cockles to generous mains (roasts, pies,
burgers, accompanied by excellent chips cooked
in goose fat). Even if you don't stay overnight
in the seductively masculine bedrooms upstairs,
you can always drop by for one of their huge
breakfasts, accompanied by various hair-of-the-
dog libations. In fact, only the excruciating

Golden Eagle. *See p70.*

Guinea. *See p70.*

slogan – 'Hops and chops, cuvées and duvets' – strikes a false note at this Smithfield treasure. *Babies & children admitted (until 7pm). Entertainment (band 7pm Mon, 2pm Sun). Disabled: toilet. Tables outdoors (2, pavement).* **Map p242 O5.**

French House
49 Dean Street, W1D 5BG (7437 2799, www.frenchhousesoho.com). Leicester Square or Piccadilly Circus tube. **Open** noon-11pm Mon-Sat; noon-10.30pm Sun. **Food served** *Bar* noon-4pm Mon-Fri. *Restaurant* noon-3pm, 5.30-11pm Mon-Sat. **Soho**
An evergreen haunt of Soho barflies, the French House should have 'La Marseillaise' playing as you walk in. Beer (house lager) is sold in halves; eau de vie comes in strawberry, pear and plum varieties; the champers is Canard Duchêne and Pol Roger; and there's Breton cider and Ricard behind the bar. The 30-strong (16 by the glass) wine list is dominated by *vins français*, Pouilly-Fuissé Monternot 2007, Brouilly 2009 and more affordable St Julien d'Aille de Provence included. This is no recent Gallic gimmick: frequented by Soho's criminal and cultural underworld after the war, this was also where Charles de Gaulle ran his London base in the Vichy era, hence the photo; more recent guests (Suggs, Francis Bacon) receive more wall space. There's a restaurant, the

Polpetto, upstairs, offering Venetian platters, and bar snacks are served until 4pm. *Babies & children admitted (restaurant).* **Map p241 K6.**

George IV
26-28 Portugal Street, WC2A 2HE (7955 7743). Holborn or Temple tube. **Open** noon-11pm Mon-Fri. **Food served** noon-10pm Mon-Fri. **Aldwych**
It's a splendid little pub, this, with a young, international clientele drawn in no small part from the nearby London School of Economics – note the foreign banknotes behind the half-moon bar counter. They're treated to a decent selection of ales on draught – Wadworth 6X, Everards Tiger and Wychwood Hobgoblin – with more timid Europeans opting for a bottle of Budvar, Corona, Beck's or Peroni. Wine prices are kept reasonable: an acceptable Codesa de Leganza crianza tempranillo at £3.10 a glass or £11.45 a bottle, with Casa La Joya sauvignon blanc coming in a touch higher. Food (soups, salads, large poppy seed bloomer sandwiches) has also been priced with the student in mind. It's a traditional pub refit job, so the wood is as shiny as can be around the spacious bar on the ground floor, and thought has gone into creating the relaxing function room upstairs. Nicely located on a traffic-free junction of three streets. *Function room (50 capacity).* **Map p243 M6.**

Golden Eagle

59 Marylebone Lane, W1U 2NY (7935 3228).
Bond Street tube. **Open** 11am-11pm Mon-Sat;
noon-7pm Sun. **Marylebone**
As Marylebone grows ever more gentrified with
each passing year, this backstreet local seems
ever more out of place in its surroundings.
No bad thing, of course. A paint job tidied
up the room a few years ago, but the Golden
Eagle remains what it's been for years: an
unpretentious, comfortable-as-old-slippers little
boozer (and we mean little; seating's limited to
a couple of tables and a string of bar stools
along the front window), not hugely charismatic
but pleasingly untouched by corporate hands
and always serving two or three well-kept ales.
Try to make it for one of the thrice-weekly piano
singalongs ('On the Street Where You Live',
'Ev'ry Time We Say Goodbye', and so on), led
by Tony 'Fingers' Pearson, which make a jolly
counterpoint to the barman's relentlessly weary
demeanour. An absolute peach.
Entertainment (pianist 8.30pm Tue, Thur,
Fri). **Map p238 G5.**

Golden Lion

25 King Street, SW1Y 6QY (7925 0007).
Green Park or Piccadilly Circus tube.
Open 11am-11pm Mon-Fri; noon-6pm Sat.
Food served noon-4pm, 5-7.30pm Mon-Fri;
11am-3pm Sat. **St James's**
Set opposite Christie's auction house, this
august Nicholson's hostelry cannot fail to attract
a discerning suit-and-tie clientele delighted to
find superior ales (George Gale Seafarer's,
Sharp's Cornish Coaster), sandwiches (honey-
and-mustard roast ham and cheddar) and mains
(home-made Aberdeen Angus burger, boeuf
bourguignon). A wine selection of 16 low- to
mid-range standards seems relatively modest
given the surroundings and customer base.
With heraldic crests set into glazed windows
that shut out the 21st century, and a dark-wood
interior as cosy as when Oscar Wilde and Lillie
Langtree imbibed between acts at the long-gone
St James's Theatre opposite, the Golden Lion
does little to dispel the feeling that you may be
getting home by horse-drawn hackney.
Entertainment (quiz 6.30pm 2nd Tue of mth).
Function room (50 capacity). Tables outdoors
(3, pavement). **Map p241 J8.**

Guinea

30 Bruton Place, W1J 6NL (7409 1728,
www.theguinea.co.uk). Bond Street or Oxford
Circus tube. **Open** 11.30am-11.30pm Mon-
Fri; 6-11.30pm Sat. **Food served** *Bar* 12.30-
2.30pm Mon-Fri. *Restaurant* 12.30-3pm,
6-10.30pm Mon-Fri; 6-10.30pm Sat. **Mayfair**
'Established 1675' says the sign outside and,
tucked down a sought-after Mayfair mews, this
venerable establishment is truly a thoroughbred
in the Young's stable. A gilt-framed portrait
of the now octogenarian royal couple in a
pre-nuptial portrait pose sets the tone amid
the pub's varnished wood and tartan. Prime
Aberdeenshire Scotch beef is the speciality of
the Guinea Grill, while the handmade pork pies
(£2.75) should satisfy smaller appetites. As well
as standard Young's ales on the centrepiece bar
counter, Bombardier, Courage Director's, Peroni
and Pilsner Urquell are also available on draught,
plus Bitburger by the bottle – although from
May, Pimm's (£4.05; £20.60 by the jug) might be
more appropriate. A somewhat limited choice of
wine stretches to a Chablis St-Claire, pleasingly
sold by the glass.
Function room (28 capacity). Wireless internet.
Map p239 H7.

Hand & Shears

1 Middle Street, EC1A 7JA (7600 0257).
Barbican tube. **Open** 11am-11pm Mon-Fri.
Food served noon-3pm Mon-Fri. **Clerkenwell**
The history displayed on a plaque outside this
cubby-hole of a pub dates back as far as 1132,
when an alehouse stood on this site. In Tudor
times, it was frequented by the tailors and
drapers who gave the pub its current name.
Oval-shaped, with an island bar of similar
outline, and black-and-white images of old
London complementing the atmosphere, the
Hand & Shears continues to preserve the
tradition it has spent centuries bolstering.
Courage Best (yes, *that* traditional), Greene King
IPA and Adnams are served from an honest
wooden bar in a room that's quiet enough to
amplify the odd sole making a scuffing sound
on the bare floorboards. The menu is of the
sausage-and-mash-for-a-fiver variety.
Children & babies admitted (upstairs only).
Function room (50 capacity). Games (darts).
Map p242 O5.

Harrison

28 Harrison Street, WC1H 8JF (7278
3966, www.harrisonbar.co.uk). King's Cross
tube/rail. **Open** 11am-11pm Mon-Fri; 5-11pm
Sat; noon-10.30pm Sun. **Food served** noon-
3pm, 6-9.30pm Mon-Fri; 6-9.30pm Sat; 12.30-
8pm Sun. **King's Cross**
In Clerkenwell, this place would almost go
unnoticed. Here, amid a Legoland of housing
estates and shops catering chiefly to custom
from the Indian subcontinent, it's practically
miraculous. Comprising a simply furnished
room of stripped wood and tables occupied
by after-work regulars, this corner pub enjoys

Punchbowl. *See p74.*

considerable local status for being a smart but unpretentious spot for a decent pint, a natter and a Sunday roast. Früli, Timothy Taylor Landlord, Erdinger, Amstel, London Pride and Staropramen pour from the beer taps lining the long bar counter, staffed by friendly foreigners. Festival tables outside offer extra seating on sunnier days. Standard gastropub fare is well put together and fairly priced. *Entertainment (bands most Sun; check website for details). Tables outdoors (12, pavement). Wireless internet.*

King & Queen
1 Foley Street, W1W 6DL (7636 5619).
Goodge Street tube. **Open** 11am-11pm Mon-Fri; noon-11pm Sat; 7-10.30pm Sun. **Food served** noon-2.30pm Mon-Fri. **Fitzrovia**
Look around this traditional boozer, displaying heraldic shields, royals through the ages in playing-card form, and pictures of the England touring cricket team to Australia in 1978-79, and you'd be hard pushed to guess that this was where Bob Dylan made one of his first London

appearances. It still has a monthly folk night but most come to this dark, expansive saloon for the range of beers, which includes St Austell Tribute, Sharp's Doom Bar, Adnam's and San Miguel. Whiskies – Macallan 10, Laphroaig and Glenmorangie all by the optic – are another speciality. Sport broadcasts from a TV on the back wall – it's not a bad place to watch the Saturday results unfold in peace and quiet. Food includes scampi and chips, and steak-and kidney pudding, and sales are rung up on an old copper cash register. *Children admitted (until 7pm). Entertainment (folk club 7.30pm monthly Fri). Function room (60 capacity). Tables outdoors (3, pavement).* **Map p240 J5.**

Kings Arms
25 Roupell Street, SE1 8TB (7207 0784).
Waterloo tube/rail. **Open** 11am-11pm Mon-Fri; noon-11pm Sat; noon-10.30pm Sun. **Food served** noon-3pm, 6-10.30pm Mon-Fri; 6-10.30pm Sat; noon-8pm Sun. **Waterloo**
The good bit: located on an impossibly handsome street of 19th-century workers' cottages, this is easily the nicest pub in the immediate vicinity. The bad news: everybody in the immediate vicinity knows it, and the Kings Arms is packed most nights as a result. Still, even if you have to battle to get served, the pub retains at least some of its charms, and keen-eyed drinkers should be able to snaffle a table in one of the two cosy, country pub-styled rooms within a half-hour or so: there's a decent amount of turnover, as occasionally boisterous after-work crowds gradually give way to more mellow locals as the evening develops. The eight ales on tap – Brakspear Oxford Gold, Sambrook's Wandle, Adnams, and Dark Star Partridge Best and Hophead, plus guests – are all well kept; the wine list is also stronger than average. *Babies & children admitted (until 5pm). Disabled: toilet. Function rooms (30, 70 capacity). Wireless internet.* **Map p250 N8.**

Lamb
94 Lamb's Conduit Street, WC1N 3LZ (7405 0713, www.thelamblondon.co.uk).
Holborn or Russell Square tube. **Open** noon-11.30pm Mon-Wed; noon-12.30am Thur-Sat; noon-10.30pm Sun. **Food served** noon-9pm daily. **Bloomsbury**
In operation for nearly three centuries, this Young's pub boasts a glorious Victorian interior, dating back to a time when stars of the stage and music hall were regulars here. Publicity shots of Lillian Braithwaite, Seymour Hicks

Queens Larder. *See p74.*

and contemporaries form two decorative rows across the walls of a cosy, varnished-wood interior, while the central horseshoe bar is ringed with original etched-glass snob screens, used to shield Victorian gentlemen when liaising with 'women of dubious distinction'. They would have been wooed by tunes from the polyphon, a 19th-century music machine still standing in the corner. The Young's beers are no more exciting here than in other pubs owned by the brewery (although they do seem to have improved since brewing was moved from Wandsworth). Still, the room is handsome enough to make up for it. Food, inevitably, is as trad as it gets.
Babies & children admitted (until 5pm).
Function room (40 capacity). Tables
outdoors (3, patio). Wireless internet.
Map p242 M4.

Lamb & Flag
33 Rose Street, WC2E 9EB (7497 9504).
Covent Garden tube. **Open** 11am-11pm
Mon-Thur; 11am-11.30pm Fri, Sat; noon-
10.30pm Sun. **Food served** noon-3pm
Mon-Fri; noon-4.30pm Sat, Sun.
Covent Garden
Rose Street wasn't always the domain of puzzled tourists sipping pints of Bombardier. Squeezed between Garrick Street and the old Covent Garden market, this dog-leg alleyway was once the haunt of whores and bare-knuckle

fighters, the latter hosted at this low-ceilinged tavern when it was called the Bucket of Blood (the poet Dryden was beaten up here in 1679). Today's regulars are now honoured with a photo and a plaque; Robert 'Bob' Townley even has his flat cap framed. Estrella and Peroni make welcome appearances as draught options, though most seem to stick to bottled Corona or Beck's. Food comprises ploughman's lunches and doorstep sandwiches; heartier meals (sausages, roasts) can be taken upstairs or in the back room. Two centuries of mounted cuttings and caricatures amplify the sense of character and continuity, although not everyone gets to see them: space is always at a premium, hence the pavement cluster on summer nights.
Babies & children admitted (lunch only).
Entertainment (band 7.30pm Sun). Games
(darts). **Map p241 L7.**

Museum Tavern
49 Great Russell Street, WC1B 3BA (7242
8987). Holborn or Tottenham Court Road
tube. **Open** 11am-11.30pm Mon-Thur;
11am-midnight Fri, Sat; noon-10pm Sun.
Food served noon-9.30pm Mon-Sat; noon-
9pm Sun. **Bloomsbury**
Inevitably pandering to tourists who flock to the British Museum opposite – note the £5 T-shirts behind the bar – this attractive, traditional hostelry also appeals to Londoners with a taste for decent ales. Harvey's Sussex Best, Timothy

Taylor Landlord, Theakston Old Peculiar, Daleside Spring Frenzy, Young's Gold, Hobgoblin and Fuller's London Pride line a bar counter also stocked with Hendrick's gin, Cockburn's port, Pimm's, and Glenmorangie, Laphroaig and Talisker whiskies – British or what? These bottles beckon before a beautiful gilt-mirrored back bar, evidence of the major mid-1800s refurb of this tavern, then the Dog & Duck, which has been operating from the 1700s (when this area was surrounded by marshes, and not crocodiles of cagouled Italians and the stench of over-priced hot dogs). The food – soup, pie, sausage, roast, puddings – exudes homely familiarity. *Children admitted (until 5pm). Tables outdoors (8, pavement).* **Map p240 L5.**

Nags Head
53 Kinnerton Street, SW1X 8ED (7235 1135). Hyde Park Corner or Knightsbridge tube. **Open** 11am-11pm Mon-Sat; noon-10.30pm Sun. **Food served** noon-9pm daily. **Belgravia**
It's unusual to see a landlord's name plastered on the front of a pub, but then there aren't many like Kevin Moran left in the trade. The Nags Head reflects Moran's exuberant eccentricity, both by design (mobiles are banned; the walls are cluttered with everything from cartoons to baseball reports, garden tools to vintage penny-slots) and, most strikingly, by accident – the rooms could scarcely be wonkier, one stepped awkwardly above the other with a bar that somehow serves them both. The ale is from Adnams and only OK, and the below-par pub food is best avoided, but the particular appeal of this place isn't really about the beer or the vittles. A Belgravia landmark of sorts. *Babies & children admitted (until 6pm). Games (antique What-the-Butler-Saw machine). Tables outdoors (2, pavement).*

Newman Arms
23 Rathbone Street, W1T 1NG (7636 1127, www.newmanarms.co.uk). Goodge Street or Tottenham Court Road tube. **Open** noon-midnight Mon-Fri. **Food served** noon-3pm, 6-10pm Mon-Fri. **Fitzrovia**
There's been a business located at this gateway to a cobbled alleyway since 1730 – see the red sign outside and etched writing over the bar – but as a pub it had its heyday in the mid 20th century, when George Orwell was a regular and Michael Powell filmed here. Both men get a decorative look-in, the pub's 101 minutes of movie fame marked by an Italian poster (1960's *L'Occhio che uccide*, aka *Peeping Tom*). Today, this is the lunchtime and post-work haunt of undemanding chaps laying into the Everard's

Beacon, George Gale Seafarers or Fuller's Honey Dew, perhaps accompanying a cheese-and-ham toastie (£1.50) or prefacing a shift upstairs from the cosy street-level bar to the pie room. There, the venison-and-mushroom or beef-and-Guinness staples can be followed by treacle sponge or rhubarb crumble. **Map p240 J5.**

Newton Arms
33 Newton Street, WC2B 5EL (7242 8797). Holborn tube. **Open** 11am-11pm Mon-Sat. **Food served** 11am-8pm Mon-Thur; 11am-3pm Fri; noon-3pm Sat. **Covent Garden**
Surrounded by *Sweeney*-era office blocks, the Newton Arms reflects a bygone era: no picture windows, no scuffed-floor makeovers and absolutely no gimmicks. You almost expect Jack and George to breeze in, slap a pack of Dillies on the bar and order two whiskies, large ones. Prices, while perhaps not pre-Thatcher, are certainly reasonable: no meal's more than a fiver, whether liver and onions, chicken curry, jacket potatoes or other anti-gastropub fare. White-shirted, tie-wearing staff pour pints of John Smith's, Courage, Adnams and San Miguel, amid mounted scenes of horse-racing and Ireland. It's the kind of place your dad might have taken you for your first shandy. *Babies & children admitted. Tables outdoors (2, pavement).* **Map p240 L6.**

Old Coffee House
49 Beak Street, W1F 9SF (7437 2197). Oxford Circus or Piccadilly Circus tube. **Open** 11am-11pm Mon-Sat; noon-10.30pm Sun. **Food served** noon-3pm Mon-Sat. **Soho**
The Old Coffee House is in fact an old pub, with old pub attitudes, drinks and decor: the vintage etched mirror still advertises MB Foster and Truman, Hanbury & Buxton; birds stay stuffed in glass frames; and the menu still consists of pies and jacket potatoes. The layout of the place, though, lies with its 18th-century roots, when such coffeehouses were debating chambers for rational political discussion. The debate today is carried out between two Sky Sports TV screens at each end of the one-room interior. The racing form is also perused, on the bar beside various handpumps (look out for the Brodie's ales). A framed display of David Beckham memorabilia contains a signed photo, close-ups of that last-minute free-kick against Greece, and a letter written by him as a teenage apprentice to 'lee', explaining how he'd just received his first match fee and bonus, and now had £250 in the bank. Like we said: vintage. *Babies & children admitted (restaurant). Function room (50 capacity).* **Map p241 J6.**

Pakenham Arms

1 Pakenham Street, WC1X 0LA (7837 6933, www.pakenhamarms.com). Russell Square tube. **Open** 10.30am-midnight Mon-Wed; 10.30am-1am Thur-Sat; 11am-11pm Sun. **Food served** noon-3pm, 5-9pm Mon-Fri; noon-7pm Sat, Sun. **Clerkenwell**

Occupying a quiet corner of Clerkenwell behind Mount Pleasant sorting depot, with red postal vans regularly passing its sun-catching front terrace, the Pakenham is simply a thoroughly decent, and decent-sized, corner boozer. Atop a long bar counter, taps of Greene King, Sambrook's Wandle, Sharp's Doom Bar and Sagres lager draw in a blokey clientele of posties and ale fans, some scarfing down a homemade pie of the day or a notable Pakenham burger topped with cheese, bacon and onion rings. Look out for the twofer meal deal for under a tenner on weekday lunchtimes. Flatscreen TVs in diagonal corners of the expansive main saloon provide entertainment for sports fans but the Pakenham is best enjoyed by day, providing the epitome of the quiet pint beneath tasteful black-and-white shots of vintage London. *Babies & children admitted. Tables outdoors (4, pavement). Wireless internet.* **Map p242 M4.**

Plumbers Arms

14 Lower Belgrave Street, SW1W 0LN (7730 4067). Victoria tube/rail. **Open** 11am-11pm Mon-Fri. **Food served** noon-8pm Mon-Fri. **Victoria**

Unassuming and well run, this corner boozer isn't interested in living off its brief footnote in history (it was here, in 1974, that Lady Lucan reported the murder of the family nanny). Guest ales are generally programmed on a week-by-week basis: Fuller's London Pride or St Austell Tribute might appear alongside regulars Black Sheep Ale and Timothy Taylor Landlord. After a brief foray into the exotic, the menu has reverted to traditional English pub food (pies, fish 'n' chips). Tradesmen still drink here, as they did when master builder Thomas Cubbitt's employees – servants and footmen too – frequented the pub erected in his honour. The boxy interior and layout is related to their relative social status. *Babies & children admitted (until 7pm). Function room (20 capacity). Games (board games).* **Map p249 H10.**

Princess Louise

208-209 High Holborn, WC1V 7BW (7405 8816). Holborn tube. **Open** 11.30am-11pm Mon-Fri; noon-11pm Sat; noon-10.30pm Sun. **Food served** noon-2.30pm, 6-8.30pm Mon-Thur; noon-2.30pm Fri. **Holborn**

With half-a-dozen ornately carved, sumptuously tiled bar areas under one high, stucco ceiling, the Princess Louise is a classic example of the kind of Victorian public house in which drinking was segregated according to social status. Today, it's an across-the-board Sam Smith's pub, with the mediocre beer priced to fly (a pint of Old Brewery bitter goes for a shade over two quid, almost comical by the standards of the area). The full Smith's range is available by the bottle in the fridges behind the horseshoe island bar; Organic Lager is probably your best bet. Sandwiches and pub grub satisfy hungrier diners, who are also accommodated in the upstairs bar (mealtimes only). London buses roll past the frosted glass windows as American tourists tentatively sample the strange dark ales at room temperature; across the bar, regulars pass carefully calculated coinage over the counter without looking up from the racing form. **Map p240 L5.**

Punchbowl

41 Farm Street, W1J 5RP (7493 6841, www.punchbowllondon.com). Green Park tube. **Open** noon-11pm Mon-Sat; noon-5pm Sun. **Food served** noon-3pm, 6-10pm Mon-Sat; noon-4pm Sun. **Mayfair**

'Camera equipment strictly prohibited' says the notice outside what was a pretty standard local pub until it was taken over by Guy Ritchie and two of his pals. Beside the warning will be the day's lunch or dinner menu: Bombardier-battered haddock with hand-cut chips, say, or a starter of smoked trout with homemade bread. Amid dark wood panelling, heavy tables and grandiose framed portraits, the distinction between drinking and dining remains, with the cosy, candlelit restaurant area set back from a main bar. The room exudes its Georgian tavern heritage, with illustrations of hunting and a large portrait of Winston Churchill among the decorative additions. Deuchars IPA, Wells Bombardier and Shepherd Neame Spitfire comprise the ales; prices by the glass and bottle for the various French, Spanish, Tuscan and New World wines are kept reasonable. *Function room (20 capacity).* **Map p239 H7.**

Queens Larder

1 Queen Square, WC1N 3AR (7837 5627, www.queenslarder.co.uk). Russell Square tube. **Open** 11.30am-11pm Mon-Sat; noon-10.30pm Sun. **Food served** noon-3pm daily. **Bloomsbury**

Although its terrace helps to create a continental atmosphere, at least when joined by others

Flask. *See p79.*

along this pedestrianised stretch, the Queens Larder is a classic British pub. The royal connections advertised in the name are, for once, legitimate: it was here that long-suffering Queen Charlotte hid the medicaments of her husband, the famously 'mad' King George III. A medical connection remains: off-duty staff from nearby Great Ormond Street are among the latter-day regulars at this wooden cubby-hole, sipping Greene King IPA and Old Speckled Hen while munching spam fritters, chips and beans or roast beef and Yorkshires (less than a tenner). Gilt-framed posters for theatre and Royal Ballet productions bring things up to date, if barely. *Babies & children admitted (until 6pm). Function room (30 capacity). Tables outdoors (8, pavement). Wireless internet.* **Map p240 L4.**

Red Lion

23 Crown Passage, off Pall Mall, SW1Y 6PP (7930 4141). Green Park or St James's Park tube. **Open/food served** 11am-11pm Mon-Sat. **St James's**

This unashamedly old-fashioned pub attracts an unashamedly old-fashioned clientele made up of neighbourhood gents and well-to-do local workers, although it would also excite overseas tourists looking for a quaintly, quintessentially English inn. With china plates lining the walls and an attractive little bar tucked in one corner, the small ground-floor room offers nowhere to hide, in keeping with the sense that most of the drinkers are on first-name terms. The musty upstairs room is often empty, but it's worth a peek for its cluttered and dated decor and gentlemen's club feel. On Saturdays, when the locals have all retreated to the country, the staff content themselves with pouring pints for the handful of exuberant blokey gangs who show up as part of the fabled Monopoly-board pub crawl: this is the nearest boozer to Pall Mall. *Babies & children admitted (until 7pm). Function room (50 capacity).* **Map p241 J8.**

Red Lion

48 Parliament Street, SW1A 2NH (7930 5826). Westminster tube. **Open** 10am-11pm Mon-Fri; 10am-9pm Sat; noon-9pm Sun. **Food served** *Bar* noon-9pm daily. *Dining room* 10am-9pm daily. **Westminster**

'A Great British Tradition' runs the wording around this 600-year-old pub. However, the Red Lion's character is defined as much by its location (it's the closest pub to Downing Street) as its history. Fuller's took over the place in 2009, but aside from a predictable and by no means unwelcome increase in the number of Fuller's beers on tap, change has been conspicuous by its absence: the decor remains traditional and woody, images of politicans past continue to look down on the drinkers, and the food still has few aspirations beyond sustenance. MP-spotters are more likely to find their prey down the road at the St Stephen's Tavern, leaving this place to a mix of tourists and civil servants. *Babies & children admitted (until 5pm). Entertainment (comedy 7.30pm Mon; quiz 7pm last Wed of mth). Tables outdoors (2, pavement). Wireless internet.* **Map p249 K8.**

Rose & Crown

*47 Colombo Street, SE1 8DP (7928 4285).
Southwark tube/rail.* **Open** 11.30am-11pm
Mon-Fri. **Food served** noon-2pm Mon-Fri.
Waterloo

Claiming origins in the 17th century, this
Shepherd Neame pub seems geographically and
stylistically at odds with the post-war mess that
is Waterloo: it's as if a village pub (with a beer
garden, no less) had been plonked here and
pointed towards some higher being. Hanging
flower baskets add colour to the grey
surroundings; it might be nice to have a beer
outside, but the view, in truth, is pretty grim.
Inside, the Rose & Crown is all dark wood,
decorated with snaps of the regulars and black-
and-white photographs of bygone local scenes.
Standard Shepherd Neame beers, from likeable
seasonals and reliable Spitfire to the ever-bland
Master Brew, complement lagery stablemates
Oranjeboom and Holsten Export. You won't find
any surprises on the food menu.
*Function room (50 capacity). Tables outdoors
(26, garden).* **Map p250 N8.**

Salisbury

*90 St Martin's Lane, WC2N 4AP (7836 5863).
Leicester Square tube.* **Open** 11am-11pm
Mon-Wed; 11am-11.30pm Thur; 11am-midnight
Fri, Sat; noon-10.30pm Sun. **Food served**
noon-10pm Mon-Sat; noon-9pm Sun.
Leicester Square

A 'sport-free pub since 1892', the Salisbury is
one of those etched-glass, carved-mahogany,
Victorian pub landmarks whose appearance has
tourists reaching for their cameras. It's a Taylor
Walker pub, so the menu's traditional – Whitby
breaded scampi from the 'Fish & Chip Shop',
Great British Pub Platter – and ales feature
prominently on the 'Beautiful Beer Menu'.
Along with Bombardier, Young's London Gold
and the brewery's own Timothy Taylor Landlord,
you'll find St Austell Tribute, Mad Goose,
Budvar and Estrella Damm, as well as Newky
Brown by the bottle. The pre-theatre crowd
rubs shoulders with the snap-happy tourists
when the pub fills in the early evening, but it's
spacious enough to fit half of London in.
*Babies & children admitted (until 5pm).
Function rooms (25, 40 capacity). Games
(board games). Tables outdoors (4, pavement).*
Map p241 L7.

Speaker

*46 Great Peter Street, SW1P 2HA (7222
1749, www.pleisure.com). St James's Park
tube.* **Open** noon-11pm Mon-Fri. **Food
served** noon-10pm Mon-Thur; 2-4pm Fri.
Westminster

As the sign outside says: 'This is a real pub.
No big screen. No music. No fruit machines'.
Indeed, you'll just find low-level chatter in the
one main room amid light-wood decor, fresh
flowers, framed caricatures and rows of
hardback novels from Macmillan-era book
clubs. Pride of place, though, goes to the
monthly changing list of guest ales chalked up
by the bar, featuring the likes of Ilkley Black
and Coastal Merry Maidens Mild. Superior
sandwiches (home-cooked roast turkey or
topside of beef) are fairly priced at £3, while
'Dennis's famous' chicken-liver pâté is similarly
own-made and served with toast. Lager
drinkers may choose between Pilsner Urquell,
Grolsch and Beck's Vier, oenophiles can opt for
the acceptable and affordable house La Casada,
or a standard merlot, Rioja or sauvignon blanc.
Map p249 K8.

Star Tavern

*6 Belgrave Mews West, SW1X 8HT (7235
3019, www.fullers.co.uk). Hyde Park Corner
or Knightsbridge tube.* **Open** 11am-11pm

Filthy MacNasty's. *See p79.*

Mon-Fri; noon-11pm Sat; noon-10.30pm Sun. **Food served** noon-4pm, 5-9pm Mon-Fri; noon-5pm Sun. **Belgravia**
During the 1950s and '60s, this tidy pub tucked away down a beautiful Belgravia mews is said to have drawn a mix of the very high and the very low: on the one hand, the wealthy locals who've long dominated the area; and on the other, the underworld types who aspired to it (the Great Train Robbery was reputedly planned upstairs). These days, it's a little less vibrant, but it's still a pleasant place, spruced up by a fairly recent refurbishment and enlivened in summer by its fabled hanging baskets. It's a Fuller's pub, which means that the beer ranges from merely reliable (Chiswick) to excellent (occasional seasonals and the unjustly maligned London Pride); food fits into the Fuller's tradition of simple, smart pub grub. *Babies & children admitted. Function room (50 capacity). Games (board games). Wireless internet.*

Three Kings of Clerkenwell
7 Clerkenwell Close, EC1R 0DY (7253 0483). Farringdon tube/rail. **Open** noon-11pm Mon-Sat. **Food served** noon-3pm, 6.30-10pm Mon-Fri. **Clerkenwell**
The royal trio of the pub's name turns out to be Elvis, Henry VIII and King Kong, a suitably eccentric trio for this most excellent of pubs. Papier-mâché rhino heads, autographed baseball photographs, twinkling fairy lights and a roaring fire provide the decor inside the intimate main room, as landlord Deke Eichler and his team of chummy, quietly efficient bar staff pour pints of decent ale and generous glasses of wine to garrulous Clerkenwell types and their associated along-for-the-ride pals. There's a gentle music theme to the place: the Monday-night music quiz is fiercely competitive and amusingly difficult, while the underused upstairs room contains a vinyl jukebox crammed with fabulous old sides that run from rare funk to unironic soft rock. The food's good enough and fairly priced; keep your eyes peeled for the occasional themed DJ nights (freak folk, classic jazz) on Saturdays. A gem. *Babies & children admitted (until 5.30pm). Entertainment (quiz 9pm Mon). Function rooms (70 capacity). Games (board games).* **Map p242 N4.**

Toucan
19 Carlisle Street, W1D 3BY (7437 4123). Leicester Square or Tottenham Court Road tube. **Open** 11am-11pm Mon-Fri; noon-11pm Sat. **Food served** 11am-3.30pm Mon-Sat. **Soho**
With its prime location right off Soho Square, its customers sipping a pavement pint on sunny afternoons, the intimate two-floor Toucan could easily be mistaken for a Guinness museum: publicity posters for the black stuff cover the walls, overlooked by a trio of toucans. At the bar two varieties of the stout (one Extra Cold), Magners and Grolsch are served, along with Jameson's on the optics and rarer whiskeys (Knappogue Castle, Clontarf Reserve). These days there are even spicy olives on the bar. In the equally small (and darker) basement, where Jimi Hendrix once played, food is served: Irish stew, Rossmore County Cork oysters (£5 for six) and anything requiring ketchup. The Toucan tapas selection includes baked beans, so it's far from pretentious. There are also Guinness cocktails, a top-of-the-range black velvet of Guinness and champagne, or the poor man's variety with cider instead. *Wireless internet.* **Map p240 K6.**

Windsor Castle
27-29 Crawford Place, W1H 4LJ (7723 4371). Edgware Road tube. **Open** 11am-11pm Mon-Thur; 11am-midnight Fri, Sat; noon-10.30pm Sun. **Food served** noon-3pm, 6-10pm Mon-Fri, Sun; 6-10pm Sat. **Marylebone**
If Alf Garnett ever redecorated heaven, it might look like this. Royals in plate, porcelain and photographic form grimace alongside sundry souvenirs of National Service; once a month, members of the Handlebar Club delicately try to keep their 'taches from drowning in ale. Plaques mark every drinking space, each dedicated to a cherished regular whose first name reflects pre-war fashion, while signed photos of lesser British celebrities (Dennis Waterman, PC Snow from *Softly Softly*) testify to a relaxed bonhomie. Visiting Americans seem to like it, perhaps plumping for Guinness over the ales (Adnams, Bombardier) or preferring a G&T to a glass of – no, really – Liebfraumilch. George Best resides atop a horseshoe bar counter, behind which an adept kitchen turns out Thai curries. Outside tables offer respite from the somewhat claustrophobic interior. *Babies & children admitted. Function room (26 capacity). Tables outdoors (4, pavement).* **Map p238 F5.**

Ye Olde Cheshire Cheese
145 Fleet Street, EC4A 2BU (7353 6170). Chancery Lane or Temple tube. **Open** 11am-11pm Mon-Fri; noon-11pm Sat; noon-4pm Sun. **Food served** noon-9.30pm Mon-Fri; noon-8.30pm Sat; noon-3pm Sun. **City**
This Fleet Street landmark was rebuilt back in 1667 ('in the reign of King Charles II'), and its

Island Queen. *See p80.*

17th-century history is in large part responsible for its 21st-century appeal. The royals to have been served thereafter are painstakingly listed outside in a higgledy-piggledy passageway, drawing in dozens of tourists a day to the pub's baffling labyrinth of rooms. Few leave disappointed – the layout, starting with the chop room on the left as you walk in, resembles a Cluedo board, and screams 'historic' as you stoop your head and dive down a cramped staircase to discover yet another bar room. The beer comes from Samuel Smith's, no better here than at the brewery's other London operations, and the food is the expected collection of historic pub grub staples ('ye famous' steak and kidney pudding, and so on).
Babies & children admitted (restaurant).
Map p243 N6.

Also recommended...
Adam & Eve (Gastropubs & Brasseries, *p128*); **Artillery Arms** (Beer Specialists, *p108*); **Betsey Trotwood** (Clubs & Music Venues, *p205*); **Coach & Horses** (Gastropubs & Brasseries, *p130*); **Eagle** (Gastropubs & Brasseries, *p131*); **Edgar Wallace** (Beer Specialists, *p109*); **Green Man** (Beer Specialists, *p110*); **Gunmakers** (Gastropubs & Brasseries, *p131*); **Harp** (Beer Specialists, *p110*); **King Charles I** (Beer Specialists, *p111*); **Lord John Russell** (Beer Specialists, *p111*); **Peasant** (Gastropubs & Brasseries, *p134*); **Queen's Head** (Beer Specialists, *p112*); **Queen's**

Head & Artichoke (Gastropubs & Brasseries, *p135*); **Seven Stars** (Gastropubs & Brasseries, *p136*); **Ship & Shovell** (Beer Specialists, *p112*); **White Swan Pub & Dining Room** (Gastropubs & Brasseries, *p137*); **Wilmington Arms** (Clubs & Music Venues, *p207*); **Ye Olde Mitre** (Beer Specialists, *p112*).

North

Compton Arms
4 Compton Avenue, N1 2XD (7359 6883).
Highbury & Islington tube/rail. **Open** noon-11pm Mon-Sat; noon-10.30pm Sun. **Food served** noon-8pm daily. **Islington**
This quiet, unassuming local is hidden away behind the Union Chapel and thus mercifully isolated from the chaos of Highbury Corner. It's a cosy place, split between a longish main room (with a TV at one end) and a smaller, squarer space on the other side of the bar. There's not much to choose between them, but if you're planning to order something from the menu of easygoing pub grub, you're more likely to find a seat in the latter. A chatty bunch of locals gathers here nightly, chewing over Arsenal's fortunes and bantering with interlopers over pints of ale (up to four on tap). It's not Islington's only real pub, of course, but it is one of its best.
Children admitted (over-14s only, until 9pm). Tables outdoors (8, garden).
Map p255 O26.

Filthy MacNasty's

*68 Amwell Street, EC1R 1UU (8617 3505,
www.filthymacnastys.co.uk). Angel tube.*
Open noon-11pm Mon-Sat; noon-10.30pm
Sun. **Food served** noon-3pm, 5.30-9.30pm
Mon-Fri; 5.30-9.30pm Sat, Sun.
Islington
Though it's been repainted in a fetching red
(it's no longer filthy or nasty), this music
landmark still pokes its tongue out. This isn't
to suggest that the staff are rude – the opposite,
in fact; they're rough diamonds to the core – but
you can't attract a regular flow of rock nuts
without a hint of attitude, especially with the
jukebox gone from the back room (there are now
rotating art exhibitions there). The tunes live on,
though, when acoustic sessions take over from
time to time, and there's also the 'Great London
Rock 'n' Roll Music Quiz' every Monday. It's
a place for ale aficionados, with the likes
of Wadworth 6X and Brains' Reverend James
('A taste of the good life') on draught, and there
are almost as many Irish whiskeys available
as from their Caledonian counterparts. Pub grub
and TV football complete the perfect weekend
haunt for the music-obsessed bloke.
*Disabled: toilet. Function room (70 capacity).
Entertainment (music quiz 7pm Mon; bands,
poetry readings; days vary; call for details).
Tables outdoors (14, pavement).*

Flask

*77 Highgate West Hill, N6 6BU (8348 7346).
Archway or Highgate tube, or bus 143, 210,
214, 271.* **Open** noon-11pm Mon-Sat; noon-
10.30pm Sun. **Food served** noon-3pm,
6-10pm Mon-Fri; noon-4pm, 6-10pm Sat;
noon-4pm, 6-9.30pm Sun. **Highgate**
When Albert Uderzo drew a timeless English
pub for a scene in *Asterix in Britain*, it looked
a lot like this traditional spot on Highgate
Hill: wooden beams, fireplaces, bottle-glass
windows and a labyrinth of snug rooms. Should
you find it, the little bar in one corner serves
a gently unusual range of beers, which has
improved since Fuller's took over the pub in 2009:
you might find the likes of Butcombe Bitter,
Hydes Original, Adnams and Fuller's own
Honey Dew on tap, with such Belgian brews as
Vedett and Duvel available by the bottle. Single
malts are another feature, though you might
prefer something chilled from the wine list
if you're taking to the side terrace in summer.
*Babies & children admitted (until 7pm).
Tables outdoors (20, garden).*

Harringay Arms

*153 Crouch Hill, N8 9QH (8340 4243).
Finsbury Park tube/rail then W3, W7 bus,
or Crouch Hill rail.* **Open** noon-11.30pm Mon-
Thur, Sun; noon-midnight Fri, Sat. **Crouch End**

Lord Clyde. *See p81.*

Swimmer at the Grafton Arms.
See p82.

Those coming this way for the first time, perhaps on the W7 bus up Crouch Hill, might miss this little Irish pub beside a branch of NatWest. The Harringay Arms' rather bland, un-publike façade hides a wood-panelled interior, an illusion of space created by judicious use of mirrors. Like it and it's 'cosy', dislike it and it's 'cramped'; still, the regulars are generally happy to move from their space at the bar should you wish to order. Beers include Courage Best and Adnams Broadside, along with standard lagers, but they could sell washing-up liquid in pints and locals would continue to come here for a natter. The history of the area can be studied in detail on a wall by the door, with maps and documents detailing old planning permission requests, while the back area acts as a wall of honour to Irish literature, with Behan, O'Brien, Yeats and others honoured in portrait form. *Entertainment (quiz 9pm Tue). Games (darts). Tables outdoors (4, garden).*

Hemingford Arms
158 Hemingford Road, N1 1DF (7607 3303, www.capitalpubcompany.com/the-hemingford-arms). Caledonian Road tube/rail. **Open** 11am-11pm Mon-Sat; noon-10.30pm Sun. **Food served** noon-4pm, 6-10.30pm Mon-Sat; noon-4pm, 6-10pm Sun. **Islington**
Don't be fooled by the all-singing, all-dancing slickness of the Hemingford's website: the pub itself is something of a shambles, and much the better for its idiosyncracies. Nothing much changes here: a baffling multitude of jumble-sale pub ephemera still hangs from the walls and the ceilings, the food is still stomach-lining Thai, the three or so ales are still good enough, and the locals are still a pleasingly talkative and egalitarian mix of classes and ages. Events run from quiz night to a weekly bluegrass session (Mondays from around 9pm), but many of the regulars only have eyes for the big-screen football. Any semblance of a sign outside has long since been covered by the ivy that drapes over almost every inch of the frontage. *Babies & children admitted (until 6pm). Entertainment (bands 9pm Mon, Thur-Sun; quiz 9pm Wed). Function room (60 capacity). Tables outdoors (9, pavement).*

Island Queen
87 Noel Road, N1 8HD (7354 8741, www.the islandqueenislington.co.uk). Angel tube. **Open** noon-11pm Mon-Wed, Sun; noon-11.30pm Thur; noon-midnight Fri, Sat. **Food served** noon-3pm, 6-10pm Mon-Thur; noon-4pm, 6-10pm Fri; noon-10pm Sat, Sun. **Islington**
This Islington backstreet is a notch above most of its N1 competitors. First, the beers: Peroni, Sierra Nevada, Leffe, Früli, Schneider Weisse, Paulaner, Pilsner Urquell and Staropramen, all on draught, complemented by tap ales such as Landlord and Doom Bar. Second, the wines: 20 in number, all but a couple available by both

bottle and glass. There's also the pub food, affordable and good enough. Inside, high ceilings tower over etched mirrors and abundant greenery; there are a couple of outdoor tables too. Even when it's busy, the height of the rooms means acoustics that allow easy conversation. But the Island Queen's main asset is that it has personality in spades: it's a proper pub for people who want a proper drink.
Babies & children admitted (until 7pm). Entertainment (quiz 8pm Tue). Function room (60 capacity). Games (board games). Tables outdoors (4, pavement). **Map p255 O2.**

Lord Clyde
340-342 Essex Road, N1 3PB (7288 9850, www.thelordclyde.com). Angel tube or Highbury & Islington tube/rail. **Open** noon-11pm Mon-Thur; noon-11.30pm Fri, Sat; noon-10.30pm Sun. **Food served** noon-3pm, 6-10pm Mon-Fri; 11am-3pm, 6-10pm Sat; noon-5pm, 6-9pm Sun. **Islington**
A quality makeover, this, a few bus stops north of the spaghetti junction of bars around the Angel. It's a big place to keep busy with return custom, with the huge interior supplemented by

Auld Shillelagh. *See p83.*

an umbrella-festooned front terrace ('The Deck'), but the owners succeed thanks to excellent food, decent ales (Harveys Sussex Best plus a guest, such as Hook Norton's Old Hooky or Cotleigh's 25) and a pub-like atmosphere with nods to modern manners. Lending itself to peaceful newspaper perusal at lunchtimes, ideally in the big armchair by the open fire, the Lord Clyde also suits the pre-party crowd, with music at conversational level, San Miguel, Amstel and Aspall Cyder on draught, and superior, own-made bar snacks (sausage rolls, scotch eggs). Lunchtime meze, Harveys-battered haddock and chips, and Sunday roasts (served until 7pm) provide further sustenance.
Babies & children (until 6pm). Entertainment (quiz 8pm Mon). Games (board games). Tables outdoors (8, garden). Wireless internet.

Old Red Lion
418 St John Street, EC1V 4NJ (7837 7816, www.oldredliontheatre.co.uk). Angel tube. **Open** noon-midnight Mon-Thur, Sun; noon-1am Fri, Sat. **Islington**
The Old Red Lion is most famous for the matchbox-sized fringe theatre that sits above it, staging no-budget productions of plays both old and (mostly) new. But the pub itself shouldn't be overlooked: it's not quite a world away from the boisterous boozers on Upper Street, but it's certainly a welcome relief. Although it could use a spruce-up, it's a handsome place at heart, part-partitioned by an etched-glass screen and otherwise furnished with old-fashioned pub booths, tables and stools. Your company at the bar will be a mix of quiet pint-nursing regulars (the beer is very decent, with Harveys Sussex Best among the five ales), pre- and post-theatre drinkers, the occasional student (City University is down the road) and refugees from the alcoholic turbulence closer to the Angel.
Babies & children admitted (until 7pm). Entertainment (theatre 7.30pm daily). Function room (40 capacity). Games (board games). Tables outdoors (4, patio).

Salisbury Hotel
1 Grand Parade, Green Lanes, N4 1JX (8800 9617). Manor House tube then bus 29, 141. **Open** 5pm-midnight Mon-Thur; 5pm-2am Fri; noon-2am Sat; noon-11.30pm Sun. **Food served** 5-10pm Mon-Fri; noon-10pm Sat, Sun. **Harringay**
The draught beers alone may justify the trek to Harringay for this popular spot. George Gale HSB, Fuller's London Pride, Discovery and Honey Dew, Belgian Palm, Rothaus, Leffe and two varieties of Litovel from the Czech Republic. Bottled, the world's your oyster: Chimays of all

colours, Erdinger, St Helier pear cider. Then again, there's room to stack a warehouse-load behind the oval bar counter. There's food too: thin-crust pizzas, salads and homemade burgers. Once you get stuck into the jukebox (*Pet Sounds, Sticky Fingers, The Gram Parsons Anthology*) or the regular music in another barn-like side room, leaving becomes a problem. Monday is quiz night, when the jukebox is out of operation. *Babies & children admitted. Disabled: toilet. Entertainment (poker 8pm Wed; bands 9pm Fri, Sat winter). Function room (120 capacity). Games (board games). Wireless internet.*

Shakespeares Head
1 Arlington Way, EC1R 1XA (7837 2581). Angel tube. **Open** 11.30am-11.30pm daily. **Food served** 11.30am-7.30pm Mon-Sat.
Islington
After a decade or so that's seen frosted pub windows across London replaced by clear glass, the Shakespeares Head may look a little daunting from the outside. Don't be shy: this salt-of-the-earth local extends a warm welcome to all. It's hard to imagine a pub with fewer pretensions than this place, done out in gloss-painted wood, standard-issue pub carpets and plump seating. The 1970s feel extends to the beer (Courage Best) and the food: main courses cost less than an average gastropub starter (spag bol for a fiver, for example). But this old-school boozer is made notable by the people in it: the staff, for whom nothing is too much trouble; and the clientele, an easygoing mix of theatregoers (Sadler's Wells is steps away) and talkative locals who've been drinking here since their dads brought them in for a pint on their 18th birthday. It's a mix mimicked on the walls, where signed photos of thesps and hoofers jostle for attention with the pictures of the locals out on a jolly. Quite a treasure, in its way. *Babies & children admitted (garden). Tables outdoors (6, garden).*

Star
47 Chester Road, N19 5DF (7272 2863, www.thestar-n19.com). Archway or Tufnell Park tube. **Open** 5-11pm Mon-Thur; 5pm-midnight Fri; noon-midnight Sat; noon-11pm Sun. **Food served** 6-10pm Mon-Fri; noon-4pm, 6-10pm Sat; 1-6pm Sun. **Tufnell Park**
Diagonally opposite an unpromising strip of kebab joints and loitering hoodies, this relaxing pub attracts many an ale aficionado and dog-walker. Along one side of a homely pub space filled with cosy, upholstered settees and bare brick, a bar counter manned by an amiable Frenchman features taps of Timothy Taylor Landlord and Sambrook's Wandle, as well as

San Miguel and Peroni lagers. Selections from the huge board of wines start at a little under £4 a glass. Below the wine board, a door leads to steep steps and a small square of gravel-surfaced back garden; the logs in the hallway come into use on wintry afternoons, when the fat candles flicker on the sturdy wooden tables. The likes of rib-eye steak and whole baked bream might feature on the changing food menu; many, though, are happy to share a pork pie or some snacking salami with their four-legged companions at their feet, a pleasure strictly forbidden to the house dog. Occasional unplugged entertainment encourages lingering. *Babies & children admitted. Entertainment (comedy, musicians; call for details). Function room (120 capacity). Games (board games). Tables outdoors (5, balcony; 10, garden). Wireless internet.*

Swimmer at the Grafton Arms
13 Eburne Road, N7 6AR (7281 4632). Holloway Road tube, or Finsbury Park tube/ rail then bus 29, 253. **Open** 5-11pm Mon-Fri; noon-11pm Sat; noon-10.30pm Sun. **Food served** 6-9pm Mon-Fri; noon-3pm, 6-9pm Sat; 1-5pm Sun. **Archway**
A large front terrace enveloped by branded umbrellas gives way to a classic, high-ceilinged pub, with one end dedicated to an open kitchen manned by a commendably grizzled southern Italian. Rump steak with chips is all well and good, but most customers are here for what the sign over the counter advertises as 'handpumped cellar-cooled real ales'. The likes of Butcombe Bitter and London Pride are complemented by Litovel, Leffe and Früli, with bottles of Duvel and Corona chilling in the fridge behind. Comfortably sparse, the interior features a fireplace surrounded by gilt-framed mirrors and swimming memorabilia: photographs of Johnny Weissmuller, Buster Crabbe and the White City pool of 1908 (the first time the Olympic sport wasn't held in open waters). *Games (board games). Tables outdoors (15, garden). Wireless internet.*

Also recommended...
Charles Lamb (Gastropubs & Brasseries, *p138*); **Drapers Arms** (Gastropubs & Brasseries, *p139*); **Duke of Cambridge** (Gastropubs & Brasseries, *p141*); **Junction Tavern** (Gastropubs & Brasseries, *p141*); **Marquess Tavern** (Gastropubs & Brasseries, *p141*); **Northgate** (Gastropubs & Brasseries, *p142*); **Oxford** (Gastropubs & Brasseries, *p142*); **Queens** (Gastropubs & Brasseries, *p142*); **Southampton Arms** (Beer Specialists, *p113*).

Nags Head

of the week. It's the kind of pub where the wine list runs to 'red or white', and where the staff are so matey and hospitable that they'll offer to bring your Guinness over to your table rather than have you hang around at the bar and wait for it to reach perfection. No wonder everybody here always seems to be in such a good mood. *Babies & children admitted (until 7pm). Entertainment (musicians 8pm alternate Fri & Sat). Tables outdoors (7, garden).*

Nags Head
9 Orford Road, E17 9LP (8520 9709, www.thenagshead17.com). Walthamstow Central tube/rail. **Open** 4-11pm Mon-Thur; 2-11pm Fri; noon-11pm Sat, Sun.
Walthamstow
This bright, homely pub accommodates quietly spoken ale drinkers, well-meaning ladies of a certain age keen on self-improvement (classes here include Egyptian dance and pilates) and, crucially, cats and those who love them. The place is dotted with images of the little darlings, refugees from a nearby rescue home; one of them, Tetley, 'the village cat', has a near-permanent place at one of the tables on the front terrace and in a lovely illuminated garden. The beer-hunters eschew Tetley (and, for that matter, Tetley's) in favour of Landlord, Woodforde's Wherry, Mighty Oak's lovely Oscar Wilde Mild and Nethergate Itinerant, brewed in the cats' honour. The Nags Head also offers jazz on a Sunday night, and gives house room to an art project investigating the origins of the Barbie doll.
Entertainment (life-drawing classes 7.30pm Mon; women's Egyptian dance classes 7pm, 8.30pm Tue; pilates 7.30pm Wed, Thur; musicians 4-8pm Sun). Tables outdoors (8, patio; 20, heated garden).

North East

Auld Shillelagh
105 Stoke Newington Church Street, N16 0UD (7249 5951, www.theauldshillelagh.com). Stoke Newington rail or bus 73, 393, 476. **Open** 11am-11pm Mon-Wed; 11am-1am Thur-Sat; noon-midnight Sun. **Stoke Newington**
The added-value attractions at this skinny little Church Street boozer are numerous: sporadic themed music nights (including the Bowie Bar on the second Thursday of the month, with films and food – Diamond Hot Dogs, anyone? – to go with the tunes), big-screen football, a surprisingly large beer garden. But the Shillelagh is at its best when it keeps things simple, as an honest, uncomplicated Irish pub (as opposed to Irish-themed pub; the difference is crucial) that draws a devoted circle of boozed-up Stoke Newingtonians most nights

Nightingale
51 Nightingale Lane, E11 2EY (8530 4540). Snaresbrook or Wanstead tube. **Open** 10am-midnight daily. **Food served** 10am-10pm Mon, Wed; 10am-4pm Tue, Thur; 10am-6pm Fri-Sun. **Wanstead**
Monika works the bar at this salt-of-the-earth pub, dispensing pints (Woodforde's Wherry, Black Sheep, Doom Bar) to first-name-terms regulars and occasionally bringing a pint to old George at his corner table as his legs only take him as far as the pub door itself. Her counter serves both the main bar and saloon bar behind it, where ruddy-faced men of brotherhood age, having forsaken manly pint-horsing for the security of married life, sit in silence with their wives, not quite out of earshot of the swearing on the other side. Both bar areas are social-club comfortable – green upholstered furniture,

red carpet – and reflect the sporting interests of the landlord (framed West Ham shirt, signed QPR one, collection of tickets to sundry matches). The food's a grab-bag of Brit dishes and more exotic imports (Thai green curry, say); there's Irish music once a week.
Babies & children admitted. Entertainment (musicians 8pm Wed). Function room (20-25 capacity). Tables outdoors (8, pavement).

Prince George
40 Parkholme Road, E8 3AG (7254 6060). Dalston Junction or Dalston Kingsland rail. **Open** 5pm-midnight Mon-Thur; 5pm-1am Fri; 2pm-1am Sat; 2-11.30pm Sun. **Dalston**
Once a mellow backstreet local, the George now swarms with rowdy, slumming-it art students in ridiculous outfits on Fridays and Saturdays, to the point where the landlord has even hired a bouncer. As the pub's popularity has risen, so have the prices; you can drink for less in Mayfair. Still, catch it on a quieter night, and this remains a great pub, a mixed coterie of longtime Dalstonians and recent arrivals shooting the breeze over pints (Pride, Seafarer, George Gale HSB) and a jukebox-led soundtrack of classic cuts and hipster-friendly obscurities. The raffish decor (yellowing walls, stuffed animals) will be familiar to anyone who's drunk at Stoke Newington's Shakespeare or the Royal Inn on the Park in Victoria Park, two of the dozen-ish pubs under the same umbrella, but the George retains its own identity to the last.

Babies & children admitted (until 8.30pm). Entertainment (quiz 8.30pm Mon). Games (board games, pool table). Tables outdoors (8, heated forecourt). Wireless internet.

Scolt Head
107A Culford Road, N1 4HT (7254 3965, www.thescolthead.com). Haggerston rail. **Open** noon-midnight Mon-Sat; noon-11.30pm Sun. **Food served** noon-3pm, 6.30-10pm Mon-Fri; noon-4pm, 6.30-10pm Sat; noon-4pm, 6.30-9pm Sun. **Dalston**
In a corner of Hackney where pool tables and a giant TV are still a prerequisite for survival, the former Sussex Arms was smartened up to good effect a few years ago. The new owners tore out the carpets and scrapped some of the scruffier furniture; however, despite the more aspirational nature of the clientele, it still feels like an old-fashioned pub. There are ales (Truman's Runner, Brewer's Gold IPA) for around three quid a pint; a brief but thoughtful wine list; and good, fairly priced British food, stretching from gastropubby mains to epic, softball-sized scotch eggs. If the pub has a problem, it's size: it has more space than it needs, and the room can feel a little empty on quieter nights. But that's a small quibble with a very likeable enterprise.
Babies & children admitted. Entertainment (quiz 8pm Mon; musicians 8pm 1st Thur of mth). Function room (250 capacity). Tables outdoors (12, garden). Wireless internet.

Palm Tree

Ye Olde Rose & Crown

*53 Hoe Street, E17 4SA (8509 3880,
www.roseandcrowntheatrepub.webeden.co.uk).
Walthamstow tube/rail.* **Open** 10am-11pm
Mon-Thur; 10am-midnight Fri, Sat; noon-
11pm Sun. **Food served** 1-3.30pm daily.
Walthamstow
A few years ago, this capacious corner pub was
straight from the old school: footy on the telly,
folk club in the function room, banter at the bar,
lager in the fridge. It was a fair old place back
then, but it's better now, spruced up by an
ambitious team who aim to return this
imposing boozer to its former status as a local
community hub. The main bar is a big, bright,
open-plan space, with a baby-grand piano and
an above-average range of ales compensating
for the lack of cosiness: you can expect to find
up to five on tap at any one time, including a
fair number of unusual varieties. Upstairs, the
old function room is now being billed as a
theatre, home not to folk nights but comedy
clubs and occasional small-scale stage shows.
*Babies & children admitted. Entertainment
(theatre 7.30pm daily; quiz 8.30pm 1st Sat
of mth). Games (board games, pool). Tables
outdoors (2, pavement). Wireless internet.*

Also recommended…

Cat & Mutton (Gastropubs & Brasseries,
p143); **Duke of Wellington** (Beer
Specialists, *p115*); **Londesborough Pub
& Dining Room** (Gastropubs & Brasseries,
p144); **Prince** (Gastropubs & Brasseries,
p144); **Prince Arthur** (Gastropubs &
Brasseries, *p144*).

East

Golden Heart

*110 Commercial Street, E1 6LZ (7247 2158).
Liverpool Street tube/rail or Shoreditch High
Street rail.* **Open** 11am-midnight Mon-Sat;
11am-10.30pm Sun. **Spitalfields**
Landlady Sandra Esquilant, regular Tracey
Emin and Lady Di are given equal profile on
the walls of this traditional Truman boozer, a
hangout for the arty crowd and Shoreditch
flotsam and jetsam. Sandra, whose 30-year
marriage to Dennis is celebrated in neon
outside (one of several Emin creations here),
provides bar-counter cheer. A sign proclaiming
'Stand Still and Rot' is another interesting
touch, but your eyes will be most drawn to the
penny-chew-coloured jukebox featuring
images of the Statue of Liberty. On our latest
visit, the CD pages were left open at 'Chas &
Dave's Street Party' and Frank Sinatra's 'My

Way, The Best of' which seemed to characterise
the place nicely. Running in bright red on the
walls are the beer names of yesteryear (Eagle
Ale, Eagle Stout, and so on); these days it's
Adnams and Leffe on draught, and affordable,
well-kept wines.
*Babies & children admitted. Function room
(45 capacity). Tables outdoors (1, pavement).*
Map p244 R5.

King Edward VII

*47 Broadway, E15 4BQ (8534 2313,
www.kingeddie.co.uk). Stratford tube/rail/DLR.*
Open noon-11pm Mon-Wed; noon-midnight
Thur-Sat; noon-11.30pm Sun. **Food served**
noon-3pm, 5-10pm Mon-Fri; noon-10pm Sat;
noon-9pm Sun. **Stratford**
On the other side of the Stratford Centre from
the ever-expanding transport hub stands a sea-
green storefront topped by a hungover image
of sleep-around monarch Edward VII. He may
have approved of what lies within: even today,
this old but sympathetically renovated pub is
divided by ornately tiled walls and frosted-
glass dividers. The sunken front bar fills with
the banter of workers from the London 2012
site, while the dark-wood saloon bar, the back
room and the verdant rear patio hum with the
chatter of young professionals. Catering to the
latter means that the pub now lays on pumpkin,
carrot and kidney bean curry and couscous, a
wine of the week and the reassuring strum of
a guitar on open-mic Thursdays. Regulars can
still look forward to a pint of Eddie's Best –
brewed for the pub by Nethergate – or
Bombardier, with whiskies such as Laphroaig,
Lagavulin and Glenlivet providing a late-night
chaser. At the risk of damning it with faint
praise, this is easily the best pub in Stratford.
*Babies & children admitted. Entertainment
(musicians 9pm Thur; quiz 8.30pm Sun).
Function room (60 capacity). Tables outdoors
(5, yard).*

Palm Tree

*127 Grove Road, E3 5BH (8980 2918). Mile
End tube or bus 8, 25.* **Open** noon-midnight
Mon-Thur; noon-2am Fri, Sat; noon-1am Sun
(last admission 10.45pm). **Mile End**
This is a glorious old East End boozer, albeit
one cast adrift in the green acres of Mile End
Park, nestled up against the Regent's Canal. You
can run through a checklist of trad features –
shelf of china plates, dried hops hung in a
corner, London Fives dartboard, signed pictures
of 'celebrity' drinkers (Jim Bowen being one of
the few you might recognise) above the oval
central bar but that doesn't do it justice. Yes, the
shiny copper-coloured metallic wallpaper

provides the wonderful light, but the place also has a great mix of punters: the more enterprising students from the university across the canal and sundry nutters from the nearby climbing wall brush shoulders with the suit-and-sovereign old blokes and their wives, who breeze in from the estate for the weekend singalongs. Beer-lovers do best, with a couple of interesting guests always on tap; wine, on the other hand, comes from a Stowells dispenser behind the bar.
Entertainment (musicians 9.45pm Fri, Sat; 9pm Sun). Games (London Fives dartboard). Tables outdoors (4, park).

Pride of Spitalfields
3 Heneage Street, E1 5LJ (7247 8933). Aldgate East tube. **Open** 11am-11pm Mon-Sat; noon-10.30pm Sun. **Food served** noon-2.30pm Mon-Fri; 1-4.30pm Sun.
Brick Lane
Down a cobbled spur off Brick Lane, this totally unfashionable boozer attracts by its very lack of pretention. Background sounds of 'Bohemian Rhapsody' battle with ambitious chatter about Leyton Orient's chances of making the play-offs as blokes sink pints of Sharp's Doom Bar, Crouch Vale Brewer's Gold, and Fuller's ESB and London Pride. Everything on the menu, served beneath an awning proclaiming 'Mary's Pantry', seems to come with chips and cost £2.50; the quite wonderful white-and-tabby tomcat treats everyone with disdain, so don't even bother trying to win his favour. Framed black-and-white photographs of the East End's past decorate a seen-it-all single bar room of faded red banquettes, and there's even a piano in the corner should you find yourself in urgent need of an old-fashioned knees-up.
Babies & children admitted.
Map p246 S5.

Ten Bells
84 Commercial Street, E1 6LY (7366 1721, www.tenbells.com). Liverpool Street tube/rail or Shoreditch High Street rail. **Open** noon-midnight Mon-Wed, Sun; noon-1am Thur-Sat.
Spitalfields
Firmly on the Shoreditch circuit, this prominent, stripped-down corner pub is party central, a century or so after its clientele included Jack the Ripper's last victim enjoying her final drink. Press cuttings and other Ripperana line the stairs to the toilets, but while the current owners have kept the pub's original tiling (amazing it is, too), they've played the alternative card by chucking in busted sofas, '60s cinema seats and a glitterball. The market traders of Spitalfields

opposite thus avoid it, despite a worthy selection of beers that includes Bombardier, Grolsch, Staropramen and John Smith's on draught, and Sol, Früli, Budvar and Brooklyn by the bottle. Ask for a glass of wine and you'll get something equally quaffable. Monday's quiz nights are taken as seriously as the need to look interesting and imbibe.
Function room (40 capacity). **Map p246 S5.**

Also recommended...
Carpenters Arms (Beer Specialists, *p116*); **Fox** (Gastropubs & Brasseries, *p144*); **Grapes** (Rooms with a View, *p163*); **Gun** (Gastropubs & Brasseries, *p145*); **Hemingway** (Good Mixers, *p188*); **Narrow** (Gastropubs & Brasseries, *p146*); **Old Fountain** (Beer Specialists, *p117*); **Princess of Shoreditch** (Gastropubs & Brasseries, *p146*); **Prospect of Whitby** (Rooms with a View, *p164*); **Royal Oak** (Gastropubs & Brasseries, *p147*); **Town of Ramsgate** (Rooms with a View, *p164*); **Wenlock Arms** (Beer Specialists, *p117*).

South East

Ashburnham Arms
25 Ashburnham Grove, SE10 8UH (8692 2007, www.ashburnhamarms.com). Greenwich DLR/rail. **Open** noon-11pm Mon-Wed, Sun; noon-midnight Thur-Sat. **Food served** noon-2pm, 6-9pm Tue-Sat; noon-4pm Sun.
Greenwich
Greenwich's Ashburnham Arms nicely bridges the gap between contemporary bar and old-fashioned local. On the one hand, there's the beer, a familiar array of Shepherd Neame beers (Master Brew, Spitfire and others) served with good grace from a neat little bar counter, and the boozer's status as a keen cricket pub, the first XI and its upcoming fixtures posted for all to see. On the other, there's the bright, lived-in interior, the funky continental bar furniture on the expansive terrace, and the idiosyncratic artistic rendition of Greenwich in map form. Natural light floods over the wooden furniture, and the conservatory and the garden suit families who are drawn to the kids' selections on the menu while themselves favouring a disparate array of unpubby surprises (pizzas, for one thing). Most wines are less than £4 a glass.
Babies & children admitted (until 7.30pm). Entertainment (quiz 9.15pm Tue). Function room (25 capacity). Tables outdoors (11, garden; 5, patio). Wireless internet.
Map p253 D2.

Lord Clyde. *See p90.*

Bear

*296A Camberwell New Road, SE5 0RP
(7274 7037, www.thebear-freehouse.co.uk).
Oval tube.* **Open** 4-10.30pm Mon; noon-11pm
Tue-Thur; noon-midnight Fri, Sat; noon-10pm
Sun. **Food served** noon-3pm, 7-10pm Tue,
Sat; noon-3pm, 6-10pm Wed-Fri; noon-4pm
Sun. **Camberwell**

It's something of a surprise to find a pub as
amiable as this on what is the least appealing
arm of Camberwell's beleaguered crossroads.
A former Victorian gin palace dominated by a
horseshoe bar, the Bear has scrubbed up
nicely and now oozes warmth, especially by
candlelight. Despite this, it's still very much a
locals' boozer, with an unusually fine selection
of cast ales (look out for the occasional beer
festival), a decent range of bottled beers
(Duvel, Peroni, Anchor, Erdinger, Chimay
Blue), a well-chosen wine list and good-
value food among the consumable attractions.
The rear room, decorated with stopped clocks
and china dogs, is an easy place to while
away an evening. There's also a popular quiz
on Tuesdays.

*Babies & children admitted. Entertainment
(quiz 8pm Tue). Function room (40 capacity).
Games (board games). Tables outdoors
(4, pavement). Wireless internet.*

Charles Dickens

*160 Union Street, SE1 0LH (7401 3744,
www.thecharlesdickens.co.uk). Southwark tube.*
Open noon-11pm Mon-Fri; noon-8pm Sat;
noon-6pm Sun. **Food served** noon-3pm,
6 8.30pm Mon-Fri; 2-8pm Sat; noon-6pm
Sun. **Bankside**

Despite the continental bar furniture placed
ambitiously outside in the unlikely event that
any streaks of sunlight should deign to invade
this dark locality, the Dickens is as English as
they come. This is yet another SE1 pub with
terrific beer: regulars crowded around the dark
wood bar may get to choose from the unusual
likes of Goffs Tournament, Nethergate Suffolk
County Best, Adnams Extra and Mighty
Oak's Oscar Wilde Mild. Further inspection
of the interior reveals a wonderful collection
of caricatures from the novels of the man
himself: look carefully and you might spy the
two Wellers and Mr Micawber, for instance,
each with a relevant quotation. The menu
includes gammon steak with eggs, pineapple
and chips, which should give you an idea as to
the other available choices.

*Babies & children admitted (until 7pm).
Entertainment (quiz 8.30pm Wed). Tables
outdoors (3, pavement; 6, garden). Wireless
internet.* **Map p250 O8.**

Commercial

*212 Railton Road, SE24 0JT (7733 8783,
www.thecommercialhotelhernehill.co.uk).
Brixton tube/rail then bus 3, 196, or Herne
Hill rail.* **Open** *noon-midnight Mon-Thur;
noon-1am Fri; 11am-1am Sat; 11am-midnight
Sun.* **Food served** *noon-10pm Mon-Thur;
noon-11pm Fri, Sat; 11am-9.30pm Sun.*
Herne Hill
On a narrow bend opposite Herne Hill station,
a short bus hop from Brixton, the Commercial
is a pleasurable pub in which to spend some
time. It's one of the more modern Mitchells
& Butlers pubs, not dissimilar in style to the
Crown & Sceptre in Fitzrovia in the way it mixes
old-fashioned pub culture with new school pub
cooking and a comparatively enlightened
approach to beer. Two expansive rooms of
stripy furniture and contemporary colours, with
Wi-Fi and board games, accommodate drinkers
and diners, while a pie slice of back garden
houses a handful of tables and umbrella heaters.
A board in the spruced-up main bar proclaims
the presence of 21 draught beers (including
Red Stripe, Paulaner, Franziskaner, Sierra
Nevada, Peroni and Beck's Vier), three ciders
and four ales (including Fuller's London Pride
and Sharp's Doom Bar). Food stretches from
bar snacks (fried chorizo, houmous) to larger,
workaday meals (burgers, Sunday roasts);
a Monday quiz diverts the locals.
*Babies & children admitted (until 7.30pm).
Disabled: toilet. Entertainment (quiz 8pm
Mon; knitting club 8pm Wed). Games (board
games). Tables outdoors (5, garden).*

Crown & Greyhound

*73 Dulwich Village, SE21 7BJ (8299 4976,
www.thecrownandgreyhound.co.uk). North
Dulwich rail.* **Open** *11am-11pm Mon-Wed;
11am-midnight Thur-Sat; 11am-10.30pm Sun.*
Food served *noon-10pm Mon-Thur; noon-
11pm Fri, Sat; noon-9.30pm Sun.* **Dulwich**
Although this fusion of two Victorian pubs is
certainly large, the Crown & Greyhound is also
surprisingly cosy, split up as it is into various
dark wood-panelled rooms with robust tables,
carved wooden seating and nicotined ceilings.
Black and red tiles chequer the floor around
the semi-circular bar, where a guest ale sits
alongside London Pride, Sharp's Doom Bar and
Harveys Sussex Best to tempt the all-and-
sundry collection of mums, nippers, builders,
students and tourists who gather here. At the
rear, alongside a restaurant section with a nice
conservatory, solid outdoor tables make light
work of the substantial portions of food brought
by the amiable staff (there's also a Sunday
carvery). Two black-hooded barbecues await

orders when summer brings hordes to a back
garden in which an enormous, seen-it-all-before
horse chestnut tree holds sway.
*Babies & children admitted (until 9pm).
Disabled: toilet. Entertainment (chess club 8pm
Mon; life-drawing class 6pm Tue; wine club
6pm Thur). Function room (100 capacity).
Games (board games). Tables outdoors
(50, garden).*

Half Moon

*10 Half Moon Lane, SE24 9HU (7274
2733, www.halfmoonpub.co.uk). Herne Hill
rail.* **Open** *noon-midnight Mon-Thur; noon-
1am Fri, Sat; noon-10.30pm Sun.* **Food
served** *5-10pm Mon-Thur; 4-10pm Fri;
noon-10.30pm Sat; noon-9pm Sun.* **Herne Hill**
A late-afternoon visit to the Half Moon can be a
sobering experience. The selection of beers on
offer – Kronenbourg, Fosters, Adnams bitter –
will be as low-key as the atmosphere, unaided by
the size of the place. Still, things improve
markedly in the evenings, when Herne Hillians
descend on this Victorian boozer and the pub's
pulse quickens. While a little tatty in places, it's
really a handsome spot, its old-school grandeur
having just about lasted down the years. At the
end of the bar is a fine snug where mirrors
painted long ago with slightly awry paintings of
water fowl adorn the walls and a La Spaziale
coffee machine gurgles in the background.
There's music in the back room, but it's unlikely
to be of much interest if you are not personally
acquainted with the people who are playing it.
*Babies & children admitted (until 8pm).
Entertainment (open mic 8pm Tue; quiz 8pm
Thur; bands 8pm Fri, Sat). Function room (220
capacity). Tables outdoors (4, pavement).
Wireless internet.*

Hare & Billet

*1A Elliot Cottages, Hare & Billet Road,
SE3 0QJ (8852 2352). Blackheath rail.*
Open *11am-11pm Mon-Wed; 11am-midnight
Thur-Sat; noon-11pm Sun.* **Food served**
*noon-3.30pm, 5.30-9pm Mon-Fri; noon-9pm
Sat, Sun.* **Blackheath**
This landmark pub on the edge of the heath has
been satisfying visitors since the 1600s. After
a yomp around the parkland, the food and drink
at the Hare & Billet is welcome, with solid dishes
such as gammon steaks or sausage and mash
(two meals for £6) offered alongside a few choice
wines. However, it seems that most drinkers still
come here for a refreshing pint after a stroll
across the wilderness outside. British ales might
include Greene King IPA and Old Speckled Hen,
with a couple of Leffes and other popular
Belgian labels by the bottle. A television offers

Avalon. *See p90.*

entertainment, but the pub doesn't have to push the boat out too far to keep the tills ringing. *Babies & children admitted (until 7pm). Entertainment (quiz 8pm Sun).* **Map p253 E3**.

Lord Clyde

27 Clennam Street, SE1 1ER (7407 3397, www.lordclyde.com). Borough tube. **Open** 11am-11pm Mon-Fri; noon-11pm Sat; noon-6pm Sun. **Food served** 11am-2.30pm, 5.30-9pm Mon-Fri. **Borough**

A haven of tranquillity in a Borough sidestreet bookended by Peabody Trust residences, the Lord Clyde is a lived-in home from home for middle-aged regulars and penny-conscious students. A Truman's landmark – note the pub sign outside and the etched mirror within ('Unrivalled Mild Ales & Double Stout') – the Clyde now offers a multitude of brewery flagship ales: Young's, London Pride, Adnams. Prices are more than reasonable, but perhaps not as affordable as the 1/6d pale ale on offer when England last won the World Cup, as revealed by a July 1966 price list mounted under a large TV linked up to Sky Sports. Draught lagers are glugged by regulars playing darts in a back room otherwise decorated by a print depicting the Lord Clyde's heroic action at the Battle of Balaclava in the Crimean War. Pictures of ships and Spitfires, and an old Player's cigarette ad, continue the armed forces theme.
Function room (30 capacity). Games (darts). **Map p250 P8**.

Princess of Wales

1A Montpelier Row, SE3 0RL (8852 5784, www.princessofwalespub.co.uk). Blackheath rail. **Open** noon-11pm Mon-Sat; noon-10.30pm Sun. **Food served** noon-10pm Mon-Sat; noon-9.30pm Sun. **Blackheath**

Although the Princess of Wales has undergone a revamp by Mitchells & Butlers, turning it into a modern bar bright with exotic beer taps, the pub hasn't quite forgotten its history. In 1871, England players gathered here before the first ever international rugby union match, an event commemorated with a modest alcove of mementoes. Elsewhere, though, the huge main bar, a corridor of tables and various back areas done out in pub-cum-lounge-bar style have been given over to a young clientele sipping selections from a global beer range (Doom Bar, Meantime Stout, Früli, Kozel) to a student-rock soundtrack. Dishes such as a large 21-day-aged rib-eye steak or Cotswolds lamb leg steak with lentils and peppers can also be enjoyed on the front terrace, in the conservatory or in the back garden.

Babies & children admitted (until 7pm). Disabled: toilet. Entertainment (quiz 8pm Tue). Function room (50 capacity). Games (darts). Tables outdoors (30, garden).

Also recommended...

Cutty Sark Tavern (Rooms with a View, *p164*); **Dog & Bell** (Beer Specialists, *p117*); **Gowlett** (Good Mixers, *p191*); **Hermits Cave** (Beer Specialists, *p119*); **Herne Tavern** (Gastropubs & Brasseries, *p147*); **Market Porter** (Beer Specialists, *p120*); **Royal Oak** (Beer Specialists, *p120*); **Trafalgar Tavern** (Rooms with a View, *p167*); **Victoria Inn** (Beer Specialists, *p121*).

South

Avalon

16 Balham Hill, SW12 9EB (8675 8613, www.theavalonlondon.co.uk). Clapham South tube. **Open** noon-11pm Mon-Wed; noon-midnight Thur; noon-1am Fri, Sat; noon-10.30pm Sun. **Food served** noon-3.30pm, 6-10.30pm Mon-Fri; noon-4pm, 6-10.30pm Sat; noon-9pm Sun. **Balham**

Certainly the most 'designed' option of the many good pubs in Balham, Avalon is worth a visit just for a peek at the HG Wells-inspired

Nightingale. *See p94.*

dining room or to enjoy the brilliant garden (huge, beautifully landscaped; feral children and barbecues in good weather). But if you just want a comfortable pub with nice sofas and a heated smoking area, it can do that too. We've had several meals in the dining room; although decent and of the meaty, solidly British variety – steaks, ox tongue, wood pigeon – they're a bit pricey unless you're taking advantage of one of the frequent meal deals. There's always a decent selection of real ales: Adnams Lighthouse, Timothy Taylor Landlord and Sharp's Doom Bar, say.
Babies & children admitted (until 8pm). Disabled: toilet. Entertainment (DJ 9.30pm Fri, Sat). Function room (22 capacity). Games (board games). Tables outdoors (35, garden/courtyard; 15, patio). Wireless internet.

Bedford

77 Bedford Hill, SW12 9HD (8682 8940, www.thebedford.co.uk). Balham tube/rail. **Open** 3pm-midnight Mon-Thur; 2pm-2am Fri; 11am-2am Sat; noon-midnight Sun. **Food served** 6.30-10pm Mon-Fri; noon-10pm Sat, Sun. **Balham**
As busy and prominent as any local can be, this corner pub in Balham attracts all-comers, who sit and commune in a nondescript interior or at outdoor tables by busy traffic. No, that doesn't sound attractive, but the Bedford succeeds because they've found the knack of making people feel comfortable. After all the developments in pub culture over the last decade, mates, dates and strangers still make that easy text-message invitation of an afternoon: 'Bedford?' By then, the place is pretty full, and the day's suggestions of steak sandwiches and pies wiped from the board behind the bar, but the likes of Timothy Taylor Landlord, O'Hanlon's Yellowhammer and Sharp's Doom Bar should still be on, and roughly ten wines should still be available. The calendar takes in cabaret, comedy, music, dance classes, quiz nights… It's still all happening at the Bedford.
Babies & children admitted (until 7pm). Disabled: toilet. Entertainment (line-dancing 7.30pm Mon; quiz 8.30pm Mon; swing dancing 8pm Tue; comedy 9pm Tue, Fri, Sat; salsa 7.45pm Wed; tango 7.15pm Thur, alternate Sun; nightclub 11pm-2am Fri, Sat). Function rooms (75, 200 capacity). Tables outdoors (4, pavement; 5, garden). Wireless internet.

Bobbin

1-3 Lilleshall Road, SW4 0LN (7738 8953, www.thebobbinclapham.com). Clapham Common tube. **Open** noon-11pm Mon-Thur; noon-midnight Fri, Sat; noon-10.30pm Sun. **Food served** noon-3pm, 6-10pm Mon-Fri; noon-4pm, 6-10pm Sat; noon-4pm, 6-9pm Sun. **Clapham**
A really mixed crowd fills this deceptively large pub, everyone from twentysomething young professionals to gents and ladies of a certain age. Recently refurbished, it offers snug nooks in the bar area (complete with board games and a dartboard – and handy as an overflow for parents needing to keep the children in check), a tranquil conservatory for diners and a lovely patio space with heaters. Some come for the ale (Harveys Sussex Best, Sambrook's Wandle), others for the lager (Bitburger, Leffe, Sagres) and others still for the wine (extensive and set at Clapham prices) and the food – the menu's had an overhaul too, with deli-inspired small plates, a charcuterie board (with an excellent piccalilli), whitebait, super chunky chips and a solid choice of sandwiches. But most choose the Bobbin for a community feel and the buzz around the invariably swamped bar counter.
Babies & children admitted (until 6pm). Entertainment (quiz 8pm Wed). Function room (40 capacity). Games (darts). Tables outdoors (11, garden). Wireless internet.
Map p252 A1.

Devonshire

39 Balham High Road, SW12 9AN (8673 1363, www.dukeofdevonshirebalham.com). Balham tube/rail. **Open** noon-midnight Mon-Fri; noon-1am Sat; noon-11pm Sun. **Food served** noon-9.30pm Mon-Thur, Sun; noon-10.30pm Fri, Sat. **Balham**
Head north from Balham station or south from Clapham South and you'll pass a few pubs, but none are as huge or attractive as this Young's operation. Wicker furniture on the terrace (weather permitting) is a nice touch; inside, the open-plan front area, kitted out with contemporary sofas and banquettes, feels both lived-in and looked after, a world away from some of the more workaday pubs owned and operated by the same brewery across the city. A dividing wall covered in memorabilia – a Clash gig ticket from the '16 Tons' tour, images of a life lived in and around music and pubs – sections off a dining area with a tasteful mural running around it. The wine list is long for a Young's pub, with more than three dozen varieties; burgers and salads are joined on the food menu by sharing platters.
Babies & children admitted (until 7pm). Disabled: toilet. Entertainment (quiz 8pm Mon). Games (board games). Tables outdoors (45, garden). Wireless internet.

Cat's Back. *See p94.*

Effra

38A Kellet Road, SW2 1EB (7274 4180).
Brixton tube/rail. **Open** noon-11pm Mon-
Thur; noon-midnight Fri; 10am-midnight Sat;
10am-10.30pm Sun. **Food served** noon-10pm
Mon-Fri; 11am-10pm Sat; 11am-9.30pm Sun.
Brixton
Four-pint pitchers of Red Stripe, ska turned
up nice and loud, tip-top Guinness, jerk chicken
and rice, unfeasibly friendly bar staff, two
pull-down screens for sports – this is a real
home from home for many Brixtonians, with
more of an Afro-Caribbean community feel
than many other watering holes found in
the neighbourhood. Touches of old-school
pubbery – framed collections of cigarette cards
(footballers, fops, racehorses), a horseshoe bar,
globe-shaped light fittings – combine with
more modern, stripped-back decorative
touches to nice effect; smokers occupy the
outdoor space at the back, done out like
a garden centre. Dominoes and the football
provide diversions during the day; after dark,
the Effra draws a younger crowd, some here to
dine in the rear space near the garden with
others showing up for the often excellent jazz.
Entertainment (musicians 8.30pm Tue-Thur,
Sat, Sun). Games (dominoes). Tables outdoors
(3, garden). **Map p252 E2.**

Fentiman Arms

64 Fentiman Road, SW8 1LA (7793 9796,
www.geronimo-inns.co.uk/thefentimanarms).
Oval tube or Vauxhall tube/rail. **Open**
noon-11pm Mon-Thur; noon-midnight
Fri, Sat; noon-10.30pm Sun. **Food**
served noon-3pm, 6-10pm Mon-Fri;
noon-4pm, 6-10pm Sat; noon-9pm Sun.
Vauxhall
Tucked away on a quiet, handsome residential
street between Vauxhall and Stockwell, the
Fentiman Arms has been designed by Geronimo
Inns to appeal to the neighbourhood's discreetly
wealthy locals. Upmarket, clean-cut and tasteful,
the pub attracts well-spoken City boys and
shiny-haired career blondes who'd rather hide
out with a decent bottle of wine and a plate
of gastropub-type food than face the mean
streets of SW8 of an evening. It's bigger than
it looks from the outside: the pleasing main
room extends into a handsome, well maintained
garden, and there's a nice room upstairs
available for private hire. Service can be hit-or-
miss, from very helpful to borderline rude; prices
are high, but the regulars either don't notice
or don't mind. Its proximity to the Oval means
it's rarely anything less than packed after close
of play; understandable, as it's the best option
within a ten-minute walk of the ground.

Cock & Hen. *See p95*.

Babies & children admitted. Entertainment (quiz 8pm Tue). Function room (80 capacity). Games (board games). Tables outdoors (25, garden). Wireless internet.

Nightingale
97 Nightingale Lane, SW12 8NX (8673 1637). Clapham South tube or Wandsworth Common rail. **Open** 11am-midnight Mon-Sat; noon-midnight Sun. **Food served** noon-10pm daily. **Battersea**
A number of elements lift the Nightingale from its apparent status as just another Young's pub. Built in 1853 by Thomas Wallis, this cosy community local offers a fireplace and blankets in winter, and a back beer garden in summer, reached through a conservatory decorated with museum artefacts depicting the history of the brewery. This vintage feel is continued with displays of Wills's cigarette cards in the main bar, where you can pick up souvenir postcards or badges of the pub. Board games include Scrabble and Taboo, and there's a popular alfresco darts set-up in the beer garden. The standard Young's ale range is complemented by 15 wines.
Babies & children admitted (until 9pm). Disabled: toilet. Games (board games, darts). Tables outdoors (18, garden). Wireless internet.

Prince of Wales
48 Cleaver Square, SE11 4EA (7735 9916, www.princeofwaleskennington.co.uk). Kennington tube. **Open** noon-11pm Mon-Sat; noon-10.30pm Sun. **Food served** noon-3pm Mon, Fri, Sat; noon-3pm, 6-9pm Tue-Thur; noon-4pm Sun. **Kennington**
Hidden in the corner of an archetypal, residential Georgian square, this traditional Shepherd Neame pub wouldn't be out of place on the edge of a village green somewhere in semi-rural Kent. Well kept inside and out, albeit with few nods to modernity, the pub has flower boxes along the front window, while the walls of the snug and cushioned interior are lined with a Victorian advert for St Jacob's Oil and framed portraits of 19th-century cricketers – it's not far from the Oval, and gets particularly busy after close of play during Test matches and one-dayers. The beers are Shepherd Neame standards, Spitfire and the like; the clientele on non-cricket days are largely made up of members of the hobnobbing local media gentry. A very agreeable little pub.
Babies & children admitted (until 9pm). Tables outdoors (3, pavement).

Also recommended...
Canton Arms (Gastropubs & Brasseries, p149); **Eagle Ale House** (Beer Specialists, p123); **Manor Arms** (Gastropubs & Brasseries, p150); **Priory Arms** (Beer Specialists, p123).

South West

Alma
499 Old York Road, SW18 1TF (8870 2537, www.thealma.co.uk). Wandsworth Town rail. **Open** 11am-midnight Mon-Sat; noon-11pm Sun. **Food served** noon-4pm, 6-10.30pm Mon-Sat; noon-9.30pm Sun. **Wandsworth**
A landmark Young's pub and rightly so, the large, Victorian-era Alma serves punters of all stripes gathered around a low, island bar. Some perch on barstools, others at tables nearer the windows: most will be gawping at the large, pull-down screen for big matches. Outside of these magic 90 minutes plus stoppages, the Alma attracts ale fans eager to sample Sambrook's Wandle, Wells Bombardier or something from the regular Young's range. Bar food is another plus: deli boards of cured meats, honey-and-mustard chipolatas, burgers with brie and bacon. For finer dining, head to the adjoining restaurant for the likes of honey-glazed Gressingham duck breast. If you don't want to leave at chucking-out time, then stay: there are 23 hotel rooms here.
Babies & children admitted. Function room (80 capacity). Wireless internet. **Map p251 B2.**

Cat's Back
86-88 Point Pleasant, SW18 1NN (8877 0818, www.catsback.co.uk). East Putney tube or Wandsworth Town rail. **Open** 11am-midnight Mon-Thur, Sun; 11am-2am Fri, Sat. **Food served** 11am-10pm Mon-Sat; 1-4pm Sun. **Wandsworth**
The land around the Cat's Back is increasingly given over to modern residential developments, but this wonderful, bohemian community pub continues to plough its own singular furrow; it's the kind of eccentric, genuinely alternative place that's all too rare in this corner of the city. Locals gather conspiratorially round the cosy main bar, a fire-warmed cabin decked out with intriguing tat: photographs of Terry-Thomas, a Christmas greetings card from Robson-era Ipswich Town, a *Johnny Suede* poster and, in opposite corners, a piano and an acoustic guitar. The real ales might include Hepworth Dark Horse mild and Sambrook's Wandle; eight wines are all sold by the glass. That whirr you hear in between three-minute snatches of indie din is a dumb waiter, lowering the likes

George IV. See p100.

of lamb kofta or rib-eye steak; you can also eat in an upstairs room where live bands play amid Nick Cave prints and vintage artwork. The cat's miaow, and no mistake. *Babies & children admitted. Disabled: toilet. Entertainment (musicians 7.30pm alternate Thur). Function room (30 capacity). Tables outdoors (8, garden).*

Chelsea Potter
119 King's Road, SW3 4PL (7352 9479). Sloane Square tube then bus 11, 22. **Open** 11am-11pm Mon-Thur; 11am-midnight Fri, Sat; noon-10.30pm Sun. **Food served** 11am-9pm Mon-Sat; noon-9pm Sun. **Chelsea**
Right on the King's Road, the Chelsea Potter has seen its share of action down the years: the Stones, it's said, were once regulars here. Old light fittings hint at the pub's pedigree, while the wooden furniture – except for a single modern sofa – exudes an antiquated charm. Today, though, you're more likely to be mingling with local ladies, a handful of should-know-better spiky-haired gents and Italian tourists with truculent offspring in tow. The resulting bonhomie takes place in a classic, one-room pub interior and a couple of tables on Radnor Street, fuelled by pints of Sharp's Doom Bar and London Pride, and assorted bottled beers (Budvar and Heineken among them). Considering the location, the wines are well priced, although the 15 choices by the glass won't get anyone over excited.

Babies & children admitted (until 9pm). Tables outdoors (5, pavement). **Map p248 D5.**

Cock & Hen
360 North End Road, SW6 1LY (7385 6021, www.cockandhenfulham.com). Fulham Broadway tube. **Open** 11am-11.30pm Mon-Thur; 11am-12.30am Fri, Sat; 11am-11pm Sun. **Food served** 11am-10.30pm Mon-Sat; 11am-9.30pm Sun. **Fulham**
Pretty much as close as the Young's chain gets to a bar rather than a pub, this huge place by Stamford Bridge is quite singular given the traditional bent of its ownership. First-time visitors will discern little from its bland, black frontage facing a church. Within, though, mirrors hang from baroque-wallpapered walls and Victorian lighting adorns the ceiling, the interior stretching right back to a raised area and garden behind. Along with the regular Young's beers, there are wines and even – another surprise for a Young's operation – familiar cocktails (cosmopolitans, mojitos). The food extends to scampi and chips, chicken goujons, steak ciabatta and Sunday roasts. The soundtrack is usually provided by the chat of the matey locals, but there are board games for quieter nights.
Babies & children admitted. Disabled: toilet. Entertainment (poker night 7.30pm Mon). Games (board games, darts). Tables outdoors (17, garden). Wireless internet.

Goldhawk. *See p100.*

Fox & Hounds

29 Passmore Street, SW1W 8HR (7730 6367, www.youngs.co.uk). Sloane Square tube. **Open** 11am-11pm Mon-Sat; noon-10.30pm Sun. **Food served** 12.30-2.30pm Mon-Fri. **Chelsea**
When Gordon, a regular who you may meet sipping a glass of red at the bar, began coming here, the Fox & Hounds was even smaller than it is now, which is to say pretty small indeed. At that time, it was part of the Grosvenor Estate; it's now linked to the Young's chain, which explains the ales. A wonderfully cosy place, it exudes a slight gentlemen's club feel these days: the friendly landlord will address you as 'Sir' when you first order, surrounded by paintings of hunting scenes and a caricature of Churchill. Honest pub grub at honest prices appears on weekday lunchtimes. Urban myth comes with the oft-repeated but never-verified rumour that this is where Tony Warren devised *Coronation Street*. Still, at least they haven't renamed it the Rovers Return. *Entertainment (quiz 8pm last Sun of mth).* **Map p248 E4.**

Leather Bottle

538 Garratt Lane, SW17 0NY (8946 2309, www.leatherbottlepub.co.uk). Earlsfield rail. **Open** 11.30am-11pm daily. **Food served** noon-10pm Mon-Sat; noon-9pm Sun. **Earlsfield**

Behind the wide front terrace, the layout of this ages-old, well-run Young's pub may be a little confusing at first, but the Leather Bottle is worthy of exploration. Spaces include the Board Room, accessed from a short staircase either end behind the main bar; a more intimate room mainly given over to diners (fish 'n' chips, burgers); and a substantial beer garden, a boon in summer. In colder months, the large old fire in the main bar comes into its own, as locals exchange chit-chat for old-school board games. The decoration isn't anything remarkable, but it's worth eyeing up the vintage memorabilia dotting the bare-brick walls, such as the photograph of the pub in its circa-1890 prime. *Babies & children admitted (until 7pm). Disabled: toilet. Entertainment (poker 8.30pm Tue; quiz 8.30pm Thur). Function rooms (30, 40, 80 capacity). Tables outdoors (70, garden). Wireless internet.*

Pear Tree

14 Margravine Road, W6 8HJ (7381 1787, www.thepeartreefulham.com). Barons Court tube. **Open** noon-11pm Mon-Sat; noon-10.30pm Sun. **Food served** noon-3pm Mon-Fri; noon-4pm, 6-9.30pm Sat; noon-4pm, 6-9pm Sun. **Fulham**
The Pear Tree sits behind Margravine Cemetery in the middle of low-rise council blocks – an oasis of comfortable calm in an unexpected location. The pub changed hands lately and has benefited from a refurbishment, with the main room centred on a horseshoe bar; adjoining is a back room used chiefly for dining (Sunday roasts provide punctuation on a food menu that reprises many gastropub favourites), and then a small, pear-tree-shaded garden complete with an area inspired by Moroccan boudoirs. Timothy Taylor Landlord and Old Speckled Hen seem the best draught options, with a standard wine selection of ten options of each colour all sold by the glass. The drinks list may not be impressive, but the garden makes this worth a special trip. *Babies & children admitted (until 8.30pm). Games (board games, darts). Tables outdoors (12, garden). Wireless internet.*

Also recommended...

Bricklayer's Arms (Beer Specialists, *p124*); **Bull's Head** (Clubs & Music Venues, *p219*); **Cadogan Arms** (Gastropubs & Brasseries, *p151*); **Fox & Grapes** (Gastropubs & Brasseries, *p151*); **Half Moon** (Clubs & Music Venues, *p220*); **Pig's Ear** (Gastropubs & Brasseries, *p152*); **Sultan** (Beer Specialists, *p124*);

Sun Inn (Rooms with a View, *p167*);
White Horse (Beer Specialists, *p124*).

West

Brook Green Hotel

170 Shepherd's Bush Road, W6 7PB
(7603 2516, www.brookgreenhotel.co.uk).
Hammersmith tube. **Open** 11am-midnight
Mon-Thur, Sun; 11am-1am Fri, Sat. **Food
served** noon-3pm, 6-10pm Mon-Fri; noon-
10pm Sat, Sun. **Hammersmith**
Its large front facing Brook Green, a peaceful
rectangle of tennis courts and relaxation tucked
behind the chaos that is Hammersmith,
this rather grand, high-ceilinged Young's pub
is comfort itself. House plants, a fireplace and
inviting sofas all contrive to create
a faintly homely feel, although you'd love this
much light and space in your own flat. You can
see halfway across the green from the picture

Old Ship. *See p102.*

windows, so pick a prime spot from which to sip
your pint of Grolsch Blond, Bath Green Ale
or Young's own London Gold. Entertainment
comes in several guises: comedy nights, a book
club, even salsa evenings. Neither the food nor
the wine are anything to get excited about.
Babies & children admitted (until 6pm).
Disabled: toilet. Entertainment (salsa 7pm
Wed; comedy 8pm 1st Thur of mth; swing
dancing 7pm Sun). Function room (100
capacity). Tables outdoors (12, garden).
Wireless internet.

Castle

225 Portobello Road, W11 1LU (7221 7103,
www.castleportobello.co.uk). Ladbroke Grove
tube. **Open** noon-11pm Mon, Tue, Thur,
Sun; noon-midnight Wed, Fri, Sat. **Food
served** noon-10pm Mon-Sat; noon-9.30pm
Sun. **Notting Hill**
Whatever the price and quality of the gastropub
fare (pork belly and mash for a tenner, roasted
root risotto at £7.50), this is a proper Portobello
local. The majority of the jolly, bohemian-
minded punters hanging around the pleasingly
sparse, open-plan interior – probably at the bar –
seem cheerfully merry whatever the time of
day, which is testament of sorts to the agreeable
atmosphere cultivated by the matey staff.
There's music three or four nights a week;
the rest of the time, it's a free for all, with
unshaven musos hammering back Black Sheep,
Staropramen, Kirin or Leffe. A couch in one
corner affords comfort to couples.
Babies & children admitted (until 7pm).
Disabled: toilet. Entertainment (open mic
8.30pm Wed; bands 8.30pm Fri, Sat). Tables
outdoors (3, pavement). **Map p247 Z5.**

Churchill Arms

119 Kensington Church Street, W8 7LN
(7727 4242, www.fullers.co.uk). High Street
Kensington or Notting Hill Gate tube.
Open 11am-11pm Mon-Wed; 11am-midnight
Thur-Sat; noon-10.30pm Sun. **Food served**
noon-10pm Mon-Sat; noon-9.30pm Sun.
Kensington
Not that most tourists would know, but there
seems to be a contradiction here. The Churchill,
a celebration of the wartime leader (they even
estimate the number of champagne bottles the
man consumed), is in fact an Irish pub – didn't
Ireland remain neutral during World War II?
Regardless, this is a fine establishment, part
homely tavern (it's a Fuller's, and the beer is
excellent) and part Thai restaurant. Character
is provided by the lived-in feel and mass
of junk – portraits of prime ministers
and American presidents, the documented

triumphs of the Clare GAA hurling team, shiny copper things. The verdant frontage, embellished by an image of Churchill giving the V, is a regular winner in its category of the London in Bloom competition. Tourists love it, yes, but the regulars here include locals, and not just the posh ones. *Babies & children admitted.* **Map p247 B8**.

Colton Arms

187 Greyhound Road, W14 9SD (7385 6956). Barons Court tube. **Open** noon-3pm, 6-11.30pm Mon-Thur; noon-3pm, 6pm-midnight Fri; noon-4pm, 7pm-midnight Sat; noon-4pm, 7-11pm Sun. **Food served** noon-3pm Mon-Fri; noon-4pm Sat. **Barons Court**
Far enough from the beaten track to attract only the occasional irregular, the delightful Colton Arms is warming in winter (trusty fireplace) and convivial in summer ('Biergarten' out back). At some point in the dim and distant, somebody seems to have tried to build a tourist trade by naming the toilets 'Sires' and 'Wenches' and hanging up all manner of tankards and horse brasses, not to mention a royal crest of unknown European heritage, but visits by the Osaka branch of the Sharp's Doom Bar Appreciation Society are rare. A sturdy cash till, guarded by a portrait of a late, lamented mastiff, registers a pre-decimal ring-up; a clock may chime while you order. If this place were a little more TARDIS-shaped (it does its best), you'd swear you'd walked into an episode of *Doctor Who*. *Children admitted (garden). Tables outdoors (4, garden).*

Cumberland Arms

29 North End Road, W14 8SZ (7371 6806, www.thecumberlandarmspub.co.uk). West Kensington tube or Kensington (Olympia) tube/rail. **Open** noon-11pm Mon-Wed, Sat; noon-midnight Thur, Fri; noon-10.30pm Sun. **Food served** noon-3pm, 6-10pm Mon-Sat; noon-9.30pm Sun. **Hammersmith**
A great find, this, a cathedral-ceilinged pub decked out in the best possible taste. On the walls are a publicity poster for Air Atlas and a classic shot of Grand Central Station bathed in sunlight, an image echoed by beams of light falling on the wooden tables and banquettes. The Cumberland circulates its beers, listing the coming attractions on the menu: as well as the familiar likes of Deuchars IPA and St Austell Tribute, you may find rarer ales from such brewers as Otter, Butcombe and Sharp's. Food's another strong suit (expect to hear regulars raving about the Andalusian oxtail casserole and goat's cheese tart), but this is more pub than gastropub. The 40-plus wines start at around £15 a bottle and run north to around £30.

Clifton. *See p105.*

Babies & children admitted (until 7pm). Games (board games). Tables outdoors (9, garden). Wireless internet.

Drayton Court
2 The Avenue, W13 8PH (8997 1019, www.fullers.co.uk). West Ealing rail. **Open** 11am-11pm Mon; 11am-midnight Tue-Thur; 11am-1am Fri, Sat; noon-11pm Sun. **Food served** noon-3pm, 5.30-10pm Mon-Fri; noon-10pm Sat; noon-8pm Sun. **Ealing**
Don't be put off by the Castle Greyskull-like exterior or the faintly eerie pub sign: this is one of the warmest and most likeable pub interiors in west London. It's huge but cosy, a feat achieved by dint of a fire (in winter only, of course), soft woody colours and pleasing carpets. During the day, kids are made to feel especially welcome to the point where staff will even host birthday parties for them. If you take your drink to the small slice of terrace at the back, the one with the contemporary furniture, you'll quickly realise why this is such a popular choice for families: the garden is enormous. At night, back inside the pub, you can watch the big game in convivial company on a large screen. The full and reliable range of Fuller's beers is available, as is a commendably affordable range of food. The nearest tube station is a bit of a trek, but there's a minicab office next door – or you could stay in one of the guest rooms themed on Ealing comedies. *Babies & children admitted. Disabled: toilet. Entertainment (quiz 8.30pm Thur; comedy 9pm Fri). Function room (120 capacity). Tables outdoors (100, garden). Wireless internet.*

Earl of Lonsdale
277-281 Westbourne Grove, W11 2QA (7727 6335). Ladbroke Grove or Notting Hill Gate tube. **Open** noon-11pm Mon-Sat; noon-10.30pm Sun. **Food served** noon-9pm daily. **Notting Hill**
A bit of a surprise, this. First, you'll see a sturdy pub, occupying the corner of Portobello Road and Westbourne Grove. Within, there are partitioned areas done out in neat, shiny wood and interconnected by chest-high doorways. The curiosities lie further back: one room is somewhere between a gentlemen's club and a tearoom at a honeymoon resort, a lounge that seems more suited to toast and coffee than pie and a pint. Among the photographs – past carnivals, touched-up images of Portobello Market – is another oddity: a wall honouring the man after whom the pub is named, the so-called Yellow Earl, who is most famous as the founder of the AA. It's a Sam Smith's pub,

which means the drinks aren't a great part of the appeal. That you have to walk over and help yourself to salt, vinegar and sauces indicates little snobbery where pub grub is concerned. *Babies & children admitted (lounge & garden until 8pm). Entertainment (quiz 8.30pm Tue). Tables outdoors (16, garden).* **Map p247 Z6.**

Elephant & Castle
40 Holland Street, W8 4LT (7937 6382). High Street Kensington tube. **Open** 11am-11pm Mon-Sat; noon-10.30pm Sun. **Food served** noon-10pm daily. **Kensington**
The crossroads of family homes and little shops the Elephant & Castle calls home could almost be a quiet village in Oxfordshire, a comparison on which you might muse as you sip a pint of London Pride or Doom Bar (joined by guests such as Thornbridge Jaipur or Stonehenge Sign of Spring) on the terrace. The interior feels lived in: regulars find their place on a studded, upholstered banquette, in a wooden booth or in an intimate back room lined with newspaper splashes of 20th-century moments (Laika, Neil Armstrong). The blurb on the menu – pies, pastas, sausages – refers to the pub's traditional attraction to journalists (it's within post-deadline range of the *Mail*'s office). These days, though, you'll mostly find residents and white-collar workers doing the *Standard* crossword. *Tables outdoors (8, pavement).*

George & Dragon
183 High Street, W3 9DJ (8992 3712, www.georgeanddragonacton.com). Acton Central tube/rail. **Open** 4-11pm Mon; noon-11pm Tue-Thur; noon-midnight Fri, Sat; noon-10.30pm Sun. **Food served** 5.30-9.30pm Mon; noon-2.30pm, 5.30-9.30pm Wed-Sat; noon-6pm Sun. **Acton**
This historic gem of a pub would be noteworthy whatever its location; amid the unpromising mess of bookies, takeaways and pound shops that together comprise Acton High Street, it stands out a mile. After 250 years and a recent spruce-up, it's now kept in excellent nick by the latest in a string of landlords, whose names – starting with 'David Simman (1759)' – are etched on to a board in the bar. Tap beers include Hoegaarden, Litovel, Palm, Leffe and a variety of Fuller's ales; in common with other pubs in the Remarkable Restaurants mini-chain, the wines are good but more expensive than they ought to be. The big decorative surprise comes with the large room to the rear, whose back bar is topped with a sign for 'Bonds and Dealers', and statues of two bare-breasted nymphs hoisting lights.

Holly Bush. See p106.

Babies & children admitted. Disabled: toilet. Entertainment (quiz 8.30pm Mon, 8pm Tue; open mic 7.30pm Thur). Function room (110 capacity). Games (board games). Tables outdoors (4, courtyard). Wireless internet.

George IV

185 Chiswick High Road, W4 2DR (8994 4624). Turnham Green tube. **Open** 11.30am-11pm Mon-Thur; 11.30am-1am Fri, Sat; noon-11pm Sun. **Food served** noon-10pm Mon-Sat; noon-7pm Sun. **Chiswick**

This is a huge Fuller's pub, right on the main drag and almost large enough to have its own microclimate. Due to its size and location, it attracts a mixed bunch of drinkers – locals, labourers, shoppers, couples, families – and the selection of food and drinks is designed to please all-comers. There's the full Fuller's ale range, for a start, with Pride, ESB, Chiswick and Discovery supplemented by seasonals such as Spring Sprinter. Fuller's have branded the place an 'Ale & Pie House', which should give you an idea what you might find on the food menu. The pub has a portrait of King George, in whose honour the pub was renamed

in the 1820s. However, it opened a half-century earlier, when it traded as the Boston Arms. Babies & children admitted (until 7pm). Disabled: toilet. Entertainment (comedy 8.30pm Fri, Sat; bands 9pm Fri, Sat). Function room (200 capacity). Games (darts). Tables outdoors (3, pavement; 7, garden). Wireless internet.

Goldhawk

122-124 Goldhawk Road, W12 8HH (8576 6921). Goldhawk Road tube. **Open** noon-11pm Mon-Wed; noon-midnight Thur-Sat; noon-11pm Sun. **Food served** noon-10pm daily. **Shepherd's Bush**

This big, black-fronted barn of a community pub hides a large, friendly interior brimming with a pop sensibility: Keith Moon (in a target T-shirt) peers down from a lookalike portrait painting on to a youthful crowd spread over sofas and chairs while Jarvis Cocker does the playlists. The beer range is equally striking: Tiger, Adnams, Mac's Gold, Grasshopper and B Bulldog all greet the spoiled-for-choice first-time visitor. Food is served all day and is just the cheaper side of expensive – chicken tagine for £9.50, burgers for a little less, good old fish-finger sandwiches further down the scale. If conversation dries up, play 'spot the album' from the vinyl backdrop on one wall. *Babies & children admitted (until 7pm). Disabled: toilet. Entertainment (musicians 8pm Thur; quiz 8.30pm Sun). Games (board games). Tables outdoors (6, pavement).*

Ladbroke Arms
54 Ladbroke Road, W11 3NW (7727 6648, www.capitalpubcompany.com). Holland Park tube. **Open** 11.30am-11pm Mon-Sat; noon-10.30pm Sun. **Food served** noon-2.30pm, 7-9.30pm Mon-Fri; 12.30-2.45pm, 7-9.30pm Sat, Sun. **Holland Park**
The prominent, self-standing pub sign on the front terrace proudly declares 'Free House', and sure enough, the Ladbroke Arms is a law unto itself. Happy to cater both to moneyed fortysomethings sinking sancerre on the sunny front terrace, and to ale aficionados after a pint of Sharp's Doom Bar or Twickenham Spring Ale, the Ladbroke stands on a quiet, residential street in Holland Park lined with police cars attached to the station opposite. The decor in the light main bar is noteworthy, with an original 1920s poster for Fap'Anis ('celui des connoisseurs' and worth a few bob) on one side, a display shelf full of decorative bottles of olive oil on the other. A back room fills with

middle-aged chatter, while one narrow corridor behind provides peace and quiet for book-readers – every pub should have one. Dining is of the smart, upscale variety. *Babies & children admitted (dining only). Tables outdoors (12, terrace). Wireless internet.* **Map p247 A7**.

Mawson Arms
110 Chiswick Lane South, W4 2QA (8994 2936, www.fullers.co.uk). Turnham Green tube. **Open** 10.30am-8pm Mon-Fri. **Food served** noon-7pm Mon-Fri. **Chiswick**
Notwithstanding a recent modest refit, little has changed at this pub for many a year. Key to its appeal is the location: down towards the Thames, a fair trek away from the nearest tube station, it's in the shadow of the Fuller's brewery, and thus plays host to many drinkers before and after tours of the grand old factory. Alongside the expected range of Fuller's beers – Discovery, Honey Dew, London Pride and others – there's also uncomplicated and cheap food: burgers, sandwiches, fish 'n' chips, and an assortment of pies (steak and ale, chicken and leek). Note the unusual opening hours: maybe Edwardian licensing laws still apply to this most traditional of pubs. *Babies & children admitted. Function room (25 capacity).*

Flask. *See p105.*

Mitre

24 Craven Terrace, W2 3QH (7262 5240, www.mitrelancastergate.com). Lancaster Gate tube or Paddington tube/rail. **Open** 11am-11pm Mon-Sat; noon-10.30pm Sun. **Food served** noon-10pm Mon-Sat; noon-9.30pm Sun. **Bayswater**

CAMRA district awards greet the visitor at this high-ceilinged Young's pub tucked behind the Bayswater Road. A large bar dominates the L-shaped wooden interior, upon which taps of Erdinger, Kirin Ichiban, Peroni, Heineken and Wells Bombardier accompany those of the usual Young's range; wines include a more-than-decent shiraz and malbec. The food is a little more imaginative than that offered at many of the Mitre's stablemates: venison burgers, for example, along with spicy potato skins in the bar-snacks category. Above the fireplace runs the Latin motto *Audere est facere*; whether or not the owners, staff and locals are Spurs fans, there's plenty of football banter around the bar. *Babies & children admitted. Entertainment (quiz 8pm Tue). Function room (50 capacity). Games (board games). Tables outdoors (8, pavement). Wireless internet.*

Old Pack Horse

434 Chiswick High Road, W4 5TF (8994 2872, www.fullers.co.uk). Chiswick Park tube. **Open** 11am-11pm Mon-Wed; 11am-midnight Thur-Sat; noon-10.30pm Sun. **Food served** noon-10pm daily. **Chiswick**

Not to be confused with the Packhorse & Talbot down the road, this traditional Fuller's pub dates back to the days of the Chiswick Empire, which explains both the 'Empire Bar' legend carved into the back bar and the posters and memorabilia in the back room. The interior is indeed a beauty, the three rooms kept in good shape by attentive staff. It's a fine, relaxing place to enjoy a football match; each of the many televisions seems to be surrounded by comfortable furniture. Groups can opt for any one of four big spreads from the Thai menu, but if you're just after a bite at half-time, a couple of the starters should do. There are no surprises among the standard wines and Fuller's ales, but sometimes no surprises is a good thing. *Babies & children admitted (until 7.30pm). Tables outdoors (3, pavement; 4, garden). Wireless internet.*

Old Ship

25 Upper Mall, W6 9TD (8748 2593, www.oldshipw6.com). Ravenscourt Park tube. **Open** 9am-11pm Mon-Sat; 9am-10.30pm Sun. **Food served** 9am-10pm daily. **Hammersmith**

It's a long walk from Hammersmith Bridge along a lazy bend in the Thames, a world away from belching buses and snarled-up traffic, but if you bypass a few pubs in favour of this one, you'll be pleased you've made the trek. The boathouse feel of the airy building is continued in the maritime-themed decor of sailing paintings and iconography. Depending on which areas have been hired out, you should have a choice of outdoor seating upstairs or down, or a spot in the classy main bar/restaurant. Bitburger or Corona by the bottle seem the best choices for lager drinkers, Young's or Wells Bombardier for ale aficionados, although there's also a long list of wines. Food features Mediterranean fish stew and tuna fish cakes alongside pork loin steak, chicken leek pie and lamb kofta couscous. *Babies & children admitted. Disabled: toilet. Function room (100 capacity). Tables outdoors (10, garden; 10, terrace; 8, patio). Wireless internet.*

Prince Alfred & Formosa Dining Rooms

5A Formosa Street, W9 1EE (7286 3287, www.youngs.co.uk). Warwick Avenue tube. **Open** noon-11pm Mon-Sat; noon-10.30pm Sun. **Food served** noon-3pm, 6.30-10pm Mon-Thur; noon-3pm, 6.30-11pm Fri, Sat; noon-9pm Sun. **Maida Vale**

An amazingly well preserved example of Victorian interior design, this pub comprises a maze of partitioned snugs around an ornate main bar, each seemingly smaller than the next (did we miss the bottle saying 'Drink Me'?). In any case, the wow factor for first-time visitors is pretty much guaranteed, and there'll be more exclamation when the price of a pint becomes apparent: your Peroni will cost upwards of four quid. That aside, the Prince Alfred is an atmospheric spot for an intimate drink, located on a quiet junction where Castellain Road, Warrington Crescent and Formosa Street meet. Once you've gawped at the interior, try and get a scuffed wooden table outside on the pretty tiled front patio. *Babies & children admitted. Disabled: toilet. Entertainment (quiz 8pm Tue). Games (board games). Tables outdoors (2, pavement). Wireless internet.*

Prince Bonaparte

80 Chepstow Road, W2 5BE (7313 9491, www.theprincebonapartew2.co.uk). Notting Hill Gate or Royal Oak tube. **Open** noon-11pm Mon-Sat; noon-10.30pm Sun. **Food served** noon-3.30pm, 6-10.30pm Mon-Fri; noon-10.30pm Sat; noon-9.30pm Sun. **Westbourne Grove**

There's a hint of gastropub-by-rote to the large, corner Bonaparte, but the formula is rendered

Sir Richard Steele.
See p106.

well. It's a big, bare-bricked, high-ceilinged space but not an unwelcoming one, with picture windows inviting an egalitarian mix of men and women inside for evenings of friendly chat over a glass of something cold. In both the lunch and the dinner menus, the starters (grilled squid, butter bean and chorizo stew; squash purée, goat's curd and toasted pine nuts with pitta bread) display a little more spontaneity than the mains, but it's all good stuff, with prices about what you'd expect given the postcode. The Bonaparte also serves the drinker well: ales from Sharp's (Own, Doom Bar, Cornish Coaster) feature on the low, half-moon bar counter, along with Moretti, Camden Hells Lager and Sagres; there are more than a dozen wines by the glass and around 40 by the bottle.
Babies & children admitted (until 6pm). Disabled: toilet. Wireless internet.
Map p247 A5.

Royal Exchange
26 Sale Place, W2 1PU (7723 3781). Edgware Road tube or Paddington tube/rail. **Open** 11am-11pm Mon-Sat; noon-10.30pm Sun. **Food served** 11am-9.30pm Mon-Sat; noon-9.30pm Sun. **Bayswater**
This quiet corner pub hides a hive of daytime activity centred on the racing industry. Form is fervently studied beneath a phalanx of flat-screen TVs switching from course to course; thoroughbreds are celebrated in painting and caricature; and a somewhat fanciful image in the conspiratorial back room depicts a winner cantering past the winning post of the pub itself. To aid concentration and gambling chatter, Greene King IPA and Brakspear join various lagers and Guinness on tap, the popularity of the latter tied in part to the pub's long-term Irish ownership. It might also explain the roast Limerick ham in some of the sandwiches, though there are also hot meals of the comfort-cooking variety (cottage pie, stews). Should your horse come in, consider ordering Louis Dornier champagne: it goes for £35 a bottle.
Babies & children admitted. Tables outdoors (4, pavement).

Victoria
10A Strathern Place, W2 2NH (7724 1191, www.fullers.co.uk). Lancaster Gate tube or Paddington tube/rail. **Open** 11am-11pm Mon-Sat; noon-10.30pm Sun. **Food served** noon-9.30pm Mon-Sat; noon-9pm Sun. **Bayswater**
Queen Vic looks down disdainfully from her sign on to a mini roundabout beside this stately pub, a favourite with Churchill, Dickens, the Dracula Society and sundry debating and speaking clubs. In a corner of London without

Roebuck. *See p106.*

too many outstanding pubs, the Victoria is a reliable option, no more and no less than a well-run corner boozer. It's perhaps best described as 'accommodating', and the trad-pub decor and unpretentious ambience will be comfortably familiar to fans of other pubs in the Fuller's group. The beer is good (Chiswick, Discovery, London Pride, Honey Dew); wines begin around £3.50 a glass and edge up towards £30 a bottle. The food is as old-school as the venue in which it's served: cheddar and chutney sandwiches, pies, pork belly. Watch yourself descending the steep staircase to the toil... sorry, 'lavatories'. *Babies & children admitted (until 6pm). Entertainment (quiz 9pm Tue). Function rooms (15, 35 capacity). Games (board games). Tables outdoors (7, terrace). Wireless internet.*

Windsor Castle

114 Campden Hill Road, W8 7AR (7243 8797, www.thewindsorcastlekensington.co.uk). Notting Hill Gate tube. **Open** noon-11pm Mon-Sat; noon-10.30pm Sun. **Food served** noon-4pm, 5-10pm Mon-Fri; noon-10pm Sat; noon-9pm Sun. **Kensington**
The layout of the Windsor Castle hasn't changed since the pub was built in 1835, when presumably people were a little shorter than they are now. The Campden, Private and Sherry Rooms are filled with wooden pews and booths that offer little room for manoeuvre, but the pub's historic imperfections are all part of its considerable charm. Decorative accents come from framed pictures that can hardly have changed in a century, along with a map of the world that dates from around the same time. But if this old-world interior isn't to your taste and the weather allows, you can take your drink (Timothy Taylor Landlord, Sambrook's Wandle, five types of draught cider, various wines) and food (sausages, lamb shank) into the surprisingly capacious garden. A characterful place, and hard to dislike. *Babies & children admitted (until 7pm). Games (board games). Tables outdoors (21, garden).* **Map p247 A8.**

Also recommended...

Carpenter's Arms (Gastropubs & Brasseries, *p152*); **City Barge** (Rooms with a View, *p169*); **Cow** (Gastropubs & Brasseries, *p153*); **Dove** (Rooms with a View, *p169*); **Duke of Sussex** (Gastropubs & Brasseries, *p153*); **Ealing Park Tavern** (Gastropubs & Brasseries, *p153*); **Havelock Tavern** (Gastropubs & Brasseries, *p153*); **Princess Victoria** (Gastropubs & Brasseries, *p155*); **Rocket** (Gastropubs & Brasseries, *p155*); **Stonemasons Arms** (Beer Specialists, *p126*); **Swan** (Gastropubs & Brasseries, *p156*);

Thatched House (Gastropubs & Brasseries, *p156*); **Warrington** (Gastropubs & Brasseries, *p156*).

North West

Clifton

96 Clifton Hill, NW8 0JT (7372 3427, www.cliftonstjohnswood.com). St John's Wood tube. **Open** noon-11pm Mon-Sat; noon-10.30pm Sun. **Food served** noon-2.30pm, 6-9.30pm Mon-Fri; noon-3pm, 6-9.30pm Sat; noon-4pm, 6.30-9pm Sun. **St John's Wood**
This former hunting lodge is, or was, a pub in disguise. Edward VII had the Clifton declared a hotel so he could pursue his paramours without being accused of doing so in a pub; a large etched mirror ('Assirati's Temperance Bar') is probably another Edwardian ruse. Today, it's simply a relaxing spot for enjoying a pint. The range of ales isn't enormous but they're in good shape, the best bets from a bar that doesn't offer many surprises. The large front terrace fills with couples and paint-spattered workmen; inside, the dormouse quiet is only broken by the clack of Othello counters or the roar of the crowds on Sky Sports on Sunday afternoons. Diners may retire to the conservatory or the secluded back garden to tuck into the pub grub. *Babies & children admitted (until 7pm). Entertainment (quiz 8.30pm Thur). Function room (40 capacity). Games (board games). Tables outdoors (12, garden). Wireless internet.*

Flask

14 Flask Walk, NW3 1HG (7435 4580, www.theflaskhampstead.co.uk). Hampstead tube. **Open** 11am-11pm Mon-Thur; 11am-midnight Fri, Sat; noon-10.30pm Sun. **Food served** noon-3pm, 6-10pm Mon-Fri; noon-10pm Sat; noon-9pm Sun. **Hampstead**
Blending perfectly with the second-hand bookstores and other arcana along this lovely, narrow pedestrianised passage, this imposing but welcoming Young's pub has benefited from a 2007 refit that spruced it up without draining its character. Decorative accents are provided by scenes from fairytales, black-and-white photos of days out and century-old posters for London Underground, but the best seats are around the tall table facing the picture window. Wines figure prominently here, perhaps more so than is common at other branches in the Young's family, but the regular beers are all present and correct. Many come here to eat, either in the pub or in the large rear dining area. You can get food to share (vegetarian or mini pie platter), as well as the traditional pub grub.

Babies & children admitted (restaurant, until 8pm). Disabled: toilet. Entertainment (quiz 8.30pm Tue). Games (board games). Tables outdoors (3, pavement). Wireless internet.

Holly Bush

22 Holly Mount, NW3 6SG (7435 2892). Hampstead tube or Hampstead Heath rail. **Open** noon-11pm Mon-Sat; noon-10.30pm Sun. **Food served** noon-3pm, 6-10pm Mon-Fri; noon-4pm, 6-10pm Sat; noon-5pm, 6-9pm Sun. **Hampstead**

Negotiate the steep steps from Heath Street up to isolated, cobbled Holly Mount to this house built in the 1790s by portrait painter George Romney. It was later taken over by Benskins, a Watford brewery, in 1928, and much more recently by Fuller's. Three low-ceilinged bar areas carry a lived-in feel, the one bar counter purveying pints of Fuller's ESB, Seafarers and London Pride, as well as Harveys Sussex Best, Leffe, Beck's and Blue Moon. Pimm's and lemonade is a summer treat, as is a spot out front; consult the chalked-up weather forecast should you be pondering another steep climb the next day, perhaps to work off the smartened-up gastropub cooking.
Babies & children admitted. Function room (45 capacity). Wireless internet.

Sir Richard Steele

97 Haverstock Hill, NW3 4RL (7483 1261, www.faucetinn.com). Belsize Park or Chalk Farm tube. **Open** 11am-midnight Mon-Sat; noon-11.30pm Sun. **Food served** noon-3pm, 6-10pm Mon; noon-3pm, 6-10.30pm Tue-Fri; noon-10.30pm Sat; noon-10pm Sun. **Belsize Park**

'Genuine London boozer' pretty much covers it when it comes to this pub. Named in honour of the Irishman who's most famous today for founding the *Spectator*, the Steele is a fabulously raffish place, defined by the boozy chaos that invariably seems to follow an evening spent jostling for attention at its central bar or crouched around one of its sticky tables. Within a dimly lit interior covered in portraits and street signs, talkative locals shoot the breeze over pints of ale (Timothy Taylor Landlord, Dark Star Hophead) and the occasional whisky; even the drunkest of drunks remain good-natured until chucking-out time. There's a grab-bag of live music – Irish folk, acoustic or open-mic, depending on the night and the week – while quiz nights and comedy clubs provide alternative entertainment.
Babies & children admitted (until 7pm). Entertainment (musicians 8.30pm Wed, 5pm & 9pm Sun; comedy 8.45pm Sat). Function room (120 capacity). Tables outdoors (16, patio). Wireless internet.

Spaniards Inn

Spaniards Road, NW3 7JJ (8731 8406, www. thespaniardshampstead.co.uk). Hampstead tube then 603 bus. **Open** noon-11pm daily. **Food served** noon-10pm daily. **Hampstead**

On a narrow bend by Hampstead Heath – where the danger of being knocked down by a school-run mum is as real to today's visitor as was being hijacked in Dick Turpin's day – you'll see signs proclaim 'Spaniards Inn 1565 AD' (said inn now stands by a large car park). They say Turpin was born here in 1705, a century before Keats wrote 'Ode to a Nightingale' in the beer garden. The range of beers (Sierra Nevada, St Austell Tribute, Adnams Broadside, London Pride, Franziskaner and others) are as big an attraction as any historic tie-in, as is the huge outdoor eating area. The food menu might include Barnsley chops with Greek salad; the cheese plate favours this green and pleasant land. Expect a tussle for tables on bank holiday weekends.
Babies & children admitted. Function room (40 capacity). Tables outdoors (80, garden).

Also recommended...

North London Tavern (Gastropubs & Brasseries, *p157*); **Roebuck** (Beer Specialists, *p126*).

Outer London

Roebuck

130 Richmond Hill, Richmond, TW10 6RN (8948 2329). Richmond tube/rail. **Open** noon-11pm Mon-Fri; 10.30am-midnight Sat; noon-10.30pm Sun. **Food served** noon-3pm, 6-10pm Mon-Fri; noon-10pm Sat, Sun. **Richmond, Surrey**

This pub's appeal isn't quite all about location, location, location. But by the same token, the views from here, a fair hike up Richmond Hill, are beautiful – take your drink outside to one of the benches and you'll be looking out towards rural Petersham and across the Thames, with only the occasional passing plane to disturb you. Inside, it's a straightforward local, untouched by current trends in pub culture: so-so beers, line-the-stomach food, uncomplicated decor, efficient staff. So far, so so – but it's the views from outside that make it worth the hike.
Babies & children admitted (until 9pm). Disabled: toilet. Function room (80 capacity). Games (board games). Tables outdoors (30, terrace).

Also recommended...

Eel Pie (Beer Specialists, *p126*); **White Swan** (Rooms with a View, *p170*).

Beer Specialists

Central	108
North	113
North East	114
East	116
South East	117
South	122
South West	124
West	126
North West	126
Outer London	126

Beer Specialists

A few decades ago, traditional British beer seemed to be on the way out – it was something only your grandfather would drink. Younger drinkers instead sought the trend of the moment, likely a foreign lager in a long-necked bottle topped with a wedge of lime. But just as the gastropub reintroduced Britons to the delights of sausage, mash and onion gravy, so real ale has made a welcome comeback. Londoners now drink more ale than they have for years, and breweries are popping up all over the place. Young's has moved its brewing base to Bedford, but Kernel in Bermondsey, Brodie's in Leyton (based at the **King William IV**), Redemption in Tottenham and the Camden Town Brewery have all opened in recent years, joining ever-reliable Fuller's and fast-rising Meantime (now with two bars of its own, the **Greenwich Union** and the **Old Brewery**) on the capital's brewing map.

Most of the 50-odd venues in this section claim real ale as a speciality. Some, such as the Fuller's-run **Artillery Arms** on the cusp of the City, and the Harveys-tied **Royal Oak** in Borough, take most or all of their ales from a single brewer; others, among them the venerable **Old Fountain** near Old Street and nearby newcomer **Mason & Taylor**, are free houses that specialise in variety. But, of course, British ale isn't the only story. Other bars specialise in beers from beyond these isles: **Zeitgeist at the Jolly Gardeners** deals in German beers; the **Dove** in Hackney and Covent Garden's **Lowlander** offer Belgian brews; and the taps and fridges at the **Euston Tap** have a global reach, including some terrific American craft brews.

Central

Artillery Arms
102 Bunhill Row, EC1Y 8ND (7253 4683).
Old Street tube/rail. **Open** noon-11pm Mon-Sat; noon-10.30pm Sun. **Food served** noon-3pm, 6-9pm Mon-Fri; noon-9pm Sat, Sun. **City**
A Fuller's boozer of dark wood, frosted glass and leather-upholstered banquettes in bottle green, the Artillery is the classic spot for the post-work quiet pint. Too petite to create an annoying bar crush, it offers its customers two modest drinking and dining spaces around the centrepiece bar counter, where George Gale Spring Sprinter is dispensed along with the standard Fuller's favourites (Chiswick, ESB, Discovery, London Pride). Food is a big draw here, the prices set for a City-based clientele, notably the pie of the day with seasonal vegetables and roast potatoes, and the leek, pea and sun-blushed-tomato risotto. Even the light bites (Welsh rarebit with salad, a humble pork pie) cost the best part of a fiver or more. Still, set on a quiet, leafy street opposite Bunhill Fields Burial Ground, it also provides smokers with a tranquil spot for outdoor chatter.

Babies & children admitted (until 8pm). Disabled: toilet. Function room (40 capacity). Wireless internet. **Map p244 P4.**

Bree Louise
69 Cobourg Street, NW1 2HH (7681 4930, www.thebreelouise.com). Euston Square tube or Euston tube/rail. **Open** 11.30am-11pm Mon-Sat; noon-10.30pm Sun. **Food served** noon-10pm Mon-Sat; noon-9pm Sun. **Euston**
Hopheads and scrumpy merchants make pilgrimages to this unassuming boozer tucked behind the utterly non-descript streets near Euston station. Their obscure objects of desire sit in (mainly) barrel form behind the bar: Art Brew Tempest Stout, Dark Star Six Hop, Bateman's XXXB feature among the '16 real ales' promised outside, with New Forest Kingston Black, Ciderniks Dab Hand and Weston's Country Perry among the 'eight cask ciders'. There's also the house brew of Bree Louise organic pilsner and a surprisingly attractive choice of food: burgers made from fresh ground beef, lamb or wild boar; Colston Bassett blue stilton among the cheeses; and, to start, a pâté of the day to go with the warm, rustic bread. There's also Heinz baked beans.

All is served in improbably unfashionable surroundings, Jack Vettriano prints and such, but that bothers the equally unfashionable and big-bellied clientele not one jot. *Babies & children admitted. Games (board games, dominoes). Tables outdoors (8, pavement). Wireless internet.*

Cask

6 Charlwood Street, SW1V 6EE (7630 7225, www.caskpubandkitchen.com). Pimlico tube. **Open** 4-11pm Mon; noon-11pm Tue-Sat; noon-10.30pm Sun. **Food served** noon-3pm, 6-10pm Tue-Fri; 12.30-9.30pm Sat, Sun. **Pimlico** There's a lot to like about this blissful beervana, which is tucked away in a gloriously ugly housing block behind Pimlico. Chief among its attributes, as you might expect from the name, is a terrific selection of beers, with Moravka (a Derbyshire-brewed pilsner) and Rothaus Weisse and Pils from the Black Forest among the taps. Half of the ten handpumps are devoted to a trio of brewers – Thornbridge Brewery from Derbyshire, Dark Star from Brighton and Scotland's Brew Dog – with guests selected only from microbreweries. And there's plenty of variety in bottled form, hailing chiefly from North America, Belgium and Denmark. Attention is also paid to the food, with the pub grub given a 21st-century, post-gastropub lift.

Green Man. *See p110.*

The room is comfortable enough, but it's the beer that really elevates this one above the norm. *Babies & children admitted. Tables outdoors (4, pavement). Wireless internet.* **Map p249 J11.**

Drayton Arms

153 Old Brompton Road, SW5 0LJ (7835 2301, www.thedraytonarmsnorthkensington.co.uk). Earl's Court or Gloucester Road tube. **Open** noon-midnight Mon-Fri; 10am-midnight Sat, Sun. **Food served** noon-4pm, 6-10pm Mon-Fri; noon-10pm Sat; noon-9pm Sun. **South Kensington** A pledge chalked up in the corridor of this comfortably trendy spot gives the first names of the bar staff, the promise of good drinks in a friendly atmosphere, and the assurance that your food will arrive in 15 minutes. Sunlight floods the large main bar through picture windows, falling on scuffed wooden tables and mismatched sofas. The selection of beer taps on the bar counter is impressive: Sierra Nevada, Kozel, Kirin Ichiban, Franziskaner; meanwhile, Spitfire, Sharp's Doom Bar, Sambrook's Wandle and Butcombe's Old Vic Porter are the four handpumped British ales. Behind the bar await many of your favourite Belgian and continental brews by the bottle. As for the food, the Drayton is big on snacks, burgers and Sunday roasts. *Babies & children admitted (until 6pm). Disabled: toilet. Entertainment (DJs 8pm Sat). Games (board games). Tables outdoors (6, pavement).* **Map p248 A4.**

Edgar Wallace

40 Essex Street, WC2R 3JE (7353 3120, www.edgarwallacepub.com). Temple tube. **Open** 11am-11pm Mon-Fri. **Food served** 11am-9.30pm Mon-Fri. **Aldwych** Named after the crime-writing regular, the Edgar Wallace has coped well with the demise of nearby Fleet Street. Much of its daytime trade now comes from the Royal Courts of Justice, and the legal trade's patronage helps to ensure standards remain high. The pub has upped its beer game, as evidenced by the 200-plus beer mats and pump clips: you'll find up to eight ales on tap, with the house brew (Edgar's Pale Ale) supplemented by the likes of Suffolk's Nethergate. The after-work crowd generally fire into the wine; menus, bearing an iconic profile of the author, offer hearty fare. Framed mementos upstairs tell of the time when Wallace ran a writers' club there, while the hallway contains a potted biography of the man. Why don't people live those kind of lives any more? *Babies & children admitted (restaurant only). Function room (40 capacity).* **Map p243 M6.**

Euston Tap

West Lodge, 190 Euston Road, NW1 2EF (3137 8837, www.eustontap.com). Euston tube/rail. **Open** 11am-11pm Mon-Fri; noon-11pm Sat; noon-10pm Sun. **Food served** 6-10pm Tue-Sun. **Euston**

Back in the day, train stations had proper pubs – and the wheel seems to be turning back that way: first, the Betjeman Arms opened at St Pancras; and now drab Euston boasts a fantastic craft-beer bar. It's a small and simple space within one of the 1830s Portland-stone lodges fronting the station. The colourful parade of taps showcases beer's full breadth of flavours and styles: 19 rare and renowned craft beers, including Erdinger Urweisse, and Matuska Raptor IPA and an unfiltered version of Bernard pilsner from the Czech Republic. Eight options play to the cask crowd, with ales from the Marble and Thornbridge breweries. Two enormous chillers stock an eclectic array of bottles: the friendly staff will help you choose from altbier, kellerbier and kolsch from Germany, pale ales and pumpkin beers from America's craft-brewing scene, Belgian classics and a Scandinavian selection.

Babies & children admitted (until 7pm). Tables outdoors (10, garden). Wireless internet.

Green Man

36 Riding House Street, W1W 7EP (7580 9087, www.thegreenmanw1.co.uk). Goodge Street or Oxford Circus tube. **Open** noon-11pm Mon-Sat; noon-10.30pm Sun. **Food served** noon-10pm Mon-Sat; noon-9.30pm Sun. **Fitzrovia**

Cider marks out the Green Man from the pack, but it's also a decent boozer in its own right. A young, loquacious crowd comes to shout over an indie soundtrack and sample London's best choice of ciders and perries: up to ten on draft, at least twice as many by the bottle, and they even have their own 'Green Man Special' cider. Purists, however, may blanch at the bottled concoctions such as pear and strawberry ciders from Brothers. Beer is also a strength, with three ales supplemented by foreign obscurities. Friendly young staff, regular events (including a monthly meeting of the London Air-Accordion Society) and a decent pub-grub menu are further attractions, as is the interior: high plastered ceilings, bare floorboards and a cosy back area with padded leather banquettes, plus a mellower, more modish bar upstairs.

Entertainment (comedy 7pm every other Mon, Tue; DJs/musicians 7pm Fri, Sat). Function room (70 capacity). Games (board games). Tables outdoors (3, pavement). **Map p240 J5.**

Harp

47 Chandos Place, WC2N 4HS (7836 0291). Charing Cross tube/rail. **Open** 11am-11pm Tue-Sat; noon-10.30pm Sun. **Trafalgar Square**

Where once fine and varied sausages were the main selling points of this well-hidden Irish pub near Charing Cross post office, now it's sought-after ales. The board outside details the current selection, while around a bar counter eminently suited to being propped up, obscure beer mats tell of ales from yesteryear. It's not only ales – at present Sambrook's, Thornbridge and Dark Star – but traditional cider and perry, too. Sausages still sizzle away on the hob beside the bar, where cheery regulars chat with the staff or study the racing form. Decor is provided by portraits of long-forgotten personalities lining the narrow walls of the one main bar, and signature harps glazing in the front windows, which open out completely as summer comes. **Map p241 L7.**

Euston Tap

Jerusalem Tavern

*55 Britton Street, EC1M 5UQ (7490 4281,
www.stpetersbrewery.co.uk). Farringdon
tube/rail.* **Open** 11am-11pm Mon-Fri. **Food
served** noon-3pm Mon-Fri. **Clerkenwell**
The Jerusalem is both fabulously historic and a
complete fabrication. Although the premises
date from the early 18th century, the current
shopfront wasn't added until 1810 and the place
didn't open as a pub until the 1990s. The wonky,
green-painted interior has two front tables and
a fireplace partially screened off from the main
room, which has a large fixed table at the back
and a sweet little table above the friendly melée
of lawyers, media workers and businessmen.
The beer in question is the full range from the
St Peter's Brewery in Suffolk, served from a row
of small wooden casks lined up behind the
counter. The decent food offerings include a
large roast pork sandwich on sourdough with
potato wedges. The place is small, however, so
avoid the immediate after-work rush if you don't
feel like sharing a table. **Map p242 O4.**

King Charles I

*55-57 Northdown Street, N1 9BL (7837
7758). King's Cross tube/rail.* **Open** noon-
11pm Mon-Thur; noon-1am Fri; 5-11pm Sat.
King's Cross
Hidden from the outside world, this homely pub
provides rare ales, many whiskies, a roaring fire
and the day's papers to the surprisingly few
regulars who frequent it. In fact, if you had to
describe what a pub was to someone from Pluto,
this would do the job. There's even a bar
billiards tables with a set of rules, just to make
it easier for them. Beer-wise, you'll find sought-
after Italian Moretti on draught, Theakston
Paradise Ale, Caledonian Flying Dutchman and
Deuchars IPA, potentially chased with Maker's
Mark, Highland Park or Glenlivet. There are
Brodie's sherries, too, and bog-standard wines
you needn't bother with. Various branches of
the deer family make a decorative appearance,
as do unusual tribal masks.
*Babies & children admitted (until 6pm).
Games (bar billiards, board games). Tables
outdoors (4, pavement). Wireless internet.*

Lord John Russell

*91-93 Marchmont Street, WC1N 1AL
(7388 0500). Russell Square tube.* **Open**
11.30am-11pm Mon-Sat; noon-10.30pm Sun.
Food served noon-2.30pm Mon-Fri; 1-9pm
Sun. **Bloomsbury**
Within walking distance but a world away from
the Bloomsbury set and the British Museum, the
Marchmont neighbourhood is a mongrel area of

the low-waged, laundrette users and long-term
ex-students. All can be found in this rather
splendid venue named in honour of the man
who twice served as prime minister in the 19th
century – and a descendant of the family that
developed Bloomsbury. It has all the markings
of a gastropub (bare boards, sturdy rustic
tables, the occasional pew and a colour photo of
the pub on the walls) but only feels the need to
serve pies and pasties. The beers – König
Pilsner, Hannibal's Nectar, Wadworth 6X,
Caledonian Flying Dutchman, Budvar light and
dark – are what bring punters here. Rugby's also
big, as are the Sunday roasts (£7.95). Smokers
gather in the attractive adjoining courtyard.
*Babies & children admitted (until 7pm). Tables
outdoors (7, pavement). Wireless internet.*

Lowlander

*36 Drury Lane, WC2B 5RR (7379 7446,
www.lowlander.com). Covent Garden or
Holborn tube.* **Open/food served** 11.30am-
11pm Mon-Sat; noon-10.30pm Sun.
Covent Garden
Brightly logoed and Benelux-themed, the smart
Lowlander's expansive, long-tabled main space
is easily filled, thanks to an impressive range of
draught and bottled beers, a fine kitchen and
likeable staff who are well up to what is, given
the bar's popularity, often a tough job. Some 15
tap beers, by the half-pint glass or two-pint jug,
include Palm Spéciale, St Louis Premium and
Poperings Hommelbier, as well as more familiar
compatriots. Of the 100 bottled varieties, Achel,
Charles Quint and St Feuillien Blond stand out
among the 20 abbey types – and you won't see
a lambic Cantillon Rose de Gambrinus in many
bars even in Belgium. The own-made *Stoemp*
stew, meanwhile, is ubiquitous there, while
mussels come in a choice of four sauces. The
attractive mezzanine is often occupied by
private parties.
*Babies & children admitted (until 6pm).
Function room (22 capacity).* **Map p240 L6.**

Porterhouse

*21-22 Maiden Lane, WC2E 7NA (7836 9931,
www.porterhousebrewco.com). Covent Garden
tube or Charing Cross tube/rail.* **Open** noon-
11pm Mon-Thur; 11am-11.30pm Fri, Sat;
noon-10.30pm Sun. **Food served** noon-9pm
Mon-Sat; noon-7pm Sun. **Covent Garden**
Irish by professed nationality but global by
nature, this gleaming hostelry with a busy
terrace does a fine line in international beers and
hearty fare. Underpinning it all are draught
stouts and ales; in the case of Wrasslers, made
to a century-old recipe. Along with the semi-
titular Porterhouse Red are An Brainblásta (at

7%, it lives up to its name), the gentler TSB and a pungent Oyster Stout. The bottled list is a tippler's travelogue: Corsican Columba, Cypriot Keo, Moroccan Casablanca. The Porterhouse Frying Pan, with smoked bacon, potatoes, chorizo and red piquillo, should soak up whatever you choose. There are also wines and cocktails, but that'd be missing the point. *Disabled: toilet. Entertainment (bands 9pm Wed-Sat; Irish band 4.30pm Sun). Function room (100 capacity). Tables outdoors (12, pavement).* **Map p241 L7.**

Queen's Head
66 Acton Street, WC1X 9NB (7713 5772, www.queensheadlondon.com). King's Cross tube/rail. **Open/food served** 4-11pm Mon; noon-midnight Tue-Sat; noon-11pm Sun. **King's Cross**
Once a tired tanking house, this has been transformed into a great little neighbourhood pub that's retained the faded Victorian splendour: well-trodden wooden floors, stained-glass windows, an upright piano. There's no cutlery laid on the unclothed tables, just candles and enough space to place a pint and a Melton Mowbray pie or, if you're properly peckish, a substantial and good-value cheese or meat board. The broad-minded range of craft beers spans several styles, with some sourced locally – Kernel, Meantime, Redemption and Camden Town – while other curiosities can be found in the fridge (De Molen from Holland); the staff know all about what they're serving. In addition to a fair-priced wine list, there's a selection of spirits weighted strongly towards whisky. *Babies & children admitted (until 7pm). Entertainment (comedy 7.30pm Tue; musicians 7.30pm Wed, Thur). Games (board games). Tables outdoors (2, pavement). Wireless internet.* **Map p242 M3.**

Ship & Shovell
1-3 Craven Passage, WC2N 5PH (7839 1311). Charing Cross tube/rail. **Open** 11am-11pm Mon-Sat. **Food served** noon-3.30pm Mon-Fri; noon-4pm Sat. **Strand**
At facing sides of the southern end of the arches, these two nautically themed pubs sharing the same title have historians tied up in knots. Are they named after the coal-heavers who also frequented the nearby Coal Hole, or are they named after the unfortunate Sir Cloudesley Shovell, who received a knighthood despite losing his fleet off the Isles of Scilly in 1707? In any case, both have a maritime theme and, as befits a brewery (Hall & Woodhouse) also founded in the 18th century, both offer ales and pub grub in a trad setting. Those ales include

Badger First Gold, Tanglefoot and Hopping Hare (alongside mainstream lagers). Foodwise, superior baguettes, lamb shank and Florentine gnocchi are consumed with gusto by white-collar lunch-breakers. Later, those in the pedestrianised space outside mingle by the queue for gay superclub Heaven. *Babies & children admitted (Sat only). Function room (20 capacity). Games (darts).* **Map p241 L7.**

Ye Olde Mitre
1 Ely Court, Ely Place, at the side of 8 Hatton Gardens, EC1N 6SJ (7405 4751). Chancery Lane tube or Farringdon tube/rail. **Open** 11am-11pm Mon-Fri. **Food served** 11.30am-9pm Mon-Fri. **Chancery Lane**
Built, as the sign inside says, by Bishop Goodrich in 1546, this traditional tavern consists of a cramped, three-room bar space fronted by an enclosed courtyard with stand-up tables, all accessed by alleyways from two separate streets. On offer here are ales and history; punters, City types and admiring tourists can choose to sip from George Gale Seafarers, Caledonian 80, Fuller's Honeydew, Adnams Broadside or Deuchars IPA beneath portraits of Henry VIII and sundry beruffled luminaries. The handful of wines – pinot noir La Lumière, pinot grigio Veneto – are well priced at around £15, while the old-school pub fare starts with toasted sandwiches, scotch eggs, pork pies and the like (£2), moving on to full, hearty meals. *Function room (30 capacity). Games (cribbage, dominoes). Tables outdoors (15 barrels, pavement). Wireless internet.* **Map p242 N5.**

Also recommended...
Anglesea Arms (Classic Pubs, *p61*); **Argyll Arms** (Classic Pubs, *p61*); **Audley** (Classic Pubs, *p61*); **Bell** (Classic Pubs, *p62*); **Betsey Trotwood** (Clubs & Music Venues, *p205*); **Castle** (Classic Pubs, *p65*); **Coach & Horses** (Gastropubs & Brasseries, *p130*); **Commercial Tavern** (Good Mixers, *p177*); **Dog & Duck** (Classic Pubs, *p67*); **Fox & Anchor** (Classic Pubs, *p68*); **Gunmakers** (Gastropubs & Brasseries, *p131*); **De Hems** (Good Mixers, *p179*); **Honey Pot** (Gastropubs & Brasseries, *p133*); **Kings Arms** (Classic Pubs, *p71*); **Lexington** (Clubs & Music Venues, *p206*); **Mark's Bar** (Cocktails & Spirits, *p28*); **Museum Tavern** (Classic Pubs, *p72*); **Peasant** (Gastropubs & Brasseries, *p134*); **St John** (Gastropubs & Brasseries, *p135*); **Salisbury** (Classic Pubs, *p76*); **Seven Stars** (Gastropubs & Brasseries, *p136*); **Speaker** (Classic Pubs, *p76*); **Star Tavern** (Classic Pubs, *p76*).

North

North Nineteen

194-196 Sussex Way, N19 4HZ (7281 2786, www.northnineteen.co.uk). Archway tube or 43, 271 bus. **Open** 4pm-midnight Mon-Thur; 4pm-1am Fri; noon-1am Sat; noon-midnight Sun. **Food served** 5-10pm Mon-Fri; noon-10pm Sat, Sun. **Hornsey**

Don't be deterred by the anonymous name and the drab housing blocks that surround North Nineteen: this is a gem of a makeover. The main bar adds a fireplace, a TV and a space for open-mic sessions to a counter offering the likes of Timothy Taylor Landlord, guest ales and beers from Skinner's in Truro (Cornish Knocker golden ale, Betty Stogs bitter); a chalkboard and an array of beermats testify to the presence of regular guest ales. Another bar, accessed via the dog-leg front terrace or through the gents', best suits the convivial enjoyment of superior pub grub (Irish stew, chargrilled chicken sandwiches and so on). Whiskies, too, are a strong point: there are 26 in all, 'plus six off-menu', according to Tony, the landlord, who'll be playing darts in the side games room on rare quiet moments. *Babies & children admitted (until 8.30pm). Entertainment (open mic 7.30pm Tue; poker*

8pm Wed; bands 8.30pm Sat; jazz 6pm Sun). Function room (50 capacity). Games (board games, darts). Tables outdoors (5, front garden; 3, back garden). Wireless internet.

Southampton Arms

139 Highgate Road, NW5 1LE (07958 780073 mobile, www.thesouthamptonarms. co.uk). Kentish Town tube. **Open/food served** noon-midnight daily. **Kentish Town**

'Ale, cider, meat' reads the sign on the outside wall, resembling a film set for a wartime drama; inside, it could be 1943 at this quite wonderful independent taproom for all you know. It's usually every two or three days that the bar welcomes a new obscure ale from a small British brewery, but a busy Saturday might see casks from small independent breweries such as Marble, Thornbridge and Dark Star run out in 'a couple of hours', according to the barman. Three barrels of cider also await (Borough Hill making regular appearances), alongside a huge hunk of pork. As the venue's seemingly reluctant website says, 'Seven real ales, eight real ciders, hot meat in baps, that's it'; a roast pork bap is £3.90, 'real money only'. Throw in a stinky coal fire, period portraiture and a small square of brick-floor back garden, and the experience is complete.

Porterhouse. *See p111.*

Babies & children admitted. Entertainment (musicians 8pm Wed, 6pm Sun). Tables outdoors (10, garden). Wireless internet.

Also recommended...

Bull & Last (Gastropubs & Brasseries, *p138*); **Charles Lamb** (Gastropubs & Brasseries, *p138*); **Clissold Arms** (Gastropubs & Brasseries, *p139*); **Drapers Arms** (Gastropubs & Brasseries, *p139*); **Duke of Cambridge** (Gastropubs & Brasseries, *p141*); **Flask** (Classic Pubs, *p79*); **Island Queen** (Classic Pubs, *p80*); **Junction Tavern** (Gastropubs & Brasseries, *p141*); **Marquess Tavern** (Gastropubs & Brasseries, *p141*); **Pineapple** (Good Mixers, *p183*); **Salisbury Hotel** (Classic Pubs, *p81*); **Swimmer at the Grafton Arms** (Classic Pubs, *p82*); **Wenlock & Essex** (Good Mixers, *p183*).

North East

Birkbeck Tavern
45 Langthorne Road, E11 4HL (8539 2584). Leyton tube. **Open** 11am-11pm Mon-Thur; 11am-midnight Fri, Sat; noon-11pm Sun.
Leyton

Regulars here cluster around the counter and banter with the amiable, larger-than-life bar lady. Walk in here again in five years' time and it'll be the same. Beers are chalked up like a Tote board. Runners and riders change almost daily: 100-1 shots might be Sweet Chariot from the excellent Mighty Oak brewery in Maldon, or Spring Cottage Biscuit from Caerphilly's Newmans Brewery. A sure bet, though, is Rita's Special, in honour of a former barmaid, sold here and here alone. Rita's costs a mere £2.90 a pint, a reasonable pricing policy that extends to tea (85p), coffee (ditto) and sandwiches (£1.60); perhaps part of the deal for being nominated for a Tetley pub award in 1992 was to keep everything at Black Wednesday prices. There's nothing grim about the surroundings: a nice walled garden hints at a previous life as a guesthouse. You'll be lucky if you get a game on the dartboard.
Entertainment (karaoke 8.30pm alternate Sat). Function room (100 capacity). Games (darts, pool). Tables outdoors (14, garden).

Dove
24-28 Broadway Market, E8 4QJ (7275 7617, www.belgianbars.com). London Fields rail. **Open** noon-11pm Mon-Thur, Sun; noon-midnight Fri, Sat. **Food served** noon-10pm Mon-Thur, Sun; noon-11pm Fri, Sat. **Hackney**

Nothing much changes at the Dove, one of only a few Broadway Market businesses to predate the street's gentrification. The staff long ago realised that the formula of great beers (mostly Belgian, plus a few real ales), uncomplicated food (stews, burgers, sausages) and simple decor (lots of wood, much of it a bit battered) was a winner that'd stand the test of time. As a result, the place now runs itself, chiefly for the benefit of Hackneyites who are quietly disdainful of the two newcomers up the road (the Cat & Mutton and Off Broadway). This autopilot approach to the business doesn't always work in its favour: the food, particularly, could do with improvement. But this place ain't going anywhere, and its regulars wouldn't have it any other way. *Babies & children admitted (until 6pm). Entertainment (jazz 8.30pm Wed, Sun). Games (board games). Tables outdoors (6, pavement). Wireless internet.*

Duke of Wellington

119 Balls Pond Road, N1 4BL (7275 7640, www.thedukeofwellingtonn1.com). Dalston Junction or Dalston Kingsland rail. **Open** 3pm-midnight Mon-Wed; 3pm-1am Thur, Fri; 11am-1am Sat; noon-11.30pm Sun. **Food served** 5.30-10pm Mon-Fri; 11am-5pm, 5.30-10pm Sat; noon-8pm Sun. **Dalston**
The 2009 conversion of this corner pub is a textbook example of how to update an old local for a younger, 21st-century clientele. In many ways, the Wellington hitches its wagon to tradition. There's an emphasis on real ales: Sambrook's Wandle is supplemented by three guest brews, and twice-yearly beer festivals bring in a broader selection. The decent and fairly priced menu (pies, burgers) won't frighten any horses. And the decor keeps things tastefully, handsomely familiar. But there's more: Saturday brunch, twice-monthly movie nights, occasional music, a broad range of spirits and late hours all add value for twenty- to fortysomething Dalstonians who find the scene on Kingsland High Street too messy for comfort. The friendly bartenders occasionally get a little over-enthusiastic with the stereo's volume dial, but this is otherwise a great find. *Babies & children admitted. Entertainment (musicians 7.30pm 1st Thur of mth; DJs 8pm 3rd Thur of mth; film screenings 8pm 1st & 3rd Sun of mth). Function room (60 capacity). Tables outdoors (6, pavement). Wireless internet.*

Jolly Butchers

204 Stoke Newington High Street, N16 7HU (7241 2185, www.jollybutchers.co.uk). Bus 67, 76, 149, 243. **Open** 4pm-midnight

Mon-Thur; 4pm-1am Fri; noon-1am Sat; noon-11pm Sun. **Food served** 5-10pm Mon-Fri; noon-10pm Sat, Sun. **Stoke Newington**
It's not true to say that Stoke Newington has been crying out for a spot like this; by and large, the locals have seemed content with the array of weary boozers, formulaic gastropubs and corny bars that dot N16. Still, the area is a lot richer for its arrival. Formerly a miserable pub, it's had its tired decor ripped out and replaced by... well, not much. The walls are plain and the furniture is wooden, a decorative ethos that seems built on the elusive phrase 'shabby chic'. It's nice enough, as is the no-messing food (burgers, pies, cassoulet, all around a tenner), but the real appeal is provided by the beer: ten handpumps offer real ciders and rarely seen brews from the likes of Crouch Vale, Dark Star and Thornbridge, plus local microbreweries such as Camden Town Brewery, Redemption from Tottenham and Brodie's from Leyton, while the bottles in the fridges head beyond Britain to Belgium. A welcome addition. *Babies & children admitted (until 8pm). Wireless internet.*

Pembury Tavern

90 Amhurst Road, E8 1JH (8986 8597, www.individualpubs.co.uk/pembury). Hackney Central or Hackney Downs rail. **Open** noon-11.30pm Mon-Thur, noon-1am Fri, Sat; noon-11pm Sun. **Food served** noon-10pm daily. **Hackney**
There's no faulting the beer at this grand old corner pub, which had lain derelict for a spell before being revived by the Individual Pubs group in 2006. The 16 handpumps on the long bar are rarely all in operation, but there's usually a wide selection of ales: regular guest ales join the core collection from Cambridge's Milton Brewery, from the gentle Minotaur mild to the lively, pungent Marcus Aurelius stout, and three beer festivals a year (March, July and November) bring further variety. Despite the best efforts of the staff and the presence of a bar billiards table (there's also pool and board games), the beer is certainly the main attraction: the vast, brightly lit bar room feels like a youth hostel canteen, and an absence of soft furnishings has created acoustics that don't aid conversation. *Babies & children admitted. Disabled: toilet. Entertainment (quiz 8pm Mon). Games (bar billiards, board games, pool). Wireless internet.*

William IV

816 High Road, E10 6AE (8556 2460). Leyton Midland Road rail. **Open** 11am-11pm Mon-Thur; 11am-1am Fri, Sat; noon-midnight Sun. **Food served** 1-9pm daily. **Leyton**

There's been a brewery at this Leyton pub for years, but it had been defunct for a while before Jamie and Lizzie Brodie took over the place in 2008. The couple hit the ground running: less than two years after they moved in and started brewing, they'd already nailed down a 20-plus range of ales, several of which can also now be found at unaffiliated pubs in London. Not all of their beers quite work, and occasionally there is a sense that the pair might be stretched a little thin – the handpumps have up to a score of Brodie's ales on the go at any one time. But it would be churlish to criticise their enterprise or their enthusiasm, especially when they sell their own beers for a mere £1.99 a pint; try the Red or the Amarilla and you'll be on safe ground. The pub itself is a capacious, unpretentious corner local.
Babies & children admitted (until 8pm). Entertainment (jazz 8pm last Thur of mth). Games (cribbage, darts). Tables outdoors (2, pavement). Wireless internet.

Also recommended...
Café Oto (Clubs & Music Venues, *p211*); Nags Head (Classic Pubs, *p83*); Off Broadway (Good Mixers, *p185*); Prince (Gastropubs & Brasseries, *p144*); Ye Olde Rose & Crown (Classic Pubs, *p85*).

North Nineteen. *See p113.*

East

Carpenters Arms
73 Cheshire Street, E2 6EG (7739 6342, www.carpentersarmsfreehouse.com). Liverpool Street tube/rail. **Open** 4-11.30pm Mon; noon-11.30pm Tue-Thur, Sun; noon-12.30am Fri, Sat. **Food served** 5-10pm Mon; 1-10pm Tue-Sun. **Brick Lane**
The buzzy Carpenters Arms looks tiny from the outside, but it's always comfortably busy rather than uncomfortably cramped. The handsome wood decor and old black-and-whites of Brick Lane are glammed up with chandeliers, mirrors and an appropriately expressionless painting of the Krays, who bought a previous incarnation of this place for their dear old ma. A second, equally cosy room opens on to a neat heated deck, which combines hanging ivy and a neoclassical statuette. The drinks selection is great: alongside three ales on draught (including Palm 'Speciale Belge'), there's a terrific range of bottles, with Belgian brews and American imports sitting alongside British specialities such as Nethergate's Old Growler porter, Olah Dubh ('black oil', and not far off in appearance) and St Peter's Organic Best Bitter. The cut-above food (boards of cheese or charcuterie, home-made chips, Sunday roasts) isn't sold at stupid prices, and the clientele is fashionably Hoxditch without making a song and dance about it.
Babies & children admitted. Games (board games). Tables outdoors (6, garden). Wireless internet. **Map p246 T4.**

Mason & Taylor
51-55 Bethnal Green Road, E1 6LA (7749 9670, www.masonandtaylor.co.uk). Liverpool Street tube/rail or Shoreditch High Street rail. **Open** 5pm-midnight Mon-Thur; 5pm-2am Fri; noon-2am Sat; noon-midnight Sun. **Food served** 5-10pm Mon-Thur; 5-10.30pm Fri; noon-10.30pm Sat; noon-9pm Sun. **Shoreditch**
The guys behind the Duke of Wellington in Dalston have taken over this two-floor, somewhat urban/industrial space to showcase boutique beer. Behind a concrete bar, a dozen draught taps draw both the obscure and the accessible: Brooklyn Lager, Bitburger and De Koninck alongside Thornstar (a collaboration from Thornbridge and Dark Star) and a milk stout from Colorado, as well as some decent ciders. The friendly staff are happy to advise on putting together a taster flight. The 40-strong bottled-beer menu changes regularly: local beers include Kernel IPA and Meantime Raspberry, and there are American craft beers, barrel-aged

Dog & Bell

brews, 'oddities', and the best of Belgium and Germany. Tapas-style small plates with a British bent include whitebait, smoked salmon with horseradish cream and roast butternut squash with bacon. On Sundays, it's all about the roasts. *Babies & children admitted. Booking advisable Fri, Sat. Disabled: toilet. Entertainment (DJs 9pm Fri, Sat). Function room (120 capacity). Wireless internet.* **Map p246 S4.**

Old Fountain
3 Baldwin Street, EC1V 9NU (7253 2970). Old Street tube/rail. **Open** 11am-11pm Mon-Fri. **Food served** noon-2.45pm, 5-9pm Mon-Fri. **Shoreditch**
Ale fans and discerning pub-goers make a beeline for this friendly, family-run boozer, set amid completely mundane surroundings in a non-descript corner of the City. Two main bar rooms await, the front one decorated with a beautiful illustration of the École des Beaux-Arts from 1865, but it's the bright red beer towels branded with the name of Brighton's Dark Star brewery that will most attract the beer-aficionado's keen eye. Kernel brews from Bermondsey, Fiery Fox red cider from Gwynt y Ddraig, and Brodie's Irish Oyster stout are also here, complemented by doorstep sandwiches (filled with the likes of home-cooked roast beef with horseradish or cumberland sausage) for

under three quid. There are also pizzas, burgers, jacket potatoes and other pub staples. First-name terms twixt staff and clientele add to an overall sense of bonhomie. *Babies & children admitted.* **Map p244 Q4.**

Wenlock Arms
26 Wenlock Road, N1 7TA (7608 3406, www.wenlock-arms.co.uk). Old Street tube/rail. **Open** noon-midnight Mon-Thur, Sun; noon-1am Fri, Sat. **No credit cards.** **Shoreditch**
Peek through the door of this single-room boozer and you'll immediately see its raison d'être: a line of handpumps along the cramped central bar counter, with a mild always among the enticing options. First opened as a pub in 1836, it survived the Blitz and was reopened in 1994, although the shabby decor makes it look and feel more like a '70s-vintage taproom. The interior is as down-at-heel as the location, but there's a real community feel to the place: how many Islington pubs have cricket and football teams? The clientele is a lovely mix of garrulous locals, ale hunters and slumming-it art students, and everyone talks to everyone else. On Friday nights, a cluster of old timers rattles through *Pennies from Heaven*-vintage tunes around the piano; there's more jazz on Saturdays and Sunday afternoons, but the regulars are on hand to provide slice-of-life entertainment all week. *Babies & children admitted (until 9pm). Entertainment (quiz 9pm Thur; blues/jazz 9pm Fri, Sat, 3pm Sun). Function room (25 capacity). Games (cribbage, darts, dominoes).*

Also recommended...
Hemingway (Good Mixers, *p188*); **Pride of Spitalfields** (Classic Pubs, *p86*).

South East

Dog & Bell
116 Prince Street, SE8 3JD (8692 5664). New Cross tube/rail or Deptford rail. **Open** noon-11.30pm daily. **Food served** noon-3.30pm, 6-9pm Mon-Sat; 12.30-3.30pm Sun. **No credit cards.** **Deptford**
It's perhaps not all the better for the refurb a little while back – whatever happened to that Empire-era map of India? – but the good old Dog & Bell still charms the local creatives and ale aficionados. Mounted art, even Fred Aylwood's wacky collage, is now neatly framed; a gas fire in the corridor linking the two rooms is surrounded by tables, thus creating a third space. Beers include treats from Dark Star

Greenwich Union

(Hophead included) and Fuller's; draught Budvar comes in regular light and dark varieties; and a string of Belgian beers (Gentse Tripel, Liefmans) is individually labelled with little Post-it strips in the fridge. Food-wise, the place has moved a little upmarket (stuffed peppers?), but you can still get a dish of pork sausages, mash and onion gravy for £5.95. Also present: bar billiards, the lyrics to 'Homeward Bound' (not the Paul Simon tune but a music hall ditty mentioning this very pub) and, yes, the regulars. *Plus Deptford, tu meurs. Entertainment (quiz 9pm Sun). Games (bar billiards, board games). Tables outdoors (4, garden).* **Map p253 C1.**

Florence

133 Dulwich Road, SE24 0NG (7326 4987, www.capitalpubcompany.com). Herne Hill rail. **Open** 11.30am-midnight Mon-Thur; 11.30am-1am Fri; 11am-1am Sat; 11am-midnight Sun. **Food served** noon-10pm Mon-Sat; 11am-9.30pm Sun. **Herne Hill**
That the people behind the light, modern Florence care about beer is obvious from the phenomenal range on offer and the helpful tasting notes on all the pumps. In fact, as the copper vats just beyond the main bar show, they care about it enough to brew their own, and their fruity Dam Tasty Beaver and Bonobo beers are in no way overshadowed by the competition at the bar (Meantime Pale Ale, Duvel Green). A regularly updated menu (slow-roast lamb, white bean chilli and the like) is well matched by an imaginative wine list. Past the vats, a roomy conservatory with a table football table and an open kitchen leads to a capacious decked terrace and a separate children's and garden room. Popular with all ages, and deservedly so. *Babies & children admitted (until 8.30pm). Disabled: toilet. Games (table football). Tables outdoors (5, pavement; 30, garden). Wireless internet.*

Greenwich Union

56 Royal Hill, SE10 8RT (8692 6258, www.greenwichunion.com). Greenwich rail/DLR. **Open** noon-11pm Mon-Fri; 11am-11pm Sat; 11.30am-10.30pm Sun. **Food served** noon-10pm Mon-Fri; 11am-10pm Sat; 11am-9pm Sun. **Greenwich**
Although its thunder has been stolen by the newer Old Brewery, the Greenwich Union remains the spiritual home of Alistair Hook's Meantime mission to bring German-style beers to the British public. Six tap options – the likes of Helles and Wheat – complement two dozen or more international labels by the bottle, including the little-seen Schneider Aventinus,

Aecht Schlenkerla Marzen (a smoked beer otherwise only available in its native Bamberg) and Cantillon Gueuze. Food runs from a humble bacon butty to chargrilled steaks; you'll also find wines, coffees and teas. Throw in imagery by Hook's schoolmate Ray Richardson, framed covers from *Picture Post* and a small front terrace, and you have a very tidy operation. *Babies & children admitted (until 9pm). Tables outdoors (16, garden). Wireless internet.* **Map p253 E2.**

Hermits Cave

28 Camberwell Church Street, SE5 8QU (7703 3188). Denmark Hill rail. **Open** noon-midnight Mon-Wed; noon-2am Thur-Sat; noon-1am Sun. **No credit cards. Camberwell**
This friendly cabin of an Irish pub has been the haunt of Camberwell's more cultured art students since Leonardo's time, it seems. Prices are still cheap, the regulars still include old locals who've been skulking around in SE5 since Macmillan told them they'd never had it so good, and the decor is still largely made up of pre-war drinks advertising ('Good Old Murphy's!') and contemporary photography. Beers might include selections from the Brodie's brewery in Leyton; such French ciders as Pays d'Aude and Fermier (each £6) offer an inappropriately continental alternative. Wine is not a selling point, but the prices are fair: all bottles are £12, with glasses at £4.20. A large TV in the saloon bar attracts football fans of the *laissez jouer* variety; conversation around the timeless wooden interior is the definition of bonhomie. *Babies & children admitted (until 6pm). Games (board games). Wireless internet.*

Katzenjammers

Hop Exchange, 24 Southwark Street, SE1 1TY (3417 0196, www.katzenjammers.co.uk). London Bridge tube/rail. **Open** noon-11pm Mon-Sat. **Food served** noon-10pm Mon-Sat. **Borough**
Although the vaulted basement rooms are very attractive, the big draw at this underground bar is the German beer. There are seven on draught, plus more than a score by the bottle; among them is Paulaner Hefe-Weizen, a wonderful wheat beer, alongside a comprehensive selection of weissbiers and dunkels, kölsch beers, dark lagers, pilsners and more. The other sides to Katzenjammers' character hold less appeal: the service can be slow; the food would shame an autobahn truck-stop (unattractively orange sauerkraut, spätzle no better than a packet version); and as for the music, which might include an oompah band playing 'Wonderwall', the less said the better. Inevitably, the room can

get rowdy with a clientele keen on recreating Oktoberfest for the other 11 months of the year. But the beers alone make it worth considering. *Babies & children admitted (until 6pm). Booking advisable Thur, Sat. Dress: no football colours. Entertainment (musicians 7.30pm Fri). Function room (42 capacity).* **Map p250 P8.**

Market Porter

9 Stoney Street, SE1 9AA (7407 2495, www. markettaverns.co.uk). London Bridge tube/rail. **Open** 6-8.30am, 11am-11pm Mon-Fri; noon-11pm Sat; noon-10.30pm Sun. **Food served** noon-3pm Mon-Fri; noon-5pm Sun. **Borough** Rare is the evening – or, for that matter, the Saturday afternoon – when this place isn't packed to the gunwales. The reasons for its popularity are plainly apparent: a handsome, old-fashioned room; a plum location; and one of the best real-ale selections in London. Spend any time here, though, and its shortcomings will become obvious: the staff who don't seem to have much idea what they're serving, a shame given the huge variety of ales and the lack of a central board detailing what's on offer; and the lack of seats in the S-shaped room, which fosters not so much intimacy but discomfort. Beer tourists will find plenty to enjoy, but there are more comfortable pubs nearby in which to spend an evening. *Babies & children admitted (weekends). Disabled: toilet. Function room (60 capacity).* **Map p250 P8.**

Old Brewery

Pepys Building, Old Royal Naval College, SE10 9LM (3327 1280, www.oldbrewery greenwich.com). Cutty Sark DLR. **Open** 10am-11pm Mon-Sat; 10am-10.30pm Sun. **Food served** noon-10.30pm Mon-Sat; noon-10pm Sun. **Greenwich** Rather than make cask-conditioned English ales for an already crowded market, Alastair Hook and his team at Meantime specialise in more unusual artisan beers, which they've rolled out in increasing numbers across London over the last few years. In 2010, he opened this ambitious operation, a microbrewery, pub and café-diner in part of the newly refurbished Old Royal Naval College. The modern bar area is small but has a huge outdoor seating area. Meantime's own beers, chiefly brewed using bottom-fermented, low-temperature continental methods, take pride of place; among them are Helles, a pale lager, and the potent Hospital Porter. But the menu extends beyond Greenwich to cover around 50 beers on draught or in bottles, arranged by style on the menu from 'hoppy ales' to 'Belgian Lambic and crisp beers'. The food, too, is excellent, billed on the menu as 'Modern British' and taking in such hearty dishes as pork terrine served with strips of pig's ear. *Babies & children admitted (until 6pm). Disabled: toilet. Tables outdoors (30, terrace). Wireless internet.* **Map p253 E1.**

Rake

14 Winchester Walk, SE1 9AG (7407 0557). London Bridge tube/rail. **Open** noon-11pm Mon-Fri; 10am-11pm Sat; noon-8pm Sun. **Borough** When asked how often his team change the draught options here, the barman casually replied that it depended on consumption: perhaps daily, perhaps every couple of days. To say that this blue-fronted spot has Aechte Schlenkerle Rauchbier (a rare smoked variety from Bamberg), Jenlain, Meteor Pils and Grisette Fruits des Bois on tap will be old news by the time you read this, but that gives you an idea of what the type of beers that appear here. The only guarantee, as advertised on a yellow sign above the bar, is that there'll be 'No crap on tap'. The tap brews, offered in third-of-a-pint measures for easy sampling, are merely the tip of a beery iceberg: as befits an operation run by the folk behind the Utobeer stall in Borough Market, there are also bottles galore from all corners of the world, an enticing selection sold at elevated prices. The room is tiny with few decorative distractions; a small covered courtyard provides extra shelter. *Babies & children admitted. Disabled: toilet. Tables outdoors (7, decking).* **Map p250 P8.**

Royal Oak

44 Tabard Street, SE1 4JU (7357 7173). Borough tube. **Open** 11am-11.30pm Mon-Sat; noon-9pm Sun. **Food served** noon-3pm, 5-9.45pm Mon-Sat; noon-7.45pm Sun. **Borough** The only London pub of the estimable Lewes brewer Harveys, this traditional Victorian corner tavern draws beer fanatics, and with good reason: the ales here, from year-round fixtures such as Sussex Mild to seasonals including Old Ale, are always in perfect condition. But the Royal Oak would be worthy of a visit even without the cask brews: this is a a lovely place to spend an evening. Civilised groups of local residents, after-work drinkers and beer tourists fill the two rooms nightly, perched at sturdy bar furniture beneath an unflashy but handsomely restored interior. The absence of canned music aids the flow of conversation; excellent, unpretentious pub cooking (roasts, hot pots) helps dissipate the effects of the beer. One of the city's best. *Function room (40 capacity).* **Map p250 P9.**

Mason & Taylor. *See p116.*

Southwark Tavern

22 Southwark Street, SE1 1TU (7403 0257, www.thesouthwarktavern.co.uk). London Bridge tube/rail. **Open** 11am-midnight Mon-Wed; 11am-1am Thur, Fri; 10am-1am Sat; noon-midnight Sun. **Food served** 11am-10.30pm Mon-Fri; noon-10pm Sat; noon-10.30pm Sun. **Borough**
Another in the string of yoof boozers cannily conceived and marketed by the Mitchells & Butlers pubco (see also the Crown & Sceptre, the Carpenters Arms and the Green Man in Fitzrovia, among numerous others), this corner pub is a pretty sizeable place, but it'll still be a struggle to get served after 6pm on a party-hearty Friday. The main room is often thronged with lively twenty- and thirtysomethings on the post-work razzle, drawn by the Southwark Tavern's easy mix of traditional pub style and youthful buzz in an area that's rich in the former but otherwise lacking in the latter. The other key to its appeal is the terrific range of beers, from British ales (some familiar, some rare) to continental and American imports. The choice of beers is much smaller in the downstairs bar (there are no handpumps, for one thing), but you'll get served a lot quicker. The food is soak-it-up pub grub. *Babies & children admitted (until 5pm). Entertainment (quiz 8pm Tue). Games (board games).* **Map p250 P8.**

Victoria Inn

72-79 Choumert Road, SE15 4AR (7639 5052). Peckham Rye rail. **Open** noon-midnight Mon-Thur; noon-1am Fri; 11am-1am Sat; 11am-midnight Sun. **Food served** noon-10pm Mon-Fri; 11am-10pm Sat; 11am-9.30pm Sun. **Peckham**
In the posher part of Peckham, the former Wishing Well has had a fair few coins tossed at it, but it's a homely rather than haughty affair. Hunkered around an oak horseshoe bar are high brown suede banquettes, robust wooden tables and worn-out leather armchairs. The open-plan kitchen turns out traditional pub tucker with a twist: chorizo scotch egg and breaded halloumi sticks for snack or starter, spicy chargrilled chilli squid for a main. Not many boozers have beer lists as broad as this, with draught Meantime, Adnams, Erdinger and Bonobo (brewed at its sister pub, the Florence), as well as a bevy of bottled beers including Duvel and Brooklyn Lager. Don't be disheartened by the wines on draught (really) from the US and Argentina – for entry-level liquids, they're a decent drop. *Babies & children admitted (until 8pm). Disabled: toilet. Games (board games, video games). Tables outdoors (17, garden). Wireless internet.*

Wheatsheaf

24 Southwark Street, SE1 1TY (7407 9934). London Bridge tube/rail. **Open** 11am-11pm Mon-Fri; 11am-11pm Sat; noon-10pm Sun. **Food served** noon-3pm, 5-9pm Mon-Thur; noon-3pm Fri; noon-9pm Sat; noon-8pm Sun. **Borough**
The demise of the Stoney Street Wheatsheaf, a cosy Young's boozer that was mercifully devoid

of the brewery's usual decorative blandness, was bemoaned by locals, but not for long: this is, after all, an area rich in terrific, traditional-ish pubs that serve excellent beer. Regardless, it soon resurfaced around the corner, under the umbrella of the small Red Car group. Whereas the original Wheatsheaf was calm, cosy and old-fashioned, version 2.0 is large and modern, and the staff's attempts to make the capacious room feel more intimate (there are even sofas, anathema to old regulars) haven't been wholly successful. But there's no criticising the beer: you'll usually find at least nine ales on tap, including many obscure varieties, with a pub grub menu to help keep your stomach on an even keel. Worthy competition to the other pubs in this neck of the woods.
Babies & children admitted (until 6pm). Games (darts). Wireless internet. **Map p250 P8.**

Zerodegrees

29-31 Montpelier Vale, SE3 0TJ (8852 5619, www.zerodegrees.co.uk). Blackheath rail. **Open** noon-midnight Mon-Sat; noon-11.30pm Sun. **Food served** noon-11pm Mon-Sat; noon-10.30pm Sun. **Blackheath**
With branches in Bristol, Reading and Cardiff, and a mission 'to create internationally inspiring gourmet dishes and exceptional freshly brewed beers', Zerodegrees brings a young clientele to its sunken restaurant and two-floor bar on the edge of Blackheath. It's an open-plan space, the preparing of fire-roasted pizzas providing entertainment when the match isn't occupying the large screen at one end: you may have to wait for a dining table or book the TV sofas on big-game nights. Behind the bar, huge copper vats contain the four house brews, uniformly priced in half-pint (£1.60), pint (£2.90) and four-pint (£10.95) measures. There's a Czech-type pilsner, a US-style pale ale, a chocolatey black lager and a Belgian-influenced wheat variety; all are available in take-home kegs. Special and seasonal ales, and fruit beers are also produced, but the bar area could do with signage so that you can assess your options more easily.
Babies & children admitted. Tables outdoors (10, terrace).

Also recommended

Bear (Classic Pubs, *p87*); **Charles Dickens** (Classic Pubs, *p87*); **Commercial** (Classic Pubs, *p88*); **Gowlett** (Good Mixers, *p191*); **Herne Tavern** (Gastropubs & Brasseries, *p147*); **Lord Clyde** (Classic Pubs, *p90*); **Trafalgar Tavern** (Rooms with a View, *p167*).

South

Draft House

94 Northcote Road, SW11 6QW (7924 1814, www.drafthouse.co.uk). Clapham Junction rail or Clapham South tube. **Open** 11am-11pm Mon-Fri; 10am-11pm Sat; 10am-10.30pm Sun. **Food served** 11am-10pm Mon-Sat; 10am-9pm Sun. **Battersea**
Clad in wood, warmed by candlelight and brightened with pop art and green furniture, the Draft House shakes beer out of its socks and sandals and dresses it in something more stylish. Served in third-, half- and full pints, the 19 beers on tap at the long, curved bar include British ales, German lagers, Budvar Half & Half and (in season) rye-based Schremser Roggen Bier, all served in the correct glassware. And over in the chiller, excellent American microbrews rub shoulders with acclaimed European efforts (perhaps Erdinger Dunkel or Alhambra Negra, depending on the time of year). Cooked in an open-plan kitchen and served by amiable staff in an unfussy dining room, food includes unusual delights such as ox tongue fritters and potted crab, plus more predictable gastropub fodder (steak and chips, burgers); it's a shame that the menu doesn't recommend beer and food pairings, but it's the only oversight in this otherwise fine operation.
Babies & children admitted. Tables outdoors (8, terrace). Wireless internet. **Map p251 E2.**

Sultan. *See p124.*

Rake. See p120.

Sun. **Food served** noon-3pm, 5.30-9.30pm Mon-Fri; noon-9.30pm Sat; 1-9pm Sun. **Stockwell**

The Priory Arms is known for its dedication to quality beers and ales. One end of the convivial interior is topped by entangled vines of dry hops; the other, around the bar counter, is encrusted with scores of multicoloured beer mats, souvenirs from ales previously featured here. You might find Hop Back's Summer Lightning alongside the output of Sharp's, Cottage Brewery and London independents: Twickenham Fine Ales, Camden Town Brewery, Tottenham's Redemption, and Sambrook's, brewed just a couple of miles to the west in Battersea. The pub is equally proud of its stock of German and Belgian brews available by the bottle, with Rothaus, Floris and Erdinger among the wheat varieties. A daily-changing menu offers around eight fairly priced main dishes, plus standard burgers. Board games and chess (note the boards on the veneered tables) provide entertainment; smokers take to the front terrace. *Entertainment (quiz 8.30pm Sun). Games (Scrabble tournament). Function room (60 capacity). Tables outdoors (5, terrace).*

Eagle Ale House

104 Chatham Road, SW11 6HG (7228 2328, www.eaglealehouse.co.uk). Clapham South tube. **Open** 2-11pm Mon-Fri; noon-11pm Sat; noon-10.30pm Sun. **Battersea**

Halfway up a steep, residential street, this pub is favoured by cheeky chaps who should know better. It looks like Billy Liar's bedroom, were Billy Liar to have been a rugby-playing Crystal Palace fan. Images of glamorous women of the Sinatra era mingle with framed programmes from Selhurst Park, memorabilia relating to England's Rugby World Cup victory and other Brit iconography (1966, Coopers Henry and Tommy, a poster for *The Italian Job*). Two fireplaces assist in creating intimacy. Ales such as BG Sips ('Blue Monkey with a handle, please, Dolores'), 6d from Dorset's Sixpenny Brewery and William Wilberforce Freedom Ale are crammed into the little half-square of bar counter. Dolores deals bravely with the weakening banter as the night rolls on. Occasional wives and girlfriends may be treated to a Coldridge chardonnay. *Babies & children admitted. Entertainment (quiz 8pm Sun). Tables outdoors (8, garden). Wireless internet.* **Map p251 E3.**

Priory Arms

83 Lansdowne Way, SW8 2PB (7622 1884, www.theprioryarms.co.uk). Stockwell tube. **Open** noon-11pm Mon-Sat; noon-10.30pm

Zeitgeist at the Jolly Gardeners

49-51 Black Prince Road, SE11 6AB (7840 0426, www.zeitgeist-london.com). Vauxhall tube/rail. **Open** noon-12.30am Mon-Thur; noon-1am Fri; 1pm-midnight Sat; 1-11pm Sun. **Food served** noon-10pm daily. **Vauxhall**

In October 2007, this spacious Victorian pub in an almost comically isolated spot behind Lambeth Bridge was spruced up by new German owners. They retained the ornate central bar, but the periphery was reupholstered in black banquettes, and the walls were painted matt black. A few German flags brighten up the pub – not something you would have seen in the middle of the last century, when this part of Lambeth was heavily bombed by the Luftwaffe. The main attraction, of course, is the list of German beers, which contains few familiar names (Beck's is about it) and covers most styles, from aromatic weiss varieties through light pilsners to darker brews. Occasional beer festivals further increase the variety. The food is just as Teutonic: schnitzel, sausages and other hearty fare constitutes the lion's share. The bar's popular with German expats, who gather to watch Bundesliga matches on two big screens. *Babies & children admitted. Tables outdoors (6, garden). Wireless internet.*

Also recommended...

Antelope (Gastropubs & Brasseries, *p148*); **Avalon** (Classic Pubs, *p90*); **Bread**

& Roses (Good Mixers, *p192*); **Canton Arms** (Gastropubs & Brasseries, *p149*); **Ink Rooms** (Good Mixers, *p192*); **Manor Arms** (Gastropubs & Brasseries, *p150*).

South West

Bricklayer's Arms

32 Waterman Street, SW15 1DD (8789 0222, www.bricklayers-arms.co.uk). Putney Bridge tube or Putney rail. **Open** noon-11pm Mon-Sat; noon-10.30pm Sun. **No credit cards. Putney**
There's something of a village-pub feel to this hostelry: Putney's first, it started life in 1826. Although it's since been surrounded by a modern housing estate, the historic prints and games of nine-pin skittles and shove ha'penny lend a rustic feel. The old-world ambience is amplified by the range of classic handpumps that draw from a daunting range of a dozen ales, often focusing on a selection from a particular guest brewery (or three). Lager drinkers may opt for Budvar, San Miguel, Pilsner Urquell or Staropramen; cider from Somerset's Perry is also available. A regular winner of CAMRA awards, the Bricklayer's has had to struggle to retain its independence of late, but the battle appears to have been won. 'We have no desire to be themed, modernised, sanitised! There's not a drizzled sun-dried tomato in sight,' it proclaims. This is a free house through and through.
Babies & children admitted (until 9pm). Games (bar skittles, board games). Tables outdoors (6, garden).

Citizen Smith

160 Putney High Street, SW15 1RS (8780 2235, www.citizensmithbar.co.uk). East Putney tube or Putney rail. **Open** 5-11pm Mon; noon-midnight Tue-Thur; noon-2am Fri, Sat; noon-11pm Sun. **Food served** 5-10pm Mon; noon-10pm Tue-Sat; noon-9pm Sun. **Putney**
Its wide-open windows facing Putney station, Citizen Smith (didn't he come from Tooting?) frequently fills to the brim with young punters on the razzle and on the pull. It's not so brash that Pimm's or jugs of elderflower pressé can't be advertised on the bar, but for the most part, a drinks selection that would be the envy of most bars south of Kensington is overlooked in favour of party-oriented hedonism. Shame. The beers are great: Sierra Nevada, Anchor Steam and Lowrider are among the draught options, with Argentine Quilmes, German Augustiner Hell and other more prevalent global brands by the bottle. The wine selection isn't shabby, either, and neither are the cocktails: mai tais with

Myers's rum, black Russians with Wyborowa and cosmopolitans with Skyy Citron vie for attention with the 'Mojitos' sign above the overflow serving hatch at the back, surrounded by urban murals featuring Grace Jones and other pop icons.
Babies & children admitted (until 7pm). Disabled: toilet. Entertainment (bands 7pm Thur, Sun; DJs 9pm Fri, Sat). Wireless internet.

Sultan

78 Norman Road, SW19 1BT (8542 4532). Colliers Wood tube then 200 bus. **Open** noon-11pm Mon-Thur, Sun; noon-midnight Fri, Sat. **Colliers Wood**
No beturbaned Muslim ruler beams out from the free-standing pub on a quiet residential road behind All Saints' Church in Mitcham: the Sultan was a black stallion who sired many a champion racehorse in the 19th century. Inside this homely community boozer, you'll find a detailed history of Selim, sire of Sultan; it's a suitable backdrop for the old geezers who sit studying the racing form and sipping affordable pints of Summer Lightning and other fine ales from the Hop Back Brewery of Salisbury. The saloon bar is named after Ted Higgins, part of the original cast of Radio 4's *The Archers*. All told, this is a lovely local, with a leafy beer garden, plenty of parking space and decent pub food. Everyone seems to know each other, but strangers can also expect a warm welcome.
Games (board games). Tables outdoors (10, garden). Wireless internet.

White Horse

1-3 Parsons Green, SW6 4UL (7736 2115, www.whitehorsesw6.com). Parsons Green tube. **Open** 9.30am-11.30pm Mon-Wed, Sun; 9.30am-midnight Thur-Sat. **Food served** 10am-10.30pm daily. **Parsons Green**
Only the lack of ceiling fans stop the main bar of this renowned hostelry from feeling like something from the days of the Raj. The Victorian ceilings are airily high, and wide windows with wooden venetian blinds let plenty of light into the bar. Chesterfield-style sofas surround huge tables, ideal for families and groups of friends, though the umbrella-covered outdoor tables are most coveted. You can expect plenty of turned-up collars and rugby shirts, but the spread of customers is wider than you might imagine. Beer is the great leveller: there are eight ales on offer at the mahogany bar, among them Harveys Sussex Best and Jaipur IPA from the Thornbridge Brewery in Derbyshire, while the glorious list of bottled brews is particularly strong on Belgian and American beers. Regular beer festivals usually

Eel Pie. *See p126.*

come with a tight focus, with May's London Beer Festival and November's Old Ale Festival well worth marking in the calendar. *Babies & children admitted. Disabled: toilet. Function rooms (18 & 35 capacity). Tables outdoors (20, garden). Wireless internet.*

Also recommended...

Harwood Arms (Gastropubs & Brasseries, *p152*); **Sun Inn** (Rooms with a View, *p167*).

West

Stonemasons Arms
54 Cambridge Grove, W6 0LA (8748 1397). Hammersmith tube. **Open** 11am-11pm Mon-Sat; noon-11pm Sun. **Food served** noon-3pm, 6-10pm Mon-Fri; noon-10pm Sat; noon-9.30pm Sun. **Hammersmith**
This light, airy, two-floor gastropub – and, on Sundays, neighbourhood film club – is a Fuller's establishment par excellence. Alongside Pride Honey Dew and seasonals such as Spring Sprinter, the taps offer Leffe, Peroni and Staropramen. A dozen or so wines of each colour gradually ascend the pricing scale until they're nearly at £30 a bottle. The Stonemasons Arms is one of those venues that could sit in several chapters within this book. We've put it in the beer section, but it's also both a good-looking, easygoing local and a fine gastropub, drawing professionals who sit in the sunken back area around the half-open kitchen and tuck into reliable British cooking as sunlight sweeps over the wooden furniture. The decor is provided by tasteful line drawings, and entertainment comes from Sky Sports. *Babies & children admitted (until 6pm). Entertainment (quiz 8pm Wed). Function room (50 capacity). Games (board games). Tables outdoors (4, pavement). Wireless internet.*

Also recommended...
Cumberland Arms (Classic Pubs, *p98*); **Ealing Park Tavern** (Gastropubs & Brasseries, *p153*); **Elephant & Castle** (Classic Pubs, *p99*); **George IV** (Classic Pubs, *p100*); **Havelock Tavern** (Gastropubs & Brasseries, *p153*); **Mawson Arms** (Classic Pubs, *p101*).

North West

Roebuck
15 Pond Street, NW3 2PN (7435 7354, www.roebuckhampstead.com). Belsize Park tube. **Open** noon-11pm Mon-Thur;

noon-midnight Fri, Sat; noon-10.30pm Sun. **Food served** noon-3pm, 5-9pm daily. **Hampstead**
This escape hatch for staff from the Royal Free was given a facelift by Young's when they took over a couple of years ago: purple floral wallpaper, mirrors and '70s swivel chairs are paired with a grandly tiled fireplace and an old piano, though don't expect anyone to hammer out 'Knees Up, Mother Brown' around closing time. The high arched windows offer a surprisingly leafy view of the hospital; alternatively, head out to the spacious paved garden, where there are barbecues in summer. Emphasis has been taken off the cocktails and placed firmly on the four handpumps, with Waggle Dance, Bombardier, and Young's Special and Bitter now typical; there's also draught Peroni, Kirin Ichinar and Addlestone's cider. The Tuesday quiz nights are popular, as are the Sunday lunches. *Babies & children admitted (until 7pm). Disabled: toilet. Entertainment (quiz 8pm Tue). Function room (60 capacity). Games (board games). Tables outdoors (16, garden). Wireless internet.*

Also recommended...

Holly Bush (Classic Pubs, *p106*); **Horseshoe** (Gastropubs & Brasseries, *p157*).

Outer London

Eel Pie
9-11 Church Street, Twickenham, Middx, TW1 3NJ (8891 1717). Twickenham rail. **Open** 11am-11pm Mon-Wed; 11am-midnight Thur-Sat; noon-10.30pm Sun. **Food served** noon-3pm daily. **Twickenham, Middx**
Halfway down narrow Church Street, parallel to the Thames and the Eel Pie Island of early 1960s music lore, this likeable old Hall & Woodhouse pub is a real rugby haunt. Walls of framed tickets, colour caricatures and signed shirts line the far end of the two-space interior, historic prints of this sleepy neighbourhood the other. Between them, the bar features taps that might offer drinkers the likes of Kronenbourg and Amstel, various Badger-branded ales (First Gold, Hopping Hare, the summery Lemony Cricket), Harveys Sussex Best and Peroni. Prices are reasonable, helping to keep this place in business when there's no Six Nations game or big-name concert up the road. Sit outside on summer weekends, when the street gets closed to traffic. *Babies & children admitted (until 9pm).*

Gastropubs & Brasseries

Central	128
North	138
North East	143
East	144
South East	147
South	148
South West	151
West	152
North West	157
Outer London	158

Gastropubs & Brasseries

Two decades on, and the wave that started when the **Eagle** coined the word 'gastropub' continues, a phenomenon that's in no small part responsible for the astonishing transformation of London into a gourmet capital. After years of eating dull or barely edible bar food – simply as ballast between pints – Londoners have come to know and love eating in pubs. And, just as pertinently, landlords have come to rely on the presence of steak pies, burgers and the ever-popular sausage, mash and onion gravy – or, indeed, much fancier dishes – to add appeal to failing alehouses. It's got to the point where just about every new pub renovation in London incorporates the addition of a kitchen or the extension of an existing one.

The venues in this chapter come in all shapes and flavours. The likes of the **Seven Stars**, the **Gunmakers** and the **Cat & Mutton** are chiefly drinking venues, convivial pubs with unusually good kitchens. Other enterprises offer two distinct environments for those after food and those who just want a drink: at the **Peasant** and Bethnal Green's **Royal Oak**, for instance, drinkers fuelled by bar snacks reside in the main space, while those looking for a more serious meal get to eat it in a quieter, smarter dining room upstairs. And still others are closer to restaurant than taproom: the **Harwood Arms** in Fulham, for instance, is tilted more at diners than drinkers. All, though, are linked by two characteristics: excellent food and worthwhile drinks, with no pressure to enjoy one without the other.

Central

Adam & Eve
77A Wells Street, W1T 3QQ (7636 0717, www.geronimo-inns.co.uk/theadamandeve). *Oxford Circus or Tottenham Court Road tube.* **Open** 11am-11pm Mon-Fri; noon-11pm Sat; noon-6pm Sun. **Food served** noon-9pm Mon-Thur; noon-4pm, 5-9pm Fri; noon-9pm Sat; noon-5pm Sun. **Fitzrovia**
Another entry in the Geronimo chain (note the bright, stand-up letters near the entrance), this makeover gastropub exudes an urban feel. It also caters to diners and drinkers with equal care. A long, shiny bar counter features varied UK and international brews, a Geronimo trademark; you might find Waggle Dance, Doom Bar and Adnams, along with Aspall Suffolk Cyder. Geronimo's wine man, John Clevely, produces a new list every month, divided into such categories as 'Warm-Hearted Reds' and 'Chardonnay Lovers & Friends'; nearly all selections come by the bottle and two sizes of glass. Food is a serious matter – 'Please wait to be seated,' says the sign – but those who just want a bite with their beer can plump for bar grub. Michael Caine and Twiggy are decoratively namechecked, while a 'Garden of Eden' (what else?) offers fresh air.
Babies & children admitted (until 6pm). Booking advisable Wed-Fri, Sun. Games (board games). Tables outdoors (2, pavement; 4, courtyard). Wireless internet. **Map p240 J6.**

Anchor & Hope
36 The Cut, SE1 8LP (7928 9898). Southwark tube or Waterloo tube/rail. **Open** 5-11pm Mon; 11am-11pm Tue-Sat; 12.30-5pm Sun. **Food served** 6-10.30pm Mon; 12.30-2.30pm, 6-10.30pm Tue-Sat; 2pm Sun. **Waterloo**
Very continental, this, but also unmistakably British. Behind an awning, spread over an otherwise prosaic Waterloo street, you'll find a daily menu chalked up on a board, and a side area for dining bistro-style. There's plenty for

Eagle. *See p131.*

the drinker to contemplate if food isn't a priority: ales such as Wells Bombardier, Young's and St Austell Tribute, for a start, plus Red Stripe on draught. An egalitarian approach to cocktail pricing – all about £5 – allows for a selection of martinis (gin, vodka, breakfast and espresso), while the wine drinker is spoiled for choice. Starting with a standard house vin de pays in each colour, the list quickly works itself up to giddier heights. Roast skate, grilled Orkney kippers and steak pie (for two to share) are typical of the attractive food options. A little art indoors and a few tables outside complete the picture.
Babies & children admitted. Booking essential Sun. Tables outdoors (5, pavement). **Map p250 N8.**

Coach & Horses

26-28 Ray Street, EC1R 3DJ (7278 8990, www.thecoachandhorses.com). Farringdon tube/rail. **Open** noon-11pm Mon-Fri; 6-11pm Sat; 12.30-5pm Sun. **Food served** noon-3pm, 6-10pm Mon-Fri; 6-10pm Sat; 1-4pm Sun. **Clerkenwell**
The Guardian's 2008 move from Clerkenwell to King's Cross led to fears that this appealing gastropub, directly behind the old newspaper offices and a local for discerning staffers since its reopening in 2003, might struggle for custom. Happily, it still seems to be chugging along

nicely. According to the website, 'We haven't messed around with the original gastropub formula because we think it works,' and that pretty much covers it: wooden panelling on the walls, decent ales (Landlord is a constant) and interesting wines behind the bar, impressive, Brit-leaning food on the menu, and good service in every corner of the operation. The front rooms are more appealing than the space at the back and the slightly pokey garden; the outdoor tables are surprisingly nice in summer. All told, a really likeable enterprise.
Babies & children admitted. Booking advisable Fri, Sun. Tables outdoors (6, garden). **Map p242 N4.**

Duke of Wellington

94A Crawford Street, W1H 2HQ (7723 2790, www.thedukew1.co.uk). Baker Street tube or Marylebone tube/rail. **Open** noon-11pm Mon-Sat; noon-10.30pm Sun. **Food served** noon-3pm, 6.30-10pm Mon-Fri; 10am-4pm, 7-10pm Sat; 12.30-4.30pm, 7-9pm Sun. **Marylebone**
Although the owners may have upped the ante at the Duke of Wellington where the kitchen is concerned (on top of the superior bar food served downstairs from a daily-changing menu, there's a full-blown restaurant upstairs), a laissez-faire approach remains around the main bar. Thus, you still see the kind of decor – pre-*Lady Chatterley* soft porn magazine

Norfolk Arms. *See p133.*

covers, the record sleeve of Vanessa Paradis' 'Joe le Taxi', Falkland-era *Sun* splashes – that would adorn the most frightful pub in Chelsea. The place retains its charmingly informal air – most tables have paper wedges under their legs – but even if you're paying £3 for a 125ml glass of the cheapest white (and certainly when it's a large glass of Côtes de Nuits Villages at £18.40), you want to be able to rest your drink securely. Altogether, the Duke provides more than 40 labels by the glass and nearly 120 by the bottle; ale aficionados are spoiled, with Sharp's Doom Bar, Black Sheep Ale and Fuller's London Pride on the pumps.
Babies & children admitted (until 7pm).
Booking advisable. Tables outdoors (6, pavement). Wireless internet. **Map p238 F5.**

Eagle
159 Farringdon Road, EC1R 3AL (7837 1353). Farringdon tube/rail. **Open** noon-11pm Mon-Sat; noon-5pm Sun. **Food served** 12.30-3pm, 6.30-10.30pm Mon-Fri; 12.30-3.30pm, 6.30-10.30pm Sat; 12.30-3.30pm Sun. **Clerkenwell**
Widely credited with starting the gastropub revolution, the Eagle celebrated its 20th birthday in 2011, and is still a highly popular fixture in this gastropub-heavy corner of town. Drinkers and diners returning to the place after a lengthy absence will find that little has changed. The food, cooked in front of you at an open kitchen along the bar, remains reliably excellent; the drinks (a couple of ales, a short wine list and, surprisingly, a few cocktails) are good enough; the service is both friendly and efficient; and the one-room bar remains raffishly comfortable, if a little cramped. The only downside, as ever, remains the throng of customers: you'll probably end up sharing a table, regardless of whether you're dining or merely drinking, and the acoustics aren't designed for conversation. But it's easy to see how this place has remained busy for two decades, and congratulations to them for not messing with a successful formula.
Babies & children admitted. Tables outdoors (4, pavement). **Map p242 N4.**

Grazing Goat
6 New Quebec Street, W1H 7RQ (7724 7243, www.thegrazinggoat.co.uk). Marble Arch tube. **Open** 8am-11pm Mon-Thur, Sun; 8am-midnight Fri, Sat. **Food served** 7.30-11.30am, noon-10pm Mon-Sat; 7.30-11.30am, noon-9.30pm Sun. **Marylebone**
This huge gastropub from the Cubitt House group is a very expensive-looking refurbishment that's transformed a neighbourhood boozer into

something akin to a wealthy country-house hotel (indeed, there are eight bedrooms). Although simple British food is a fine thing, the kitchen's preferences seem to be a homage to the pub food of the Beefeater era – fish and chips, burgers, steaks, Sunday roasts – though there are more-modern dishes, such as a starter of chilli salt squid. The service is chirpy and the food is nicely prepared, but not impressive enough in itself to make Grazing Goat a destination eaterie. As for drinking, the wine list easily outshines the beers, with Deuchars IPA the only real ale on tap on our visit; the score of wines by the glass are well chosen, with most priced between a fiver and a tenner.
Babies & children admitted. Disabled: toilet. Function room (100 capacity). Tables outdoors (6, pavement). **Map p238 F6.**

Green
29 Clerkenwell Green, EC1R 0DU (7490 8010, www.thegreenec1.co.uk). Farringdon tube/rail. **Open** noon-11pm daily. **Food served** noon-3pm, 6-10pm Mon-Sat; noon-8pm Sun. **Clerkenwell**
Not to be confused with the nearby Green Tavern, this classy, food-oriented corner venue looks like a typical neighbourhood pub, but takes a distinctly continental approach to proceedings. Below a huge antique clock, smartly dressed types loosen their ties and tuck into upscale bar snacks (homemade Cumberland sausage rolls, warm pork scratchings with apple sauce) or more substantial mains (steamed sea bass, perhaps, or risotto of cauliflower, sorrel and truffle oil). There are around 30 wines, a dozen or so of which are available by the glass; draught options include Bee Sting Pear Cider, Licher Weizen, Bitburger and Adnams, with Duvel and Bellevue Kriek sold by the bottle. The square of terrace by the front door catches the sun quite nicely, while upstairs is a slightly more formal dining room.
Babies & children admitted. Disabled: toilet. Function room (70 capacity). Tables outdoors (7, pavement). Wireless internet. **Map p242 N4.**

Gunmakers
13 Eyre Street Hill, EC1R 5ET (7278 1022, www.thegunmakers.co.uk). Farringdon tube/rail. **Open** noon-11pm Mon-Fri. **Food served** noon-3pm, 6.30-9pm Mon-Fri. **Clerkenwell**
'The finest ale and eating house in Clerkenwell' says the board outside – and the Gunmakers does present a very good case. One of many gastropubs in the area, the Gunmakers also operates as a bar, with plenty of natter around the cosy front room. The cask ales – Mad

Goose Purity, Thornbridge Jaipur, Woodford's Wherry and Redemption Fellowship Porter – are consumed as readily as the wines from a list of 16 varieties, whose Italian influence harks back to the time when this area was Little Italy (frame-makers and organ-builders worked here, as did Hiram Maxim, inventor of the machine gun – hence the pub name). Chilean El Descanso merlot and Türk Eiswein von Grüner Weltliner dessert wine might bookend your pork chop and asparagus, or rib-eye steak with French fries, rocket and garlic Pastis butter. Two bright spaces behind provide dining comfort. *Babies & children admitted (until 5pm). Booking advisable Fri. Tables outdoors (7, conservatory).* **Map p242 N4.**

Honey Pot
20 Homer Street, W1H 4NA (7724 9685). Edgware Road tube or Marylebone tube/rail. **Open** noon-11pm Mon-Sat; noon-5pm Sun. **Food served** noon-10pm Mon-Sat; noon-4pm Sun. **Marylebone**

There's much to admire at this tapas tavern, whatever you're after – terrific small plates, courteous and attentive service, and a wealth of wine. A former Victorian boozer, it's brightened by enormous windows and a rear conservatory, while the main bar area is partitioned from a small crowd of dining tables using sherry barrels, all surrounded by dangling jamón, wine decanters and cans of olive oil. Confidently cooked classic tapas such as salt cod fritters and padrón peppers mingle with more unusual dishes (snails with chorizo and fried egg); or choose from the array of charcuterie and steaks. There's a solid selection of Meantime beers on tap as well as the pub's Honey Pot lager, brewed at London Bridge. The wine list, numbering some 130 bins, offers 32 wines by the tumbler. *Babies & children admitted. Disabled: toilet. Tables outdoors (6, pavement).* **Map p238 F5.**

Norfolk Arms
28 Leigh Street, WC1H 9EP (7388 3937, www.norfolkarms.co.uk). Euston tube/rail. **Open** 11am-11pm Mon-Sat; noon-10.30pm Sun. **Food served** noon-3pm, 6-10.15pm Mon-Fri; noon-4pm, 6-10.15pm Sat; noon-10.15pm Sun. *Tapas* noon-10.15pm daily. **King's Cross**

Spanish hams, garlic and peppers are strung around this convivial little corner pub-eaterie, whose offerings place it above many tapas bars. There are Iberian touches to the drinks selection too: the house El Muro La Mancha in two colours, sangria by the glass or pitcher, Sagres on draught. However, you'll also find

Opera Tavern. *See p134.*

an Austrian Kremstal grüner veltliner and an Alsatian Jean Baltenweck organic riesling among the 15 white wines; a Massolino Barolo and a Château St-Jean Châteauneuf-du-Pape among the 20 reds; and British Greene King IPA and Theakston's Best among the draught beer choices. Prices are generally reasonable (£10 for a charcuterie platter), and the outdoor seating brings a touch of civilisation to this otherwise drab locality of dismal two-star hotels and takeaways. *Babies & children admitted. Booking advisable. Function room (10 capacity). Tables outdoors (15, pavement). Wireless internet.*

Only Running Footman
5 Charles Street, W1J 5DF (7499 2988, www.therunningfootman.biz). Green Park tube. **Open** 7.30am-11pm daily. **Food served** 7.30am-10.30pm daily. **Mayfair**

Environs: a handsome, pub-style room with blue leather banquettes and picture windows let down by scuffed tables and poor acoustics. Menu: British-inflected, aspirational pub food that might read better than it tastes (spelt spaghetti with clams, chilli, garlic and wild fennel, for instance), despite the presence of some high-quality ingredients born from an ethical sourcing policy. Drinks: a couple of real ales on tap (Bombardier, Young's) and a well-constructed wine list, with some intriguing bottles at the lower end. But the service is less than perfect. On a recent visit, the only running footman was a pleasant young waitress; the rest of the staff were hanging out behind the bar and displaying no interest in their customers. *Babies & children admitted. Booking advisable Thur, Fri. Disabled: toilet. Function rooms (40 capacity). Tables outdoors (10, pavement). Wireless internet.* **Map p239 H7**.

Opera Tavern

23 Catherine Street, WC2B 5JS (7836 3680, www.operatavern.co.uk). Covent Garden tube. **Open** noon-11pm Mon-Fri; noon-midnight Sat; noon-3pm Sun. **Food served** noon-11.30pm Mon-Sat; noon-3pm Sun. **Covent Garden**
Occupying two floors in a grand old pub that's had a major refit, Opera Tavern is low-lit, looks on-trend and is immediately appealing. The extensive list of pricey bar snacks craftily meshes Italianate small plates and Spanish tapas – five-year-aged pata negra, a good selection of Italian cheeses – and there are nods to New York fashion (mini pork-and-foie-gras burgers). The cooked dishes are put together with aplomb (a tower of braised short rib of beef balanced on a disc of polenta, for example). The Italian and Spanish wines by the glass alone make this a destination bar, with a small selection of dry sherries (perfect with the charcuterie), and a catarratto from Sicily at only £3.85. The service is delightful, but this place is already the worst-kept secret in Covent Garden, which could turn your quest for a table into a drama.
Babies & children admitted. Booking advisable. Function room (45 capacity). Tables outdoors (3, terrace). **Map p241 L6**.

Orange Public House & Hotel

37 Pimlico Road, SW1W 8NE (7881 9844, www.theorange.co.uk). Sloane Square tube. **Open** 8am-11.30pm Mon-Thur; 8am-midnight Fri, Sat; 8am-10.30pm Sun. **Food served** 8-11.30am, noon-9.30pm daily. **Victoria**
Once the Orange pub and microbrewery, this building was reborn in 2009 as the third in Cubitt House's string of four quality gastropubs (the others are the Pantechnicon, the Thomas Cubitt and the Grazing Goat). Stripped wood, black-and-white photographs of the locale as was, a Barnum & Bailey circus handbill and an 1833 cutting from *The Times* complete the decorative suggestion that you're in a pub, as do the presence of Harveys Sussex Best, Adnams and Deuchars IPA on the bar. However, from the bar snacks (house-baked breads with pumpkin-seed oil) to more substantial dishes (slow-cooked shoulder of pork), the food is quality stuff. There are wood-fired pizzas in two sizes, to be enjoyed with a glass of house white Via Fordulo pinot grigio or red Vincent Bouquet merlot in the bar or the equally neat dining space. A modest cocktail selection includes a sunny alliance of blood orange and champagne.
Babies & children admitted. Booking advisable. Disabled: toilet. Function rooms (120 capacity). Tables outdoors (5, pavement).

Pantechnicon Public House & Dining Room

10 Motcomb Street, SW1X 8LA (7730 6074, www.thepantechnicon.com). Hyde Park Corner or Knightsbridge tube. **Open** noon-11pm Mon-Fri; 9am-11pm Sat, Sun. **Food served** noon-9.30pm Mon-Sat; noon-9pm Sun. **Belgravia**
This grand old spot was once a repository for works of art, stored in a high-ceilinged space behind Doric columns. Faithfully restored, it's now flooded with natural light and lined with oak tables and leather chairs – a place for art dealers in smart, stripy shirts to entertain and network over braised pork belly or saddle of Devon lamb. There's also an upstairs dining room with a slightly more contemporary feel. The ground-floor area is bookended by a bar, where Adnams is the standout beer. A 15-strong cocktail list includes a Moscow Mule with Belvedere vodka, while the wine list covers most bases, beginning with a Hungarian pinot grigio and a Languedoc merlot.
Babies & children admitted. Booking advisable. Function rooms (80 capacity). Tables outdoors (7, pavement).

Peasant

240 St John Street, EC1V 4PH (7336 7726, www.thepeasant.co.uk). Angel tube or Farringdon tube/rail. **Open/food served** noon-11pm Mon-Sat; noon-10.30pm Sun. **Clerkenwell**
Close to City University but by no means a typical student hangout, this is a textbook example of how to run a quality kitchen while retaining the character of a corner boozer. Done out with classic pub trappings and boyish accents (a poster for an Iggy gig in San Sebastián, a wooden sign relating to speedway), the Peasant's large, L-shaped space fills most nights with discerning but unpretentious punters, here to mix easily over an extensive drink selection: alongside good ales (Burton Bridge Stairway to Heaven, Inveralmond Ossian, Crouch Vale Brewers Gold), there's draught Leffe, Camden Wheat Beer, Truman's Runner and one or two Meantime brews; a tremendous array of bottled beers; and some 50 wines. The fine roster of gastropub dishes expands to roasts

Peasant

on Sundays; there's smarter, pricier food upstairs in the more formal dining room.
Babies & children admitted (until 9pm). Booking advisable Thur-Sun. Tables outdoors (4, garden terrace; 5, pavement). **Map p242 O4.**

Queen's Head & Artichoke

30-32 Albany Street, NW1 4EA (7916 6206, www.theartichoke.net). Great Portland Street or Regent's Park tube. **Open** 11am-11pm Mon-Sat; noon-10.30pm Sun. **Food served** noon-3pm, 6-10.15pm Mon-Fri; 12.30-4pm, 6-10.15pm Sat; noon-10.15pm Sun.
Marylebone
The management runs a tidy gastronomic operation from these roomy premises on a quiet corner near Regent's Park. Most people seem to patronise this converted pub for the food, enjoyed in a simple wooden interior flooded with sunlight. A daily-changing menu of eight starters and six mains might include goat's cheese and English asparagus tart or chicken liver pâté, while a huge selection of tapas includes many Mediterranean standards and also Dorset rock oysters. However, it's also absolutely fine to just rock up for a drink: the atmosphere is convivial and there's usually room to spare. On tap are Marston's Pedigree, Timothy Taylor Landlord, Adnams, Bitburger and San Miguel. Wines, 40 in number, are joined by standard cocktails, nicely priced at around £6.50 each.
Babies & children admitted. Booking advisable Thur-Sun. Tables outdoors (4, garden; 8, pavement). Wireless internet. **Map p238 H4.**

St John

26 St John Street, EC1M 4AY (7251 0848, www.stjohnrestaurant.com). Barbican tube or Farringdon tube/rail. **Open** 11am-11pm Mon-Fri; 5-11pm Sat; noon-5pm Sun. **Food served** noon-3pm, 6-11pm Mon-Fri; 6-11pm Sat; 1-3pm Sun. **Clerkenwell**
Diners will need to book well ahead for Fergus Henderson's pioneering British restaurant, but you don't need reservations for the spacious adjoining bar: show up in the evening and you should be able to snag a table, offering a more casual opportunity to sample the kitchen's singular style. As in the restaurant, the decor in the high-ceilinged space (a former smokehouse) is stark and straightforward: white walls, wooden furniture – and that's more or less it. Dispensed by ever-friendly staff, drinks include an excellent list of wines by the glass, a couple of ales (Wadworth 6X and Black Sheep Ale, perhaps) and brews from Meantime. You don't have to eat here, but the excellence

Bald-Faced Stag. See p138.

of the food, from doorstep ham sandwiches and chunky Welsh rarebit to the signature eccles cake with Lancashire cheese, means you'd be foolish not to.
Babies & children admitted. Booking essential (restaurant). Disabled: toilet. Function room (18 capacity). **Map p242 O5.**

Seven Stars

53 Carey Street, WC2A 2JB (7242 8521). Chancery Lane or Holborn tube. **Open** 11am-11pm Mon-Fri; noon-11pm Sat; noon-10.30pm Sun. **Food served** 1-9.30pm daily. **City**
Located behind the Royal Courts of Justice, the tiny, charismatic Seven Stars is the spot where barristers bring their clients for celebratory champagne or commiseratory scotch after a big case. A glass display case holds a copy of landlady Roxy Beaujolais's cookbook *Home from the Inn Contented*, a sign that the simple pub food advertised on the blackboard is going to be impressive. Real ales are the tipple of choice among many of the locals – alongside Adnams Bitter and Broadside, you might find beers from smaller breweries such as Dark Star – but there's also a short, sound list of wines by the glass. Seats at the tables covered with green and white checked oilcloths are hard to come by, but considerate bar staff do their best to alert customers to vacancies.
Map p243 M6.

Somers Town Coffee House

60 Chalton Street, NW1 1HS (7691 9136, www.somerstowncoffeehouse.co.uk). Euston
tube/rail. **Open** noon-11pm Mon-Sat; noon-10.30pm Sun. **Food served** noon-10pm Mon-Sat; noon-9pm Sun. **Euston**
The Somers Town Coffee House is a huge place, imbued with a French sensibility. It's divided in two – a spacious front bar, and a restaurant – with additional space on the front terrace, in the back garden and in the rear room (complete with fireplace). Nothing seems too much trouble for the excellent staff, whether you're here for food or simply a drink. If you're in the latter category, you'll find ales (Wells Bombardier, Wadworth 6X), lagers (Red Stripe, Kirin Ichiban) and, best of all, a good wine list, organised into descriptive categories by the two sisters from Normandy who are behind the enterprise: 'dense and concentrated red, oak ageing', for example. Authentic French food runs from fish soup with all the trimmings to magret of duck with orange sauce, golden beetroot and glazed turnips. The bar menu tempts with such savouries as own-made crab beignets with salsa verde.
Babies & children admitted (until 5pm). Booking advisable. Disabled: toilet. Tables outdoors (20, garden; 20, terrace). Wireless internet.

Temperance

74-76 York Street, W1H 1QN (7262 1513, www.thetemperance.co.uk). Edgware Road or Marylebone tube. **Open** noon-11pm Mon-Sat; noon-10.30pm Sun. **Food served** noon-3pm Mon; noon-3pm, 6-10pm Tue-Fri; noon-8pm Sat; noon-4pm Sun. **Marylebone**

Simple but effective, this large, dark and sometimes lively bar on a quiet Marylebone street provides quality sustenance to diner and drinker alike. The Temperance's lunchtime menu, which changes daily, moves beyond gastropub clichés to take in the likes of black-eyed pea, chickpea and aubergine stew; after 5pm, it's Brit-style tapas along the lines of mini chipolatas and whitebait with tartare sauce, as well as an appetising cheeseboard. Beer drinkers will find San Miguel, Sharp's Doom Bar, Ringwood and Beck's Vier on the bar, plus bottles of Moretti and Corona behind it, while some 15 wines come by the glass. There's also a dining room upstairs, and pavement seating for smokers.
Babies & children admitted. Booking advisble Thur-Sat. Function room (40 capacity). Tables outdoors (3, pavement). Wireless internet. **Map p238 F5.**

Thomas Cubitt

44 Elizabeth Street, SW1W 9PA (7730 6060, www.thethomascubitt.co.uk). Victoria tube/rail. **Open** noon-11pm daily. **Food served** noon-9.30pm daily. **Victoria**
After a little refit in spring 2010, this upmarket brasserie is busy nearly every mealtime, a Belgravia clientele venturing towards Victoria

coach station in order to partake in roast rack and braised shoulder of lamb, and a pumpkin, spinach and pine nut wellington. The Sunday roasts are worthy of a Waitrose TV ad, but you'll pay £27 for the 28-day-aged fillet from the Castle of Mey estate in Caithness. The layout of the main bar lends itself more to dining, but you can drink there. A 30-strong wine selection includes a dozen at around £6.50 a glass (Levin Wines sauvignon blanc from the Loire Valley, De Alto Rioja) or £22 a bottle. Cocktails include a Basil Fawlty (Belvedere vodka, apple juice, passionfruit and own-made ginger syrup). You'll find Asahi and Bitburger among the bottled beers, plus Deuchars and Adnams on tap.
Babies & children admitted. Function rooms (12, 20, 30, 42 capacity). Tables outdoors (8, pavement). **Map p249 H10.**

White Swan Pub & Dining Room

108 Fetter Lane, EC4A 1ES (7242 9696, www.thewhiteswanlondon.com). Chancery Lane tube. **Open** 11am-midnight Mon-Thur; 11am-1am Fri. **Food served** noon-3pm, 6-10pm Mon-Fri. **City**
British food, quality wines and intimate but comfortable surroundings are the keys to this City gastropub, cloistered away in a little-known corner by the Breams Building. No, it's not

Drapers Arms. *See p139.*

cheap – £14.95 for fish 'n' chips with pea purée tells its own story. However, discerning and well-salaried regulars can look forward to a choice of two dozen wines by the glass (from French pinot noirs to British vintages from Kent's Chapel Down vineyard), eight varieties of classic and classic-inspired cocktail (whisky sours, cosmopolitan and the like, priced at a reasonable £7.50) and two or three ales on tap (London Pride, Adnams Broadside). Diners can settle down in the comparatively informal main bar at street level, overlooked by prime bar seats in the curved mezzanine, or in the brighter and more formal dining room upstairs.
Babies & children admitted. Booking advisable (dining room). Function room (50 capacity). Wireless internet. **Map p243 N6.**

Also recommended...

1 Lombard Street (Cocktails & Spirits, *p20*); **28°-50° Wine Workshop & Kitchen** (Wine Bars, *p48*); **Anthologist** (Good Mixers, *p172*); **Bar Battu** (Wine Bars, *p49*); **Barrica** (Wine Bars, *p49*); **Benugo Bar & Kitchen** (Good Mixers, *p173*); **Bleeding Heart Tavern** (Wine Bars, *p50*); **Brasserie Max** (Hotel Bars, *p41*); **Camino** (Good Mixers, *p175*); **Capote y Toros** (Wine Bars, *p51*); **Cellar Gascon** (Wine Bars, *p52*); **Cinnamon Club** (Cocktails & Spirits, *p22*); **Circus** (Clubs & Music Venues, *p205*); **Cottons** (Cocktails & Spirits, *p22*); **Dollar** (Cocktails & Spirits, *p23*); **Ebury Wine Bar & Restaurant** (Wine Bars, *p52*); **Endurance** (Good Mixers, *p177*); **Folly** (Good Mixers, *p178*); **Fox & Anchor** (Classic Pubs, *p68*); **Guinea** (Classic Pubs, *p70*); **Hakkasan** (Cocktails & Spirits, *p26*); **Hawksmoor** (Cocktails & Spirits, *p27*); **Kings Arms** (Classic Pubs, *p71*); **Lexington** (Clubs & Music Venues, *p206*); **Mark's Bar** (Cocktails & Spirits, *p28*); **Medcalf** (Good Mixers, *p179*); **Newman Arms** (Classic Pubs, *p73*); **Punchbowl** (Classic Pubs, *p74*); **Shochu Lounge** (Cocktails & Spirits, *p30*); **Skylon** (Rooms with a View, *p161*); **Terroirs** (Wine Bars, *p54*); **Vinoteca** (Wine Bars, *p54*); **Zuma** (Cocktails & Spirits, *p31*).

North

Bald-Faced Stag
69 High Road, N2 8AB (8442 1201, www. realpubs.co.uk). East Finchley tube. **Open** noon-11pm Mon-Wed, Sun; noon-11.30pm Thur; noon-midnight Fri, Sat. **Food served** noon-3.30pm, 6-10.30pm Mon-Fri; noon-4.30pm, 6-10.30pm Sat; noon-9.30pm Sun. **East Finchley**

This fine contemporary drinkerie-restaurant stays true to its previous guise as a long-established local (note the pre-war photographs of social gatherings, crowded omnibuses and Finchley's old skating rink), but now offers the kind of environment designed to please today's demanding urbanite – the bar stools have smooth, soft-leather seats, which should give you the general idea. While not the be-all and end-all, beers are a strength: ales from Sharp's, among others, plus the continental likes of Moretti and Bitburger. The bar food is decent and far from snobbish, especially considering the restaurant serves the elevated and expensive likes of pork loin (£15): a lamb kofte is £6, and there's a simple deli board of cured meats and pickles. Wines are numerous and notable.
Babies & children admitted. Disabled: toilet. Entertainment (quiz 6.30pm Wed; jazz musicians 7.30pm 1st Wed of mth). Tables outdoors (23, garden). Wireless internet.

Bull & Last
168 Highgate Road, NW5 1QS (7267 3641, www.thebullandlast.co.uk). Kentish Town tube/rail then 214, C2 bus, or Gospel Oak rail then C11 bus. **Open** noon-11pm Mon-Thur; noon-midnight Fri, Sat; noon-10.30pm Sun. **Food served** noon-3pm, 6.30-10pm Mon-Fri; 12.30-3.30pm, 6.30-10pm Sat; 12.30-3.30pm, 7-9pm Sun. **Kentish Town**

Ideal for a post-prandial stroll on Parliament Hill Fields, this gastropub is at times a victim of its own success: at busy times, you may find your hunger being whetted to a keen edge. Which is no bad thing, as the cooking is pretty special, after all – a seasonal menu of well-reared ingredients combined in ways that hark to the past yet seem thoroughly modern. Lamb ploughman's comes with an anchovy beignet and bleu d'auvergne cheese; a flaky-topped pie is made with ox cheek accompanied by roast bone marrow. You'll find around six bottles under £20 on the wine list, plus bin end deals, but the Bull & Last is serious about its ales, including Black Sheep, Doom Bar and Mad Goose. Finish with a superb own-made ice-cream.
Babies & children admitted. Booking advisable. Function room (80 capacity). Tables outdoors (5, pavement). Wireless internet.

Charles Lamb
16 Elia Street, N1 8DE (7837 5040, www.thecharleslambpub.com). Angel tube. **Open** 4-11pm Mon, Tue; noon-11pm Wed-Sat; noon-10.30pm Sun. **Food served** 6-9.30pm Mon, Tue; noon-3pm, 6-9.30pm Wed-Sat; noon-6pm Sun. **Islington**

Named after the famed 18th-century essayist who lived around the corner on Colebrooke Row, the Charles Lamb opened quietly in 2007. However, this upscale corner local feels like it's been here for a good deal longer, such is the degree to which it's become part of the fabric of the surrounding neighbourhood (it was at the heart of the area's Royal Wedding street party celebrations, for example). The regulars are a highbrow, high-spirited bunch; some are here simply for the drinks, which usually include three or more ales, Breton cider and Kernel IPA in bottles, while others tackle the aspirational gastropub cooking that generally impresses. All this is served by friendly staff in a pair of small, handsome rooms – spruced up in April 2011 – with wooden floors, decorated with menu blackboards, letterpress prints and other tasteful ephemera. You'd like it in your part of town.
Babies & children admitted. Bookings not accepted. Games (board games). Tables outdoors (6, pavement). Map p255 O2.

Clissold Arms
105 Fortis Green, N2 9HR (8444 4224, www.clissoldarms.co.uk). East Finchley tube. **Open** noon-11pm Mon-Thur; noon-midnight Fri, Sat; noon-10.30pm Sun. **Food served** noon-4pm, 6-10pm Mon-Sat; noon-9pm Sun. **Muswell Hill**

The Clissold Arms is famed as the site of the Kinks' first gig (Ray and Dave Davies grew up nearby in Denmark Terrace), so it's no surprise that there's now a whole room dedicated to the Kinks, inventively called 'The Kinks Room'. Most of the pub is now given over to a rather bright, scrubbed-oak and beige restaurant area designed to appeal to well-heeled Muswell Hill diners, with plenty of space for families at weekends; there's also a covered terrace, heated in winter, open-air in summer. Food follows a familiar gastropub style (pork loin, sirloin steak) but sometimes comes with more full-on flavours: pan-fried fillet of Cornish sea bass with ratatouille, red pepper velouté and sage tapenade, for instance. The cask ales are well kept and the wine list is extensive but pricey.
Babies & children admitted. Booking advisable. Disabled: toilet. Function room (70 capacity). Tables outdoors (30, terrace).

Drapers Arms
44 Barnsbury Street, N1 1ER (7619 0348, www.thedrapersarms.com). Highbury & Islington tube/rail. **Open** 11am-midnight Mon-Fri; 10am-midnight Sat; 10am-11pm Sun. **Food served** noon-3pm, 6-10.30pm Mon-Sat; noon-4pm, 6.30-9.30pm Sun. **Islington**
Renovated and reopened in 2009 by Nick Gibson and Ben Maschler (son of restaurant critic Fay), this is Islingtonian gastropub culture at its most gorgeous, offering top-notch, seasonal fare in spotless eggshell-blue

Duke of Cambridge. *See p141.*

Pantechnicon Public House & Dining Room. *See p134.*

surroundings. Those just here for the beer may choose from a long line of taps dispensing ales (Truman's Runner, Dark Star Hophead, Thornbridge Jaipur) and continental beers (Bitburger, Staropramen); six wines of each colour come by the glass, half-litre or bottle, with 60 others by the bottle in the full list. The drinks accompany a daily-changing menu, featuring the likes of grilled razor clams, braised short ribs and slow-cooked lamb shoulder. The pub's name is reflected in a scissors mural, complementing three fireplaces, shelves of paperbacks and a pile of board games; a verdant beer garden exudes an equal amount of class.
Babies & children admitted. Booking advisable weekends. Function room (50 capacity). Games (board games). Tables outdoors (8, garden). Wireless internet. **Map p255 N1.**

Duke of Cambridge
30 St Peter's Street, N1 8JT (7359 3066, www.dukeorganic.co.uk). Angel tube.
Open noon-11pm Mon-Sat; noon-10.30pm Sun. **Food served** 12.30-3pm, 6.30-10.30pm Mon-Sat; 12.30-3.30pm, 6.30-10pm Sun.
Islington
The organic bandwagon continues to roll all over the city, and this long-serving gastropub continues to do the towing. The Duke of Cambridge opened in 1998, long before the countrywide trend for organic food, and is still going strong, serving a mix of drinkers and diners in its capacious, airy corner premises. The enterprise remains much as it ever was: largely excellent gastropub food, made with seasonal local ingredients and served at prices that range from above-average to eye-watering; service that jumps from fabulous to indifferent, sometimes within the course of a single meal; and a decent range of drinks, including Pitfield ales, Freedom lagers and some unusual wines. Pleasingly, drinkers are made to feel as welcome as diners, not always the case at a venue with such a reputation for its food.
Babies & children admitted. Booking advisable. Function room (100 capacity). Tables outdoors (4, pavement). **Map p255 O2.**

Junction Tavern
101 Fortess Road, NW5 1AG (7485 9400, www.junctiontavern.co.uk). Tufnell Park tube or Kentish Town tube/rail. **Open** noon-11pm Mon-Fri; 11.30am-11pm Sat; noon-10.30pm Sun. **Food served** noon-3pm, 5.30-10.30pm Mon-Fri; noon-4pm, 6.30-10.30pm Sat; noon-9.30pm Sun. **Kentish Town**

This place has clearly been built around the classic gastropub formula, but it's hard to complain when that formula is delivered quite so well. Mac, the bear-like house dog, wanders through the pub but is generally discouraged from the dining area, where the menus change frequently with a nice eye to seasonality. While not over-long, they still offer an attractive and consistently enjoyable choice of inventive dishes and old favourites. The pub's three spaces (big wooden tables around the front bar, a spacious conservatory, and a leafy terrace for summer) make it ideal for long, leisurely lunches, though you can just drink here: the wine list is very well priced and user-friendly, and the beer is also a strength, with regular festivals complementing the five year-round handpumps. Despite the place's popularity, the welcoming staff never seem overrun or flustered.
Babies & children admitted (until 7pm). Tables outdoors (15, garden). Wireless internet. **Map p254 J24.**

Lansdowne
90 Gloucester Avenue, NW1 8HX (7483 0409, www.thelansdownepub.co.uk). Chalk Farm tube or bus 31, 168. **Open** noon-11pm Mon-Sat; noon-10.30pm Sun. **Food served** noon-3pm, 6-10pm Mon-Fri; 12.30-3.30pm, 6-10pm Sat; 9-11.30am, 12.30-3.30pm, 6-9.30pm Sun. **Chalk Farm**
You'll find a mixed bunch of punters, from young families to dog walkers, gathered in this expansive, communal-dining-room-cum-pub. Tables are uncomfortably squeezed together in the main bar; stools at the counter act as a holding area before tables become free, or offer mid-afternoon relaxation after a walk around nearby Primrose Hill. For the ale hunter, there's Wells Bombardier and Truman's Runner on draught; the wine drinker is spoiled for choice, with many options by the glass. Those not keen on sitting down to a whole black bream with romesco sauce or braised lamb shank with cinnamon, greens and pearl barley can opt for a steak sandwich. A few tables outside catch the afternoon sun.
Babies & children admitted. Booking advisable. Disabled: toilet. Function room (50 capacity). Tables outdoors (10, pavement). Wireless internet. **Map p254 G26.**

Marquess Tavern
32 Canonbury Street, N1 2TB (7354 2975, www.themarquesstavern.co.uk). Angel tube or Highbury & Islington tube/rail. **Open** 5-11pm Mon-Thur; 4pm-midnight Fri; noon-midnight Sat; noon-10.30pm Sun. **Food served** 6-10pm Mon-Fri; noon-5pm, 6-10pm Sat; noon-5pm, 6-8pm Sun. **Islington**

Prince Arthur. See p144.

The board outside advertises the Marquess as 'the pub to try before you die'. It isn't quite *that* good, but it does a fine job of catering to diner and drinker alike. Run by five former customers, the pub attracts a lively professional crowd to its busy, four-square counter, behind which are almost as many beers and whiskies as wines. On tap, a row of Young's, Heineken, Peroni (albeit at £4.10 a pint) and Leffe complement 30 bottled options from Belgium, Scotland (Kelpie's Seaweed Ale, gooseberry-flavoured Grozet Premium), Germany (Jever Pilsener, Köstritzer Schwarzbier), Australia (Cooper's Pale and Sparkling) and Epping (the new home of the Pitfield Brewery). Seasonal fare is offered in the back room, though the award-winning gastropub meals are now restricted to Fridays and Saturdays; the rest of the week, it's classic thin-crust pizzas and Sunday roasts. *Babies & children admitted (until 7pm). Entertainment (quiz 8pm Tue). Function room (12 capacity). Tables outdoors (6, patio). Wireless internet.* **Map p255 P26.**

Northgate
113 Southgate Road, N1 3JS (7359 7392). Essex Road rail or bus 21, 141. **Open** 5-11pm Mon-Thur; 5pm-midnight fri; 11am-midnight Sat; noon-10.30pm Sun. **Food served** 6.30-

10.30pm Mon-Fri; 11.30am-3pm, 6.30-10.30pm Sat; noon-4pm, 6.30-9.30pm Sun. **Islington** Neatly named for its location on the corner of Northchurch and Southgate Roads, this pub conversion has been overshadowed by two newer openings, the Duke of Wellington to the north and the Scolt Head to the east. Still, it retains a band of loyal regulars, happy to take root for the evening in the expansive pub space or the plain but popular streetfront beer garden. Inside, blackboard menus, an abundance of wood, a few decent ales and a large, separate dining area with an open kitchen all suggest an archetypal modern gastropub, but this place does it better than many. On tap you'll find a few real ales, and the decent wine menu has several options by the glass. *Babies & children admitted. Booking advisable Fri-Sun (restaurant). Tables outdoors (10, patio).*

Oxford
256 Kentish Town Road, NW5 2AA (7485 3521, www.theoxfordnw5.co.uk). Kentish Town tube. **Open** noon-11.30pm Mon, Tue; noon-midnight Wed-Sat; noon-10.30pm Sun. **Food served** noon-3.30pm, 6-10pm Mon-Wed; noon-3.30pm, 6-10.30pm Thur, Fri; noon-4pm, 6-10.30pm Sat; noon-10pm Sun. **Kentish Town** The floor tiles at the entrance spell out the year 1863, but the makeover at this convivial venue ensures it belongs to post-Blair London. The expansive, high-ceilinged one-room space is divided between a dining area and open kitchen on the far side, and a lived-in bar as you walk in. Coat hooks are provided beneath a bar counter begging to be propped up; chesterfields and olive-coloured divans complement the pews and regular bar seating. This is an authentic pub with contemporary touches. Pumps of quality ales – Harveys Sussex Best, Timothy Taylor Landlord, Shepherd Neame Bishop's Finger – line up with taps of Sagres and Heineken, with wines numbering a dozen. Copies of the daily menu are placed on each table (28-day-aged Scotch rib-eye steak, Mersea Island rock oysters, pork board for two to share). A 45-cover upstairs dining room copes with overflow and private bookings. *Babies & children admitted (until 8pm). Booking advisable evenings. Disabled: toilet. Entertainment (musicians 8pm Mon; quiz 7.45pm Tue; comedy 7.45pm Wed, Thur). Function room (80 capacity). Tables outdoors (7, pavement). Wireless internet.*

Queens
49 Regent's Park Road, NW1 8XD (7586 0408, www.youngs.co.uk). Chalk Farm tube or bus 31, 168, 274. **Open** 11am-11pm

Mon-Sat; noon-10.30pm Sun. **Food served** noon-3pm, 6-10pm Mon-Fri; noon-10pm Sat; noon-8pm Sun. **Primrose Hill**
Close enough to Primrose Hill to attract hikers and dog walkers, the Queens has re-entered the Young's fold (the Young's sign hanging outside remained a constant through the changes in management), with Kronenbourg and Peroni accompanying the signature brews on draught. Customers at the raised front tables overlooking the street, and in the tartan-tinged back area, are served by the one narrow strip of bar – when things get busy, the decked outdoor area fills up. There are great views from the upstairs dining room and terrace, where lunches (Cumberland sausage sandwich, 8oz rump steak) and dinners (fresh oysters, pan-fried salmon) are served.
Babies & children admitted (restaurant). Booking advisable. Entertainment (quiz 7.30pm Thur). Function room (60 capacity). Tables outdoors (4, balcony; 2, pavement). Wireless internet.

Also recommended...
Crown & Goose (Good Mixers, *p183*); **Star** (Classic Pubs, *p82*); **Swimmer at the Grafton Arms** (Classic Pubs, *p82*).

North East

Cat & Mutton
76 Broadway Market, E8 4QJ (7254 5599). London Fields rail. **Open** noon-11pm Mon-Wed, Sun; noon-midnight Thur; noon-1am Fri; 11am-1am Sat. **Food served** noon-3pm, 6.30-10pm Mon-Fri; 11am-4pm, 7-10pm Sat; noon-7pm Sun. **Hackney**
Show up at this corner pub on a Sunday lunchtime and you'll think you've walked into an estate agent's advertisement for urban living. Artfully scruffy and unnecessarily sunglassed thirtysomethings wake up with a pint and dissect last night's adventures; affluent couples tuck into decent gastropub cooking; bar staff mill about looking like everyone's cooler older brother or sister. It's all very New Hackney, a far cry from the days when this was the kind of pub in which drinkers occasionally got glassed at the bar. Every Tuesday, there's a quiz hosted by the presumably pseudonymous Quizzee Rascal and Lethal Quizzal; if you chuckled at the pop-culture reference, then this just might be your kind of place.
Babies & children admitted. Disabled: toilet. Function room (80 capacity). Tables outdoors (5, pavement).

Princess of Shoreditch.
See p146.

Londesborough Pub & Dining Room

36 Barbauld Road, N16 0SS (7254 5865, www.thelondesborough.com). Stoke Newington rail or bus 73, 393, 476. **Open** 5-11pm Mon-Thur; 5pm-midnight Fri; noon-midnight Sat; noon-10.30pm Sun. **Food served** 6-10.30pm Mon-Fri; noon-10.30pm Sat; noon-9.30pm Sun. **Stoke Newington**

This backstreet Stokey local, buried in the complicated network of residential streets behind Church Street, has been spruced up lately after some time in the doldrums. It's a big place, even bigger than it looks from its street-corner location, and a difficult one to fill. The deepish dining room can feel somewhat tumbleweedy when it's not busy, which is often the case early in the week, and the bare-brick decor doesn't encourage intimacy. As a result, you're better off staying at the front, close to the big picture windows and the imposing bar. Still, that shouldn't detract from its virtues: a couple of ales, worthwhile cocktails, sturdy gastropub grub, a cosy garden and staff who are keen to make you feel at home. Worth a second look. *Babies & children admitted. Entertainment (DJs 10.30pm Fri, Sat; see website for details). Tables outdoors (10, garden). Wireless internet.*

Prince

59 Kynaston Road, N16 0EB (7923 4766, www.theprincepub.com). Stoke Newington rail or bus 73, 393, 476. **Open** 5-11pm Mon-Thur; noon-midnight Fri, Sat; noon-10.30pm Sun. **Food served** 5-11pm Mon-Thur; noon-11pm Fri, Sat; noon-9pm Sun. **Stoke Newington**

Tucked away in the residential labyrinth behind the corner of the High Street and Church Street in Stoke Newington, this is one of the nicer drinking options in a part of London with more than its share of mediocre pubs. The first thing you see as you walk through the corner door is four handpumps (Sharp's Doom Bar, Black Sheep Ale and others). But there are also novel ciders and a pretty decent wine list, among other drinking options. Food is a selling point – gastropub-style cooking that's perhaps a little too pricey but, especially at Sunday lunchtimes, ticks most of the comfort-cooking boxes. The locals are a friendly bunch, as are the staff. *Babies & children admitted. Disabled: toilet. Function room (50 capacity). Tables outdoors (8, garden).*

Prince Arthur

95 Forest Road, E8 3BH (7249 9996, www.theprincearthurlondonfields.com). Bus 38, 242, 277. **Open** 4-11pm Mon-Thur; 3-11pm Fri; 10.30am-11pm Sat, Sun. **Food served** 6-10pm Mon-Thur; 6-10pm Fri; noon-4.30pm, 6-10pm Sat; noon-9pm Sun. **Hackney**

The Prince George pretty much had this area to itself for years, but the comparatively recent renovations of the Spurstowe and this corner gastropub, formerly the Lady Diana, have provided it with much-needed competition. The Prince Arthur is the smartest of the various gastropubs run by Tom and Ed Martin – others include the Gun (*see right*) in Docklands and the Botanist in Belgravia – but it wears its upmarket status easily. While there's an understandable emphasis on the food (good but pricey), drinkers are by no means excluded: this is still a place to enjoy a quiet pint, whether at the handsome, dark wooden bar or at one of the plain, pubby tables. London Pride, Bitburger and a strong wine list fuel conversations in a room that, quite unlike its local competitors, usually remains low-key. *Babies & children admitted. Disabled: toilet. Entertainment (quiz 8pm Mon). Games (board games). Tables outdoors (4, pavement). Wireless internet.*

Also recommended...

Dove (Beer Specialists, *p114*); **Scolt Head** (Classic Pubs, *p84*).

East

Fox

28 Paul Street, EC2A 4LB (7729 5708, www.thefoxpublichouse.co.uk). Old Street tube/rail. **Open** noon-11pm Mon-Fri; 6-11pm Sat; noon-5pm Sun. **Food served** noon-3pm, 6-10pm Mon-Fri; 6-10pm Sat; noon-4pm Sun. **Shoreditch**

The Fox is an after-work magnet on Thursdays and Fridays, when you can hardly see the bar for bodies. Outside peak hours, though, it's a very pleasant place for a drink, just far enough from Shoreditch's main drag to ensure that it isn't dominated by bright young things. Plus points include an attractive ground-floor room, modernised but not ruined, with a big central bar and etched-glass windows, moreish bar food dished up as small plates by the same kitchen that serves the lovely first-floor restaurant, and a generally relaxed vibe. The fine range of wines is complemented by a couple of ales; Harveys Sussex Best usually seems to be among them. Worth considering if you're in the area. *Babies & children admitted. Disabled: toilet. Function room (12 capacity). Tables outdoors (6, terrace; 3, pavement). Wireless internet.* **Map p244 Q4.**

Narrow. *See p146.*

Gun
*27 Coldharbour, E14 9NS (7515 5222,
www.thegundocklands.com). Blackwall or
Canary Wharf DLR.* **Open** 11am-midnight
Mon-Sat; 11am-11pm Sun. **Food served**
noon-3pm, 6-10.30pm Mon-Fri; noon-4pm,
6-10.30pm Sat; noon-4pm, 6.30-9.30pm Sun.
Docklands
The Gun occupies a Grade II-listed building
that Tom and Ed Martin reopened in 2004 after
a three-year restoration. The brothers have
since rolled out their formula – essentially,
'posh gastropub' – all over the city, from the
Botanist in Belgravia to the Prince Arthur (*see
left*) in Hackney, but the Gun remains in fine
fettle. In front of dark-wooden shelving
punctuated by tiled columns, good-humoured
staff dole out draught ales and lagers to
standing drinkers. The back room, so bijou that
you'll have no choice but to socialise, maintains
an air of tipsy bonhomie; in summer, you could
do worse than take a glass of viognier out on
to the rear terrace and marvel at the view of
the O2 while enjoying something from the
barbecue. Back inside, contented chatter
provides the soundtrack to diners sampling
dishes such as Welsh salt-marsh saddle of
lamb at the tables beyond the main bar.

*Babies & children admitted. Booking
advisable. Disabled: toilet. Function rooms
(16, 22, 74 capacity). Tables outdoors
(11, riverside terrace). Wireless internet.*

Morgan Arms
*43 Morgan Street, E3 5AA (8980 6389,
www.capitalpubcompany.com). Mile End
tube.* **Open** noon-11pm Mon-Thur, Sun;
noon-midnight Fri, Sat. **Food served**
noon-3pm, 7-10pm Mon-Sat; noon-3.30pm,
7-9pm Sun. **Bow**
A large, significantly upgraded corner pub
on a quiet residential street, the Morgan has
a country-kitchen vibe. Its gastropub status is
signalled by a large triptych of garlic and fresh
produce on the wall of the main bar area, the
continental awning outside and the separate
dining area with a chalked-up daily menu at its
entrance. Food doesn't disappoint: diners may
find mains such as chargrilled 21-day-aged rib-
eye steak; roast cod with mash and purple
sprouting broccoli; or roast pork belly stuffed
with prune, sage and apple. But drinkers are not
forgotten: Sharp's Doom Bar, Adnams and
Bitburger are served from a small bar counter,
and there'll be about three dozen wine choices
on the regularly updated list.

Babies & children admitted. Disabled: toilet. Function room (40 capacity). Tables outdoors (4, pavement; 3, garden). Wireless internet.

Narrow
44 Narrow Street, E14 8DP (7592 7950, www.gordonramsay.com/thenarrow). Limehouse DLR. **Open** noon-11pm Mon-Sat; noon-10.30pm Sun. **Food served** 11.30am-3pm, 6-11pm Mon-Fri; noon-4pm, 5.30-11pm Sat; noon-4pm, 5.30-10.30pm Sun. **Limehouse**
The conservatory-styled restaurant area along the outside of this Gordon Ramsay gastropub offers a fine view of the revamped Limehouse dock. Inside the red-bricked building itself, through a surprisingly small front hallway, the main bar is roomy and traditionally decorated, the walls adorned with period photographs. Draught beers include Leffe, Peroni and offerings from the reliable Meantime, which also provides some bottled options. Bar food ranges from pickled whelks and cockles to Gloucester Old Spot sausages with grain-mustard mash and red-pepper relish. Wine lovers are well served here, with a 2009 bacchus from Chapel Down in Kent, and a sweet Hungarian Tokaji 5 Puttonyos, just two of many possibilities. While there's the vague sensation of upmarket Wetherspoons about the place,

the Narrow is popular enough to suggests that Ramsay has hit upon a successful formula. *Babies & children admitted (restaurant). Booking advisable. Disabled: toilet. Entertainment (quiz 8pm Mon). Function room (14 capacity). Tables outdoors (36, riverside terrace).*

Princess of Shoreditch
76-78 Paul Street, EC2A 4NE (7729 9270, www.theprincessofshoreditch.com). Old Street tube/rail or bus 55. **Open** noon-11pm daily. **Food served** *Bar* noon-3pm, 6.30-10pm Mon-Fri; noon-4pm, 6.30-10pm Sat; noon-8pm Sun. *Restaurant* noon-3pm, 6.30-10pm Tue-Fri; 6.30-10pm Sat; noon-8pm Sun. **Shoreditch**
The previous Princess gastropub lasted four years, a lifetime in Shoreditch terms. There wasn't much wrong with the old place, which might be why the current owners haven't altered its appearance too much. Originally dating from 1742, the two-storey corner site has big Georgian windows, gaps in the floorboards you can see through and a cast-iron spiral staircase that links the lively ground-floor pub and the smarter first-floor dining room. Downstairs, Shoreditch creatives drown their sorrows as art budgets plummet, tweeting and texting over pints of

Garrison

Tring's straw-coloured Side Pocket for a Toad. There's good pub food on offer here: sausage and mash, crumble and custard. But the eats are better and pricier in the dining room (where bookings are accepted, unlike the bar), whose antique is feel enhanced by large photographic portraits of a Victorian music-hall diva. *Babies & children admitted (until 6.30pm). Booking advisable (restaurant). Function room (15 capacity). Wireless internet.* **Map p244 Q4.**

Royal Oak

73 Columbia Road, E2 7RG (7729 2220, www.royaloaklondon.com). Hoxton rail or bus 26, 48, 55. **Open** 5-11pm Mon-Fri; noon-11pm Sat; 11am-10.30pm Sun. **Food served** *Bar* 6-10pm Mon-Fri; noon-4pm, 6-10pm Sat; 11am-4pm, 6-9pm Sun. *Restaurant* 7-9pm Tue-Sat; noon-4pm Sun. **Shoreditch**
To misquote the late Brian Moore, this is a pub of two halves. Upstairs is a cultured, calm and almost sedate dining room, within which nouveau Eastenders tuck into expensive but impressive Modern European cooking. Downstairs in the good-looking pub, built around a handsome central bar, the scene is more boisterous, as easily distracted staff deliver pricey wines and ales to an assortment of vintage-clad creatives who keep the hum of conversation going throughout the night. It's at its best earlier in the week: Fridays and Saturdays can be uncomfortably frantic, and the flower market on the doorstep means Sundays can be a crush. Keen-eyed sitcom enthusiasts may recognise the Royal Oak from its starring role in *Goodnight Sweetheart*, although the current owners seem strangely reluctant to advertise the source of the pub's 15 minutes. *Babies & children admitted. Booking advisable (dining). Tables outdoors (4, yard).* **Map p246 S3.**

Also recommended...

Book Club (Good Mixers, *p186*); **Boundary Rooftop** (Rooms with a View, *p163*); **Carpenters Arms** (Beer Specialists, *p116*); **Hemingway** (Good Mixers, *p188*); **Mason & Taylor** (Beer Specialists, *p116*); **Owl & Pussycat** (Good Mixers, *p189*).

South East

Garrison

99-101 Bermondsey Street, SE1 3XB (7089 9355, www.thegarrison.co.uk). London Bridge tube/rail. **Open** 8am-11pm Mon-Thur; 8am-midnight Fri; 9am-midnight Sat; 9am-10.30pm

Canton Arms. *See p149.*

Sun. **Food served** 8-11.30am, noon-3pm, 6-10pm Mon-Fri; 9-11.30am, 12.30-4pm, 6-10pm Sat; 9-11.30am, 12.30-4pm, 6-9.30pm Sun. **Bermondsey**
Behind the smoked-glass windows of its green-tiled exterior, the Garrison is assuredly more restaurant than public house. Cat-swingers might be challenged, but diners on various configurations of seating looked happy enough on a spring lunchtime. The bar – where sweeping chrome pipes dispensing draught Franziskaner and Staropramen graze on a bevelled, white-tiled front – stands next to the open kitchen, edged at one end by hanging baskets of fruit and vegetables. From here, dishes such as lamb neck navarin, and asparagus, broad bean and pea risotto are ferried through clustered tables and affably quirky decor to an eager clientele. Both the menu and the wine list are extensive. *Disabled: toilet. Function room (35 capacity).*

Herne Tavern

2 Forest Hill Road, SE22 0RR (8299 9521, www.theherne.net). East Dulwich or Peckham rail, or bus 12, 197. **Open** noon-11pm Mon-Thur; noon-1am Fri, Sat; noon-10.30pm Sun. **Food served** noon-2.30pm, 5.30-9.30pm Mon-Fri; noon-3pm, 5.30-9.30pm Sat; noon-4pm Sun. **East Dulwich**
Is there a better pint in London than the light and hoppy Hogs Back Summer Ale served here? No wonder this operation – 'a traditional family pub,' proclaims the website – is as attractive

Brown Dog. *See p151*

to the workmen at the wood-panelled bar as it is to the families that pack the happily shabby back garden. The Herne was renovated a few years ago, and locals have since come to regard it as a reliable option in this slightly pub-starved part of town. The ales are always good, and the food is another selling point: starters such as own-made gravadlax and scotch duck egg; beautifully rare burgers; chocolate brownie for dessert. Perhaps understandably, given the demographic make-up of the area, families are made to feel very welcome here.
Babies & children admitted (until 9pm). Entertainment (quiz 7.30pm Sun). Function room (60 capacity). Tables outdoors (25, garden).

Rosendale
65 Rosendale Road, SE21 8EZ (8761 9008, www.therosendale.co.uk). East Dulwich or West Dulwich rail. **Open** noon-11pm daily. **Food served** noon-10pm daily. **Dulwich**
The Rosendale is now a resolutely upmarket venture, its sights trained on moneyed diners and on maintaining its reputation as a popular venue for social events. Spacious and blessed with natural light, the huge primary dining area is a split-level affair with high ceilings. A sizeable

Rothko-red painting hangs on the wall to the left of the bar, which offers Everards Tiger and London Pride ales along with an impressive choice of rums; the owner's passion for wine is reflected in the mind-boggling selection. Snacks include fried whitebait, aïoli and sour cream, as well as tempting own-made chocolate cakes. Roll up here in the afternoon, and you may share the space with mothers and kids.
Babies & children admitted (until 7.30pm). Disabled: toilet. Function rooms (45, 100 capacity). Tables outdoors (48, garden).

Also recommended...
Green & Blue (Wine Bars, *p55*);
Old Brewery (Beer Specialists, *p120*);
Royal Oak (Beer Specialists, *p120*);
Victoria Inn (Beer Specialists, *p121*);
Woolpack (Good Mixers, *p191*).

South

Antelope
76 Mitcham Road, SW17 9NG (8672 3888, www.theantelopepub.com). Tooting Broadway tube. **Open** 4pm-midnight Mon-Thur; 4pm-1am Fri; noon-1am Sat; noon-10.30pm Sun.

Food served 4-10.30pm Mon-Fri; noon-4pm, 6-10.30pm Sat; noon-5pm Sun. **Tooting** Tooting's first bona fide gastropub, put together by the people behind the Balham Bowls Club and the Tooting Tram & Social, is a grand Victorian building with many original features. A solid, dark wood bar dominates the drinking area at the front; wooden panelling, saloon lights, velvet bar stools and autumnal colours give the place a cosy feel, the better to enjoy cask-conditioned ales such as Purity UBU, St Austell Tribute and up to five guests. In the back room, the Antelope becomes a full-blown gastropub, specialising in the kind of dishes that a good home cook would relish making: onion tarte tatin; wild garlic, broad bean and pecorino risotto; organic pork cutlet with apple and walnut stuffing. A large function room at the back of the building contains a billiards table, a dartboard and a huge dropdown screen for sports events. *Babies & children admitted. Booking advisable. Disabled: toilet. Entertainment (quiz 8pm Tue; comedy 8pm last Sun of mth). Function room (150 capacity). Tables outdoors (25, garden). Wireless internet.*

Le Bouchon Bordelais
5-9 Battersea Rise, SW11 1HG (7738 0307, www.lebouchon.co.uk). Clapham Junction rail

or bus 35, 37. **Open** 5-11pm Mon; 10.30am-11pm Tue-Thur; 10.30am-midnight Fri, Sat; 10.30am-10pm Sun. **Food served** 6-10pm Mon-Thur; 6-11pm Fri; noon-11pm Sat; 12.30-10pm Sun. **Battersea** This popular enterprise is a classy, continental establishment with a double life as yet another spot in the Clapham/Battersea orbit where as yet unnested grown ups go to drink and find each other. It's all pretty upmarket: rugby plays on TF1 while City types mingle in bistro surroundings and commune over wine (also available by the carafe), Moretti lager or Bulmers cider by the bottle, or a pint of Theakston's, Amstel or Guinness. Excellent food is available (rib-eye steak baguettes with melted emmental, charcuterie platters), but the plastic being casually waved around at the end of the evening is just as likely to be for booze-only carousing. *Babies & children admitted. Function room (60 capacity). Tables outdoors (14, terrace). Wireless internet.* **Map p251 E2.**

Canton Arms
177 South Lambeth Road, SW8 1XP (7582 8710, www.cantonarms.com). Stockwell tube. **Open** 5-11pm Mon; 11am-11pm Tue-Sat; noon-10.30pm Sun.

Cadogan Arms. *See p151.*

Food served 6-10pm Mon; noon-2.30pm, 6-10pm Tue-Sat; noon-4pm Sun. **Stockwell** Not so long ago, this pub was all swirly carpets, warm pints and cigarette smoke, but it's now been Botoxed. The lovely leaded windows with their stained-glass remain; however, the wood-panelled walls have been painted in oxblood and the boards have been laid bare, and Edwardian drawing-room mirrors now hang as ornaments. The drinks have improved: there are now four real ales on tap, which might include Betty Stogs from the Skinner's brewery in Cornwall or O'Hanlon's Port Stout from down in Devon; a well-chosen selection of wines, with eight by the glass; and cheap cocktails. The dining area at the back is the domain of chef Trish Hilferty, formerly of such notable enterprises as the Fox in Shoreditch, Great Queen Street in Covent Garden and the Anchor & Hope in Waterloo, who conjures up modern British dishes in a St-John-moved-on style.
Babies & children admitted (until 9pm). Tables outdoors (7, patio). Wireless internet.

Manor Arms
13 Mitcham Lane, SW16 6LQ (3195 6888, www.themanorarms.com) Streatham rail or bus 249. **Open** 11am-11pm Mon-Thur; 11am-1am Fri, Sat; noon-midnight Sun. **Food served** noon-3pm, 6-10pm Mon-Sat; noon-9pm Sun.

Streatham
A sweeping, pewter-clad bar dominates the ground floor of this art deco pub; behind the bar there's a big and busy open kitchen. Original 1930s oak panelling lines the walls, yet it's light and refreshingly modern in look. Cheery staff intercept you as you walk in and guide you to a table, but it's still a proper pub, with hand-pulled pints including Sambrooks Wandle from Battersea, Purity Pure Gold and Adnams Broadside. But most people are here to dine: a salad of mixed beets, soft goat's cheese and pickled walnuts makes a good start; rib steak is a cut above, accompanied by chips of the skinny, french fry variety. There's a good selection of wines and a diverting Wayne Collins cocktail, but it's the congenial atmosphere and the friendly service that are the real draw.
Babies & children admitted. Booking advisable Thur-Sun. Disabled: toilet. Games (board games). Tables outdoors (16, garden). Wireless internet.

Also recommended...
Draft House (Beer Specialists, *p122*).

Honey Pot. *See p133.*

South West

Brown Dog

28 Cross Street, SW13 0AP (8392 2200, www.thebrowndog.co.uk). Barnes Bridge rail. **Open** noon-11pm daily. **Food served** noon-3pm, 7-10pm Mon-Fri; noon-4pm, 7-10pm Sat; noon-4pm, 7-9pm Sun.
Barnes
It's quite hip, the Brown Dog. Certainly hipper than any place at the end of a complacent residential street with aspirational, French-style door numbers should be. First, there's the interior: Polaroids of dogs, Soviet and Chinese propaganda posters, and a decorative obsession with green cobras. Second, the bar counter, a half-moon shared equally between the Rose Bar and the Saloon Bar, upon which Stowford Press cider, Sambrook's Wandle, Weizen Gold, Twickenham Original and rare Stiegl lager from Stuttgart await inspection. There are some 30 wines and quality food (which can also be enjoyed in the back garden): baked dressed Dorset crab with chips and salad, say, or own-made beefburger. Drawing kits and dog bowls demonstrate that the Brown Dog caters for the whole nuclear family, though it's generally discerning young professionals who drift in with purpose.
Babies & children admitted. Games (board games). Tables outdoors (12, garden). Wireless internet.

Cadogan Arms

298 King's Road, SW3 5UG (7352 6500, www.thecadoganarmschelsea.com). Sloane Square tube then bus 19, 22, 319. **Open** 11am-11pm Mon-Sat; 11am-10.30pm Sun. **Food served** noon-3.30pm, 6-10.30pm Mon-Fri; noon-10.30pm Sat; noon-9pm Sun.
Chelsea
In 2009, this welcoming Chelsea pub was given a countrified look by the Martin Brothers (the Gun in Docklands, Islington's Peasant and others), complete with stuffed creatures and encased fly-fishing displays on the walls. It's still a proper boozer with good ales, but it's also now worth visiting for its cooking, served towards the back in the snug and smoothly run dining area. In summer, you can expect the likes of vivid green pea soup garnished with pancetta, double cream and microgreens; and duck breast, neatly cut into fingers (with the fat rendered away) and placed on a salad of green beans, beetroot and potato. Puddings tend towards the old school, such as a rum and raisin sticky toffee pudding, served with butterscotch sauce and vanilla ice-cream. The wine list offers many intriguing

choices, and there's also a good cheeseboard. A formula Martin Brothers gastropub, perhaps – but what a formula.
Babies & children admitted. Entertainment (quiz 7.30pm Mon). Function room (50 capacity). Wireless internet. **Map p248 C5.**

Earl Spencer

260-262 Merton Road, SW18 5JL (8870 9244, www.theearlspencer.co.uk). Southfields tube. **Open** 11am-11pm Mon-Thur; 11am-midnight Fri, Sat; noon-10.30pm Sun. **Food served** 12.30-2.30pm, 7-10pm Mon-Sat; 12.30-3pm, 7-9.30pm Sun.
Wimbledon
Although the blue frontage and blue-painted terrace tables are somehow at odds with the humdrum surroundings, this is a very smart joint. Both food and drink are worth a trip. Sought-after ales (Hook Norton's Old Hooky, Sharp's Doom Bar, Fuller's London Pride) and standard lagers line the long, low bar that joins two spacious areas of the large, high-ceilinged interior. Wines and bar food are also superior: a choice of almost 30 wines (with a handful by the glass) can be matched with nibbles such as Normandy oysters and Atlantic prawns. A photocopied daily menu might list chargrilled sardines or lamb shoulder goulash with steamed rice; children are treated to small portions of old-school favourites. Little wonder punters are beating a path to SW18.
Babies & children admitted. Function room (100 capacity). Tables outdoors (10, patio). Wireless internet.

Fox & Grapes

9 Camp Road, SW19 4UN (8619 1300, www.foxandgrapeswimbledon.co.uk). Wimbledon tube/rail. **Open** noon-11pm Mon-Thur; 11am-midnight Fri, Sat; noon-10.30pm Sun. **Food served** noon-3pm, 6-9.30pm Mon-Sat; noon-4pm, 6-9pm Sun.
Wimbledon
This pub has long had one of London's best locations, on the edge of Wimbledon Common, well away from traffic; the area feels, and looks, like rural Surrey. The old Fox & Grapes was a bit of an underachiever, but Claude Bosi and his team have taken it over, given it a huge refurb, added three guest rooms and begun serving smart gastropub food at smart restaurant prices. A menu based around British pub favourites has been deconstructed, refined, and put back together. It changes by the season but might include starters of pork pie, or a salad of warm beetroot, endive, goat's cheese and walnuts, and mains such as roast pork belly accompanied by rich black pudding, or a fillet

of pollock on a bed on puy lentils. The wine list, featuring many organic varieties by small growers, likewise changes regularly. Symonds cider, Amstel, Sharp's Doom Bar and Black Sheep Bitter are among the draught options. *Babies & children admitted. Function room (50 capacity). Wireless internet.*

Harwood Arms
Corner of Walham Grove & Farm Lane, SW6 1QP (7386 1847, www.harwoodarms. com). Fulham Broadway tube. **Open** 5-11pm Mon; noon-midnight Tue-Sat; noon-11pm Sun. **Food served** 6.30-9.30pm Mon; noon-3pm, 6.30-9.30pm Tue-Sat; 12.30-4pm, 7-9pm Sun. **Fulham**
Snagging a table has become far more difficult since a Michelin star was awarded to this terrific gastropub – a source of frustration, surely, for the locals who saw it as a neighbourhood watering hole that happened to serve brilliant food. How spoiled they are, with the bar stocked with an excellent range of real ales on draught, an affordable wine list and a menu conscious of both provenance and seasonality. Co-owner Mike Robinson shoots all the venison used in dishes such as a platter of roe deer starters (scotch egg, rissole, tartare, smoked ham), and grilled fallow deer chops; snails with stout-braised oxtail and bone marrow has become a signature dish. The posh-country feel is created via rustic design details (hessian napkins, slabs of wood for presentation), and service is smart-shirted, laid-back and friendly. *Babies & children admitted. Booking advisable. Entertainment (quiz 7.30pm Tue).*

Pig's Ear
35 Old Church Street, SW3 5BS (7352 2908, www.thepigsear.info). Sloane Square tube then bus 19, 22, 319. **Open** noon-11pm Mon-Sat; noon-10.30pm Sun. **Food served** 12.30-3pm, 7-10pm Mon-Fri; noon-11pm Sat; noon-10.30pm Sun. **Chelsea**
Surely the only gastropub in London with a framed jacket covered in badges from the punk rock era – authentically personal, it seems – this is a classic-looking boozer often filled with loud Chelsea chatter. There's a huge photo of *Exile*-era Keef in one room, and mounted mementoes relating to seminal moments in music of that era: publicity for 'Pretty Vacant', a photo of the Ramones circa 'Pinhead', a newspaper cutting of Richards' Toronto bust. Pints of Fuller's London Pride and Greene King IPA are passed over the busy bar, behind which lurk bottles of Breton cider, house claret and pinot grigio. A lunch menu – lamb neck fillet, slow-cooked duck leg – is set against a backdrop of a newspaper

billboard declaring: 'George Best Slips Away'. Upstairs, the Blue Room is a different matter, with more complex dishes served in more formal white-tablecloth surroundings. *Babies & children admitted. Booking advisable (dining room). Games (board games).* **Map p248 C5.**

West

Anglesea Arms
35 Wingate Road, W6 0UR (8749 1291, www.capitalpubcompany.com). Goldhawk Road or Ravenscourt Park tube. **Open** 11am-11pm Mon-Sat; noon-10.30pm Sun. **Food served** 12.30-2.45pm, 7-10.30pm Mon-Fri; 12.30-3pm, 7-10.30pm Sat; 12.30-3.30pm, 6.30-9.30pm Sun. **Shepherd's Bush**
At the end of a peaceful, residential street, the Anglesea is good taste itself. Divided between a pleasant bar with a warming fire and a dining area behind, it goes big on wines (20 types available by the glass) and ales (Otter Ale, Otter Bitter, guests such as Jennings Cocker Hoop), with a handful of lagers to boot (Pilsner Urquell, Peroni and San Miguel, plus a few standard international brands by the bottle). Food prices aren't cheap: a pint of prawns costs £8.95 and rock oysters are £9.95, and these are bar snacks. But as befits one of the original gastropubs, the food is superior and always worth ordering: expect the likes of pollock with beetroot and shallot salad, or grilled veal kidneys with potato hash. *Babies & children admitted. Tables outdoors (10, pavement).*

Carpenter's Arms
91 Black Lion Lane, W6 9BG (8741 8386). Stamford Brook tube. **Open** 11am-11pm Mon-Sat; noon-10pm Sun. **Food served** noon-3pm, 6-10pm Mon-Fri; noon-4pm, 6-10pm Sat, Sun. **Hammersmith**
But for the tables outside, you might think that this was a shop. But a pub it is, and a popular one at that: head here on a Friday evening, and you'll probably find 'reserved' signs hanging on most of the dozen or so tables that hug the edge of this intimate venue. A stripped-down menu of simple mixed drinks (Stoli or Smirnoff with ginger ale, Gordon's and grapefruit, Captain Morgan and Coke) cuts nicely to the chase, but most stick to reliable wines or the beers, which might include Adnams on draft. As those 'reserved' signs make plain, food's a big part of the appeal, and with reason: it's both excellent and keenly priced. The staff who serve it are absolute darlings, genuinely delighted to

Ealing Park Tavern

see you. Little images of *The Sweeney* and the Duke of Edinburgh provide offbeat levity. *Babies & children admitted. Tables outdoors (8, garden).*

Cow

89 Westbourne Park Road, W2 5QH (7221 0021, www.thecowlondon.co.uk). Royal Oak or Westbourne Park tube. **Open** noon-11pm Mon-Sat; noon-10.30pm Sun. **Food served** noon-3.30pm, 6-10.30pm Mon-Fri; noon-10.30pm Sat; noon-10pm Sun. **Westbourne Grove**
First impressions are of an old-school Irish pub, but this is a very savvy culinary operation. As a bar, it works perfectly: the enclosed front terrace of wooden tables just in from the busy road; the main mural, part-piscine and part-pastoral; the knowingly retro touches, the red-and-green writing on the mirrors, the timeless scenes of Ireland, the Guinness ads. This was, of course, a corner pub in a previous life – check out the tiling in the toilets. Atop the long, professionally run bar are taps of Beck's, Red Stripe, Hoegaarden, Pilsner Urquell, London Pride and Timothy Taylor Landlord. Wines start at £5 for a small glass (sauvignon blanc D'Orpin and malbec Vicien Mendoza). Dine on Irish rock oysters, smoked eel or fruits de mer here, or in a compact room on the first floor. *Babies & children admitted (dining room only). Booking advisable (dining room). Function room (32 capacity). Tables outdoors (2, pavement).* **Map p247 B5.**

Duke of Sussex

75 South Parade, W4 5LF (8742 8801). Chiswick Park tube. **Open** 5-11pm Mon;

noon-11pm Tue-Thur, Sun; noon-midnight Fri, Sat. **Food served** 6-10.30pm Mon; noon-10.30pm Tue-Sat; noon-9.30pm Sun. **Chiswick**
'A beautiful restoration of a Victorian boozer on the Chiswick/Acton border,' says a notice in this – yes! – beautifully restored Victorian boozer on the Chiswick/Acton border. It's no idle boast; note, in particular, the etched glass and green-tiled fireplace from the days of Empire. Overlooking the common (which explains the many dogs), the Duke of Sussex feels faintly rural. A big horseshoe bar offers ales from the St Austell, Fuller's and Camden breweries, and a huge tap of Bitburger. There may be a forest of fresh flowers, framed black-and-white photographs, a good choice of wine and some quality food (celeriac soup, 28-day-aged steak) but the Duke isn't too proud to install a TV screen for sports by the picture windows. A garden to the side and at the back, and park benches outside, offer respite if the rugby's on. *Babies & children admitted. Disabled: toilet. Entertainment (quiz 8pm Sun). Tables outdoors (30, garden).*

Ealing Park Tavern

222 South Ealing Road, W5 4RL (8758 1879, www.ealingparktavern.com). South Ealing tube. **Open** 11am-11pm Mon-Thur; 11am-11.30pm Fri, Sat; noon-10.30pm Sun. **Food served** noon-3pm, 5-9.45pm Mon-Fri; noon-9.45pm Sat, Sun. **Ealing**
Behind its grey-fronted, manor-like exterior, this feels like a big old pub. Pints of Twickenham Naked Ladies, Sharp's Doom Bar and Harveys Sussex Best are served over a large, zinc-topped L-shaped bar to local regulars happy to relax in a high-ceilinged space amid tall houseplants and a fireplace. There are six standard wine selections by the glass, perhaps accompanied by rib-eye steak. TV sport plays in a back room decorated with Brit iconography (a still of Bob Hoskins in *The Long Good Friday*, a poster from Joe Cocker's 'Mad Dogs & Englishmen' tour). In a separate dining area to the right of the main door, reached through a grey curtain divider, diners tuck into such dishes as Gressingham duck and tandoori john dory. *Babies & children admitted (until 6.30pm). Tables outdoors (10, garden). Wireless internet.*

Havelock Tavern

57 Masbro Road, W14 0LS (7603 5374). Hammersmith or Shepherd's Bush tube, or Kensington (Olympia) tube/rail. **Open** 11am-11pm Mon-Sat; noon-10.30pm Sun. **Food served** 12.30-2.30pm, 7-10pm Mon-Sat; 12.30-3pm, 7-9.30pm Sun. **West Kensington**

This blue tile-fronted former neighbourhood boozer is stripped down and ready for business. Between mealtimes, young professionals break away from freelance duties to stake out a scuffed-wood table and sup pints of Sharp's Doom Bar, Ubu Purity, Sambrook's Wandle and Atlantic IPA (the selection changes regularly). Bitburger is the best option as far as draught lager goes; the wine choice is extensive. A daily-chalked menu lists about 20 dishes. Standards are high, but then so are the prices: Thai green chicken curry with steamed rice was £12.50 on one visit. Seating outside lends itself to summer evenings, although there's little to look at but other houses.
Babies & children admitted. Tables outdoors (6, garden; 2, pavement).

Hillgate

24 Hillgate Street, W8 7SR (7727 8566). Notting Hill Gate tube. **Open** 11am-11pm Mon-Sat; noon-10.30pm Sun. **Food served** noon-3pm, 6-10pm Mon-Fri; noon-4pm, 6-10pm Sat; noon-9pm Sun. **Notting Hill**
Previously renowned as a genuine local that belied its salubrious surroundings, this corner pub is under new ownership. It's had a serious spruce-up, and now, perhaps, feels more at home on its road of pastel-coloured cottages and

Sam's Brasserie & Bar

Victorian townhouses. The interior is a touch cold, but they've done a good job with a fairly sizeable space, retaining the finer features (dimpled glass windows, a U-shaped mahogany bar) while adding other decorative touches (big rugs, antlers adorned with fedoras and scarves, candlelit tables unencumbered by tablecloths, *Punch* magazine wallpaper in a separate snug). The choice of cask ales includes Sharp's Doom Bar and Sambrook's Wandle; the French-leaning wine list has five reds and whites by the glass; and the food doesn't venture too far away from top-end gastropub territory.
Babies & children admitted. Disabled: toilet. Entertainment (quiz 8pm Mon). Tables outdoors (15, pavement). Wireless internet.

Mall Tavern

71-73 Palace Gardens Terrace, W8 4RU (7229 3374, www.themalltavern.com). Notting Hill Gate tube. **Open** noon-midnight Mon-Sat; noon-11pm Sun. **Food served** noon-10pm Mon-Sat; noon-9pm Sun. **Notting Hill**
The Perritt brothers have ploughed a pretty penny into making the Mall Tavern's pair of double-aspect rooms look plush and pretty. New life has been breathed into the original wooden floorboards that lap around a striking central bar, while swish chandeliers hang from the ceiling and enormous glass cabinets showcase an assortment of classic culinary knick-knacks and antiques. Jesse Dunford Wood's menu carries cheeky, almost childish nods to nostalgia: expect the likes of chicken kievs, fish fingers and mushy peas, and a chunky, Desperate Dan-style cow pie complete with horns made from bone marrow. But you can also drink here: a broad range of whiskies, the bar's major strength, is supplemented by three cask ales, some craft ciders, a short, classic cocktail list and some 30 wines.
Babies & children admitted. Booking advisable evenings. Function room (16 capacity). Tables outdoors (6, garden). Wireless internet.
Map p247 B7.

Metropolitan

60 Great Western Road, W11 1AB (7229 9254, www.themetropolitanw11.co.uk). Westbourne Park tube. **Open** noon-11.30pm Mon-Thur; noon-midnight Fri, Sat; noon-10.30pm Sun. **Food served** 6-10.30pm Mon; noon-3.30pm, 6-10.30pm Tue-Fri; noon-10.30pm Sat, Sun. **Westbourne Grove**
The Westway's version of the Met bar is a sassy, urban mix of quality global food, well-chosen wines (a dozen by the glass), decent ales and lagers (including Sagres), and a regular agenda of worthwhile sounds, both from the DJ decks

and a small, unplugged stage in the corner. The fact the Metropolitan both regularly hosts buskers and proffers an acceptable chablis says everything about it – this is the kind of place London does very well. To a tower-block horizon backdrop, punters spill out on to the pavement or, in summer, hit the roof terrace. Without and within is Cash-black, offset by brown banquettes and the constant blur of traffic through the picture windows. Food ranges from rib-eye steak to bacon sandwiches, with two-for-one gourmet burgers at the start of the week. *Babies & children admitted (until 7pm). Booking advisable. Entertainment (musicians 7.30pm Thur; DJs 6.30pm Sat, 5.30pm Sun). Function rooms (150 capacity). Tables outdoors (6, terrace; 14, garden). Wireless internet.*

Mitre
40 Holland Park Avenue, W11 3QY (7727 6332, www.themitrew11.co.uk). Holland Park or Notting Hill Gate tube. **Open** noon-midnight Mon-Fri; 9am-midnight Sat; 9am-11pm Sun. **Food served** noon-11pm Mon-Fri; 9am-11pm Sat; 9am-10pm Sun. **Holland Park**
Run by the Realpubs team, this grey-fronted 'pub & brasserie' is a class act, with a restaurant cleverly interwoven behind and around the bar. Ales such as Sharp's Doom Bar, Hogs Back Spring Ale and Fuller's Chiswick complement Bitburger, Moretti, Sagres, Amstel, Heineken and two ciders (Aspall Suffolk and Symonds) atop a lovely circular zinc counter. Tasteful but lived in, it echoes the style adopted elsewhere in the expansive space. Belgian favourites, plus Tiger, Peroni and Cruzcampo, come by the bottle; affordable cocktails (£7) and a long wine list complete the picture. The all-day bar menu offers oysters at £2 each and snacks such as smoked salmon with soda bread. Tourists staying locally enjoy the view through the picture windows of passing London buses; some stop to admire the century-old shots of Ladbroke Grove and Westbourne Park. Mind your head when visiting the toilets. *Babies & children admitted. Booking advisable evenings, weekends. Disabled: toilet. Tables outdoors (11, terrace). Wireless internet.* **Map p247 Z7.**

Princess Victoria
217 Uxbridge Road, W12 9DH (8749 5886, www.princessvictoria.co.uk). Shepherd's Bush tube. **Open** 11.30am-11pm Mon-Thur, Sun; 11.30am-midnight Fri, Sat. **Food served** noon-3pm, 6.30-10.30pm Mon-Sat; noon-4.30pm, 6.30-9.30pm Sun. **Shepherd's Bush**

The sheer size of the Princess Victoria gives it an edge over many competitors: there's room here for cheerfully loud drinkers as well as dining couples and families. Tables are plentiful in both the bar and the dining room of this former gin palace, although you can also hang out around the horseshoe-shaped, marble-topped bar. Beers include Ruddles County, Summer Lightning and Timothy Taylor Landlord, while the sensational wine list offers a choice of carafe sizes plus 175ml glasses; diners are encouraged to mix and match with their food. On one recent visit, our waiter, a qualified sommelier, confessed that he knew more about wine than the cooking – fine British fare cooked with flair and finesse – but worked conscientiously to ensure that everything was just so. A terrific gastropub. *Babies & children admitted. Booking advisable (dining). Function room (80 capacity). Tables outdoors (10, garden). Wireless internet.*

Rocket
11-13 Churchfield Road, W3 6BD (8993 6123, www.therocketw3.co.uk). Acton Central tube. **Open** 10am-11pm Mon-Thur; 10am-midnight Fri, Sat; 10am-10.30pm Sun. **Food served** noon-3pm, 6-10.45pm Mon-Fri; noon-4pm, 6-10.45pm Sat; noon-5pm, 6-9.45pm Sun. **Acton**
The name and pub sign of this place, right by Acton Central station, celebrate railway pioneer George Stephenson. The airy, light interior is large enough to incorporate disparate decorative impulses: there's an area for dining at the back, decked out like a 1920s hotel suite, for instance. The long bar, however, feels like a proper bar, embellished as it is by tributes to the team line-up of Acton United FC. Harveys Sussex Best, Fuller's London Pride, Hoegaarden and Grolsch are the beer taps. The provision of Connect 4, Ludo and Scrabble help make this an ideal weekend kick-back spot. *Babies & children admitted. Function room (70 capacity). Games (board games). Tables outdoors (10, terrace). Wireless internet.*

Sam's Brasserie & Bar
11 Barley Mow Passage, W4 4PH (8987 0555, www.samsbrasserie.co.uk). Chiswick Park or Turnham Green tube. **Open** 9am-midnight Mon-Wed, Sun; 9am-12.30am Thur-Sat. **Food served** 9am-10.30pm Mon-Sat; 9am-10pm Sun. **Chiswick**
Although it has an industrial feel, the decor at Sam Harrison's well-regarded establishment is softened by vast white lampshades, a large

retro cinema poster and a row of cool black seats opposite the bar, itself elegantly designed. The bar and the dining area are clearly separated, but most people tuck in wherever they sit. Superior bar snacks include small plates, crayfish rolls and burgers; from the brasserie menu, try crispy salt and pepper squid followed by risotto primavera. Cocktails use top-notch ingredients, imaginatively mixed – note the Grey Goose caipiroska, the pear and almond daiquiri and the bellinis in white peach and raspberry varieties. Beers on tap are workaday, but ale aficionados will be pleased to find bottles of Sharp's Doom Bar and Chalky's Bark. The wine list has some 25-plus options by the glass. *Babies & children admitted. Booking advisable Thur-Sat. Disabled: toilet. Entertainment (musicians 7pm 2nd & 4th Sun of mth). Wireless internet.*

Swan
Evershed Walk, 119 Acton Lane, W4 5HH (8994 8262, www.theswanchiswick.co.uk). Chiswick Park tube or bus 94. **Open** 5-11pm Mon-Fri; noon-11pm Sat; noon-10.30pm Sun. **Food served** 6-10pm Mon-Thur; 6-10.30pm Fri; noon-3pm, 6-10.30pm Sat; noon-10pm Sun. **Chiswick**
Behind a lemon-yellow façade, set on a quiet, pedestrianised corner brightened with clusters of bright flowers, this Irish-run hostelry is a real home from home. It's pretty pub-like in feel, but the Swan is also rated for its food (salmon and dill fish cakes, roast wild pigeon breast). Drinkers are taken care of with Sharp's Doom Bar and guest ales, and tap lagers that include San Miguel and Peroni, plus a seasonal wine list with a dozen or so choices by the glass. In the wood-panelled interior, two areas – one for dining and drinking, the other just for drinking – are divided by a professionally staffed bar. Diners are treated to bright, tasteful images of Paris by Tim Johnston, drinkers to a fire and sofa seating arrangement around a flatscreen TV. There's also a small outside plot at the back, and festival tables at the front. *Babies & children admitted (until 7pm). Games (board games). Tables outdoors (30, garden).*

Thatched House
113 Dalling Road, W6 0ET (8748 6174, www.thatchedhouse.com). Ravenscourt Park tube. **Open** noon-11pm Mon-Sat; noon-10.30pm Sun. **Food served** noon-3pm, 6-10pm Mon-Fri; noon-10pm Sat; noon-9.30pm Sun. **Hammersmith**
This cosy corner pub was Young's first ever, opened in 1832. Now, under revamped Young's management and with a new chef and fresh

look, it exudes culinary confidence and a homely, rustic feel with its roaring fire, deep leather sofas and dark oak tables and floors. It deftly juggles drinking and dining with a couple of Young's ales, a guest ale and a row of lager fonts (Peroni, Grolsch Blonde, Estrella Damm), and more than a dozen wines available by the glass. The hearty, jingoistic cooking unashamedly caters for meat-lovers. Starters include wild boar, venison and rabbit terrine on toast; mains might include spatchcocked quail or the house speciality, mussels and chips; roasts are served all day Sunday. The conservatory and sizeable garden come into play in summer, when there are regular barbecues. *Babies & children admitted (until 7pm). Booking advisable weekends. Disabled: toilet. Entertainment (live music 2pm Sun). Games (board games). Tables outdoors (10, garden). Wireless internet.*

Warrington
93 Warrington Crescent, W9 1EH (7592 7960, www.gordonramsay.com/thewarrington). Maida Vale tube. **Open** noon-11pm Mon-Thur; noon-midnight Fri, Sat; noon-10.30pm Sun. **Food served** 6-10pm Mon-Wed; noon-2.30pm, 6-10pm Thur-Sat; noon-2.30pm, 6-8.45pm Sun. **Maida Vale**
Built in 1857, the Warrington eventually became the haunt of has-been glam-rockers and the Fulham punk fraternity; the Boys' 'Ballad of the Warrington' summed up the scene nicely. Fast-forward 30 years from those heady days and it's a slightly different story. Upstairs is a Gordon Ramsay gastropub, decorated in bland browns and beiges. Downstairs has also had a spruce-up, not to mention some attention paid to its choice of drinks; but it's still the same old Warrington, all marble columns and art-nouveau friezes. Gawp at the cherubs over the bar as you sip a Meantime or Greene King ale, or perhaps something from a wine list that includes many varieties rarely available by the glass. You'll pay above average for your ploughman's or bangers and mash from the bar menu, but it'll be a cut above the norm. *Babies & children admitted. Booking advisable. Disabled: toilet. Entertainment (quiz 7.30pm Mon). Function room (16 capacity). Tables outdoors (10, pavement).*

Also recommended...
Grand Union (Rooms with a View, *p169*); **Kensington Wine Rooms** (Wine Bars, *p58*); **Negozio Classica** (Wine Bars, *p58*); **Prince Bonaparte** (Classic Pubs, *p102*); **Stonemasons Arms** (Beer Specialists, *p126*).

Princess Victoria. See p155.

North West

Hill
94 Haverstock Hill, NW3 2BD (7267 0033, www.thehillbar.com). Belsize Park or Chalk Farm tube. **Open** noon-midnight Mon-Sat; noon-11pm Sun. **Food served** noon-3pm, 6-10pm daily. **Belsize Park**
This smart, large, two-room gastropub stands right by the stop for the 168 bus, although the Hill's clientele tend to be mainly locals – young professionals treating their parents to apple-and-celeriac soup followed by duck breast with parsnip purée and foie gras. Although quite formal, the Hill is keen to promote itself as a drinks venue, with wine evenings, a summer beer garden and encouragement for potential punters to watch major football tournaments *chez eux* – presumably while sinking pints of Sagres, Amstel, Adnams or Guinness rather than the two-dozen wines on offer (Domaine de la Chézatte Sancerre; St Hallett Blackwell Barossa Valley shiraz). Around a dozen come by the glass. *Babies & children admitted. Function room (30 capacity). Tables outdoors (15, garden). Wireless internet.*

Horseshoe
28 Heath Street, NW3 6TE (7431 7206). Hampstead tube. **Open** 10am-11pm Mon-Thur; 10am-midnight Fri, Sat; noon-10pm Sun.

Food served noon-3.30pm, 6-10pm Mon-Thur; noon-3.30pm, 6-11pm Fri; 10am-4.30pm, 6.30-11pm Sat; noon-4.30pm, 6.30-9.30pm Sun. **Hampstead**
Hampstead shoppers drop into this bright corner for light meals, hearty gastropub fare and more sophisticated choices (crisp-skinned pollock with samphire and nuggets of crayfish, for example), plus special deals such as Red Poll beef burger with chips and a glass of house wine or OJ (£7). Vegetarians might opt for broccoli and pine nut wellington. It's worth forgoing the (not bad) wine list to explore the beers as the pub brews its own ales, and there's a great choice of bottled options, including Coopers and Little Creatures from Australia, and Belgian raspberry beer Bacchus. Service can be too laid-back, not least because staff seem to enjoy each other's company, but if you're happy to chill, the Horseshoe makes a relaxing afternoon destination. *Babies & children admitted. Booking advisable Fri-Sun. Tables outdoors (2, pavement). Wireless internet.*

North London Tavern
375 Kilburn High Road, NW6 7QB (7625 6634, www.northlondontavern. co.uk). Kilburn tube or Brondesbury rail. **Open** noon-11.30pm Mon-Wed; noon-midnight Thur; noon-1am Fri, Sat; noon-11pm Sun. **Food served** 6-10.30pm Mon;

noon-3.30pm, 6-10.30pm Tue-Fri; noon-5.30pm, 6-10.30pm Sat; noon-9.30pm Sun. **Kilburn** Despite a substantial and sympathetic refit in the spring of 2010 by the fast-growing Realpubs group, this remains at heart a tiled-exterior local boozer, where the impressive culinary offerings need not dissuade the drinker from strolling in for a quiet pint. In expansive, high-ceilinged, wood-panelled surroundings, pull up a bar stool and sup on lagers such as Sagres, Bitburger and Moretti, or ales including Brains Milkwood and Deuchars IPA, with Vedett, Duvel, Budvar and Chimay (of both colours) brightening the fridge behind. Wines include a dozen choices by the glass, rising to feature the likes of a Tremblay chablis at around £25 to £30 a bottle. The superior food menu might include pan-fried Cornish sardines, Lancashire hotpot and poached haddock, with occasional forays into continental variety (seafood, chicken and smoked sausage paella). Music and monthly comedy nights should bring customers from further afield than NW6.
Babies & children admitted (until 6pm).
Booking advisable Fri-Sun. Disabled: toilet.
Entertainment (quiz 8.30pm Mon; musicians
8pm Tue, Wed; comedy 8pm 3rd Thur
of mth; jazz 8.30pm Sun). Function room
(80 capacity). Tables outdoors (8, pavement).
Wireless internet.

Old White Bear
1 Well Road, NW3 1LJ (7794 7719,
www.theoldwhitebear.co.uk). Hampstead tube.
Open 5-11.30pm Mon; noon-11.30pm Tue-Thur; noon-midnight Fri, Sat; noon-10.30pm Sun. **Food served** 6.30-10.30pm Mon; noon-3pm, 6.30-10.30pm Tue-Sun. **Hampstead** In its former guise as Ye Olde White Bear, this Hampstead hostelry was a traditional ale house, pure and simple. However, new owner Jasper Gorst (who also looks after the Oak in Notting Hill) has stripped the name of its faux-historic grandeur, traded its tankards for tablecloths and taken a deliberate stride away from stand-up-and-drink territory and towards a sit-down-and-eat ambience. The rustic factor has been ramped up with a plethora of pine dressers and tables, while the tweeness has been toned down by mosaic tiles sunk into the parquet floor, slim, chrome old-school radiators and an array of Anglepoise lamps. The emphasis is now on the food, and with good reason: the modern European cooking is excellent. Still, you can just drink if you like, choosing from a selection of wines and a couple of ales (Pride, Abbot).
Babies & children admitted. Disabled: toilet.
Function room (14 capacity). Tables outdoors
(7, pavement).

Wells
30 Well Walk, NW3 1BX (7794 3785,
www.thewellshampstead.co.uk). Hampstead
tube. **Open** noon-11pm Mon-Sat; noon-10.30pm Sun. **Food served** noon-3pm, 6-10pm Mon-Fri; noon-4pm, 7-10pm Sat; noon-4pm, 7-9.30pm Sun. **Hampstead** The Wells offers both history and contemporary class. Formerly the Wells Tavern, linked to Hampstead spa from 1702 and a venue for clandestine post-spa liaisons, it's now the kind of place where you can order pan-fried sea bass with sautéed potatoes and gremolata beurre blanc or a blackberry martini. From the outside, it still resembles a classic pub by the village church, ringed with sturdy tables; the interior, though, is deceptively sleek and filled with arty photographs. An upmarket menu might offer venison stew, grilled octopus, or lamb steak with minted peas, and the wine list features a dozen by the glass. Staff know how to mix a June Bug (Midori and Appleton white rum) and pour a pint of Black Sheep. A treasured local gastropub.
Babies & children admitted. Disabled: toilet.
Function room (12 capacity). Games
(board games). Tables outdoors (8, patio).
Wireless internet.

Outer London

Botanist on the Green
3-5 Kew Green, TW9 3AA (8948 4838,
www.thebotanistkew.com). Kew Gardens
tube/rail or bus 65, 391. **Open** noon-11pm Mon-Thur; noon-midnight Fri, Sat; noon-10.30pm Sun. **Food served** noon-3pm, 6-10pm Mon-Fri; noon-10pm Sat; noon-9pm Sun. **Kew, Surrey** Taking its cue from Kew Gardens, this light, flowery bar-restaurant a short hop south of Kew Bridge offers the illusion that you're drinking beer in a greenhouse. There's plenty of choice: Sagres, Greene King IPA and Erdinger Weiß, plus Symonds and Aspall Suffolk ciders. Anchor Steam Ale, Estrella and Duvel number among the bottled options. Cocktails (available by glass or pitcher) include a Botanist of gin, passion fruit and sundry juices; the wine list is equally user-friendly. Quality bar snacks are typified by the meze platter with Exeter Street Bakery focaccia. Kids' drawing kits encourage ice-cream pitstops after a trawl through Kew Gardens. The one flaw: brusque-almost-rude bar service on our most recent visit.
Babies & children admitted. Disabled:
toilet. Entertainment (quiz 8.30pm
Wed). Tables outdoors (6, courtyard).
Wireless internet.

Rooms with a View

Central	160
North	163
East	163
South East	164
South West	167
West	168
Outer London	170

Rooms with a View

What makes a great view? Opinions are probably as varied as the vistas from the pubs in this chapter. The historically minded can seek out echoes of London's maritime past in Wapping's **Prospect of Whitby** and the **Town of Ramsgate**, and even more so at the **Grapes**, downriver. The upper reaches of the tidal Thames offer bucolic slices of countryside, with the river literally lapping at the steps of the **White Cross** and **White Swan** pubs. For a more urban experience, you can rise above Shoreditch with fine drinks and above-par food at Terence Conran's **Boundary Rooftop**, take a breather from the hubbub of Camden Market at the **Lockside Lounge** or keep an eye out for the latest trend of pop-up rooftop bars in less likely locations such as Dalston or Peckham. And for some, the goal is to get a grand overview of the capital with a suitably fine cocktail: **Vertigo 42** in the old NatWest Tower and the **Oxo Tower Bar** both offer sweeping views of the City and London's landmarks, but as we've been watching the glass cladding creeping up the Shard, we're thinking the best panorama with a drink in hand is yet to come.

Central

5th View

Waterstone's, 5th floor, 203-206 Piccadilly, W1J 9HA (7851 2468, www.5thview.co.uk). Piccadilly Circus tube. **Open** 9am-9pm Mon-Sat; noon-8pm Sun. **Food served** 9am-9pm Mon-Sat; noon-5pm Sun. **Piccadilly**
This lounge bar-restaurant atop Waterstone's has injected irony into its cocktail selection. Among the selections, a Dusty Springfield of vodka, fresh apple juice and vanilla syrup is described as 'sultry, fruity, sour and tortured – like the singer', while the My Man Godfrey Vodkatini is 'our own little homage to David Niven'. Quality base spirits are used throughout: Grey Goose or Ketel One for the poured-at-your-table martinis, for instance. Wine-wise, you'll find 10 by bottle and glass; there's a similar number of bottled beers, including Timothy Taylor Landlord and London Pride; and the day menu features a variety of antipasti. Avert your gaze from the 40 years of Booker Prize winners on the walls and you'll be able to make out the Houses of Parliament from your low, brown-leather, two-person sofa.
Babies & children admitted. Disabled: lift, toilet. Function rooms (up to 120 capacity). Wireless internet. **Map p241 J7.**

Oxo Tower Bar

Oxo Tower Wharf, Barge House Street, SE1 9PH (7803 3888, www.harveynichols.com/oxo-tower-london). Waterloo tube/rail or Temple tube. **Open** noon-11pm Mon-Fri; 11am-11.30pm Sat; noon-10.30pm Sun. **Food served** noon-11pm Mon-Sat; noon-10pm Sun. **Waterloo**
Diners at the restaurant and brasserie have long gazed across to St Paul's Cathedral and Somerset House but it's only since owners Harvey Nicks reshuffled things that drinkers can also properly enjoy uninterrupted views. Bar designer Shaun Clarkson has updated the interior too, the most notable addition being a slick boomerang-shaped white bar behind which an army of attentive, bartenders bustle. It's not the cosiest of places, and it still conjures up a cruise ship feel, but the refit has also brought better booze. The cocktail list covers the classics using some house-made ingredients – lime cordial in the gimlet, an OXO-branded ice cube in the negroni – while the Earl Grey Mar-tea-ni comes in teacups for two. The extensive French-leaning wine list offers enough choice of wines by the glass; bottled beers include Meantime Pale Ale and Schneider Weisse. The bar menu brings sharing plates with charcuterie, manchego and quince, and boutique snacks such as as mini truffled honey chorizo.

Vertigo 42. *See p163.*

Babies & children admitted. Booking advisable. Disabled: lift; toilet. Entertainment (musicians 7.30pm daily). Function room (65 capacity). Tables outdoors (5, terrace). **Map p250 N7.**

Skylon

Royal Festival Hall, Belvedere Road, South Bank, SE1 8XX (7654 7800, www.dandd london.com). Waterloo tube/rail. **Open** 11.30am-midnight daily. **Food served** *Grill* noon-11pm daily. *Restaurant* noon-2.30pm Mon-Sat; noon-4pm Sun. **Waterloo**
Passing the throngs listening to Hindustani drumming in the Royal Festival Hall foyer, take the lift to the third floor, turn left and enter this light space. A nice blend of contemporary style and retro chic (look out for nods to the 1951 Festival of Britain), it makes terrific use of its cathedral ceilings and vast windows, which afford views of river, skyline and people on the move. In the middle of the room, surrounded by restaurant tables, is a cocktail oasis, consisting of a slate bar counter, swivel bar stools, banquettes and, nearer the window, seats for sipping *à deux*. It's not cheap: wines start at £5.55, beer's £4.50 a bottle, and the excellent cocktails, both classics (margaritas with Don Agustin) and variations such as the signature

Skylon (muddled grapes and ginger with Ciroc vodka, Manzana Verde, lime and apple juice) go for a tenner-plus. But as destination drinking venues go, this one can't easily be topped.
Babies & children admitted. Booking advisable. Disabled: toilet. **Map p250 M8.**

Skylounge

Mint Hotel, 7 Pepys Street, EC3N 4AF (7709 1043, www.minthotel.com). Tower Hill tube. **Open** 9am-2am daily. **Food served** 10.30am-10.30pm daily. **City**
The Skylounge at the recently opened Mint Hotel offers Londoners a whole new perspective. The views over the Tower of London, Tower Bridge and the ever-rising Shard are lovely – especially at night, and most particularly from the rooftop terrace. Unless you're happy with the after-work crush, the best night to go is Sunday – otherwise you may have to cool your heels in the ground-floor bar until space becomes available upstairs. There's the full range of beers, wines and spirits that you'd expect from a hotel bar; cocktails here include the Millionaire Mojito (muddled mint and fresh lime, Element 8 gold rum, angostura bitters and gum syrup, served in a chilled martini glass with a champagne float) and London Calling (vanilla and root ginger-infused Tanqueray gin, shaken with Cointreau,

Boundary Rooftop

lemon bitters, vanilla sugar and lemon juice in a chilled martini glass). Note that reservations are taken for the bar, but the outdoor tables are on a first-come, first-served basis. *Booking advisable. Disabled: lift, toilet. Tables outdoors (20, terrace). Wireless internet.* **Map p245 R7.**

Vertigo 42

Tower 42, 25 Old Broad Street, EC2N 1HQ (7877 7842, www.vertigo42.co.uk). Bank tube/DLR or Liverpool Street tube/rail. **Open** noon-4.30pm, 5-11pm Mon-Fri; 5-11pm Sat. **Food served** noon-2.30pm, 5-9.30pm Mon-Fri; 5-9.30pm Sat. **City**
You'll need to make a reservation, promise a £10 minimum spend, head through airport-style security gates ('no coins, keys or mobiles?'), take the escalator to your left and then find the lift dedicated to level 42. But the views make it worth the effort. By day, they're amazing, even discombobulating – the sort of clichéd bird's-eye views not even aeroplane windows can deliver. Within a small circle of bar space with a walk-round mirror at its core, you see 360° views of building upon building for mile after mile. As you gawp from a sci-fi retro chair in Teletubby colours (purple predominates, of course), champagne is the way to go, from entry-level Pannier Brut (£58.50) to a magnum of Krug Clos du Mesnil (£820). House wine is a shade over £9, but house wine you can have in the real world. *Booking essential. Disabled: lift, toilet. Dress: smart casual.* **Map p245 Q6.**

Also recommended...
Galvin at Windows (Hotel Bars, *p43*).

North

Lockside Lounge

75-89 West Yard, Camden Lock Place, NW1 8AF (7284 0007, www.lockside lounge.com). Camden Town tube. **Open** noon-midnight Mon-Thur; noon-3am Fri, Sat; noon-1am Sun. **Food served** noon-9pm daily. **Camden**
A pleasant ten-minute walk past an array of bars clustered around the bridge, this first-floor boathouse-like venue above Caffe Crema makes great use of its location. It's occasionally hired for private parties but when it's open to all, you can gaze over the twinkling lights around the lock and the bobbing barges as you sip your Erdinger. If it's too nippy, the interior is long and artily loft-like, and fairly relaxed – at least compared to the glug-'em-quick vibe on the main drag. Bottled beers, everyone's favourite

Belgians, are preferable to standard tap lagers; cocktails are at prices just high enough to keep out spiky-haired young backpackers. There's food, but most are happy to sit around and gaze; or, when DJs amp up the atmosphere at weekends, to take to the floor. *Babies & children admitted (until 7pm). Disabled: toilet. Entertainment (backgammon 7pm 1st & 4th Wed of mth; comedy 7pm alternate Thur; DJs 7pm Fri-Sun). Tables outdoors (10, terrace).* **Map p254 H26.**

East

Boundary Rooftop

2-4 Boundary Street, E2 7DD (7729 1051, www.theboundary.co.uk). Shoreditch High Street rail. **Open** *Apr* noon-8pm Wed-Sun. *May* noon-9.30pm daily. *June-mid Sept* noon-10.30pm daily. *Mid-late Sept* noon-8.30pm Wed-Sun. **Food served** *Apr, mid-late Sept* noon-7pm Wed-Sun. *May* noon-4pm, 5.30-8.30pm daily. *June-mid Sept* noon-4pm, 5.30-9.30pm daily. **Shoreditch**
This unsurprisingly popular spot is perched atop the Terence Conran-designed Boundary Project, which also contains a boutique hotel, a restaurant (Boundary), a café (Albion) and a deli. The alfresco rooftop retreat in the heart of Shoreditch offers impressive panoramic views of London, with the City skyline at its most dramatic after dark. There's restaurant seating for 48, with diners choosing from grills and lighter snacks from the deli downstairs. However, you can also lounge about on wicker chairs and summer seats surrounded by shrubbery, heaters, the smoky scent of cigars and a wood-burning fire. The range of bottled beers includes Meantime Wheat and Meteor pilsner from France; pitchers of house-designed cocktails and jugs of sangria; and more than a dozen wines offered by the glass, half-bottle and bottle. The downside's an obvious one: you're at the mercy of the weather. *Babies & children admitted. Disabled: lift, toilet. Tables outdoors (45, terrace). Wireless internet.* **Map p244 R4.**

Grapes

76 Narrow Street, E14 8BP (7987 4396). Westferry DLR. **Open** noon-3pm, 5.30-11pm Mon-Wed; noon-11pm Thur-Sat; noon-10.30pm Sun. **Food served** noon-2.30pm, 7-9.30pm Mon-Sat; noon-3.30pm Sun. **Limehouse**
If you're wondering what the Thames docks might have felt like before their Disneyfication into Docklands, these narrow, ivy-covered and

etched-glass premises aren't a bad place to start. The downstairs room of this riverside pub, which dates from 1720, is all wood panels and nautical jetsam (and is mercifully devoid of mobile ringtones and music); a tight stairway leads up to a more plain restaurant room that accommodates the Sunday roast overspill. The ales (Landlord, Broadside and the like) are good, but a half-dozen wines of each colour (by glass and bottle), plus jugs of kir royale in summer and glasses of port in winter, also please the cheerful clientele of well-heeled locals and grown-up heritage junkies. Watch out for your shoes if you step out of the main bar room on to the tiny deck at high tide.
Booking advisable (restaurant).

Prospect of Whitby
57 Wapping Wall, E1W 3SH (7481 1095).
Wapping rail. **Open** noon-11pm Mon-Sat; noon-10.30pm Sun. **Food served** noon-10pm Mon-Sat; noon-9pm Sun. **Wapping**
Dwarfed by residential new-builds on either side, the Prospect proclaims its history from the off. 'Built c1520', offers the sign at the front; inside, signs on the walls suggest that the pub was a regular haunt of everyone from Captain Kidd to Samuel Pepys, Richard Burton to Princess Margaret. (Who now regularly haunt it. Possibly.) Behind the Prospect's bowed, boiled-sweet windows is a solid, barrel-studded, black wooden bar that now offers draught Erdinger and Staropramen alongside such real ales as Wells

Bombardier, Sharp's Doom Bar and Young's London Gold. Steak and ale pie and Sunday roasts echo the beams-galore tradition of the decor. For those who prefer a good vista with their food and drink, excellent views of the Thames can be had from the raised eating section just to the left of the bar or outside on the terrace. *Babies & children admitted. Disabled: toilet. Function rooms (up to 150 capacity). Tables outdoors (6, balcony; 7, garden).*

Town of Ramsgate
62 Wapping High Street, E1W 2PN (7481 8000). Wapping rail. **Open** noon-midnight Mon-Sat; noon-11pm Sun. **Food served** noon-9pm daily. **Wapping**
Long and narrow it may be, but the Grade II-listed Town of Ramsgate seems bright, friendly and open, not unlike the staff tending to the needs of the contented mix of locals, office workers and tourists who mingle easily within it. The food includes own-made cream of tomato soup, and beef, beetroot and mozzarella salad, while the bar continues to earn plaudits for the quality of its guest and constant real ales. Hoegaarden, Leffe and Peroni are on draught for those who favour a continental brew; wine-lovers plump for Tin Roof shiraz or Marlborough sauvignon blanc. Out back, the bijou, decked terrace delights the lucky punters who manage to grab a table in summer, watching the moorhens as the tide slaps against the stone steps leading down to the Thames from the adjacent alleyway. *Babies & children admitted (until 7pm). Entertainment (quiz 8.30pm Mon). Games (board games). Tables outdoors (12, riverside garden).*

Also recommended...
Narrow (Gastropubs & Brasseries, p146).

South East

Cutty Sark Tavern
4-6 Ballast Quay, SE10 9PD (8858 3146, www.cuttysarktavern.co.uk). Cutty Sark DLR or Greenwich DLR/rail. **Open** 11am-11pm Mon-Sat; noon-10.30pm Sun. **Food served** noon-9pm Mon-Fri, Sun; noon-10pm Sat. **Greenwich**
The history may be confusing, but the location can't be beat. A Georgian freehouse since either 1695 or 1795, depending on whether you believe the sign outside or the writing in the coloured glazed panes in the front door, this hostelry was converted to its present state in the early 19th century. At that time, the waterfront was a busy and thirsty place; this landmark remains, beside an eyesore power station but with perfect

views encompassing the Dome, Docklands and beyond. Some of the tables are set by river-view windows; in summer, ten Thameside terrace tables come into their own. Within the pub, beer-barrel seats, maritime knick-knacks, low ceilings and creaking floorboards make it feel like a smugglers' haunt; you half expect a bag of shiny doubloons to be plonked down at the bar while you order. Gales' Seafarers Ale is among the draught options, along with other Fuller's-related beers. There's a spacious first-floor area, but the best seats are in the Smoke Room, an intimate corner of comfortable leather chairs tucked away by the front door. *Babies & children admitted (until 9pm). Tables outdoors (10, terrace).*

Frank's Café & Campari Bar

10th floor, Peckham multi-storey carpark, 95A Rye Lane, SE15 4ST (07580 545 837, www.frankscafe.org.uk). Peckham Rye rail. **Open** *July-Sept* 11am-10pm Thur-Sun. **Food served** 6-10pm Thur-Sat; 11am-noon Sun. **No credit cards. Peckham**
Frank's Café emerged on top of Peckham's multi-storey car park in summer 2007 as part of the Bold Tendencies sculpture exhibition. It's run by duo Frank Boxer and Michael Davies, who met

while working at The Cut's Anchor & Hope. Peckham is not famed for being scenic, but sit under the illuminated red canopy at twilight and you can drink in unparalleled views across London along with your Campari-based cocktail, prosecco or bottled beer. The simple bistro fare verges on a posh picnic and changes daily: you might get Toulouse sausages or buttery courgettes on toast. On Sundays, a buck's fizz or bloody mary sets the pace for atypical brunch dishes such as mushrooms with gremolata on toast, or bacon collar with egg mayo. Frank's burgeoning popularity as it has moved from one-off pop-up to regular summer fixture means the crowd is becoming more mixed, a solid yuppie following picking up on the vibe generated by the early-adopter art students and young creatives. It's a bit hard to find, and details may change, so check the website before heading over.

Mayflower

117 Rotherhithe Street, SE16 4NF (7237 4088). Rotherhithe tube. **Open** 11am-11pm daily. **Food served** noon-2.30pm, 6-9.30pm Mon-Fri; noon-3pm, 6-9.30pm Sat; noon-3.45pm, 6-8.45pm Sun. **Bermondsey**
Dating back to 1620, the Mayflower certainly looks the part: appearing suddenly along the

Frank's Café & Campari Bar

Mayflower. *See p165.*

Thames path, its white and black-timbered frontage set with diamond-leaded windows positively oozes tradition. Inside, beyond the counter, the small main bar area (cosy alcoves, open fire) leads to a deck outside at the rear. So far, so apparently authentic, but the prices tagged both to the drinks (a fairly uninspiring selection of beers punctuated by the odd real ale) and the food (fish a speciality of sorts) are pure 21st century, and the nagging suspicion of being in a tourist trap is hard to shake off. For all that, the pub has been a thriving local over the years: in the front room, brass plaques on the back of the dark wooden seats commemorate deceased regulars and serve as a testament to the loyalty that the Mayflower once inspired. A waterfront terrace makes up for any disappointment.
Babies & children admitted (restaurant). Tables outdoors (10, riverside jetty).

Trafalgar Tavern
Park Row, SE10 9NW (8858 2909, www.trafalgartavern.co.uk). Cutty Sark DLR or Maze Hill rail. **Open** noon-11pm Mon-Thur, Sun; noon-1am Fri, Sat. **Food served** noon-10pm Mon-Sat; noon-5pm Sun. **Greenwich**
Thanks to the Thames lapping against its wall and the resulting busy tourist trade, this place is something of a local landmark. Built in 1837 and regally restored in 1968, it feels more historic than it is, with photographs of maritime scenes and portraits of braided admirals aiding the illusion; there are rooms named after Nelson, Hardy and Howe. In fact, the place is huge: downstairs alone there are five spaces, in addition to the side terrace guarded by a statue of Horatio. The very end space looks quite contemporary, but everything else here is visitor-pleasing traditional. Draught beers include British ales (Sharp's Doom Bar, Adnams Bitter) and Belgian brews (Palm, Estaminet), with plenty more Beneluxuriant options in the fridge. A bar menu offers snacks such as traditional Greenwich whitebait, fat chips and burgers, but the culinary highlight remains the Sunday roasts.
Babies & children admitted (until 7pm). Function rooms (up to 250 capacity). Tables outdoors (20, riverside). **Map p253 E1.**

South West

Sun Inn
7 Church Road, SW13 9HE (8876 5256, www.thesuninnbarnes.co.uk). Barnes Bridge rail. **Open** 11am-11pm Mon-Wed, Sun; 11am-midnight Thur-Sat. **Food served** noon-10pm Mon-Sat; noon-9.30pm Sun. **Barnes**

Priceless Tip
In London, you won't see champagne bubbles rise any higher than at Vertigo 42 (*see p163*), with striking views from 600 feet up in the air. It's magical looking over the Thames as the sun sets.

Unlike some of its local rivals, the Sun Inn doesn't enjoy a view of the Thames, but it's got the next best thing: from the large front terrace, drinkers can gaze out on to Barnes Green and its village-like duck pond. The interior amplifies the old-fashioned nature of the place, with bar staff and customers on first-name terms in the cramped, low-ceilinged space. Although it feels like one of those City pubs rebuilt after the Great Fire, the Sun Inn doesn't make much of its history but lets the drinks do the talking: ales such as Sharp's Doom Bar, Adnams Wheat Beer and Timothy Taylor Landlord are all attractive finds on draught. There are a few treasures by the bottle, too, mainly Belgian: Duvel and Vedett, for example. Wines start with a cheapish but acceptable Italian at £13; tippling is encouraged over conversation with strangers on Wednesdays at the pub's In Vino Veritas theme nights.
Babies & children admitted (until 8pm). Disabled: toilet. Entertainment (quiz 7.30pm Mon). Tables outdoors (15, terrace).

Waterfront
Baltimore House, Juniper Drive, SW18 1TS (7228 4297, www.waterfrontlondon.co.uk). Wandsworth Town rail or 295 bus. **Open** noon-11.30pm Mon-Thur, Sun; noon-midnight Fri, Sat. **Food served** noon-10pm Mon-Sat; noon-9pm Sun. **Wandsworth**
Its appearance in keeping with the swish, neutral look of the show apartments and community facilities of Battersea Reach ('defining riverside living with style') around it, this well-conceived place is atypical of the Young's stable. It feels 21st-century, for a start, with floods of natural light coming from the river-facing floor-to-ceiling windows, beyond which is a decked terrace. Regrettably, the opposite bank is an eyesore. Even so, tucked far away from a busy Wandsworth roundabout, between two Thames bridges, this seems like a world unto itself. The furniture helps: the bar stools are practically armchairs on stilts, the clock is Grand Central Station massive and the images of waterside life are nicely chosen. Along with the standard Young's beers, there's Leffe and Peroni; wines are also common to the brand, and both affordable and acceptable.

Trafalgar Tavern. *See p167.*

Babies & children admitted. Disabled: toilet.
Tables outdoors (35, riverside terrace).
Wireless internet. **Map p251 B1**.

Ye White Hart
*The Terrace, Riverside, SW13 0NR (8876
5177). Barnes Bridge rail.* **Open** 11am-11pm
Mon-Thur; 11am-midnight Fri; 10am-midnight
Sat; 10am-11pm Sun. **Food served** noon-
10pm daily. **Barnes**
Right on the river, this capacious barn of a bar
makes best use of its prime location. It's a
Young's pub, so it's well looked after, providing
the usual range of ales from the brewery stable,
as well as reliably satisfying steak pies and
Sunday roasts. What really brings in the punters,
though, is the chance to sink into a chesterfield
by the fire, or find a spot to stand on the river-
view first-floor veranda, down a pint and talk
about the rugby match that's just played out on
the big screen. On Boat Race day, the towpath
resembles Trafalgar Square on New Year's Eve,
crowds packed around a hog roast and staff
working like stevedores. On the other 364 days
of the year, it's busy but civilised, the dark-wood
interior lending a slight sense of grandeur.
*Function room (120 capacity). Tables outdoors
(6, balcony, riverside terrace; 8, garden; 12,
towpath). Wireless internet.*

West

Bridge House
*13 Westbourne Terrace Road, W2 6NG (7266
4326, www.thebridgehouselittlevenice.co.uk).
Warwick Avenue tube or Paddington tube/rail.*
Open noon-11pm Mon-Thur; noon-11.30pm
Fri, Sat; noon-10.30pm Sun. **Food served**
noon-10pm Mon-Sat; noon-9.30pm Sun.
Maida Vale
Can any theatre bar in London be as convivial
as this one? Beneath the Canal Café, the Bridge
House comprises a waterside terrace and a
spacious, relaxing interior. If it's sunny, sit
outside and listen to the lapping of the Regent's
Canal; when it's chilly, curl up around the
fireplace. Refurbishments are planned, but for
now the place has a charged, slightly naughty
feel, thanks to velvety banquettes, bright red
beaded lightshades and Anna Runefelt's faintly
erotic photos on the wall; even the toilets are
concealed behind thick curtains. In the middle
of the room, a bar dispenses ales (Landlord,
London Pride and the like) and continental
beers (Kozel, Franziskaner, Peroni), plus a list
of wines available by both glass and bottle. An
all-day kitchen deals with an extensive
and affordable seasonal menu, snacks (crab and
wasabi cakes, mini pies) complemented by

smartened-up pubby mains (pork belly with bacon and sage mash, crispy duck salad, four types of Sunday roast). *Babies & children admitted (until 7pm). Disabled: toilet. Entertainment (comedy 7.30pm & 9.30pm Mon-Sat, 7pm & 9pm Sun). Games (board games). Tables outdoors (8, terrace).*

City Barge

27 Strand-on-the-Green, Kew, W4 3PH (8994 2148). Gunnersbury tube/rail or Kew Bridge rail. **Open** 11am-11pm daily. **Food served** 11am-10pm daily. **Chiswick**
Beside a muddy but peaceful stretch of the Thames, facing a little island straight out of Arthur Ransome, this higgledy-piggledy pub offers tranquillity both inside and out. The honking of multitudinous geese all but drowns out the regular passing of Heathrow-bound aircraft; the nearest bridge welcomes trains only rarely, and you're just as likely to see an oarsman breaking the water. Inside, everyday folk sit and chat about *EastEnders*, lads on the Greene King IPA while ladies take to the house chardonnay (less than £3 a glass). Artefacts related to the location – sepia waterside scenes of yesteryear, an old wooden 'Beware of the Weir' sign – decorate the raised main bar area, leading to the back terrace. Intimate alcoves in the lower bar and riverside festival seating await couples and close friends enjoying a memorable catch-up. *Babies & children admitted. Booking advisable Sat, Sun. Tables outdoors (11, riverside terrace).*

Dove

19 Upper Mall, W6 9TA (8748 9474). Hammersmith or Ravenscourt Park tube. **Open** 11am-11.30pm Mon-Sat; noon-11pm Sun. **Food served** noon-3pm, 6-9pm Mon-Thur; noon-9pm Fri, Sat; noon-7pm Sun. **Hammersmith**
Several pubs stand amid the rowing clubs, dog-walkers and strategically placed park benches on the Upper Mall embankment upriver from Hammersmith Bridge; this one is perhaps the best (and certainly a prime spot from which to watch the Boat Race). The Dove makes much of its history: a handbill details the comings and goings of Charles II and Nell Gwynn, while an 1897 photograph is one of the many visual nods to its prime location. As Mr Fuller was one of the gentlemen involved in a 1796 takeover of the enterprise, it's no surprise to find the full range of Fuller's ales at the bar; the great-but-pricey food includes sandwiches, a house burger and pub-grub mains such as slow-roasted pork belly with celeriac mash. Inside, it's basically a classic duck-your-head heritage pub experience, but most drinkers come here to sit in the vine-entangled conservatory or the riverside terrace overlooking the houseboats. *Tables outdoors (11, riverside terrace).*

Grand Union

45 Woodfield Road, W9 2BA (7286 1886, www.grandunionlondon.co.uk). Westbourne Park tube. **Open** 11am-11pm Mon-Thur;

Dove

11am-midnight Fri, Sat; noon-10.30pm Sun. **Food served** noon-10pm Mon-Sat; noon-9pm Sun. **Westbourne Park**
From the outside, set on a busy traffic bridge, this looks like an archetypal JAG (Just Another Gastropub) makeover. Head through the pub to the terrace, though, and the scenery changes completely: table after table after table beneath large black umbrellas, all overlooking the slow-flowing canal. This terrace is the Grand Union's greatest asset, to be sure. However, the interior is also attractive, done out with post-war propaganda photographs of the catering and drinking industries. There's enough chat-level indie din to bring in the twentysomethings, but there are couple-friendly low brown sofas in the street-level main bar area. The beers are decent – Litovel, San Miguel and Becks Vier alongside Fuller's ales – although there are few surprises in the cocktail or wine lists. There are gastro-standard mains; the highlight of the food menu is the dozen mix and match tapas plates. Not such a JAG after all.
Babies & children admitted (until 6pm). Entertainment (quiz 8pm Thur; open-mic 8pm alternate Sat). Function room (40 capacity). Tables outdoors (20, canalside terrace). Wireless internet. **Map p247 A4.**

Waterway
54 Formosa Street, W9 2JU (7266 3557, www.thewaterway.co.uk). Warwick Avenue tube. **Open** noon-11pm Mon-Fri; 10am-11pm Sat, Sun. **Food served** noon-3.30pm, 6.30-10.30pm Mon-Fri; 10.30am-3.30pm, 6.30-10.30pm Sat; 11am-3.30pm, 6.30-10pm Sun.
Maida Vale
The chief selling point of this stylish bar-restaurant is its wide terrace, so close to the Regent's Canal that you can touch the bobbing barges. It's quite pricey, but the clientele are happy to keep ordering as long as the sun keeps shining (you may find the interior completely empty of a July lunchtime), and it's not as if the venue is cutting corners in its provisions. Cocktails (around £8) come in fairly standard categories, but the quality of the mixes and the spirit bases need little gimmickry, and all syrups and purées are made on-site. The wine list is long: of the 50-ish varieties, a dozen are served by the half-litre carafe, the bottle or two sizes of glass; if you're just after a *vin de pays* to plonk into an ice bucket near the lap of the water, it'll come in around £16. A flatscreen TV has been placed in front of a sofa for rainy days, though it's just as nice to watch the barges from inside.
Babies & children admitted (until 9pm). Tables outdoors (40, terrace). Wireless internet.

Outer London

White Cross
Water Lane, Richmond, TW9 1TH (8940 6844, www.youngs.co.uk). Richmond tube/rail. **Open** 9.30am-11pm Mon-Sat; 9.30am-10.30pm Sun. **Food served** 9.30am-10pm Mon-Sat; 9.30am-9pm Sun. **Richmond, Surrey**
The Young's website stiffly bills this place as a 'Traditional Historic Riverside Pub'. The use of initial caps is clumsy, but it's oddly appropriate for this grande dame of Thameside boozers. In many regards, the White Cross is a by-the-book Young's operation: solid if unspectacular ales (plus a guest), uncomplicated pub grub, friendly and competent staff, decor that doesn't leave much of an impression either way. But most by-the-book Young's operations aren't right on the river like this one, to the point where the White Cross is often cut off by high tides in spring. Your company on the terrace or at the bar will be provided by a variety of longtime locals and just-arrived tourists, with assorted rugger buggers thrown into the mix on Twickenham match days. If you haven't got tickets, worry not: major games are screened in the pub.
Babies & children admitted (restaurant & garden only). Tables outdoors (30, garden). Wireless internet.

White Swan
Riverside, Twickenham, TW1 3DN (8744 2951, www.whiteswantwickenham.com). Twickenham rail. **Open** noon-11pm Mon-Sat; noon-10.30pm Sun. **Food served** noon-3.30pm, 6-9.30pm Mon-Fri; noon-9.30pm Sat; noon-8.30pm Sun.
Twickenham, Middx
This venerable riverside pub has had a quietly turbulent time recently, thanks to a couple of ownership changes. However, it seems to be settling down again, not that anyone's in any great hurry for it to change. The main selling point is the location: set on a particularly rural bend of the Thames, it's in a peach of a spot, and the views over the river are wonderfully bucolic. But if the weather rules against sitting outside, the interior's far from ugly, wearing its 300-year history with ease. Unsurprisingly, the offerings from both bar (decent ales) and kitchen (pub grub) don't divert much from tradition, but that's just the way the locals and the occasional interloping tourists like it.
Babies & children admitted. Entertainment (musicians 8.30pm Wed). Tables outdoors (25, balcony; 15, garden). Wireless internet.

Also recommended...
Roebuck (Classic Pubs, *p106*).

Good Mixers

Central	172
North	183
North East	184
East	185
South East	191
South	192
South West	195
West	196
North West	198

Good Mixers

The bars in this section are a wildly disparate bunch, with little in common save a lack of focus on one particular strength. If that sounds damning, it's not meant to be. Quite the contrary, in fact: most of these venues are excellent all-rounders that offer different pleasures to different drinkers, with variety a speciality of sorts.

Some of these bars are pubby in spirit: the **Hemingway** and the **Woolpack** both update traditional pub aesthetics for the 21st century. Others are built on bar culture: **Idlewild** blends upscale cocktails with smartened, gastropub-esque cooking, while **Off Broadway** attempts to bring an American-style bar to Hackney. And others defy categorisation: **CAMP** falls halfway between café and club; the **Bloomsbury Bowling Lanes** offers everything from American comfort cooking to rockabilly bands; and **Lost Angel** advertises itself as 'Bar, Restaurant, Boozer', which seems to cover all bases.

But then there are the two enormous new ventures in the City that, with recession-defying bravado, attempt even more: between them, the **Anthologist** and **Folly** have spaces and times set aside for the functions of café, restaurant, deli, cocktail lounge, champagne bar, florist, and wine and pop-up shops.

At some of these bars, you'll find both cocktails and real ales; at others, great chefs and great DJs are both on the payroll. In other words? A mixed bag.

Central

Alphabet
61-63 Beak Street, W1F 9SL (7439 2190, www.alphabet-bar.co.uk). Oxford Circus or Piccadilly Circus tube. **Open** noon-11pm Mon-Sat. **Food served** noon-9pm Mon-Sat. **Soho**
Little has changed at Alphabet since its days at the forefront of the Soho boho bar circuit. The street-level dining area is bookended by a bar counter and skylight at one end and sofas and a picture window at the other, while the walls feature long-in-the-tooth graffiti. The drinks list includes several fruity, quaffable numbers (apple martinis, raspberry mojitos); spirits are unspecified, but the back bar is lined with high-end brands. The wine list plays it safe, and there are various bottled continental lagers. Food is a bigger deal these days, with modestly priced small plates (chorizo and new potatoes, pan-fried squid) and comforting mains (Aberdeen Angus burger, king prawn and avocado salad).
Wireless internet. **Map p241 J6.**

Anthologist
58 Gresham Street, EC2V 7BB (0845 468 0101, www.theanthologistbar.co.uk). St Paul's tube or Bank tube/DLR. **Open** 7.30am-11pm Mon-Fri; 10pm-3am Sat. **Food served** 7.30am-10pm Mon-Fri. **City**
This enormous and ambitious undertaking comprises a pair of cocktail lounges, restaurant, bar, suitably rustic deli and wine shop in a vast space that resembles a more edgy, metropolitan All Bar One. While there's the clichéd wine cellar theme, some of the more 'daring' design touches include bell-jar lamps dangling from curtain rails, a 1950s kitchen and lots of large, loud orange tables. City boys and girls (all in suits) are seduced by the large list of champagnes, or dabble in the 'wine flights' (actually three standard measures of 125ml). Cocktails are segregated into either 'skinny' – the Russian Rose Martini weighs in at 80 calories – or 'signature' sections. Starting at 8am serving big breakfasts and brunch, the open-plan kitchen offers burgers, fish pies and sharing platters, including a seafood option of oysters, lobster and clams served in a bank deposit box.
Babies & children admitted. Booking advisable. Disabled: toilet. Entertainment (DJs 10pm Sat). Funcion room (35-75 capacity). Wireless internet. **Map p245 P6.**

Bar Polski
11 Little Turnstile, WC1V 7DX (7831 9679). Holborn tube. **Open** 4-11pm Mon; 12.30-11pm

Tue-Thur; 12.30-11.30pm Fri; 6-11pm Sat.
Food served 4-10pm Mon; 12.30-10pm
Tue-Fri; 6-10pm Sat. **Holborn**
This diminutive Polish hideaway stocks some
50 different vodkas, categorised according to
descriptions such as 'clean and clear', 'dry and
interesting' and 'nice and sweet'. It's a flat-rate
£2.90 for your shot, whether that's rowanberry-
flavoured Jarzebiak, the cherry Wisniowka,
caraway seed-tinted Kminkowy or sweet
aniseed Zacheta. To chase the chaser, avoid the
draught options and go for a Polish brew from
the well-stocked fridge (Zubr, Zywiec, Tatra or
Lech, perhaps). Hearty *bigos* stew, *pierogi* and
herring are among the comestibles. The merry
throng is overlooked by a large, folk art-style
mural of a cockerel.
Babies & children admitted. **Map p243 M5.**

Barrio Central

*6 Poland Street, W1F 8PS (3230 1002,
www.barriocentral.com). Oxford Circus tube.*
Open noon-1am Mon-Sat. **Food served**
5-10pm Mon-Thur; noon-10pm Fri, Sat. **Soho**
Where once shone the Amber bar, you'll now
find the strikingly Latino Barrio Central. The
main street-level bar comprises a narrow room
lined with glass-topped tables, effectively display
cases for comics, games and knick-knacks that
exude playful character. A park bench and
greenery at the back also offer decorative
variety. The drinks menu, 'in Spanglish', is
categorised by region or country: a Brazilian
Lady (Abelha cachaça and passionfruit)

complements manly Quilmes beer from Buenos
Aires; a Mayan Magic (dark chocolate, chilli,
agave and Cazadores tequila) represents
Central America; a Hispaniola Spell (Brugal
rum, shochu, jasmine, mint and ginger), the
Caribbean; and so on. Bloody big Barrio burgers,
sandwiches and burritos are filled with slow-
roasted pulled pork and other grilled meats.
*Entertainment (bands/DJs 7pm Tue-Sat).
Wireless internet.* **Map p241 J6.**

Benugo Bar & Kitchen

*BFI Southbank, Belvedere Road, SE1 8XT
(7401 9000, www.benugo.com). Waterloo
tube/rail.* **Open** 9.30am-11pm daily. **Food
served** 11am-10pm daily. **Waterloo**
After years of struggle, BFI Southbank has
finally figured out its catering. Or, rather, they
got Benugo to figure it out for them. The low
ceiling, square dimensions and lack of natural
light have long hampered the riverfront space,
and Benugo haven't succeeded in making it into
an appealing venue. But it's a different story in
the newer bar further back, always busy with a
mix of cinephiles and other revellers who've
realised that this is the best place to drink on the
South Bank. In a roomy space decked out in
kitchen-sink fashion with an artful jumble of
furnishings, the efficient staff serve unusual
lagers and decent wines at slightly above-
average prices, plus food that runs from the
serious to the cheeky. The evening atmosphere's
always lively, a welcome change from the dreary
bars elsewhere on this stretch.

Barrio Central

Babies & children admitted. Disabled: toilet.
Wireless internet. **Map p250 M8**.

Bloomsbury Bowling Lanes

Basement, Tavistock Hotel, Bedford Way,
WC1H 9EU (7183 1979, www.bloomsbury
lanes.com). Russell Square tube. **Open** 1pm-
midnight Mon-Wed, Sun; 1pm-2am Thur;
1pm-3am Fri; noon-3am Sat. **Food served**
1-10pm Mon-Fri; noon-10pm Sat, Sun.

Bloomsbury
Looking like the kind of place where Shaggy
and his gang might congregate after solving
yet another mystery, the BBL offers a splendid
mix of authentic Americana and knowing
kitsch. Alongside the lanes, rentable by the
hour, sit walls of Apollo-era ads for bowling
balls and bags (priced in dollars); bright signs
advertise such unavailable delicacies as
'Hamm's on tap' and 'Whitman's refrigerated
fresh chocolates'. Food includes ice-creams and
burgers, although visitors over the age of 18
often prefer to pull up one of the tatty, bottle-
green swivel seats in the shadow of the
Bernard beer tap and call up one of five hard
shakes (Gutter Ball, with spiced rum; Brooklyn
Hit, with Jack Daniel's, peanut butter, vanilla
ice-cream and maple syrup). Private karaoke
booths and club nights (see www.bloomsbury
live.com) complete the picture at this messy but
altogether quite glorious place.

Café Kick

Babies & children admitted (until 4pm).
Disabled: toilet. Entertainment (bands
9pm Thur-Sat). Games (bowling, pool,
table football). Wireless internet.
Map p240 K4.

Bourne & Hollingsworth

28 Rathbone Place, W1T 1JF (7636 8228,
www.bourneandhollingsworth.com). Goodge
Street or Tottenham Court Road tube. **Open**
5pm-12.30am Mon-Wed; 5pm-1am Thur-Sat.
Fitzrovia
This basement cocktail bar has given a little pep
to an otherwise long-established after-work bar
scene in Media Central. Tucked down a flight of
stairs, it feels like a private members' club, at
least until you clock the granny's-house decor:
a china cup on each of seven tables, a white-rose
design on the wallpaper, a frilly lampshade.
The empty bottles of Mumm are perhaps
wishful thinking on behalf of the management,
although it's easy to do some serious damage to
the cocktail menu. In addition – and this is
where granny's cups come into the picture –
there are four teatime cocktails, including a
Chimps Tea of Monkey Shoulder, peach liqueur,
Earl Grey tea syrup and orange zest. A solitary
Asahi tap caters to lager drinkers.
Entertainment (DJs 8pm Thur-Sat).
Map p240 K5.

Bradley's Spanish Bar

42-44 Hanway Street, W1T 1UT (7636
0359). Tottenham Court Road tube. **Open**
noon-11pm Mon-Sat; 3-10.30pm Sun. **Fitzrovia**
Is it the all-vinyl jukebox? Is it the tatty velvet
furniture? Is it old habits dying hard? Whatever
the reason, London still loves Bradley's, a two-
floor cornucopia of straw-donkey-level Spanish
tack just off the wrong end of Oxford Street. A
hotch-potch of local workers, weary shoppers
and amorous foreign-exchange students fills the
cramped two-floor space, enraging passing taxi
drivers as they spill on to the narrow street
outside. All are happy to pay slightly over the
odds for draught Cruzcampo, San Miguel and
Budvar, the highlights of a fairly limited drinks
selection that's more about quantity than
quality. By contrast, no one's exactly happy to
use the toilets, but their poor condition is
generally seen as a price worth paying.
Map p240 K5.

Café Kick

43 Exmouth Market, EC1R 4QL (7837
8077, www.cafekick.co.uk). Angel tube or
Farringdon tube/rail. **Open** noon-11pm
Mon-Thur; noon-midnight Fri, Sat;
1-10.30pm Sun. **Food served** noon-3pm,

6-10pm Mon-Thur; noon-3pm, 6-10.30pm
Fri, Sat; 1-10pm Sun. **Clerkenwell**
This estimable landmark echoes the days when
Europe was exotic and Eusebio was king, and a
trip to France or Spain meant table football, odd
beers and little plates of delicious snacks. Staff
dish out Estrella Damm, Nastro Azzurro, Super
Bock and Sagres from a counter festooned with
bright bottle labels and blackboard promises
of tasty tapas (in the evening). Groups here for
table-football tournaments, played out on tables
filling the scarf-and-programme-lined space
between bar counter and terrace, can opt for
meat or vegetarian platters; other options
include sandwiches, salads and cheese boards.
There are wines and cocktails, though you'd fit
in better with beer. Oh, and who put that
Shrewsbury Town scarf among the illustrious
colours of Milan, Fiorentina and St Etienne?
Babies & children admitted (until 6pm).
Games (table football). **Map p242 N4.**

Camino

3 Varnishers Yard, Regents Quarter, N1 9FD
(7841 7331, www.camino.uk.com). King's
Cross tube/rail. **Open** 8am-midnight Mon-
Wed; 8am-1am Thur-Sat; 10am-11pm Sun.
Food served 8am-11pm Mon-Sat; 10am-
10pm Sun. **King's Cross**
Tucked in a redeveloped courtyard near King's
Cross station, Camino is a tapas bar – but don't
groan, as it's got a kind of industrial feel and
urban atmosphere. It's also got some serious
cocktails – a Zombie 66 features 66 12-year-old
rum, Wray & Nephew *and* El Dorado three-
year-old – sold by the glass or four-glass pitcher.
Beers (Estrella Damm or Amstel) are served by
the pint or 12oz frozen mug; bottled varieties
hail from Andalucia (Alhambra), Aragon
(Ambar) and Catalonia (Estrella Damm Inedit),
plus there's El Gaitero cider from Asturias.
You'll also find traditionally produced cava
Vilarnau, sherries and blancos, rosados and
tintos from all over Spain. The more popular,
such as the modern Rioja Elaboración Especial
Beronia 2009, is available by the bottle, carafe
or two sizes of glass. Oh yes, there are all your
favourite tapas too: pulpo a la parrilla,
manchego cheese, and so on.
Babies & children admitted (until 9pm).
Disabled: toilet. Entertainment (DJs 8pm
Thur-Sat). Games (table football). Tables
outdoors (8, courtyard). Wireless internet.

Cellar Door

Aldwych, WC2E 7DN (7240 8848,
www.cellardoor.biz). Covent Garden or
Temple tube. **Open** 4pm-1am daily.
Covent Garden

A gaudy neon arrow points the way to this tiny basement, where cabaret, lounge singers and drag acts ensure things go with a swing. Classic cocktails are mixed with three categories of high-end brands, and priced accordingly: if you'd prefer your martini made with Tanqueray 10 or U'luvka, expect to pay a couple of quid extra. House cocktails include the Starbucks Must Die (Martell VS, Kahlua, own-made vanilla-infused vodka and a shot of espresso); a compact wine list caters for cocktail refuseniks and snuff is available in assorted flavours (snorting straw provided). Customers arriving before 8pm can enjoy cut-price drinks. *Booking essential. Entertainment (cabaret 9pm daily). Wireless internet.* **Map p243 M7.**

Commercial Tavern

142 Commercial Street, E1 6NU (7247 1888). Liverpool Street tube/rail or Shoreditch High Street rail. **Open** *5-11pm Mon-Fri; noon-11pm Sat; noon-10.30pm Sun.* **City**
Its authentically traditional pub exterior jutting out into Commercial Street like a ship's prow, the Commercial Tavern is a wantonly wacky revamp outpost of the Hoxton boho bar beat. Polaroids of 24-hour party people, a whole wall of *Interview* magazine covers and a cluster of retro lampshades all point towards the venue's underground bent, although the pretty young bar staff will still provide your change on a silver platter. It'll be too dark to see the beer taps on the brightly tiled bar counter, but ale drinkers should enjoy a pint of Meantime Helles or London Pale Ale, or Young's Special. If chat and early Bowie over the speakers start to lose their appeal, there's a pool table filling most of a small side room; upstairs has its own bar. *Disabled: toilet. Games (pool). Tables outdoors (3, pavement).* **Map p244 R5.**

Driver

2-4 Wharfdale Road, N1 9RY (7278 8827, www.driverlondon.co.uk). King's Cross tube/ rail. **Open** *noon-midnight Mon-Fri; 5pm-midnight Sat; noon-6pm Sun.* **Food served** *noon-3pm, 6-10pm Mon-Fri; 6-10pm Sat; noon-6pm Sun.* **King's Cross**
Set in the tangle of unpromising streets behind King's Cross, the Driver is a stylish gastropub, with a 'vertical garden' and a decked roof terrace, complemented by three more floors of dining and drinking space, above a street-level bar and restaurant of equally interesting design. There you can sip a San Miguel, Blue Moon or St Austell Tribute beneath a reindeer head in the loungey area by the fireplace or at the bar, itself hewn out of a jagged tree trunk. The tables are for diners (seared kangaroo rump, grilled skate wing), while

drinkers can partake of cocktails such as the house mojito with a dash of Frangelico. Wines start at £4.40/£15 and run up to a Château Haut-Bages Averoux at £70. *Babies & children admitted (until 10pm). Booking advisable. Disabled: toilet. Entertainment (DJs 7pm Fri). Function rooms (100 capacity). Tables outdoors (4, pavement; 5, terrace). Wireless internet.*

Endurance

90 Berwick Street, W1F 0QB (7437 2944, www.thetemperance.co.uk/endurance). Leicester Square, Oxford Circus or Tottenham Court Road tube. **Open** *12.30-11pm Mon-Wed, Sat; 12.30-11.30pm Thur; noon-11.30pm Fri.* **Food served** *12.30-4pm Mon-Fri.* **Soho**
It's now more food-focused than during Berwick Street's golden era of retro vinyl emporia, but the former King of Corsica still gathers a music-savvy Soho crowd to dine by day and wine away the night. The 100-tune jukebox (Strokes, Kings of Leon, classics) remains sacrosanct but with the volume kept low over lunch, as cosmopolitan types sit at black banquettes tucking into Thai curry, spicy sausages or rib-eye steak. Bar-like in appearance, bear-like in design with its ursine sign and mounted taxidermy, the Endurance acts as the local pub after the local offices close, awash with gossip and chat-up lines around a central, octagonal bar counter over pints of Red Stripe, San Miguel and London Pride. *Babies & children admitted (until 6pm). Booking advisable Thur, Fri. Wireless internet.* **Map p241 J6.**

Fellow

24 York Way, N1 9AA (7833 4395, www. thefellow.co.uk). King's Cross tube/rail. **Open** *noon-11pm Mon; noon-midnight Tue-Sat; noon-10pm Sun.* **Food served** *noon-3pm, 6-10pm Mon-Sat; noon-6pm Sun.* **King's Cross**
Pitching itself as 'an alternative drinking and dining destination in King's Cross', this gastropub comprises two imbibing areas, each a standout in this rapidly changing locality. Offset from the restaurant that takes up most of the ground-floor space, a holding bar has a counter lined with taps of Otter, Peroni and Sharp's Doom Bar; Pimm's by the jug (£11.50) is a popular alternative. Upstairs, a pretty walled garden adjoins an evening-only lounge bar with low seating, cocktails and regular DJ sets. To complement the Mersea Island wild oysters and whole baked Tunworth cheese, the dozen wines by the glass range from an entry-level Cantiga Viura (£2.90/£15.50) to quality Chablis, Sancerre and an unusual Hatziadakis Cuvée 17 from Santorini in the £30 bracket. The

upstairs cocktail list has its own recherché menu featuring Trealy Monmouthshire air-dried ham and Barkham blue cheese. *Babies & children admitted (until 5pm). Booking advisable. Entertainment (DJs 7pm Thur, Fri). Function room (80 capacity). Games (board games). Tables outdoors (5, pavement; 4, terrace). Wireless internet.*

Fluid
40 Charterhouse Street, EC1M 6JN (7253 3444, www.fluidbar.com). Farringdon tube/rail. **Open** noon-midnight Mon-Wed; noon-2am Thur; noon-4am Fri; 7pm-4am Sat. **Food served** noon-10pm Mon-Fri. **Clerkenwell**
Asahi, saké and sushi prevail in this two-floor Japanese-themed urban retreat. Brightly coloured vinyl stencils over the windows and retro computer games feature on the ground floor; downstairs, a brash mural of Tokyo by night has customers gawping, while DJs spin most evenings. Guinness and Asahi lager on draught and Kirin, Sapporo and Asahi Super Dry by the bottle complement almost two dozen cocktails (£7): among them is the powerful Tokyo Ice Tea, involving Midori, tequila, vodka, gin and Cointreau. Assorted sakés and shochus round off the drinks menu, along with Nikka, Gingko and Suntory whiskies and a few wines. Sushi, sashimi and tempura feature on the menu, and there are various bento boxes. *Babies & children admitted (until 9pm). Entertainment (DJs 7pm Tue-Sat). Games (retro video games). Function room (100 capacity). Tables outdoors (3, pavement). Wireless internet.* **Map p242 O5.**

Folly
41 Gracechurch Street, EC3V 0BT (0845 468 0102, www.thefollybar.co.uk). Monument tube. **Open** 7.30am-1am Mon-Fri; 10.30am-1am Sat; 10.30am-7pm Sun. **Food served** 7.30am-10pm Mon-Fri; 10.30am-10pm Sat; 10.30am-5pm Sun. **City**
A vast, yawning venue, spread over two floors and multiple levels with a look that's part industrial and part *Country Living*, this chameleon tries to be a lot of things. It's a deli and restaurant (and florist) during the day and, later, a brash, buzzy cocktail and champagne bar. Upstairs, an open kitchen opposite an array of long picnic tables serves sharing platters, gourmet sandwiches, seafood and pub staples made posh. Drinkers head down to couches and tables for two lit by birdcage lanterns, or the private vaults. Bartenders will create cocktails to your design using fresh ingredients, or you can choose from twists on

Market Place

standard classics, such as an apple and honey margarita, or 'skinnies'. The wine list isn't overly extortionate (house wine is under £14), but a lot of bubbly – mainly prosecco and Pommery – gets poured. *Babies & children admitted (until 7pm). Booking advisable. Disabled: toilet. Function room (35-80 capacity). Wireless internet.* **Map p245 Q7.**

Freud
198 Shaftesbury Avenue, WC2H 8JL (7240 9933, www.freud.eu). Tottenham Court Road tube. **Open** 11am-11pm Mon-Wed; 11am-1am Thur, Sat; 11am-2am Fri; noon-10.30pm Sun. **Food served** noon-4.30pm daily. **Covent Garden**
Back in the late 1980s, this was the place to be. A hidden cellar with a faintly industrial feel, it carried with it a certain easy-going democracy, a welcome change from style-trial nightclubs and members-only enterprises such as the Groucho. After what seems a lifetime, it hasn't changed a bit. The 40-odd affordable cocktails (£5.50-£7.25), stencilled above the busy bar counter, are strong and served with ceremony: a Holy Freud Lemonade contains vodka, lychee, lemonade and elderberry, while mojitos come in several varieties. Some 15 types of bottled beer include Meantime, Budvar and Zywiec, while wine starts at a bargain £3.35 a glass. Rotating art exhibitions dot the aged-concrete walls; it does, after all, say 'Café Bar

Gallery' in red neon outside. Who'd have thought it would survive so long? *Babies & children admitted (until 4.30pm).* **Map p240 L6.**

De Hems

11 Macclesfield Street, W1D 5BW (7437 2494, www.nicholsonspubs.co.uk). Leicester Square tube. **Open** 10am-midnight Mon-Sat; noon-10.30pm Sun. **Food served** 10am-10pm Mon-Sat; noon-10pm Sun. **Chinatown**
This famous old Dutch pub was once a refuge for homesick Dutch sailors, then later became a rallying point for the Dutch Resistance during World War II. Dotted with retro beer ads and faux Dutch Masters, it now attracts punters savvy about their Benelux brews, with taps offering the likes of Hoegaarden, Lindeboom, Franziskaner, Früli and Leffe. The bottled options fill one of the venue's natty menus: Kwak, Delirium Tremens and Chimay all come in their own logoed glasses, although the gift-wrapped Bacchus is pretty enough without. The food menu mixes English and Dutch cuisines, along with the kind of bar snacks – *bitterballen, loempia* – you might find in any Amsterdam café. *Babies & children admitted (until 7pm). Disabled: toilet. Entertainment (DJs 8pm Fri, Sat). Tables outdoors (3, pavement).* **Map p241 K6.**

Kanaloa

18 Lime Office Court, Hill House, Shoe Lane, EC4A 3BQ (7842 0620, www.kanaloaclub. com). Chancery Lane tube. **Open/food served** 4pm-3am Mon-Fri; 9pm-3am Sat. **City**
The cover of this tiki bar's menu promises 'fanciful drinks and exotic concoctions'; inside, cheery illustrations depict kitsch Polynesian-themed cocktails and punches, served in suitably outré vessels. Coconuts are filled with tequila, orange bitters and a hot sauce, while a Krakatoa (wasn't that Indonesia?) comprises a mini volcano of Kanaloa Grog (overproof and caramel rum blends) and sundry, inappropriate fruit juices. Those of a macabre bent may enjoy a Dead Man's Chest (£100, serves eight), a coffin brimming with Seven Tiki white rum, maraschino cherries and claret. It's all complete nonsense, of course, but bags of fun on the right night and in the right company. Stave off inebriation with dim sum, lobster tempura or salt and chilli squid. *Booking advisable. Disabled: toilet. Entertainment (hula girls 7.30pm Wed-Fri). Function room (150 capacity). Tables outdoors (6, pavement). Wireless internet.* **Map p243 N6.**

Market Place

11-13 Market Place, W1W 8AH (7079 2020, www.marketplace-london.com). Oxford Circus tube. **Open** 11am-midnight Mon-Wed; 11am-1am Thur; 11am-2am Fri; noon-2am Sat; 1-11pm Sun. **Food served** noon-11pm Mon-Sat; 1-11pm Sun. **Fitzrovia**
A gregarious crowd gathers at this urban bar-diner, both in the main, street-level bar and in the larger space downstairs where DJs play. It's an industrial space with wooden-slatted walls, exposed iron columns and an open kitchen. The mixed clientele tucks into a food selection that runs from snacks such as smoked salmon and cream cheese bagels to main courses of grilled squid, butter beans and lamb's lettuce. Pilsner Urquell, König, Bitburger and Köstritzer Schwarzbier are the pricey continental draught options, accompanied by a dozen wines by the glass. For cocktails, sample the signature Market Place Punch (Pimm's No.1, Finlandia Grapefruit vodka, fresh mint, strawberries, cucumber, citrus fruits and cloudy apple juice). *Disabled: toilet. Entertainment (DJs 8pm Thur-Sat). Tables outdoors (8, terrace). Wireless internet.* **Map p240 J6.**

Medcalf

38-40 Exmouth Market, EC1R 4QE (7833 3533, www.medcalfbar.co.uk). Farringdon tube/rail or bus 19, 38, 341. **Open** noon-11pm Mon-Thur, Sat; noon-12.30am Fri; noon-5.30pm Sun. **Food served** noon-3pm, 6-10pm Mon-Thur; noon-3pm, 6-10.30pm Fri; noon-3.30pm, 6-10pm Sat; noon-4pm Sun. **Clerkenwell**
Foodies and creatives gather in the main dining room and the arty side space of this quality meal-time haunt, which also offers tables outside on Exmouth Market and on a decked terrace at the back. The narrow interior space reflects the building's previous function as a butcher's shop; today, rustic breads have replaced meat pies garlanded by plastic parsley. Food is still paramount here – oak-smoked salmon and Hereford rib of beef might be among the daily-changing options – but Medcalf is also at pains to provide a surprising array of beers. Brooklyn, Rothaus, Paulaner and Meantime Helles line the

tall bar counter amid the bare light bulbs and art in the main room; by the bottle, you'll find Colonel Pale Ale, Estrella Damm and Boon Kriek, among others. Prices are reasonable, encouraging a Hoxton-like vibe as dinner drifts to social drinks. *Babies & children admitted (until 7pm). Booking advisable. Disabled: toilet. Function room (50 capacity). Games (darts). Tables outside (5, garden; 7, pavement). Wireless internet.* **Map p242 N4.**

Mustard Bar & Lounge

2 Old Change Court, Peter's Hill, EC4M 8EN (7236 5318, www.mustard-bar.com). St Paul's tube. **Open** noon-11pm Mon-Wed; noon-1am Thur, Fri. **Food served** noon-3pm, 5-9pm Mon-Fri. **City**

An oasis of contemporary bar culture in a locality dotted with wine bars and traditional pubs, Mustard is of its own. It stands off the main street, a seemingly small, streamlined pavilion that turns out to be much larger inside. Red predominates in a space surrounded by low, padded benches, while images of the Far East line a raised lounge area. A second, downstairs bar handles the overflow on clubbier nights. Cocktails include a Mustard Bison of Smirnoff, Chambord, crème de cassis and raspberries; a Mustard Kiwi makes use of vodka and fresh fruit. Absolut and Beefeater feature in the seven martinis; a handful of them are sold at cut rates during the nightly happy hour. Wines include a £41.50 Laroche Chablis and a Castillo de Clavijo Rioja (£30.50); food is tarted-up comfort cooking (burgers, sharing platters), with a curry of the day and other Indian dishes added to the mix. *Babies & children admitted (until 5pm). Disabled: toilet. Entertainment (DJs 8pm Thur, Fri). Tables outdoors (25, garden).* **Map p245 P7.**

Nordic

25 Newman Street, W1T 1PN (7631 3174, www.nordicbar.com). Tottenham Court Road tube. **Open** noon-11pm Mon-Thur; noon-midnight Fri; 6pm-midnight Sat. **Food served** noon-3pm, 5.30-10pm Mon-Thur; noon-3pm, 6-11pm Fri; 6-11pm Sat. **Fitzrovia**

It's now looking a little ragged at the edges, but the party-hearty drinkers who frequent this basement either don't mind or don't notice the slight shabbiness or the faintly dated decor as long as the drinks remain cheap, the atmosphere remains cheerful and the triptych of Max von Sydow sinking an akvavit remains on the wall. There are beers and wines, but the main points of interest on the menu are the cocktails, all

based on Scandinavian ingredients and recipes: the Northern Light, for instance, is a sweet concoction of muddled fresh mint, mango and white peach purée, mandarin vodka and blue curaçao. The shots (£3) are as cheeky as their names (Flaming Volvo, Björn's Balls). *Function room (50 capacity). Wireless internet.* **Map p240 J5.**

Phoenix Artist Club

1 Phoenix Street, WC2H 8BU (7836 1077, www.phoenixartistclub.com). Leicester Square or Tottenham Court Road tube. **Open** 5pm-2.30am Mon-Sat. **Food served** 5-9pm Mon-Sat. **Soho**

Kitsch, messy and a late-night legend, this basement bar attracts a regular crowd of debauched luvvies and miscreants. Play spot-the-soap-extra as you order a pint of Red Stripe, Kirin Ichiban, Heineken or Wells Bombardier at the bar, which is surrounded by signed black-and-white publicity shots of not-quite-familiar faces. The club is members only, but the trick to enjoying its way-past-midnight hospitality is to arrive before 8pm and stay put. After work, you can find a spot beneath the hand-painted glass panels and theatrical memorabilia: a dark and cosy alcove, perhaps, or prepare for take-off in one of the aeroplane seats. Being an artists' club, there are naturally two stages for cabaret, and a big screen for the seventh art. *Function room (100 capacity). Wireless internet.* **Map p241 K6.**

Positively 4th Street

119 Hampstead Road, NW1 3EE (7388 5380, www.positively4thstreet.co.uk). Euston tube/rail. **Open** 5-11pm Mon, Tue; noon-3pm, 5-11pm Thur; noon-3pm, 5pm-1am Fri; 7pm-1am Sat. **Food served** 5-10.30pm Mon, Tue; noon-3pm, 5-10.30pm Thur, Fri; 7-10.30pm Sat. **Euston**

You got a lotta nerve to put a New York-styled ersatz speakeasy on a corner in the no-man's land between Euston and Mornington Crescent. But does it work? Mostly. Low lighting and quirky decorative touches help create an atmospheric room, and the cocktails are decent and keenly priced: a Japanese cosmopolitan (vodka, Midori, lime and cranberry) goes for six quid. It can feel forlorn when it's empty, and the airless basement is far less appealing than the ground-level room. But on the whole, and despite the baffling name (the only other nod to Bob Dylan is the appearance of a cocktail called a Zimmerman Revisited), this is fun. Curiously, the food is Thai. *Entertainment (jazz 8pm Mon; DJs 8.30pm Fri). Function room (30 capacity).*

Simmons

*32 Caledonian Road, N1 9DT (7278 5851).
King's Cross tube/rail.* **Open/food served**
4pm-midnight Mon-Wed; 4pm-2am Thur;
4pm-3am Fri, Sat. **King's Cross**
This now evening-only DJ bar still attracts a
studenty, music-savvy crowd to what looks like
a cross between an old-style corner newsagents
and a Shoreditch-like retro bar. *Fantastic Four*
comic albums, board games in tatty boxes and
furniture both wobbly and ratty are juxtaposed
with a disco ball and a United Nations of beer
cans displayed on a shelving unit. As for actual
liquid nectar, there's no drinks menu ('Nah mate,
we just don't bother'), only taps of Amstel and
Tiger atop a tiny bar counter behind which
packets of Refreshers and Wizz Fizz offer
childhood allure. A fridge contains bottles of
Moretti, Tsingtao and Singha beers; standard
cocktails are mixed according to request; and,
on Mondays, everything seems to cost £2.50.
*Babies & children admitted (until 7pm).
Disabled: toilet. Entertainment (DJs 9pm
Thur-Sat). Function room (60 capacity).
Games (board games). Tables outdoors
(2, pavement). Wireless internet.*

Slaughtered Lamb

*34-35 Great Sutton Street, EC1V 0DX
(7253 1516, www.theslaughteredlambpub.
co.uk). Barbican tube or Farringdon tube/rail.*
Open noon-11pm Mon-Thur, Sun; noon-1am
Fri, Sat. **Food served** noon-10pm Mon-Sat;
1-8pm Sun. **Clerkenwell**
The Slaughtered Lamb's expansive main room
is centred on a busy bar counter, surrounded by
mismatched tables and chairs, and the odd
slouchy sofa. It's a popular place, with punters
queuing two deep. The bar is large enough to
accommodate an impressive array of taps
(Paulaner, Camden Hells, Red Stripe, Directors,
Bombardier, Erdinger, Sleeman Pale Ale);
behind it, the fridges are packed with bottles of
Pacifico, Brooklyn Lager and others. The menu
sticks to classic crowd-pleasers, as does the
compact wine list. Old portraits and maps of
Britain complete the decor, while downstairs a
somewhat menacing, Masonic-looking red neon
pentangle is the backdrop for gigs.
*Babies & children admitted (until 8pm).
Disabled: toilet. Entertainment (bands 8pm
daily; DJs 8pm Fri, Sat). Wireless internet.*
Map p242 O4.

Social

*5 Little Portland Street, W1W 7JD (7636
4992, www.thesocial.com). Oxford Circus tube.*
Open noon-midnight Mon-Wed; noon-1am
Thur-Sat. **Food served** noon-11pm Mon-Fri;
5-11pm Sat. **Fitzrovia**
Neil Thomson's photographs of the Social's
tenth birthday celebrations sum up this most
successful of music bars. Featured party acts
Doves, Saint Etienne and the Magic Numbers
link the Social with Heavenly Recordings, the
indie label with whom its roots lie. More than
a decade in, and the mission remains the same:
to provide proper cocktails, decent global beers,
awesome jukebox tunes, solid DJ bookings and
prole grub for the masses. Five booths
accommodate music-savvy thirtysomethings
munching square pies and fish-finger salads.

Medcalf. *See p179.*

Folly. *See p178.*

Cocktails (£8) also carry a musical theme: Chambord, peach purée, fresh lime and ginger beer introduce themselves in Sympathy for the Devil. Among the draught beer offerings are Amstel and Sagres; Heineken and Estrella are available by the bottle.
Babies & children admitted (until 5pm). Entertainment (bands/DJs 7pm Mon-Sat). Tables outdoors (2, pavement). Wireless internet. **Map p240 J5.**

Sun & 13 Cantons

21 Great Pulteney Street, W1F 9NG (7734 0934, www.fullers.co.uk). Oxford Circus or Piccadilly Circus tube. **Open** noon-11pm Mon-Fri; 6-11pm Sat. **Food served** noon-3pm, 6.30-10pm Mon-Fri. **Soho**
The Sun stands out from its many Soho rivals by virtue of its enthusiasm for music and its surprising Thai food. The 13 cantons of its name refers to the area's Swiss heritage of the late 1800s, although the decorative focus these days is on post-war pop culture. Stylish photographs of *Raw Power*-era Iggy, Bonds-era Clash, Cash and Dylan tower over taps of Litovel, San Miguel and Peroni. As there's a stylish dining room, wine hasn't been overlooked. An inexpensive selection of Thai food runs from curries in various colours to fragrant noodles and spicy soups. DJs provide the crowds of after-work drinkers with a soundtrack for their gossipy conversation.
Babies & children admitted (until 6pm). Entertainment (DJs 7pm occasional Thur, Fri). Wireless internet. **Map p241 J6.**

Two Floors

3 Kingly Street, W1B 5PD (7439 1007, www.barworks.co.uk). Oxford Circus or Piccadilly Circus tube. **Open** noon-11.30pm Mon-Thur; noon-midnight Fri, Sat. **Soho**
With separate entrances at either end and a few outdoor tables in Kingly Court, Two Floors feels more spacious than it is. The first floor sees Hoxtonesque bar bohemia, with regular rotations of young artists' work offsetting a dark interior. The short row of taps – two Red Stripe, two Camden Hells – gives the minimum of choice in draught selection, but Estrella, Brooklyn, Modelo Especial and Goose Island come by the bottle. There are four wines of each colour, with democratic pricing and crowd-pleasing selections: a South African chenin blanc, Chilean cab sauv. Down in the basement is Handy Joe's Tiki Bar, a kitsch Hawaiian-themed affair complete with bamboo panelling and illuminated tiki masks.
Function room (80 capacity). Tables outdoors (3, courtyard). Wireless internet. **Map p241 J6.**

North

Crown & Goose

100 Arlington Road, NW1 7HP (7485 8008,
www.crownandgoose.co.uk). Camden Town
tube. **Open** noon-midnight Mon-Thur, Sun;
noon-2am Fri, Sat. **Food served** noon-3pm,
6-10pm Mon-Fri; noon-5pm, 6-10pm Sat;
noon-10pm Sun. **Camden**
Set a little way from the main Camden beat, this
is a delightfully relaxed gastropub, a polite
young professional in casual after-work clothing.
The bar and the dining area fit around a half-
hexagon bar counter, with the whole intimate
single space imbued with the wafts of gravies
and sauces from the kitchen at the back.
A soundtrack of Janis, Aretha and the Velvets
plays as regulars sup on Sagres, Adnams or
Guinness (or bottles of Leffe, Budvar and
Moretti) against a backdrop of framed
butterflies and circular brass light-holders.
Laphroaig, Bushmills and other whiskies are
served over the cramped bar counter, while diners
at the back tuck into pan-fried salmon, butternut
squash Thai curry and the inevitable steaks.
Babies & children admitted (until 7pm).
Disabled: toilet. Function room (50 capacity).
Tables outdoors (8, pavement). Wireless
internet. **Map p254 J1.**

Pineapple

51 Leverton Street, NW5 2NX (7284 4631).
Kentish Town tube/rail. **Open** noon-11pm
Mon-Sat; noon-10.30pm Sun. **Food served**
noon-3pm, 6-10pm Mon-Fri; noon-10.30pm
Sat, Sun. **Kentish Town**
Tucked away in a maze of backstreet terraces,
this justifiably popular pub sits conveniently out
of earshot of the Kentish Town bustle. The bar
counter will greet you before the aromas of Thai
food: it's an ornate, carved Victorian affair not
three paces from the front door, with an
impressive array of beery choices. Ales from
Adnams, Redemption and Sambrook's join Leffe,
Beck's Vier and Staropramen in the narrow
space; beer festivals each Easter further extend
the choice. The bar is framed by two corridors
each side, with a conservatory housing a back
dining area and a garden beyond it; decor is an
easy-going mix of trad pub furniture and
handsome contemporary touches. The Pineapple
is more of a drinking house than a culinary
destination, though the Thai food and £5 lunches
are decent value and seem to please the punters.
Babies & children admitted (until 7pm).
Entertainment (quiz 8pm Mon; bands 8.30pm
Tue). Function room (35 capacity). Games
(board games). Tables outdoors (15, garden).
Wireless internet. **Map p254 J24.**

Tufnell Park Tavern

162 Tufnell Park Road, N7 0EE (7281 6113,
www.tufnellparktavern.com). Tufnell Park
tube. **Open** *Bar* noon-11pm Mon-Sat; noon-
10.30pm Sun. *Deli* 8am-5pm daily. **Food**
served noon-3pm, 6-10pm Mon-Sat; noon-
3pm, 6-9.30pm Sun. **Tufnell Park**
Banks of large windows let plenty of light into
this airy space containing a pub, restaurant and
deli. Large blackboards encircle the interior,
displaying a menu that runs from Maldon
oysters to Spanish tortilla. The adjoining deli
serves a range of delicious-looking pizzas with
interesting toppings such as Turkish lamb and
pine nuts, or field mushrooms, garlic and
thyme. Informal diners can take to the leather
sofas dotted around the pub, or the more
intimate dining area kitted out with wooden
chairs and tables. Ale drinkers are catered for
with offerings such as Sharp's Doom Bar, but
there's also a selection of the usual lagers,
including Staropramen. Bottled options are
more varied, with Sagres, Bitburger and Leffe
available. The large raised wooden deck in the
garden is perfect for soaking up the rays while
tucking into your deli purchases.
Babies & children admitted. Booking advisable
Thur-Sun. Disabled: toilet. Entertainment (quiz
8pm Mon; pétanque 6.30pm Thur). Function
room (10-300 capacity). Games (board games).
Tables outdoors (22, garden). Wireless internet.

Wenlock & Essex

18-26 Essex Road, N1 8LN (7704 0871,
www.wenlockandessex.com). Angel tube. **Open**
noon-11.30pm Mon-Thur, Sun; noon-2am Fri,
Sat. **Food served** noon-9.30pm Mon-Thur,
Sun; noon-10.30pm Fri, Sat. **Islington**
This big bar rocks an urban bordello and
burlesque look with its ruby-red ceiling, tassel
lampshades and candelabras, with a solid Wild
West saloon-style bar top on which to lean, and
the separate 'Satan's Circus' mini-club with
dancefloor. But the whole thing kind of works.
Sort of. The cocktail list is classic and concise,
with mai tais, margaritas and martinis all at £7,
while wines are confined to half a dozen reds
and whites. The great draughts include wheat
beers and lager from Bavaria, a Canadian IPA,
a couple of cask ales and a trio of fine brews
from Camden Town Brewery; bottles cover a
similar geographical spread. Smaller dishes
include ploughman-esque 'pincho' dishes such
as pickles and pork pies, while larger plates take
in butternut and pea risotto, venison pie or
mussels and chips. The £5.50 'Workers Lunch'
(noon-4pm) includes a half of Camden beer;
brunches are big on Saturday; and on Sunday,
it's roast o'clock.

Babies & children admitted (until 9pm).
Booking advisable. Disabled: toilet.
Entertainment (quiz 8pm Tue; DJs 8pm
Fri, Sat). Tables outdoors (4, pavement).
Map p255 O1.

Also recommended...
Old Queen's Head (Clubs & Music
Venues, *p211*).

North East

Alibi
91 Kingsland High Street, E8 2PB (7249
2733, www.thealibilondon.co.uk). Dalston
Junction or Dalston Kingsland rail. **Open**
5pm-2am Mon-Wed, Sun; 5pm-3am Thur-Sat.
Dalston
It's easy to think of the Alibi as the naughty kid
brother to the Dalston Superstore just up the
street. While the Superstore beckons in punters
with a large, open storefront and promises of
cocktails and comfort-cooking, the Alibi offers
little hint of what lies within, and walking down
the thin staircase to the basement for the first
time can be a little unnerving. Still, don't be
shy: they're a friendly bunch down there, if
dauntingly hip. The bar's run by the Real Gold
'creative collective' (their description), which
stages an edgy mix of DJ nights throughout the
week. Drinks aren't anything special, but this is
a good spot regardless.
Entertainment (DJs 9pm Wed-Sat).
Wireless internet.

Biddle Bros
88 Lower Clapton Road, E5 0QR (no phone).
Clapton or Hackney Central rail. **Open**
6pm-midnight Mon-Fri; 11am-12.30am Sat;
11am-11pm Sun. **Clapton**
This bar is named after the business that
previously occupied the premises: as the sign out
front advertises, the Biddle brothers were
builders' merchants. These days, the tools have
been replaced by art on the walls, and the
brickies buying trowels have been usurped by
students drinking pints. It's a strange shape for
a bar, long and thin and a little awkward, but the
loungey feel is an appealing one, and the layout
does allows you to escape the open-mic nights
and other unnecessary entertainment that take
place here from time to time. The drinks list
doesn't offer any surprises: most people, chiefly
locals who appreciate the bar's location on a
scruffy stretch between Hackney and Clapton,
are only here for the beer.
Entertainment (DJs, musicians, nights vary).
Wireless internet.

Dalston Jazz Bar
4 Bradbury Street, N16 8JN (7254 9728).
Dalston Junction or Dalston Kingsland rail.
Open 5pm-3am Mon-Thur; 5pm-5am Fri, Sat;
5pm-2am Sun. **Dalston**
Dalston's incoming hipsters tend to congregate
at newer bars such as Alibi (*see left*) and the
Dalston Superstore (*see p211*), leaving this place
to a fabulously mixed – and, more often than
not, fabulously drunk – collection of locals for
whom last orders is something to be avoided at
all costs. Plonked in the middle of what looks
like a municipal car park and reminiscent of a
1960s library, it's filled with books and retro
sofas, not so much vintage as just plain old. The
beers are bottled and the large, messy cocktails
are a fiver. The random crowd dance, carouse
and stumble about until the wee small hours to
a shuffle mix of tunes that runs from the Cure
to the soundtrack of *The Jungle Book*, but rarely
seems to take in any jazz. Why would it?
Entertainment (DJs 10pm daily).

Haggerston
438 Kingsland Road, E8 4AA (7923 3206).
Haggerston rail or bus 67, 149, 242, 243.
Open noon-1am Mon-Thur; noon-3am
Fri-Sun. **Food served** 6-11pm Mon-Thur;
6-10pm Fri, Sun; noon-10pm Sat. **Haggerston**
Longtime denizens of E8 remember this place
as Uncle Sam's, an altogether fairly shambolic
pub that found fame in the area thanks to its
unexpectedly fine Sunday-night jazz sessions.
Led by guitarist Alan Weekes, the jazz remains,
but this corner pub has otherwise changed a lot
since it was taken over in 2008. It's still not a
room in which intimacy is easily fostered, and
it usually seems to be either uncomfortably
quiet (early in the week) or unbearably busy
(Thursday onwards). But at its best, the bar has
a vibrant, kinetic feel, packed with matey
refugees from the busier, younger scenes in
Shoreditch and Dalston who like to party but
prefer to do so in jeans that allow a little
breathing room.
Babies & children admitted (until 7pm).
Entertainment (DJs 9.30pm Thur-Sun).
Function room (70 capacity). Tables outdoors
(6, pavement; 6, yard). Wireless internet.

Junction Room
578 Kingsland Road, E8 4AH (7241 5755,
www.junctionroom.co.uk). Dalston Junction
or Dalston Kingsland rail, or bus 67, 76,
149, 242, 243. **Open** 11am-midnight
Mon-Wed, Sun; 11am-2am Thur-Sat. **Food**
served noon-9pm daily. **Dalston**
This episode in the ongoing gentrification of
Dalston arrived at the same time as the East

Dalston Jazz Bar

London Line extension, appropriate for a venue that lacks the kind of edge that defines so many neighbouring bars. It's deliberate, we think; at any rate, it's a worthwhile change from the norm in E8. Done out in smart, faintly industrial fashion with a nice window on to the street, the Junction Room is a casual café-cum-diner during the day, dispensing burgers and other comfort-food staples to the locals. After dark, the kitchen's still open, but you can also choose from a short cocktail list and a few beers and wines. DJs deliver a soundtrack at weekends.
Babies & children admitted. Disabled: toilet. Entertainment (jazz 7pm Tue; DJs 8pm Thur-Sun). Function room (70 capacity). Wireless internet.

Off Broadway

63-65 Broadway Market, E8 4PH (7241 2786, www.offbroadway.org.uk). Bethnal Green tube or bus 26, 48, 106, 254, 388. **Open** 4pm-midnight Mon-Fri; 10am-midnight Sat, Sun. **Food served** 4-10pm daily. **Hackney** Housed in a former art gallery and shop, this inappropriately named hangout – it's actually right on Broadway Market – has won a loyal following since it opened at the end of 2008. The owners have said that it's modelled on a now-defunct bar in New York's East Village, and

you can kind of see what they mean without having been there. Certainly, the menu's mix of notable beers (Brooklyn on tap, along with a number of other excellent bottled American imports) with worthwhile cocktails (rooted in tradition, but modified for the modern drinker) is unusual for the UK but pretty common across the ocean. The vibe is low-key, but atmosphere develops easily in the dimly lit, L-shaped room as the place fills, which it does most evenings. Events across the main bar and the downstairs room include regular gigs and a knitting club.
Babies & children admitted (until 8pm). Entertainment (bands/DJs 9pm Fri-Sun). Function room (50 capacity). Tables outdoors (4, pavement). Wireless internet.

East

Bar Kick

127 Shoreditch High Street, E1 6JE (7739 8700, www.cafekick.co.uk). Old Street tube/rail or Shoreditch High Street rail. **Open** 10.30am-11pm Mon-Wed; 10.30am-midnight Thur; noon-midnight Fri, Sat; noon-10.30pm Sun. **Food served** noon-3.30pm, 6-11pm Mon-Wed; noon-3.30pm, 6pm-midnight Thur, Fri; noon-midnight Sat; noon-10.30pm Sun. **Shoreditch**

Sister to Clerkenwell's Café Kick, good-natured Bar Kick is more expansive than its sibling. Most obviously, it's spread over two floors. The bar at street level, the nicer of the two rooms, is a wide, lived-in space of retro continental allure with nearly a dozen table-football tables. As at Café Kick, drinks and snacks have a Latin flavour – Sagres, Super Bock and Estrella beers; grilled chorizo sandwiches; platters of Spanish cheeses, cured meats and olives; and even *pan bagnats*, baps stuffed with tuna, egg and tomato usually sold from vans around Provence. Entertainment stretches to poetry readings, stand-up comedy and speed-dating events.
Babies & children admitted (until 6pm). Disabled: toilet. Entertainment (table football tournament 7pm last Thur of mth). Function room (150 capacity). Games (table football). Tables outdoors (4, terrace). Wireless internet. Map p244 R4.

Bistrotheque Napoleon Bar
23-27 Wadeson Street, E2 9DR (8983 7900, www.bistrotheque.com). Bethnal Green tube/ rail or Cambridge Heath rail or bus 55. **Open** 6pm-midnight Tue-Sat; 6-11pm Sun.
Bethnal Green
Don't look for any garish neon signs: a few picnic tables, usually full of animated young smokers, is all that marks the entrance here. The bar runs down the side of the building; in contrast to the light, white and airy eaterie above, it's all dark woods, plush armchairs and flickering lights. Glasses of wine come in dinky little tumblers, a nice touch. Cocktails include a passionfruit caipirinha (Sagatiba Cachaca rum with fresh passionfruit, lime and passionfruit syrup). On performance nights, the tiny cabaret room next door keeps the bar full to bursting before and after shows. Sound levels vary; sit close to the door and you'll hear occasional flushing water from the pipes. But this lo-fi, unpolished approach is part of what makes Bistrotheque a much-loved place.
Disabled: toilet. Entertainment (cabaret 8.30pm Fri, Sat). Function rooms (80 capacity). Tables outdoors (4, courtyard). Map p246 U3.

Book Club
100-106 Leonard Street, EC2A 4RH (7684 8618, www.wearetbc.com). Old Street tube/rail or Shoreditch High Street rail. **Open** 8am-midnight Mon-Wed; 8am-2am Thur, Fri; 10am-2am Sat; 10am-midnight Sun. **Food served** 8am-10pm Mon-Fri; 10am-10pm Sat, Sun.
Shoreditch
This commendable bar-club comprises one expansive room – divided by a wall with an oval

hole in the middle, giving the illusion that half of Hoxton is here – and a small pool room downstairs. Cocktails are scrawled up in black felt tip on white tiles by the bar, most in the £7 range and given in-joke names such as a Shoreditch Twat (Jägermeister, tequila and Chartreuse shaken with vanilla and egg) and Don't Go to Dalston (Bombay Sapphire gin, Martini Bianco and falernum). All but one of the dozen wines – Marqués de Morano rioja crianza, Mâcon-Villages Beauvernon Thorin – come by the glass, while the draught beer option is Sagres. Sharing platters include fajitas and English barbecue ribs, while light bites (£2.50-£6) involve whitebait with garlic aïoli and own-made pork scratchings.
Babies & children admitted (until 8pm). Entertainment (bands/DJs 7pm Thur-Sat). Function room (100 capacity). Games (board games, ping-pong, pool). Wireless internet. Map p244 R4.

Café 1001
1 Dray Walk, 91 Brick Lane, E1 6QL (7247 9679, www.cafe1001.co.uk). Liverpool Street tube/rail or Shoreditch High Street rail. **Open/food served** 6am-midnight daily.
Brick Lane
Café 1001 forms part of a pedestrianised eating and shopping strip that recalls nothing so much as Friday afternoon at the Glastonbury Festival, as food stalls and barbecue grills compete for attention with record stores (Rough Trade's expansive shop) and watering holes (the Big Chill Bar is at the opposite end of the stretch). The entrance to the café welcomes a friendly bohemian crowd who gather to check emails by day, then glug lager and catch a DJ after dark. Most take their cans in with them, climbing the short staircase to a loungey area (not unlike a glorified sixth-form common room) and a music space at the back. There are other drinks, among them standard cocktails (£6.50-£7) and top-notch fresh juices. Food involves salads, soups, burgers, bagels and own-made cakes, served from early morning until late at night.
Babies & children admitted (until 7pm). Disabled: toilet. Entertainment (bands/DJs 7pm daily). Function room (200 capacity). Tables outdoors (12, courtyard). Wireless internet. Map p246 S5.

CAMP
70-74 City Road, EC1Y 2BJ (7253 2443, www.thecamplondon.com). Old Street tube/rail. **Open** noon-midnight Mon-Wed; noon-1am Thur; noon-4am Fri, Sat. **Food served** noon-3pm, 5-10pm Mon-Fri.
Shoreditch

Note the capitals here – this is not a gay bar but an arty hangout provided by the City Arts & Music Project, hence the acronym. Shoreditch creative James Priestley is behind it, so it's a funky, urban spot, quite bare and open-plan, currently lined with photos taken by students for end-of-year grades. It's a DJ venue too, with decks set up by a long bar counter where taps of Amstel and Heineken complement a short cocktail menu that includes a gin-and-elderflower smash and a CAMP spring punch. The furniture feels somewhat institutional – empty, you'd expect an evening class to be starting pretty soon – but excitable early-evening chatter quickly lends a youthful, everything-to-live-for vibe.
Babies & children admitted (until 8pm). Entertainment (DJs/bands 8pm Fri, Sat). Wireless internet. **Map p244 Q4.**

Carnivale

2 White Church Lane, E1 7QR (8616 0776, www.carnivale.co.uk). Aldgate East tube. **Open/food served** noon-1am daily. **Whitechapel**
Although Carnivale's sign is illegible, the converted church the bar occupies is prominent enough. The entrance leads into an airy, open space, with a modest stage immediately to the right and splash-art paintings overlooking a solitary music stand. Cinema seats surrounded by retro seven-inch single sleeves (Bananarama, Adam & the Ants) provide pop-culture comforts; the bar at the rear also serves the little rectangle of terrace at the back. Pints of Erdinger and Pilsner Urquell are served promptly by a good-looking bunch of staff, and food is a cut above standard bar fare (handmade pizzas, fillet steak, roast duck); the expansive mezzanine is a lovely space in which to dine. Drop by for Monday night comedy, or open-mic acoustic music on Tuesdays.
Booking advisable Thur-Sun. Disabled: toilet. Entertainment (comedy 8pm Mon; open-mic music 8pm Tue). Function room (75 capacity). Tables outdoors (5, garden). Wireless internet. **Map p246 S6.**

Dreambagsjaguarshoes

34-36 Kingsland Road, E2 8DA (7729 5830, www.dreambagsjaguarshoes.com). Old Street tube/rail or Hoxton rail. **Open** noon-1am daily. **Food served** noon-11pm daily. **Shoreditch**
Arty, grungy and unexpectedly charismatic, this amalgam of two workaday wholesale shops (hence the name) continues to thrive amid the Shoreditch hubbub. Surrounded by bits and pieces from what looks like the film set to a German Expressionist classic of early cinema, creative types gather on tatty sofas to swig bottles of Quilmes or Liberty Ale and talk concepts. Art exhibitions play as much of a role in proceedings as the well-chosen if self-consciously edgy background music. Standard wines start at £15 a bottle; there are few surprises in the cocktail selection. Staff suffer from a reputation of being more interested in posing than pouring, but there were no complaints on our most recent visit. And no complaints about the pizzas, dispatched from the adjoining Due Sardi, either.
Function room (100 capacity). Wireless internet. **Map p244 R3.**

Electricity Showrooms

39A Hoxton Square, N1 6NN (7739 3939, www.electricityshowrooms.co.uk). Old Street tube/rail or Shoreditch High Street rail. **Open** noon-midnight Mon-Thur, Sun; noon-1am Fri, Sat. **Food served** noon-10.30pm daily. **Shoreditch**
What was once a hip and minimalist venue is now quite happy to be trashy and party-minded. Sat in a main room crowded with chattering, flirty youngsters, the circular main bar is lined with draught options, including Camden Hells Lager, Camden Wheat Beer, Sleeman India Pale Ale, Erdinger, Red Stripe and Bombardier. The wine list, a half-dozen of each colour, runs from £4.10 for a glass of house. The aim of the game is to follow the peacock, a gaudy neon display of the bird lighting up in concentric circles over the door leading to karaoke and DJ parties downstairs. A few solitary light bulbs hark back to the Showroom's previous guise.
Babies & children admitted (until 7pm). Disabled: toilet. Entertainment (DJs 8pm Thur-Sat). Function room (180 capacity). Wireless internet. **Map p244 R3.**

Florist

255 Globe Road, E2 0JD (8981 1100). Bethnal Green tube. **Open/food served** 11am-11pm Mon-Sat; noon-10.30pm Sun. **Bethnal Green**
This great little spot is well worth the ten-minute walk from Bethnal Green tube: most of the people who'll be filling the place will be regulars but by no means neighbours. Fresh flowers are dotted around the homely, cosy room and the pub name is etched into the mirror, though few other decorative details will be visible for the throng of sozzled grown-ups engaged in chat by the bar and seats around it. Stowford Press cider, Brewer's Gold, Camden Hells and Rothaus Pils come on draught, with Modelo Especial, Negra Modelo, Jupiler, Flensburger and Crabbie's Ginger Beer by the bottle. There are also mixed drinks, such as a sloe and elderflower bramble (gin, sloe gin and elderflower liqueur) and a classic champagne cocktail, and decent pizzas

(with gluten-free options). Entertainment is provided by DJs and a piano in the corner; the rest of the time, it'll be Neil Sedaka, the Bay City Rollers and other tacky faves. *Entertainment (quiz 8pm Mon; DJs 8pm Fri, Sat). Wireless internet.* **Map p246 U3**.

George & Dragon
2 Hackney Road, E2 7NS (7012 1100). Old Street tube/rail or Shoreditch High Street rail. **Open** 6pm-midnight daily. **Shoreditch**
A cornucopia of tack awaits the fussy crowd in this once-tatty Shoreditch boozer, popular with both gays and straights. The interior is quite disturbing: Chinese masks, doctored romantic paintings, cut-out black hearts and so on. Focus often falls on the sounds emitting from the DJ's decks, set between the door and the bar-cum-funfair-stall. You don't need to hook a duck or shoot a gun at a playing card: pints of Moretti, Früli and Sagres are sold over the beaten-up bar for the usual Shoreditch prices, to drinkers sporting Jimmy Edwards moustaches and the kind of outfits that you might once have expected to see in the queue for a midnight screening of *The Rocky Horror Picture Show*. New-found couples may get amorous in the bar's many darker corners. *Disabled: toilet.* **Map p244 R3**.

Hemingway
84 Victoria Park Road, E9 7JL (8510 0215, www.thehemingway.co.uk). Mile End tube then bus 277 or 425. **Open** noon-midnight Mon-Thur, Sun; noon-1am Fri, Sat. **Food served** noon-10pm Mon-Sat; noon-9pm Sun. **Hackney**
A trio of London bartenders spruced up this old boozer on the edge of Victoria Park nicely. It's not overly eclectic – art deco mirrors, smart chandeliers, gun chairs – and feels as if it's been here for ages. A small open-plan kitchen serves a dining room to the rear, where the frequently rotated menu might include grilled prawns and tapenade, or scotch egg, oozing yolk and served with piccalilli, with roasts on Sundays. There's a striking selection of spirits, with bourbons and rums especially well represented. The range of draught beers includes Meantime Wheat, Konig Pilsener and Heineken, with Deuchars IPA and Doom Bar on handpull and Peroni Gran Reserva in the fridge. It feels like a pub to spend time in: plenty of board games, piles of retro magazines, (non-Sky) football on the projection screen and – this being Hackney – single-speed cycling sorts chilling out front. *Babies & children admitted. Booking advisable Thur-Sun. Disabled: toilet. Entertainment (quiz 8pm 1st Tue of mth). Function room*

(15 capacity). Games (board games). Tables outdoors (14, patio). Wirelesss internet.

Hoxton Square Bar & Kitchen
2-4 Hoxton Square, N1 6NU (7613 0709, www.hoxtonsquarebar.com). Old Street tube/rail. **Open** 10.30am-midnight Mon; 10.30am-1am Tue-Thur; 10.30am-2am Fri, Sat; 10.30am-12.30am Sun. **Shoreditch**
This bar-restaurant attracts a friendly mix of creatives, tourists and City boys. It comprises a small square of terrace and a large sunken bar area, where action buzzes around the long bar counter. The back room is usually fenced off for shows by indie hopefuls (the Shout Out Louds, Field Music, et al). As well as attractive draught beer choices – Red Stripe, Sleemans, Kirin Ichiban and Erdinger – the venue offers more than a dozen by the bottle, among them beers from Sierra Nevada, Samuel Adams and Goose Island. Some 15 standard cocktails – plus an Avenue of Buffalo Trace bourbon, Calvados and passion-fruit syrup – are priced around £7. Hoxton burgers and big, big brunches (until 5pm) are the main attractions on the food menu. *Babies & children admitted (until 6pm). Disabled: toilet. Entertainment (bands 9pm Mon-Thur, Sun; DJs 9pm Fri, Sat). Tables outdoors (10, patio). Wireless internet.* **Map p244 R3**.

Kenton
38 Kenton Road, E9 7AB (8533 5041, www.kentonpub.co.uk). Homerton Rail or bus 26, 30, 388, 425. **Open** 4-11pm Mon-Thur; 4pm-midnight Fri; noon-midnight Sat; noon-11pm Sun. **Food served** 4-10pm Mon-Thur; 4-8pm Fri; 1-8pm Sat, Sun. **Hackney**
One of Hackney's hidden gems, this eclectic boozer draws a crowd of loyal locals to an interior that mixes candlelit antiques and modern curiosities. Food during the week comes courtesy of Pieminister, with tasty, traditional roasts on a Sunday. On summer weekends, they fire up the barbecue for juicy burgers, fillets of sea bass and grilled halloumi, accompanied by all the salad you can eat. Cocktails (around £8) are a hit, especially when they're half price on Thursday's Ladies' Night (which also includes homemade cupcakes and a vintage clothing sale), though a bloody mary with horseradish seems the favourite on weekend afternoons. Draughts are less exciting, with Red Stripe, Staropramen, Stella Artois, Timothy Taylor Landlord and a guest ale on tap. The varied calendar of events also includes foreign films (with free popcorn) on Mondays, while DJs and musicians enliven the weekends.

Dreambagsjaguarshoes. *See p187.*

Babies & children admitted (until 7pm). *Entertainment (film screenings 8pm Mon; quiz 8pm Tue; musicians 8pm Wed; vintage clothing fair 8pm Thur; DJs 8pm Fri, Sat; rock 'n' roll bingo 8pm Sun). Games (board games). Tables outdoors (4, garden). Wireless internet.*

Look Mum No Hands!

49 Old Street, EC1V 9HX (7253 1025, www.lookmumnohands.com). Barbican tube or Old Street tube/rail. **Open/food served** 7.30am 10pm Mon-Fri, 9am-10pm Sat; 9.30am-10pm Sun. **Shoreditch** This 2010-vintage café, bar and bike-repair shop is a must-visit if you're a fan of two-wheeled transports of delight. During the day, there's Square Mile coffee and some fairly basic food (cakes and pastries, cold deli platters, pies, sandwiches and salads); later, visitors switch to one of four not-bad wines (from £3 a glass) or something from the small but tidy beer list (continental lagers; a bottled ale or two, such as something from local brewer Kernel). Cycling events are shown on a big screen, and there's even some outdoor seating next to some 'secure' cycle parking (but use your bike lock anyway – this is Old Street, after all). Two wheels or no wheels, this is a lovely little hangout. *Babies & children admitted. Disabled: toilet. Tables outdoors (8, garden). Wireless internet.* **Map p244 P4.**

Owl & Pussycat

34 Redchurch Street, E2 7DP (3487 0088, www.owlandpussycatshoreditch.com).

Shoreditch High Street rail or Liverpool Street tube/rail. **Open** noon-11pm Mon; noon-midnight Tue-Thur, Sat; noon-12.30pm Fri; noon-10pm Sun. **Food served** 1-3pm, 6-10pm Mon-Sat; noon-4.30pm Sun. **Shoreditch** The gentrification of trendy Redchurch Street continues as this former east-end boozer returns in a familiar gastropub guise. Fashionably mismatched Chesterfields, stripped tables and antique fittings furnish the lilac-coated main bar, which serves pints of Peroni and Heineken, a selection of four rotating ales, and wines by the glass (£6.15 for a large glass of Sauvignon de Touraine). Post-work, the pub can get uncomfortably crowded with designers from nearby agencies and itinerant City boys happy to pay the above-average prices, but ample seating in the well-heated rear terrace provides a useful retreat. Upstairs, a Victorian-style dining room offers a modern British menu that might include guinea fowl in red wine sauce or stewed duck (mains £14 to £18, with an additional charge for sides) and an extended wine list, featuring 30 options in each colour. *Babies & children admitted (until 5pm). Booking advisable. Disabled: toilet. Games (board games). Tables outdoors (9, garden). Wireless internet.* **Map p244 R4.**

Prague

6 Kingsland Road, E2 8DA (7739 9110, www.barprague.com). Old Street tube/rail or Hoxton rail. **Open/food served** noon-midnight Mon-Thur, Sun; noon-1.30am Fri, Sat. **Shoreditch**

With its dim lighting, ghostly atmosphere and woodcut artwork, entering Prague is a little like walking into a Kafka novel. Although it's on the bar vortex where Kingsland Road meets Old Street, it's often overlooked – a shame, as it's pretty good. The menu tucked into empty bottles placed on each tabletop lists 30-plus cocktails (around £7), but many drinkers are here for the Czech beers, among them the rarely found Budvar Dark on tap, and for cheap Czech-influenced snacks such as roll mops, marinated cheese and pickled sausage. The presence here of the St Vitus Gallery adds a weird, creative touch to some of the artwork; the place is filled with paintings and illustrations by local artists. *Babies & children admitted (until 6pm). Wireless internet.* **Map p244 R4.**

Red Lion
41 Hoxton Street, N1 6NH (7729 7920). Old Street tube/rail or Hoxton rail. **Open** 5-11pm Mon; noon-11pm Tue-Sun. **Food served** 5-10.30pm Mon; noon-10.30pm Tue-Sun. **Shoreditch**
A Courage cockerel stands guard above the bar of this madeover pub, formerly a bog-standard boozer but now a wannabe-boho hangout. Here congregate comparatively grown-up drinkers, slightly more sensible than the hedonists and cutting-edge creatives who fill other Hoxton spots; they gather in the main bar, beads of illuminated baubles strung around it like a fairground, alleviating the otherwise accurate impression that you're standing in a bashed-up pub. The fireplace and the glitterball add to the confused decorative impression. There are more rooms on the upper two floors, but few venture up there. The beers are standards, as are the snacks (toasties, ciabattas, tortilla) and the mains (pizzas, fish 'n' chips). *Babies & children admitted (restaurant only). Disabled: toilet. Function room (50 capacity). Wireless internet.* **Map p244 R3.**

Redchurch
107 Redchurch Street, E2 7DL (7729 8333, www.theredchurch.co.uk). Liverpool Street tube/rail or Shoreditch High Street rail. **Open** 1.30pm-1.30am Mon-Thur, Sun; 1.30pm-3.30am Fri, Sat. **Food served** 1-10pm daily. **Brick Lane**
Its decor a cross between a bordello and a corner pub, Redchurch is a quirky curveball to throw into any Brick Lane bar crawl. Narrow and (yes!) red, it's a DJ bar at heart, which grows lively as the clock nears midnight, but the bar also prides itself for 'working for over a decade with mixologists who specialise in punches'. Quite so: there are other cocktails, including bloody marys (with Finlandia) and bloody marias (with tequila), but it's the punches that catch the eye, serving four to 20 people at £9.50 a head. House cocktails include a house mojito with Bacardi, elderflower, ginger ale and a suspicion of gingerbread, and a Chinese cosmopolitan (£11) with lychees, citrus and

Balham Bowls Club. *See p192.*

Grey Goose Le Citron. You'll find Sagres, Duvel and Cusqueña among the beers, a variety of Rekorderlig fruit ciders, and nondescript house wine from £4.50 a glass. *Entertainment (musicians 8pm Tue; DJs 8pm Thur-Sun). Wireless internet.* **Map p246 S4.**

Also recommended...

Big Chill Bar (Clubs & Music Venues, *p213*); **Charlie Wright's International Bar** (Clubs & Music Venues, *p214*); **Star of Bethnal Green** (Clubs & Music Venues, *p216*).

South East

Gladstone Arms

64 Lant Street, SE1 1QN (7407 3962). Borough tube. **Open** noon-11pm Mon-Thur; noon-midnight Fri, Sat; noon-10.30pm Sun. **Food served** noon-10pm daily. **Borough**
Now independently owned, the Glad is no longer a staid, empty corner pub. While the Victorian prime minister from whom the place takes its name still glares from a massive mural on the outer wall, the interior is now funky, freaky and candlelit. Gigs take place at one end of a cosy one-room space; opposite, a bar dispenses pints of Red Stripe, Beck's Vier, St Austell Tribute and Doom Bar, while pies provide sustenance, and a crammed back bar embellished by a retro 'On Air' studio sign manages to find space for bottles of Moretti, Sol, Corona, Peroni and Budvar. The retro feel is completed by the kind of clock you still might see on the platform of a provincial railway station in Slovakia. Lovers of board games should choose a Monday or Tuesday for that slow, strategic game of Risk or head upstairs to the quieter salon-style room, which also has more upmarket food. *Babies & children admitted (until 7pm). Entertainment (musicians 8pm Thur, Sat, Sun). Games (board games). Wireless internet.* **Map p250 P9.**

Gowlett

62 Gowlett Road, SE15 4HY (7635 7048, www.thegowlett.com). East Dulwich or Peckham Rye rail, or bus 12, 37, 40, 63, 176, 185, 484. **Open** noon-midnight Mon-Thur; noon-1am Fri, Sat; noon-11.30pm Sun. **Food served** 12.30-2.30pm, 6.30-10.30pm Mon-Fri; 12.30-10.30pm Sat; 12.30-9pm Sun. **Peckham**
This family-friendly, CAMRA-decorated pub in a residential street succeeds thanks to its simple formula of providing decent drinks in a comfortable atmosphere. With London Pride and three guest ales from such breweries as Harveys, Brakspear and St Austell, plus Leffe blond on tap, this is a pub that hasn't let down its guard as far as beer is concerned. The wine list is heavy on organic fair-trade varieties, some of which come from Namaqualand in South Africa. The pub's all-things-to-all-people approach extends to stone-baked pizzas (pretty good), a covered terrace (appealing), a pool table (competitive), a weekly quiz (ditto), high chairs and toys for kids (laudable), DJs on Sundays (mellow) and local art (largely rubbish). Good stuff, all told. *Babies & children admitted (until 9pm). Disabled: toilet. Entertainment (quiz 8.30pm last Sun of mth; DJs 6pm Sun). Games (pool). Tables outdoors (3, heated terrace; 4, pavement). Wireless internet.*

Royal Albert

460 New Cross Road, SE14 6TJ (8692 3737, www.antic-ltd.com). New Cross rail. **Open** 4pm-midnight Mon-Thur; 4pm-1am Fri; noon-1am Sat; noon-midnight Sun. **Food served** 5-10pm Mon-Fri; noon-5pm, 6-10pm Sat; noon-5pm Sun. **Deptford**
Away from the contrived Rocklands scene nearby, this corner pub has rediscovered its mojo and its old name. A former dive and quite fantastic music venue in the late 1980s before it became the clubby but unsuccessful Paradise Bar, the Albert has pushed its prices slightly higher. The beers are a major attraction: guest ales on the four pumps might include the output of breweries such as Purity, Harviestoun and Thornbridge, while bottled Duvel, Brooklyn and Chimay complement a succinct, mid-range wine list. Picture windows overlook a raised front terrace with a commanding view of the 53 bus. *Babies & children admitted (until 8pm). Disabled: toilet. Entertainment (quiz 7.30pm Mon; DJs 9pm Fri). Games (board games). Tables outdoors (8, terrace). Wireless internet.* **Map p253 B2.**

Woolpack

98 Bermondsey Street, SE1 3UB (7357 9269, www.woolpackbar.com). London Bridge tube/rail. **Open** 11am-11pm Mon-Fri; 10am-11pm Sat; 10am-10.30pm Sun. **Food served** 11.30am-3.30pm, 5-10pm Mon-Fri; 10-11.30am, 12.30-9pm Sat, Sun. **Bermondsey**
The Woolpack is a down-to-earth alternative to the Garrison opposite (*see p147*). The location is prosaic – a side street branching off from the London Bridge rail estuary – but that shouldn't detract from what's a quality two-floor pub-restaurant. Beer-wise, you'll find the likes of Kirin Ichiban, Leffe and Hoegaarden, while the dozen-strong wine list (by the glass and bottle)

includes a few unusual offerings. Mains are of the beer-battered haddock and chips or Cumberland sausage and mash variety, and cost around a tenner. The smaller, tiled downstairs space feels lived-in and traditional, while upstairs is even more relaxed. *Babies & children admitted (until 5pm). Function room (50 capacity). Tables outdoors (25, garden). Wireless internet.*

Also recommended...

Amersham Arms (Clubs & Music Venues, *p217*); **Southwark Tavern** (Beer Specialists, *p121*).

South

Balham Bowls Club

7-9 Ramsden Road, SW12 8QX (8673 4700, www.antic-ltd.com). Balham tube/rail. **Open** 4-11pm Mon-Wed; 4pm-midnight Thur, Fri; noon-midnight Sat; noon-11pm Sun. **Food served** 6-9.30pm Tue-Fri; noon-3.30pm, 6-9.30pm Sat; 1-5pm Sun. **Balham**
Despite its upper-crust appearance, the BBC welcomes all-comers to its clubhouse. The bowls club's history has been sensitively preserved, with a warren of small, wood-panelled rooms decorated with rosettes, chesterfields and an old wooden scoreboard. The bar itself is cosy and crowded, with a fire in winter; draught Ubu, Peroni and Grolsch are served along with bottled Honey Dew, Fursty Ferret and Abbot. Food is a focus, with sharing platters of cured meats, comfort-food mains and generous Sunday lunches. There's plenty of space in the back rooms to dine in comfort – space enough, in fact, for two snooker tables. A crazy-paved front terrace accommodates smokers. *Babies & children admitted (until 8.30pm). Entertainment (quiz 8pm Tue). Function room (50 capacity). Tables outdoors (10, garden; 4, terrace). Wireless internet.*

Bar Estrela

111-115 South Lambeth Road, SW8 1UZ (7793 1051). Stockwell tube or Vauxhall tube/rail. **Open/food served** 8am-midnight Mon-Sat; 10am-11pm Sun. **Stockwell**
Considered by many to be the best drinking option in Little Portugal, the Star Bar is certainly the finest spot at which to watch European football, beamed in on Portuguese TV. Cold Super Bocks, custard tarts and portions of stew and sundry pork dishes served in half or full measures add to the Iberian atmosphere. You can stand at the bar, but it's more of a sit-down-and-be-served kind of place, with the uniformed

waiters gradually getting used to a pace of life a few notches faster than Portugal's. You may have to catch someone's attention if you've bagged a terrace seat. Otherwise, Estrela is relaxed and informal, even on big-match nights. *Babies & children admitted. Tables outdoors (13, pavement).*

Bread & Roses

68 Clapham Manor Street, SW4 6DZ (7498 1779, www.breadandrosespub.com). Clapham Common or Clapham North tube. **Open** 4.30-11.30pm Mon-Thur; 4.30pm-12.30am Fri; noon-12.30am Sat; noon-10.30pm Sun. **Food served** 2-10.30pm Sun. **Clapham**
Created and run by the Workers Beer Company and the Battersea & Wandsworth Trades Union Congress, Bread & Roses (named after the James Oppenheim poem inspired by an early industrial textile strike) is about more than just fundraising or class struggle – it's a very good bar. Taps of Sharp's Doom Bar, little-seen Stiegl, Budvar, Erdinger, Beck's Vier, San Miguel, and Thatchers and Aspall ciders line the bar counter, behind which a fridge contains bottles of Vedett and Sierra Nevada, among others. Wines start with a £3.25 South African shiraz and Chilean sauvignon blanc. Entertainment is provided on some nights by a DJ and/or a large screen for TV sports in the conservatory at the back, which gives access to the beer garden. A very likeable enterprise. *Babies & children admitted (until 9.30pm). Disabled: toilet. Entertainment (DJs 9pm Sat). Function room (100 capacity). Games (board games). Tables outdoors (15, garden; 8, patio; 8, conservatory). Wireless internet.* **Map p252 B1.**

Ink Rooms

14 Lavender Hill, SW11 5RW (7228 5300, www.inkrooms.co.uk). Clapham Junction or Wandsworth Road rail. **Open** 5pm-midnight Mon-Thur, Sun; 4pm-2am Fri, Sat. **Food served** 5-10pm Mon-Thur, Sun; 4-10pm Fri, Sat. **Battersea**
The folk behind Lost Society and Lost Angel have remodelled this place as an American dive bar, albeit one without the drunks, the divey-ness or, for that matter, the Americans. Decked out in black leather banquettes and stools, the main bar is coated in 1950s Sailor Jerry-style tattoo art, with the odd flash of neon and an old-school jukebox. Purple drapes partition a laid-back lounge area; downstairs, the cellar room leads out into a beer garden. The 60-strong, American-accented beer list contains superb craft brews, including Cutthroat Porter from Odell and Doggie Style Pale Ale from Flying Dog, as well

as a selection of Trappist beers; the dozen taps pour the likes of Brooklyn Lager and Sierra Nevada, and you might see Truman's among the ales. The back bar offers a well-chosen selection of spirits, including such lesser-known labels as small-batch Old Pogue bourbon. *Babies & children admitted (until 6pm). Entertainment (bands 7.30pm Thur, 6.30pm Sun; DJs 9pm Fri, Sat). Tables outdoors (10, garden). Wireless internet.* **Map p251 E1.**

Lost Angel

339 Battersea Park Road, SW11 4LF (7622 2112, www.lostangel.co.uk). Battersea Park rail. **Open** 5-11pm Tue, Wed; 5pm-1am Thur; 4pm-2am Fri; noon-2am Sat; noon-11pm Sun. **Food served** 5-10pm Tue-Thur; 4-10pm Fri; noon-10pm Sat, Sun. **Battersea**

You don't expect to find a bar like Lost Angel along this sorry-looking stretch of the Battersea Park Road, but there is a precedent: this building was once home to Dusk, which brought a little glamour to the street. The frontage now reads 'Bar, Restaurant, Boozer', more a sign of true versatility than of an incipient identity crisis. The range of drinks covers most bases: the three ales may include Otter Ale, while the cocktail list is split between classics and shouldn't-work-but-do reinventions (mojitos made with pomegranate juice and gin, for instance). It's all served within an eye-catching interior that falls between corner pub (tiles, dark wood) and modish bar (trumpets on the ceiling, white

phone box); there's also a nice little garden. The kitchen offers poshed-up bar food, and entertainment runs from DJs to quiz nights; service couldn't be friendlier. Lovely. *Babies & children admitted (until 6pm). Entertainment (quiz 8pm Tue; DJs 9pm Fri, Sat; bands 6.30pm Sun). Tables outdoors (15, garden). Wireless internet.*

Lost Society

697 Wandsworth Road, SW8 3JF (7652 6526, www.lostsociety.co.uk). Clapham Common tube, Wandsworth Road rail or bus 77. **Open** 5-11pm Tue, Wed; 5pm-1am Thur; 5pm-2am Fri; 2pm-2am Sat; noon-11pm Sun. **Food served** 5-10pm Tue-Fri; 2-10pm Sat; noon-10pm Sun. **Battersea**

Lost Society? You must be joking! They're all here, supping cocktails, gossiping in the small courtyard garden and picking at the platters. The 60-long cocktail list is a handsome one, with some unlikely but successful inventions: the Black Cherry Manhattan mixes Sazerac rye whiskey with Red Stag cherry bourbon, dry vermouth and bitters, for instance. Beers are bottled and some quite obscure, whether from Scotland (Midnight Sun Porter), America (Old Scratch from Maryland's Flying Dog brewery, Goose Island's 312 Urban Wheat Ale) or beyond. It all gets a bit more frantic at weekends, when DJs crank out tunes for party-keen Claphamites happy to dress up and pay a fiver to get in. The same folks run the fine Lost Angel (*see left*) in Battersea Park Road.

Lost Angel

Trailer Happiness. *See p198.*

*Babies & children admitted (until 5pm).
Entertainment (DJs 9pm Fri, Sat). Tables
outdoors (4, front garden; 5, back garden).*
Map p252 A1.

Lounge
*56-58 Atlantic Road, SW9 8PZ (7733 5229,
www.loungebrixton.co.uk). Brixton tube/rail.
Open/food served 11am-11pm Tue-Thur;
11am-midnight Fri, Sat; 11am-5pm Sun.*
Brixton
Its open windows facing the Front Line Brixton
Ltd grocery store across Atlantic Road, the
Lounge offers a relaxed retreat amid buzzy
Brixtonia. By day it deals mainly in food,
serving own-made burgers, all-day breakfasts,
toasted panini and the like, along with a simple,
inexpensive kids' menu. Come the evening,
things shift up a gear, with fried plantain, salt-
fish fritters and spicy chicken wings among the
small plates, plus sharing platters, grills and
salads. By then drinks will have come to the fore,
including cocktails (£5-£6.50), such as the
Loungin' Beauty of brandy, red vermouth and
ruby port. The entertainment schedule is more
varied, incorporating monthly Brixton-themed
film screenings, occasional music sessions and
rotating exhibitions.
*Babies & children admitted. Disabled: toilet.
Entertainment (bands 9pm Thur; film
screenings 7pm 1st Sun of mth). Wireless
internet.* **Map p252 E2.**

Tooting Tram & Social
*46-48 Mitcham Road, SW17 9NA
(8767 0278, www.antic-ltd.com). Tooting
Broadway tube. Open 5pm-midnight
Tue-Thur; 4pm-2am Fri; noon-2am Sat;
noon-midnight Sun.* **Tooting**
Hard to spot but impressive once you find it,
this converted tram shed incorporates a
cavernous, chandelier-lit main bar and a
smaller mezzanine, filled with decorative
quirks and televisions for football viewing.
Don't expect a laddish crowd, though: the
offbeat tone is set by a pair of winkle-pickers
displayed under glass as you walk in, while
Lionel Ritchie beams a Lionel Ritchie smile
from an album cover mounted on the back bar.
It's a laid-back bunch that mingles here, either
parked on turquoise-topped bar stools or
lounging on the banquettes and antique
armchairs. There's draught Purity Mad Goose,
Doom Bar and Grolsch, with ten wines by the
glass among the 20-strong selection.
*Disabled: toilet. Entertainment (bands/
cabaret/DJs 8pm days vary). Games (board
games). Tables outdoors (4, pavement).
Wireless internet.*

Also recommended...
Antelope (Gastropubs & Brasseries,
p148); **Dogstar** (Clubs & Music Venues,
p218); **White Horse** (Clubs & Music
Venues, *p219*).

South West

Normanby
*231 Putney Bridge Road, SW15 2PU
(8874 1555, www.thenormanby.co.uk). East
Putney tube or Putney rail. Open noon-11pm
Mon-Thur; noon-midnight Fri; 11am-midnight
Sat; 11am-11pm Sun. Food served noon-
10pm Mon-Fri; 11am-10pm Sat; 11am-9pm
Sun.* **Putney**
A booze-devoted party crowd a few years past
the age of consent aspire to mingle in the gene
pool here. Oiling this engagement are San
Miguel and Sharp's Doom Bar on draught, other
bottled beers and entry-level wines. Food begins
with the house breakfast (£6.75, or double
everything for £9.75), then extends to burgers
and other easy-to-consume dishes that suit
punters gawping at the screens showing TV
sports. Those uninterested in sport or the love
parade would do well to sit outside and perch
on one of the high stools. Back inside, DJs
occasionally spin from decks by the fireplace.
*Babies & children admitted (until 9pm).
Disabled: toilet. Entertainment (bands/DJs
9pm Fri, Sat; open mic 7pm Sun). Games
(darts, pool table). Tables outdoors (4, garden).
Wireless internet.*

Suburban Bar & Lounge
*27 Hartfield Road, SW19 3SG (8543 9788,
www.suburbanbar.com). Wimbledon tube/rail.
Open 5-11pm Mon-Thur; 5pm-midnight Fri,
Sat; 5-10.30pm Sun.* **Fulham**
This is a party bar for party people: simple as
that. The laconic Aussie staff serve a regular
clientele, captured and framed in Polaroids on
the walls, who gather in a pub-like interior to get
merry on two-fer cocktails and forget that work
will ever happen again. The drinks list, prefaced
by a neat logo also available across a T-shirt
(£15), features more than 50 concoctions, all in
the £7 range. With Makers Mark bourbon used
in the Rock Star and Brugal rum in the mojitos,
the drinkers here are taking in some quality
produce. An undemanding rock soundtrack
provides a backdrop for the chat-up banter; a
small square of garden hosts smokers and
move-to-second-base intimacy.
*Disabled: toilet. Entertainment (musicians
8pm Sun). Tables outdoors (8, garden).
Wireless internet.*

Also recommended...

Citizen Smith (Beer Specialists, p124).

West

Builders Arms

1 Kensington Court Place, W8 5BJ (7937 6213, www.thebuildersarmskensington.co.uk). High Street Kensington tube. **Open** 11am-11pm Mon-Fri; 10am-11.30pm Sat; 10am-10.30pm Sun. **Food served** noon-10.30pm Mon-Fri; 10am-10.30pm Sat; 10am-10pm Sun. **Kensington**

Less well known than many Kensington pubs because of its location – hidden among the maze of avenues behind the High Street – this establishment has a great local feel. Beer drinkers can enjoy continental lagers, Heineken and Früli or one of four rotating ales from the bar, which stands beneath a tropical mosaic of fronded palms. There are also four ciders (Aspall Perronelle's Blush and Brother's Festival among them) on offer and an array of spirits and cocktails, including the Kraken (spiced rum and Chase vodka). In summer, you can repair to the outside decking area under the green frontage to tuck into goat's cheese risotto or free-range Gloucester Old Spot sausages and mash from the British gastropub menu, or just balance your well-poured pint on one of the barrels that are used as tables.

Babies & children admitted (until 6.30pm). Disabled: toilet. Entertainment (comedy 9pm Mon). Function room (60 capacity). Tables outdoors (6, patio).

First Floor

186 Portobello Road, W11 1LA (7243 0072, www.firstfloorportobello.co.uk). Ladbroke Grove. **Open** noon-11pm Mon-Thur; 11am-midnight Fri, Sat; noon-10.30pm Sun. **Food served** noon-5pm, 7-10pm Tue-Thur; noon-5pm Fri-Sun. **Notting Hill**

A superior kind of West London bohemian generally lands here, the moneyed professional rather than the cadging layabout. The tone of this cosmopolitan drinkerie and eaterie is set by the entrance: a revolving door, which gives the place the feel of an international hotel lobby. It's a bright, colourful place, buzzy on occasion, though the punters who head here surely aren't drawn by the unmemorable range of drinks (Red Stripe, Kirin and Warsteiner on tap, along with wines and cocktails). The bar snacks are superior – triple-cooked chips, mini Cumberland sausages – but the real culinary action is in the restaurant upstairs, from which this ground-floor bar takes its needlessly confusing name.

Babies & children admitted. Entertainment (musicians 8pm Tue, 6pm Sun). Function rooms (up to 40 capacity). Tables outdoors (7, pavement). Wireless internet. Map p247 Z6.

Idlewild

55 Shirland Road, W9 2JD (7266 9198, www.ruby.uk.com/idlewild). Warwick Avenue tube. **Open** 4-11pm Mon-Thur; 4pm-midnight Fri; noon-midnight Sat; noon-10.30pm Sun. **Food served** 6-10pm Mon-Thur; 6-11pm Fri; noon-4pm, 6-11pm Sat; noon-4pm, 6-10pm Sun. **Maida Vale**

Part of the Ruby mini-chain of cocktail bars, Idlewild graced the cover of our Bars, Pubs & Clubs Guide a couple of years back, and remains something of a looker. Billing itself as a 'pub deluxe', this artistically designed joint attracts a well-turned-out crowd looking for a little more of a night out than most of the other local drinking holes can provide. Downstairs, it's comparatively mellow, an ambience due in no small part to the presence of a full menu (pork belly, poshed-up shepherd's pie) from which to choose. Things are usually a little livelier upstairs, as drinkers select from a cultured, traditional cocktail list to a DJ-built soundtrack at weekends.

Babies & children admitted (until 7pm). Entertainment (DJs 9pm Fri, Sat). Function room (80 capacity). Tables outdoors (4, garden; 2, pavement). Wireless internet.

Lodge Tavern

53 The Mall, W5 3TA (8567 0173). Ealing Broadway tube/rail. **Open** 11am-midnight Mon-Thur, Sun; 11am-1am Fri; 11am-2am Sat. **Food served** 11am-3pm, 5.30-10pm Mon-Thur; 11am-10pm Fri-Sun. **Ealing**

Sexy and sassy, surprisingly so given its location in ever-demure Ealing (weary shoppers laden with bags will be an incongruous feature of a daytime visit), the Lodge has a wooden cabin feel, at least if wooden cabins were fitted out with DJ decks and staffed by experienced cocktail mixers. The drinks list has been compiled with bravery and exuberance: a Citron Cosmopolitan features Absolut Citron, Triple Sec, cranberry juice, lime juice and flamed orange peel, while a Blueberry Amaretto Sour blends Disarrono with blueberry purée, lemon juice, sugar and optional egg white; and orange marmalade, red bell peppers and rhubarb jam are not items you expect to find on too many cocktail menus in town. Beer-wise, the Lodge stocks Zywiec and Moretti by the bottle; DJs and occasional live acts provide the soundtrack.

Paradise by Way of Kensal Green. *See p198.*

Entertainment (DJs 9pm Fri, Sat; musicians 8.30pm Sun). Tables outdoors (15, garden).

Miss Q's

180-184 Earl's Court Road, SW5 9QG (7370 5358, www.missqs.com). Earl's Court tube. **Open** 5-11pm Mon-Wed; 5pm-2am Thur-Sat. **Food served** 5-10pm Mon-Wed; 5-11pm Thur-Sat. **Earl's Court**
A rather unexpected find in the nightlife desert of Earl's Court, Miss Q's pitches itself as a rock 'n' roll pool joint and an unapologetic shrine to Americana. While a trio of pristine pool tables take centre stage (and are responsible for the name of the venue), the sizeable subterranean vault also features two bars, a kitsch flashing dancefloor, a pinball den and a stage for occasional live music. The drinks include Zatec, a snappy Czech beer, and Grolsch Weizen, a Dutch wheat beer; surprisingly, given the American theme, they're the pick of the beer pumps. Ample servings of US tucker – ribs, burgers and so on – are available, and all at less than a tenner. DJs play at weekends; one Saturday was advertised as 'a night of rockabilly, classic rock, '80s classics, chart toppers and commercial dance', which sounds like the most bet-hedging club in history. *Entertainment (DJs 8.30pm Fri, Sat; bands 8pm Wed). Function room (70 capacity). Games (pool). Wireless internet.*

Ruby & Sequoia

6-8 All Saints Road, W11 1HH (7243 6363, www.ruby.uk.com/sequoia). Ladbroke Grove or Westbourne Park tube. **Open** 6pm-12.30am Mon-Thur; 6pm-2am Fri; 11am-2am Sat; 11am-12.30am Sun. **Food served** 6-10.30pm Mon-Fri; 11am-4pm, 6-10.30pm Sat, Sun.
Notting Hill
This urban cocktail house, one of several fine Ruby-tied venues around town, has split its contemporary space into drinking and dining areas. All are treated to squishy brown seating and little candles in glasses, and most likely your seat will be close to a framed photograph of some pop icon or other (the Stones circa '66, Lydon, Weller). The impressive cocktail menu includes classic martinis and extends to seasonal selections: you might be treated to a Lilikoi (made with eight-year-old Bacardi, fresh passionfruit, vanilla liqueur and orange). Peroni, Budvar and organic cider, plus a 40-strong wine list, cater to those with less adventurous tastes. The music is imaginative and well-chosen; a sweet-scented basement hosts late-night shenanigans. It's slick, to be sure, and this is one of the better options in this corner of town. *Babies & children admitted (restaurant until 6pm Sat, Sun). Disabled: toilet. Entertainment (DJs 9pm Thur-Sat). Tables outdoors (2, pavement). Wireless internet.* **Map p247 Z5.**

Tiroler Hut

27 Westbourne Grove, W2 4UA (7727 3981,
www.tirolerhut.co.uk). Bayswater or Queensway
tube. **Open** 6.30pm-1am Tue-Sun. **Food
served** 6.30pm-12.30am Tue-Sun.
Westbourne Grove
József fled his Hungarian homeland after the
Uprising of 1956 to entertain boat passengers
on the Swiss lakes before opening this Tyrol-
themed basement in 1967, and he still presides
over it today. Beneath a Dortmunder Union pub
sign squeezed between the shopfronts, making
the narrow descent feels like gatecrashing a
Central European wedding party, with steins
and shots being necked as dirndl-clad maidens
squeeze between the throng. *Magyar csárda*
tunes and Danubian favourites have everyone
up and dancing, sweating off the reasonably
priced goulash and schnitzels. This is one of the
few places in London to sell Unicum, Hungary's
answer to Jägermeister, whose secret recipe left
with the exodus of '56.
*Babies & children admitted. Entertainment
(musicians 8.30pm Tue-Sun). Function
room (60 capacity). Wireless internet.*
Map p247 B6.

Trailer Happiness

177 Portobello Road, W11 2DY (7065 6821,
www.trailerhappiness.com). Ladbroke Grove
or Notting Hill Gate tube. **Open** 6pm-midnight
Tue-Sat. **Food served** 6-11.30pm Tue-Sat.
Notting Hill
Remaining laudably tongue-in-cheek while the
rest of Ladbroke Grove drowns in chichi spots,
Trailer Happiness is not a cocktail bar as such
– with its deliberately tacky decor (Tretchikoff
paintings galore) and DJ hatch, it's far too
informal for that. However, the drinks here
are taken seriously, with many of them made to
vintage American recipes, and both the mai tai
(Appleton V/X rum, orange curaçao, orgeat
syrup, bitters, fresh lime) and the Cotton Mouth
Killer (Elements 8 Platino, Mount Gay and Wray
& Nephew rums, lime, apple, guava juice,
apricot brandy, Galliano) do justice to the legend.
The recommended beer is not American but
König Pilsener from the German town of
Duisberg; ingredients for the food, among them
'TV dinners' such as beef fajitas, are sourced
as much as possible from the area.
*Entertainment (DJs 8pm Thur-Sat). Tables
outdoors (4, pavement). Wireless internet.*
Map p247 Z6.

Troubadour

263-267 Old Brompton Road, SW5 9JA
(7370 1434, www.troubadour.co.uk). West
Brompton tube/rail. **Open** 9pm-midnight

Mon-Thur, Sun; 9pm-2am Fri, Sat.
Food served 9-11pm daily. **Earl's Court**
In folk circles, the Troubadour is a legend:
Bob Dylan, Paul Simon, Joni Mitchell and Nick
Drake all played here, amid a '60s scene whose
resonances live on more than four decades later.
In a cramped, cosy space brimming with copper
utensils and Macmillan-era signage advertising
British Railways and the renowned pens of
MacNiven & Cameron, tourists and regulars lay
into all-day breakfasts and plates of pie, mash
and liquor, sipping on pints, glasses of shiraz
and cups of tea. Rothaus is the house beer, also
in malt (Märzen) and shandy (Radler) varieties,
with Hefeweizen and Pils coming by the bottle.
There's also a Troubadour Blonde from Belgium
and Fuller's London Pride on draught. Down in
the cellar, bands and poets still take to the stage.
*Entertainment (bands 7.30pm Mon-Sat).
Function room (120 capacity). Wireless internet.*

Also recommended...

Notting Hill Arts Club (Clubs & Music
Venues, *p220*).

North West

Paradise by Way of Kensal Green

19 Kilburn Lane, W10 4AE (8969 0098,
www.theparadise.co.uk). Kensal Green tube/
rail or Kensal Rise rail. **Open** 4pm-midnight
Mon-Wed; 4pm-1am Thur; 4pm-2am Fri;
noon-2am Sat; noon-midnight Sun. **Food
served** 6.30-10.30pm Mon-Thur; 6.30-11pm
Fri; noon-4pm, 6.30-11pm Sat; noon-9pm Sun.
Kensal Green
Paradise makes decorative use of its name,
taken from GK Chesterton's poem 'The Rolling
English Road', by filling its high-ceilinged
interior with religious icons, angels, cherubs and
flowery chandeliers, even extending the effect to
two huge stone vases of flowers on the bar
counter. When you reach it, you'll find prices to
be more than reasonable for the quality of
mixing (very good) and service (ditto). Beers
include Guinness, plus standard lagers at
standard prices; there are also plenty of wines.
With its banquet-sized dining hall, courtyard
garden and roof terrace, Paradise does a roaring
trade in private dining, and bar snacks here are
a notch above the norm: Poole harbour rock
oysters and shallot dressing, for instance.
Comedy nights, movie screenings and DJs
provide entertainment.
*Babies & children admitted (until 8pm).
Entertainment (bands/DJs 7pm Fri, Sat).
Function rooms (up to 150 capacity). Tables
outdoors (10, garden). Wireless internet.*

Gay Bars

Central	200
North East	202
East	202
South	202

Gay Bars

Although there are outliers, with gay-friendly pubs as far flung as Hampstead, Greenwich and Richmond, London's gay scene is largely split between three neighbourhoods. The most prominent, varied and central is Soho, anchored on Old Compton Street and a crowd-pleaser for years. The scene around Vauxhall is more hedonistic, attracting muscle marys, bears and others to full-on clubs that strictly enforce a leather, rubber and uniform dress code, or after-after-hours club nights (well, afternoons, actually). However, it's also home to **RVT**, the shabby Royal Vauxhall Tavern of legend, beloved by gay men and women for decades.

The final corner of London's gay triangle is East London, mostly around Shoreditch and Hoxton. At the likes of the **George & Dragon** and, further north, the **Dalston Superstore**, you'll be rubbing shoulders with fashion's latest *wunderkinder* to soundtracks constructed by ferociously underground DJs. Exclusively gay bars are few, but that's part of the attraction: a lot of the bars around here are properly mixed, which makes the neighbourhood ideal for a night out with straight mates.

The following is just a sample of the capital's diverse scene. For a far more comprehensive guide to where to go, pick up a copy of the *Time Out Gay & Lesbian London Guide*, or visit www.timeout.com/london/gay for this week's events.

Central

Admiral Duncan
54 Old Compton Street, W1D 4UB (7437 5300). Leicester Square tube. **Open** noon-11pm Mon-Thur; noon-midnight Fri, Sat; noon-10.30pm Sun. **Soho**
A triumph of brash fun over basic flirting, this Soho stalwart attracts party-oriented punters to its one-room bar in the middle of Old Compton Street. The board of shooters encourages Friday nights of inebriated abandon; lager drinkers have the choice of draught Peroni, Stella, Carlsberg, Carling or Heineken, or bottled Sol or Peroni. A jukebox provides musical offerings that are conveniently categorised by the decade. Despite all of this unabashed bonhomie, as an obvious target for dangerous homophobes, the good Admiral has been beset by tragedy, most notably by a bomb that killed three regulars on a busy night in 1999. **Map p241 K6**.

Candy Bar
4 Carlisle Street, W1D 3BJ (7287 5041, www.candybarsoho.com). Tottenham Court Road tube. **Open** 4pm-3am Mon-Sat; 4pm-12.30am Sun. **Soho**
Kim Lucas, who founded this flagship lesbian venue in 1996, upped sticks in 2008 and escaped the recession, but the Candy Bar's new owners are working hard to keep the party vibe alive. Mostly open from late afternoon only, the door policed by a uniformed lady with an ominous luminous armband ('pay in after 9pm,' she'll declare at weekends), it's a tiny venue, especially considering the publicity it has generated. Seating space is at a premium, whether at the window or on bright pink bar stools at the counter. Beneath gaudy disco balls, reasonably priced standard cocktails are served to girls who drink fast during generous happy hours and then just keep on going. DJ Wicked spins tunes when attention is focused on the erotic dancing: this was the first women-only bar in the UK to be granted a striptease licence (pole dancing takes place in the bijou basement). *Disabled: toilet. Entertainment (DJs 9pm Tue-Sun).* **Map p240 K6**.

Edge
11 Soho Square, W1D 3QE (7439 1313, www.edgesoho.co.uk). Tottenham Court Road tube. **Open** noon-1am Mon-Sat; 2-11.30pm Sun. **Soho**
Set on a corner of Soho Square, the Edge draws visitors of all kinds but caters mainly to a gay crowd: diners and coffee-sippers by day, clubbers by night. It's divided into four floors: the street-level main bar and terrace tables; the first floor Hygge Lounge and 'alfresco' second floor, both designed by Saatchi & Saatchi

Freedom Bar

with chichi decor to match; and the third-floor Club Bar, which has great views over the square. Downstairs, to a backdrop of music videos over the bar and a woozy display of 15 colour-changing squares over one wall, customers tuck into stomach-lining grub beneath a Sputnik-esque starburst ball of light. There are cocktails here as well, including the fun-loving likes of a Bomberry Sling (Bombay Sapphire, Chambord, strawberry purée, lime juice and pineapple juice). San Miguel and Carlsberg Cold are the draught lager standards.
Entertainment (pianist 9pm Wed, Sun; DJs 9pm Thur-Sat). Function room (50-100 capacity). Tables outdoors (6, pavement).
Map p240 K6.

Freedom Bar
66 Wardour Street, W1F 0TA (7734 0071, www.freedombarsoho.com). Piccadilly Circus tube. **Open/food served** 4pm-3am Mon-Thur; 2pm-3am Fri, Sat; 2-11pm Sun. **Soho**
Looking out on to the gay vortex where Brewer Street, Wardour Street and Old Compton Street merge, with the gaudy green neon boast that it's 'open till 3am' above its front window, Freedom can't really fail to bring in the punters. It draws a party crowd, women and straights included,

who fill the cream-coloured banquettes that line the main space all the way to the glittery bar counter. Quality and location considered, prices are more than reasonable: seven types of martini (£8-£9), mixed with Bombay Sapphire gin or Zubrówka, Absolut Vanilla and flavoured Stoli vodkas; champagne cocktails in a similar price range; and an array of additional mojitos, cosmos and the like. Happy hour runs all the way until 3am five nights a week (why didn't they put *that* in green neon?), by which time staggering up the stairs from the basement disco may prove a challenge.
Disabled: toilet. Entertainment (cabaret 10pm Mon). Function room (200 capacity). Tables outdoors (3, pavement). Wireless internet.
Map p241 K6.

Green Carnation
4-5 Greek Street, W1D 4DB (8123 4267, www.greencarnationsoho.co.uk). Tottenham Court Road tube. **Open** 4pm-2am Mon-Sat; 4pm-12.30am Sun. **Admission** £5 Mon-Thur, after 11pm Fri, Sat. **Soho**
'The only way to get rid of temptation is to yield to it,' reads the quote that runs across the wall of the reception area of this relatively ambitious, comparatively off-beat gay bar, set between Soho Square and the archway of Manette Steet. The nearby portrait of the quote's originator, Oscar Wilde (who else?), is no gimmick: the dark-fronted bar stages occasional literary and Wilde-themed events. Downstairs, though, you could be in any gay Soho basement, with pumping electro beats and flirty Latin staff. Mention must be made of the drinks: nearly 20 'long and fruity' cocktails in standard combinations based on Finlandia and Krupnik vodkas and Bombay Sapphire gin. House specialities include the 'short and snazzy' Carnation Kiss (Amaretto and Maraschino). Little fuss has been made of the beers, but wines run to a Charles Vienot chablis (£28.50) and a similarly priced pinot noir from the same stable.
Entertainment (cabaret 10pm Mon; pianist 10pm Thur; DJs 9pm Fri, Sat). Tables outdoors (2, pavement). Wireless internet.
Map p241 K6.

Retro Bar
2 George Court, off Strand, WC2N 6HH (7839 8760). Charing Cross tube/rail. **Open** noon-11pm Mon-Fri; 5-11pm Sat; 5-10.30pm Sun. **Strand**
Gay and straight aficionados of post-punk pop flock to this sympathetic little hideaway, found down a short flight of steps at the Charing Cross end of the Strand. Along with a Wall of Shame containing portraits of regulars in

Polaroid form, this red-fronted cabin of nostalgia is lined with black-and-white images of bygone stars (Siouxsie, Kate Bush, Ian Curtis); the Thunder jukebox cranks out music of a similar vintage. Ahead as you walk in, a small bar counter is staffed by some of the sweetest pourers in town, dispensing pints of Heineken and John Smith's, bottles of Corona and Beck's, wines and simple cocktails. Love seats in a side alcove aid communication, and there's more intimacy in the bar upstairs. Quiz nights and other themed evenings help maintain the bar's genuine sense of community.
Entertainment (quiz 9pm Tue; DJs 8pm Sat; musicals quiz 7pm Sun). Games (board games). **Map p241 L7.**

Rupert Street
50 Rupert Street, W1D 6DR (7494 3059). Leicester Square or Piccadilly Circus tube. **Open** noon-11pm Mon-Fri; 11am-midnight Sat; 11am-10.30pm Sun. **Soho**
Absolutely jam-packed heaving most evenings, this large-windowed bar transforms the corner of Rupert and Brewer Streets into gay party central. Everyone seems pretty, flirtatious and keen to socialise, abetted by attractively priced cocktails, cosmopolitans, mules and mojitos that come in at not much more than £6. Equally affordable shots and double vodka Red Bulls are devoured by the troughload. It's not all hedonism: there's half-decent dining to be had, too. Burgers, fish and chips and pies provide sustenance before the end-of-week DJ sessions.
Music (DJs 8pm Fri-Sun). Tables outdoors (5, pavement). **Map p241 K6.**

North East

Also recommended...
Dalston Superstore (Clubs & Music Venues, *p211*).

East

Also recommended...
George & Dragon (Good Mixers, *p188*).

South

RVT (Royal Vauxhall Tavern)

RVT (Royal Vauxhall Tavern)
372 Kennington Lane, SE11 5HY (7820 1222, www.rvt.org.uk). Vauxhall tube/rail. **Open** 7pm-midnight Mon, Wed, Thur; 6pm-midnight Tue; 7pm-2am Fri; 9pm-2am Sat; 2pm-midnight Sun. **Food served** 7-10.30pm Mon, Wed-Fri; 6-10.30pm Tue; 9-10.30pm Sat; 2-10.30pm Sun. **Vauxhall**
Standing firm and proud as a major traffic hub has been developed around it, the RVT dates from 1863, and remains true to its century-old tradition as a cabaret venue. It's been serving confirmed bachelors since before Kylie was born and is now the royal palace of Voho, the gay village of Vauxhall. On any given night, star names may be draped banner-big across its traditional pub frontage (Lily Savage got her start behind the bar), and the place may be absolutely jammed. The main attraction is Duckie, Amy Lamé's wilfully eccentric Saturday club night. Get here in the early evening and you'll have time and space to fire into some beef stew or a burger, but otherwise it's shots, shooters and standard lagers all the way. In the evening, muscle marys whip off their tops and gear up for an evening of debauchery at the many nearby clubs.
Disabled: toilet. Entertainment (bingo 8.30pm Mon; cabaret 8.30pm Wed, Thur; DJs 10pm Fri, 9pm Sat, 2pm Sun). Tables outdoors (6, pavement).

Clubs &
Music Venues

Central	204
North	209
North East	211
East	212
South East	217
South	218
South West	219
West	220

Clubs & Music Venues

A few years ago, many of London's more popular clubbing venues were a short stroll from a central tube station. Today, though, even with the arrival of the East London Line extension, finding the most cutting-edge nightlife in the city requires a little more effort. You'll have to head out to the wilds of north-east London for the likes of the **Dalston Superstore** and **Café Oto**, for instance.

That said, the hub of the capital's nightlife circuit remains comparatively accessible Shoreditch, especially the daunting array of clubs and DJ bars dotted between Brick Lane and Hoxton Square. From the ancient **Dublin Castle** to the modern **Lock Tavern**, Camden remains king for indie kids, though there's also a scene in New Cross. Staying south of the river, Brixton is livelier than it's been for a while. And then there are the outliers: great jazz in Barnes at the **Bull's Head**, burlesque in the City at **Volupté**, and the multifarious nights at the **Notting Hill Arts Club**.

In this section, we've focused on smaller music venues, bar-clubs and DJ bars where you could just as easily pop in for a drink as make a whole night of it. For full-on club nights and big-name concert listings, pick up a copy of this week's *Time Out* or visit www.timeout.com/london.

Central

Ain't Nothin' But...
20 Kingly Street, W1B 5PZ (7287 0514, www.aintnothinbut.co.uk). Oxford Circus tube. **Open/food served** 6pm-1am Mon-Thur; 5pm-2.30am Fri; 3pm-2.30am Sat; 3-11pm Sun. **Soho**
When the owners of this cluttered temple to *da blooze* hit upon the idea of using a Georgia White song title as its name, they could have plumped for 'Hot Nuts' or 'Take Me For a Buggy Ride'. Yet it's the risqué singer's 78 of 'The Blues Ain't Nothin' But...' that's been given pride of place facing a cabin-like bar counter where pints of Adnams Bitter and Broadside, as well as Bitburger, Murphy's and Mad Goose Purity are dispensed and duly taken back to a saloon-style back room accommodating the seating. That's where the live music takes place most nights of the week, performed by tail-shakers happy to have a residency and equal acclaim from tourists and local enthusiasts. The staircase down to the toilets is decorated with caricatures of great names in blues and wider genres (the one of Screamin' Jay Hawkins is a work of art).

Overall, a likeable student-bohemian vibe sets this place apart from the trendier spots along bar-lined Kingly Street.
Entertainment (musicians 9.30pm Mon, Wed-Sat, 6pm & 9.30pm Tue, 4pm & 9.30pm Sun; open-mic 4pm Sat). **Map p241 J6.**

Bathhouse
7-8 Bishopsgate Churchyard, EC2M 3TJ (7920 9207, www.thebathhousevenue.com). Liverpool Street tube/rail. **Open** 5pm-midnight Thur; 5pm-2am Fri; 5pm-4am Sat. **Food served** 6.30-9.30pm Thur, Fri. **Admission** free-£7. **City**
Built at the end of the 19th century, this old Victorian Turkish bathhouse has found a new lease of life as a fresh and interesting party palace. Done out with marble and gilt mirrors, the space is perfectly appropriate for decadent happenings and the showgirl, burlesque and neo-cabaret stars who perform at them. The rest of the time, the Bathhouse sees a mix of entertainment, from simple DJ nights to musical bingo sessions. The cocktail list takes in familiar classics and relatively cultured novelties (the Dorian Gray blends Chase vodka with balsamic vinegar and strawberries);

Betsey Trotwood

the restaurant's set menu might include smoked-salmon lasagne or guinea fowl suprême. *Entertainment (cabaret 8.30pm Thur, 8pm Fri; DJs 9pm Sat). Function rooms (50-80 capacity).* **Map p245 Q6.**

Betsey Trotwood

56 Farringdon Road, EC1R 3BL (7253 4285, www.thebetsey.com). Farringdon tube/rail. **Open** noon-11pm Mon-Wed; noon-11.30pm Thur; noon-1am Fri, Sat. **Food served** noon-3pm, 6-9pm Mon-Fri. **Admission** *Gigs* free-£7. **Clerkenwell**
The Betsey, as it's universally known around Clerkenwell, has never quite managed to settle on an identity, but its all-things-to-some-people approach works in its favour. The character of your fellow drinkers on any given night will largely be determined by whether or not the pub is staging a gig, either in the amazingly pokey basement space or in the roomier, prettier upstairs bar. Acts are usually indie hopefuls, alt-country twangers and winsome singer-songwriters, though there's usually a surprise or two on the venue's gig roster. Away from the entertainment, this is a roomy but ultimately pretty straightforward corner boozer, with beers by Shepherd Neame and uncomplicated pub grub by a kitchen that knows its limitations. *Babies & children admitted (until 6pm). Entertainment (musicians 8pm alternate Thur; bands/comedy Fri, Sat; check website for details). Function rooms (50 capacity). Tables outdoors (4, pavement). Wireless internet.* **Map p242 N4.**

Big Chill House

257-259 Pentonville Road, N1 9NL (7427 2540, www.bigchill.net). King's Cross tube/rail. **Open** noon-midnight Mon-Thur, Sun; noon-2am Fri, Sat. **Food served** 8am-11.30pm, noon-10pm Mon-Thur; 11am-10pm Fri-Sun. **Admission** free-£5. **King's Cross**
Poor ticket sales at the 2009 Big Chill festival led to the event seeking voluntary liquidation, at which point it was purchased by the Festival Republic behemoth. Happily, the two London bars have proven more stable, and continue to earn acclaim from fans who are inspired by the artwork and tickled by the signage ('brothers' and 'sisters' on the toilet doors). Housed in a large, difficult building, the King's Cross branch can feel a little tumbleweedy on quiet nights; it's best to head here when there are DJs, generally Thursdays to Sundays with occasional events on other evenings. From the drinks list, cocktails (served in glasses or pitchers) are more enticing than the dull beer list (Amstel, Heineken, Budvar); food includes individual dishes (burgers, burritos) and sharing platters. An upstairs patio comes into its own in summer. *Babies & children admitted (until 6pm). Disabled: toilet. Entertainment (bands/DJs 8pm Thur-Sun). Tables outdoors (7, terrace). Wireless internet.*

Circus

27-29 Endell Street, WC2H 9BA (7420 9300, www.circus-london.co.uk). Covent Garden tube. **Open** 5pm-midnight Mon-Wed;

5pm-1am Thur; 5pm-2am Fri, Sat. **Food served** 5-10.30pm Mon-Sat. **Covent Garden** Despite the name, the entertainment here comes not from clowns in collapsible cars or daring young men on the flying trapeze but from a new breed of cabaret acts: the long banquet table doubles as a catwalk-cum-stage for fire-eaters, burlesque acts and dancers. If the entertainment doesn't make your retinas wince, then the gleaming white floors and walls might. The bar and dining areas are a little spartan, but there's a softer lounge area if it all seems too clinical. The drinks list delivers classic cocktails with a twist: bellinis made with blood peaches, margaritas made with hibiscus juice and agave nectar. The food is high-end (that is, pricey) pan-Asian dishes: star anise duck confit, Josper beef fillet steak. The scene gets clubby at weekends with regular DJs and even dancing on the tables. *Booking advisable. Disabled: toilet. Dress code: smart casual. Entertainment (cabaret dinner daily).* **Map p240 L6.**

Gramaphone

60-62 Commercial Street, E1 6LT (7377 5332, www.thegramaphone.co.uk). Aldgate East tube or Liverpool Street tube/rail. **Open** noon-1.30am Mon-Thur; noon-2.30am Fri; 8pm-2.30am Sat. **Food served** noon-10pm Mon-Fri. **Admission** free-£10. **City**
Such are the economic conditions these days, not to mention Gramaphone's location a little too far from the Brick Lane beat, that during the week, Thai food takes precedence over the musical entertainment (from funk to dubstep via drum 'n' bass and most points in between). Outside, meanwhile, a board lures punters with the promise of £2 Stellas and £12 jugs of sangria rather than nights of smartly mixed abandon. Still, Gramaphone is a perfectly acceptable bar-restaurant, and you're almost guaranteed a table – no bad shout to kick off a night's trawl around E1. Cocktails (£6-£7.50) include a Gramaphone Delight of Southern Comfort, Cointreau and peach purée; Bitburger is the best draught option. Wines come eight by the bottle, four by the glass. And, yes, that aforementioned Thai food is well conceived and well presented. The cosy sofa corner and music-related photographs hark back to a trendier era. *Babies & children admitted (until 8pm). Disabled: toilet. Entertainment (bands/DJs 8pm Mon-Thur; DJs 9pm Fri, Sat). Function room (200 capacity). Tables outdoors (3, pavement), Wireless internet.* **Map p246 S6.**

Lexington

96-98 Pentonville Road, N1 9JB (7837 5371, www.thelexington.co.uk). Angel tube. **Open** noon-2am Mon-Thur; noon-4am Fri, Sat; noon-midnight Sun. **Food served** noon-3pm, 5-10pm daily. **Admission** *Gigs* free-£10. **King's Cross**

Big Chill House. *See p205.*

In the building that formerly housed La Finca, the Lexington is an unexpectedly handsome place. Many punters head here for the first-floor music venue, which stages an assortment of indie-ish bands and club nights. But the ground-floor bar is open to all (you only need to pay an admission fee if you go upstairs), and is worth a look. There's little pretence at intimacy: this is basically a big, tall corner room with bells on (plush lampshades, heavy red curtains). The main selling point is the array of American drinks: beers include flavourful brews from the likes of Goose Island in Chicago and the Brooklyn Brewery (in addition to closer-to-home Camden Wheat Beer), and the array of rare American whiskeys (including 43 bourbons) is, if anything, even more tempting. Food options include po'boys, alongside fish 'n' chips and pork katsu. The clientele consists chiefly of people taking a break from the show above, preferring the appetising jukebox to the presumably avoidable support bands.
Babies & children admitted (until 7pm). Entertainment (bands 8pm daily; quiz 8pm Mon). Games (table football). Tables outdoors (4, pavement). Wireless internet.

Lexington

Volupté
7-9 Norwich Street, EC4A 1EJ (7831 1622, www.volupte-lounge.com). Chancery Lane tube. **Open** 5pm-1am Tue-Thur; 5pm-3am Fri; 1pm-3am Sat; 1-6pm Sun. **Food served** 7pm Tue, Wed; 6.30pm, 9.30pm Thur, Fri; 2.30pm, 6.30pm, 9.30pm Sat; 3pm Sun. **Admission** free-£30. **City**
Expect to suffer wallpaper envy as you enter the ground-floor bar and then head down to this cabaret-cum-burlesque club, located, rather bizarrely, not far from Chancery Lane tube in the heart of the City. Those daring enough to descend into the basement can expect to enjoy some of the best cabaret talent in town from tables set beneath absinthe-inspired vines. Afternoon Tease combines burlesque with high tea most Saturday afternoons; other events look back as far as the Jazz Age for inspiration. The food's pricey – fettuccine with spinach and sun-dried tomatoes for £16.50 seems a little steep – but the cocktails, both traditional and modern, are more reasonable at around £8 apiece.
Entertainment (burlesque cabaret 8pm Tue-Fri, some Sat). Function room (200 capacity). **Map p243 N5.**

Wilmington Arms
69 Rosebery Avenue, EC1R 4RL (7837 1384, www.thewilmingtonarms.co.uk). Angel tube or Farringdon tube/rail. **Open** noon-11.15pm Mon-Thur; noon-12.15am Fri, Sat; noon-10.30pm

Sun. **Food served** noon-9.30pm Mon-Thur; noon-3pm Fri; noon-9pm Sat, Sun. **Admission** *Gigs* free-£5. **Clerkenwell**
The jaunty slogans that usually grace the blackboards outside this Clerkenwell pub, twinned with the Hawley Arms in Camden, reflect the cheery nature of the entire enterprise. On the left is a happy-go-lucky pub, not especially handsome but comfortable enough. The drinks list is led by two ales, both guests; food is solid pub grub. On the right, meanwhile, is a separate room given over to gigs and club nights, which works equally well as an all-standing space for gigs by guitar-slinging indie hopefuls and a cabaret-style set-up with tables and chairs. The make-up of the clientele in the pub depends on who's playing in the gig space, but pointy shoes and tight jeans are usually in abundance. A well-run operation.
Babies & children admitted (until 7pm). Booking advisable Thur, Fri. Disabled: toilet. Entertainment (bands/cabaret/comedy 7.30pm daily). Tables outdoors (4, pavement). Wireless internet. **Map p242 N4.**

Also recommended...
Bloomsbury Bowling Lanes (Good Mixers, *p174*); **Floridita** (Cocktails & Spirits, *p24*); **Golden Eagle** (Classic

Pubs, *p70*); **Green Carnation** (Gay Bars, *p201*); **Market Place** (Good Mixers, *p179*); **Ruby Lounge** (Cocktails & Spirits, *p30*); **Slaughtered Lamb** (Good Mixers, *p181*); **Social** (Good Mixers, *p181*); **Three Kings of Clerkenwell** (Classic Pubs, *p77*).

North

Blues Kitchen
111-113 Camden High Street, NW1 7JN (7387 5277, www.theblueskitchen.com). *Camden Town tube.* **Open** noon-midnight Mon-Wed; noon-1am Thur; noon-3am Fri; 11am-3am Sat; 11am-midnight Sun. **Food** served noon-10.30pm Mon-Fri; 11am-10.30pm Sat; 11am-10pm Sun. **Admission** free-£4. **Camden**

This lively, contemporary bar-diner on the main Camden drag celebrates American musical heritage in song (live shows, DJs, free harmonica lessons), spirits and sustenance. There are around 50 bourbons in a variety of categories, some used as bases for cocktails. Rarer types (Blanton's Gold, Sazerac 18-Year-Old Rye, Woodford Reserve 1838 Sweet Mash) go for a tenner or more, but otherwise you'll be paying £3.50 to £6. 'America's native spirit' is how Kentucky bourbon is described, with Ancient Age and Evan Williams typical examples; Tennessee, 'the first cousin of Kentucky', is honoured with a full suit of Jack Daniel's labels. Food stays in transatlantic character. It's all decked out with colourful impressions of legendary bluesmen Blind Willie McTell, Skip James – with the occasional torn gig poster. Oh, to have been in Paris for that Leadbelly show... *Babies & children admitted (until 7pm). Entertainment (musicians 9.30pm daily). Wireless internet.* **Map p254 J1.**

Boogaloo
312 Archway Road, N6 5AT (8340 2928, www.theboogaloo.org). Highgate tube. **Open** 6pm-midnight Mon-Wed; 6pm-1am Thur; 6pm-2am Fri; 2pm-2am Sat; 2pm-midnight Sun.* **Highgate**

Come here for the drinks (spirits and mixers, predictable lagers, the dreaded Magners) or the service (distracted at best) and you'll leave both quickly and disappointed. But although it's not as cool or as interesting as it thinks it is, and there's always a danger that you'll find yourself surrounded by wearying indie scenesters up from Camden for the night, this Highgate pub is not without appeal. The chief attractions are the string of themed DJ nights, highlighted by the retro Gerry's Joint; the casual Sunday music sessions with the excellent Walbourne Brothers; the popular monthly movie quiz; and the jukebox, a pleasing mix of canonical rock-snob classics and unexpected obscurities. Regulars include Shane MacGowan, for whom the place appears to be something of a second home on his visits to London. *Babies & children admitted (until 7pm). Disabled: toilet. Entertainment (quiz 8.30pm some Tue; musicians 8.30pm Sun). Tables outdoors (15, garden).*

Dublin Castle
94 Parkway, NW1 7AN (7485 1773, www.bugbearbookings.com). Camden Town tube. **Open** noon-1am Mon-Wed; noon-2am Thur-Sun. **Admission** *Gigs* £4.50-£6. **Camden**

A longtime fixture on the Camden pub circuit, the Dublin Castle has witnessed the launch of many a career. Note, for instance, the signed poster of Madness by the bar, behind which stands a framed photograph of Amy; Blur and Travis paid their dues on the stage in the back room. (The management has also seen fit to put up a huge Deaf School poster.) The front bar is a simple affair, purveying pints of Red Stripe, Murphy's and London Pride, bottles of Estrella, Peroni and Budvar, and unspecified wines at under £4 a glass. Bell's, Jim Beam, Jack Daniel's and Sailor Jerry are the most popular chasers, judging by optic pours on a typically busy early evening. Bands these days play under such unappetising names as Rosamojo & the White Rabbit and Die! Chihuahua, Die!, but you might get lucky with a next-big-thing or two. *Babies & children admitted (until 7pm). Entertainment (bands 8pm daily).* **Map p254 H1.**

Lock Tavern
35 Chalk Farm Road, NW1 8AJ (7482 7163, www.lock-tavern.co.uk). Chalk Farm tube. **Open** noon-midnight Mon-Thur; noon-1am Fri, Sat; noon-11pm Sun. **Food served** noon-3pm, 5-10pm Mon-Fri; noon-4pm, 6-10pm Sat, Sun. **Camden**

The bass notes pounding through the pub floor into the soles of your shoes, the spiky-haired twentysomethings, the scattering of gob-smacked students from the continent – it could only be Camden. This old local has been transformed into a DJ and music venue with room for a serious number of punters in the main bar, the large garden (accessed via a short flight of steps) and a sassy upstairs space, complete with a neon sign knowingly admitting that this is 'a tarted-up pub'. On offer are pints of Amstel, Moretti and Guinness, bottles of Modello, Leffe and Tiger, and ten wines. Music

tends towards educated indie dance, with the likes of Richard Fearless and Jon Carter sometimes behind the decks. The food is useful for lining the stomach in a bar where excess is not so much tolerated as encouraged. *Entertainment (bands 7pm Thur-Sun; DJs 7pm Thur-Sat). Games (board games). Tables outdoors (4, roof terrace; 12, garden). Wireless internet.* **Map p254 G26.**

Old Queen's Head

44 Essex Road, N1 8LN (7354 9993, www. theoldqueenshead.com). Angel tube. **Open** noon-midnight Mon-Wed, Sun; noon-1am Thur; noon-2am Fri, Sat. **Food served** 5-10pm Mon-Fri; noon-10pm Sat; noon-9pm Sun. **Admission** £4 after 8pm Fri, Sat. **Islington**
Seen by day, the Old Queen's Head is a large, attractive pub, its big fireplace surrounded by upholstered sofas and gilt-framed portraits in a church-like interior. None of this will be visible most evenings, when young, urban musos gather in force around pints of Guinness or bottles of lager. A dozen cocktails are also offered – nothing too complicated or sophisticated, but nice enough – as well as around ten wines at fair prices. The food is pretty manly (burgers, steak baguettes and so on), but otherwise it's a good cosmopolitan mix, with the crowd on any given night split roughly 50-50 between girls and boys. On weekend nights, everyone spills outside. Entertainment is generally of the up-for-it DJ variety (think of it as a spruced-up, expanded Social), though there's also a fine folk series staged in the comfortable upstairs room. *Babies & children admitted (until 7pm). Entertainment (bands 7.30pm Mon-Thur, 4pm Sun; quiz 7pm Tue; DJs 9pm Fri & Sat, 4pm Sun). Tables outdoors (6, garden; 6, pavement). Wireless internet.* **Map p255 O1.**

Proud

Horse Hospital, Stables Market, NW1 8AH (7482 3867, www.proudcamden.com). Chalk Farm tube. **Open** 11am-1.30am Mon-Wed; 11am-2.30am Thur-Sat; 11am-12.30am Sun. **Admission** free-£10. **Camden**
North London guitar-slingers and the college-age indie kids that love them both get to act like rock stars with debauched impunity at this former equine hospital, now converted into a bar and a photographic gallery that's chiefly engaged in rock 'n' roll myth-making (U2, Kings of Leon, the Libertines). With cocktail or beer bottle in hand, the artfully shambolic punters drape themselves over the luxurious textiles in the individual stable-style booths, sink into deck chairs on the outdoor terrace, or spin around in

the main band room to trendinista electro, indie and alternative sounds. Look out for under-the-radar live sets from the likes of Johnny Borrell, Carl Barât and other alt-rock journeymen. *Babies & children admitted (until 6pm). Booking advisable Thur-Sat. Entertainment (bands and/or DJs 8pm Mon-Fri, noon Sat, Sun). Games (consoles). Tables outdoors (8, terrace). Wireless internet.* **Map p254 I12G.**

Also recommended...

Filthy MacNasty's (Classic Pubs, *p79*); **Lockside Lounge** (Rooms with a View, *p163*).

North East

Café Oto

18-22 Ashwin Street, E8 3DL (7923 1231, www.cafeoto.co.uk). Dalston Junction or Dalston Kingsland rail. **Open** 9.30am-1am Mon-Fri; 10.30am-midnight Sat, Sun. **Food served** 11.30am-3pm Mon-Fri. **Admission** free-£10. **Dalston**
The unexpected conversion of Dalston from an avoidable backwater to a countercultural focal point has thrown up no more interesting venue than this, tucked away behind the north-eastern corner of Dalston Junction and housed in a plain, warehouse-like space with huge glass windows that look on to a quiet street outside. It's chiefly a music venue ('Oto' means 'sound' in Japanese), staging an on-the-edge programme that takes in alternative folk, thoughtful electronica, free jazz and other niche genres for crowds who are happy to kill the conversation during the performances. But it's also open during the day, dispensing snacks, coffees and unusual alcoholic drinks (Pitfield ales, Breton ciders, Japanese plum wine) for the benefit of artistically minded sorts with laptops in tow. *Babies & children admitted. Disabled: toilet. Entertainment (musicians 8pm days vary). Tables outdoors (8, pavement). Wireless internet.*

Dalston Superstore

117 Kingland High Street, E8 2PB (7254 2273). Dalston Junction or Dalston Kingsland rail. **Open** 10am-3am daily. **Food served** 10am-4.30pm, 6-9.30pm daily. **Dalston**
Suited to its surroundings in tipping-point East London, the Dalston Superstore is a carefully indifferent, confidently cool and slightly camp New York-styled ersatz dive bar split between two floors, clad in cement, brick and steel vents. The decor is enlivened by fluoro flashes, graffiti and a long, wooden bar, but the designers have

taken a casual, less-is-more approach to the place. The food and drinks lists are just as spare: beer in familiar bottles, a brief cocktail list, and substantial burgers, sandwiches, salads and cakes. In studiously aloof fashion, there's no website on which to discover what's on; but turn up unbidden and you might stumble into a club night, an exhibition after-party or some other faintly arty event favoured by the moustache-wearing, fixed-wheel-bicycle-riding clientele. Expect to queue at weekends. *Babies & children admitted (until 6pm). Disabled: toilet. Entertainment (DJs 9pm daily). Tables outdoors (2, pavement). Wireless internet.*

East

333

333 Old Street, EC1V 9LE (7739 5949, www.333mother.com). Old Street tube/rail or Shoreditch High Street rail. **Open** 8pm-2am Mon; 8pm-3am Tue-Thur; 10pm-3am Fri-Sun. **Admission** *Club* free-£10. **Shoreditch**
The capacious, messy 333 was one of the first clubs to colonise this corner of town, and did as much as any venue to put the neighbourhood on London's nightlife map. It's no longer the be-all and end-all of East End clubbing, and the programme in the main room is a little thinner than in previous years. Even so, this three-floored clubbing institution still draws queues for indie-rave mash-ups at weekends. The basement's dark and intense, which works well for the dubstep talent on show. Before it was the 333, the site was home to a faintly seamy gay bar called the London Apprentice; a gay night named in its honour is held here every Sunday. Upstairs is the tatty Mother Bar, responsible for countless lost evenings. There's no food up there besides the iconic nut machines, but really, if you'd eaten earlier, you probably wouldn't have wound up there in the first place. *Entertainment (DJs 10pm daily). Wireless internet.* **Map p244 R4.**

Bethnal Green Working Men's Club

42-44 Pollard Row, E2 6NB (7739 7170, www.workersplaytime.net). Bethnal Green tube. **Open** varies; check website for details. **Admission** free-£8. **Bethnal Green**
The sticky red carpet and the broken lampshades at this unusual Bethnal Green venue – which, as the bemused looks on the faces of the regulars vividly proves, still functions as a working men's club – perfectly

Volupté. *See p207.*

Proud. See p211.

suits the programme of quirky lounge nights, vintage rock 'n' roll sessions, cheesy-listening clubs and fancy-dress burlesque parties that make up the lion's part of the programming here. The mood is friendly, the playlist is usually upbeat and the air is full of artful, playful mischief. The drinks aren't anything special, to say the least, but they're at least served at prices that won't leave too much of a dent in your '50s-vintage jumble-sale purse.
Entertainment (film screenings 7pm Tue; various events, check website for details). Wireless internet. **Map p246 T4.**

Big Chill Bar
Old Truman Brewery, off Brick Lane, E1 6QL (7392 9180, www.bigchill.net). Liverpool Street tube/rail or Shoreditch High Street rail. **Open** noon-midnight Mon-Thur; noon-1am Fri, Sat; noon-midnight Sun. **Food served** noon-10pm Mon-Fri; noon-8pm Sat, Sun. **Brick Lane**
This music-oriented venue is an essential part of the Truman Brewery complex. Italian squat renegades and Japanese voyeurs join dog-on-string types and pot-bellied ex-longhairs to partake in pints of Heineken, Amstel and Budvar, or bottles of Kiwi Steinlager, Iberian

Sagres and Scottish Innis & Gunn, while DJs spin several nights a week and all day on Sundays. There's plenty of room to stretch out in the main lounge and on the front terrace for smokers. Cocktails come by the glass or the four-measure pitcher: the Big Chill Punch of vodka, champagne, passion fruit and white peach purées, for example. House burgers come with beef, chicken and vegetarian options.
Babies & children admitted (until 6pm). Disabled: toilet. Entertainment (DJs 7pm Wed & Thur, 8pm Fri & Sat, 2pm Sun). Tables outdoors (7, terrace). Wireless internet. **Map p246 S5.**

Cargo
Kingsland Viaduct, 83 Rivington Street, EC2A 3AY (7739 3440, www.cargo-london. com). Old Street tube/rail or Shoreditch High Street rail. **Open** noon-1am Mon-Thur; noon-3am Fri, Sat; noon-midnight Sun. **Food served** noon-midnight daily. **Admission** free-£12. **Shoreditch**
The bricks and arches of cavernous Cargo keep Shoreditch music fans in a blissful state of whatever-nextness. Happily, it's just far enough from the main drag to ensure that it escapes the

Dalston Superstore. See p211.

stag parties and bridge-and-tunnel revellers who roam Shoreditch at weekends, and as such has retained an atmosphere that stands slightly apart from its fashionable neighbours. The music programming remains gloriously varied, taking in everything from indie-rock hopefuls to Fela Kuti tribute acts. Also worthy of mention: the great street-food café (pizzas, burgers, £5 lunch specials) and the Shepard Fairey-styled street art in the garden. A noble endeavour, and one still worth backing.
Babies & children admitted (until 6pm). Disabled: toilet. Entertainment (bands/DJs evenings daily). Tables outdoors (14, yard). Wireless internet. **Map p244 R4.**

Catch
22 Kingsland Road, E2 8DA (7729 6097, www.thecatchbar.com). Old Street tube/rail or Shoreditch High Street rail. **Open** 6pm-midnight Mon-Wed; 6pm-2am Thur, Fri; 7pm-2am Sat; 6pm-1am Sun. **Admission** free-£5. **Shoreditch**
Advertising free pool and Carlsberg at £2 a pint before 10pm, Catch does its best to keep in the riff-raff, preferring to let the bohos, musos and pseuds waste away their existence in the Pragues and Dreambagsjaguarshoes of this world. Thus, unpretentious couples and groups randomly fill

the five booths that line the narrow space opposite the bar counter, upon which taps of Budvar, Bitburger and Grolsch (and behind which bottles of Tiger, Beck's and Peroni) help fuel conversation. At the back of the room is the pool table in question, red-topped and squeezed into a small space by the toilets. Between the bar area and the front door is a staircase leading to a seemingly tinier space where bands or DJs let loose most nights.
Entertainment (bands/DJs 8pm daily). Function room (100 capacity). **Map p244 R3.**

Charlie Wright's International Bar
45 Pitfield Street, N1 6DA (7490 8345). Old Street tube/rail. **Open** noon-1am Mon-Wed; noon-4am Thur, Fri; 5pm-4am Sat; 5pm-2am Sun. **Food served** noon-3pm, 5-10pm Mon-Fri; 5-10pm Sat, Sun. **Admission** £4 after 10pm Fri, Sat; £3 Sun. **Shoreditch**
Tucked down a dark street away from the Old Street hubbub, and named after an East End boxer who owned the place a half-century ago, this uncomplicated, late-opening Shoreditch favourite remains as mixed and welcoming as can be. In terms of food and drink, it lives up to its international billing. Taps offering Asahi, Staropramen, Oranjeboom, Leffe (blonde and

brown), Belle-Vue Kriek, Franziskaner and Guinness line the bar, while behind them sit bottles of Duvel, Chimay (red, white and blue), Red Stripe, Corona, Desperado, Beck's, Spitfire and Kopparberg cider. Wines and cocktails cover the standards, which is more than can be said for the forward-thinking jazz musicians who offer regular entertainment alongside frequent club nights (soul, funk, world music). The food, naturally enough, is Thai, with most mains priced around £6.

Entertainment (DJs/musicians 8pm, nights vary). Games (darts). Wireless internet. Map p244 Q3.

East Village

89 Great Eastern Street, EC2A 3HX (7739 5173, www.eastvillageclub.com). Old Street tube/rail or Shoreditch High Street rail. Open *Bar* 5pm-1am Thur; 5pm-3.30am Fri; 9pm-3.30am Sat; 2pm-1am Sun. *Club* 9pm-3am Thur; 9pm-3.30am Fri, Sat; varies Sun. Admission free-£10. Shoreditch
Stuart Patterson, one of the Faith crew who have been behind all-day house-music parties across London since 1999, has transformed the late and not especially lamented Medicine Bar into this two-floor, 'real house' bar-club that punches several divisions above its weight. The array of top-notch DJs on the regular roster should delight sophisticated clubbers: depending on the month and the nightly theme, you can expect to see the likes of Chicago house don Derrick Carter, legendary reggae selector Aba Shanti-I and London's own Mr C behind the decks. Food is fill-me-up club grub, perfect fuel for a night on the dancefloor; the drinks list includes an array of cocktails that claim a New York influence, plus familiar lagers (Stella, Leffe and Staropramen among the taps, Brahma, Kirin and Peroni by the bottle), wines and other niche libations.
Disabled: toilet. Entertainment (DJs 9pm Thur-Sat; varies Sun). Wireless internet. Map p244 Q4.

Favela Chic

91-93 Great Eastern Street, EC2A 3HZ (7613 4228, www.favelachic.com). Old Street tube/rail or Shoreditch High Street rail. Open 6pm-1am Tue-Thur; 6pm-2am Fri, Sat; 3pm-midnight Sun. Food served 7-10.30pm Tue-Sat. Admission free-£10. Shoreditch
The poor will be with us forever, but this bar, on a busy, part-pedestrianised junction, has changed hands a few times since the Shoreditch revolution a decade or more ago. The latest incarnation, attached to a Parisian venue of the same name and concept, is much better than its

title suggests (although, in fairness, it could hardly be worse). The large, church-like main room is done up with paper chains, a huge disco ball, vast plants and a doctored mural of Marianne defending the barricades, along with the kind of religious iconography the poverty-stricken put up lest the sky fall in on them. Caipirinhas are sold by the glass or pitcher in five fruit flavours (watermelon, mango and passionfruit included); the altogether more crass Lagerinha (beer and caipirinha) is mercifully served by the glass only. Beer choice has been pared down to Brahma and Peroni, but the variety of music on offer is broader: you could be beckoned on to the dancefloor by anything from modish electronica to '70s Latin funk.
Entertainment (DJs 9pm Fri, Sat). Tables outdoors (20, terrace). Map p244 Q4.

Horse & Groom

28 Curtain Road, EC2A 3NZ (7503 9421, www.thehorseandgroom.net). Old Street tube/rail. Open noon-midnight Mon-Wed; noon-2am Thur; noon-4am Fri, Sat; 4pm-2am Sun. Admission free-£7. Shoreditch
London's trend for pub-clubbing continues apace in this revamped Shoreditch spot. During the day, it's a good old East End boozer, but at night, the two-floor space turns into a disco hotspot. Thanks to some quality programming from Neil Thornton, some of the scene's best DJs, including the likes of Fabric's Craig Richards, Secretsundaze's James Priestley and the legendary Greg Wilson, have played in one of the pub's three rooms. A recent addition, the Boudoir, could rival fellow pub-club the Lock Tavern as having the capital's dinkiest dancefloor, which makes for an intense dancing experience. Further perks include a late licence and the purse-friendly cover charges.
Babies & children admitted (until 6pm). Entertainment (bands/DJs 8pm daily). Function roon (80 capacity). Wireless internet.

Old Blue Last

38 Great Eastern Street, EC2A 3ES (7739 7033, www.theoldbluelast.com). Liverpool Street or Old Street tube/rail, or Shoreditch High Street rail. Open noon-midnight

Mon-Wed; noon-12.30am Thur, Sun; noon-1.30am Fri, Sat. **Admission** free-£10. **Shoreditch**
This shabby, two-floored Victorian boozer was transformed in 2004 by hipster handbook *Vice* into... well, a shabby, two-floored Victorian boozer with a large PA. It's received a little more attention of late: early 2010 saw a refurbishment that covered everything from the sound systems to the frankly notorious toilets. But at heart, it's still the same old Shoreditch shambles that it was before the builders moved in. Arctic Monkeys, Amy Winehouse and Lily Allen are among those who've played secret shows in the sauna-like upper room, helping to bolster the venue's high-fashion status; more common are gigs from such too-cool-for-school outfits as Frankie & the Heartstrings and Feldberg, and giddily fashionable club nights. *Entertainment (bands/DJs 9pm daily). Function room (140 capacity). Wireless internet.* **Map p244 R4.**

Queen of Hoxton
1 Curtain Road, EC2A 3JX (7422 0958, www.thequeenofhoxton.co.uk). Old Street tube/rail or Shoreditch High Street rail. **Open** *Summer* 1pm-midnight Mon-Wed, Sun; 1pm-2am Thur-Sat. *Winter* 5pm-midnight Mon-Wed, Sun; 5pm-2am Thur-Sat. **Shoreditch**
This imposing, dark-fronted building on the corner of Curtain Road and Worship Street does little to advertise itself, but it always manages to bring in punters thanks to the quality of its music programme. As a bar, it feels industrial, with a heavy stone bar counter from which cocktails are dispensed. You'll be splashing out around £7 for caipirinhas, mojitos or – good grief – apple-strudel martinis. Beside the notices for wine and food (burgers, salt-beef wraps), DJ decks await action: the programme goes heavy on contemporary trends, albeit with indie-retro twists. The pool scene is serious enough to warrant a row of cues acting as a room divider before the row of low, squishy sofas by the window. In summer, head up to the roof terrace for a break from the action. *Disabled: toilet. Entertainment (DJs 8pm Thur-Sat). Tables outdoors (9, roof terrace).* **Map p244 R5.**

Star of Bethnal Green
359 Bethnal Green Road, E2 6LG (7729 0167, www.starofbethnalgreen.com). Bethnal Green tube. **Open/food served** 11.30am-midnight Mon-Thur; 11.30am-2am Fri, Sat; noon-midnight Sun. **Admission** free-£5. **Bethnal Green**

A bold red and silver star adorns the wall behind the stage in this intimate boozer, which has fast become the epitome of scruffy East End cool. A young, up-for-it crowd enjoy a laid-back, pubby vibe, but most of them are really here for the music: low-key gigs from big bands and youthful hopefuls, and an eclectic yet funky-fresh line-up of disco to house to indie nights, burlesque freak shows and wacky quiz nights (cash for the winners, free pasta for everyone). Watch out for madcap bash Bastard Batty Bass on monthly Thursdays, and various free or cheap sessions from Europe's best underground DJs, such as Mark 7, Ray Mang and Mulletover resident Geddes. The Tuesday-night quiz is a big hit with locals, and not solely because of the free food; Sundays are all about tasty roasts. *Babies & children admitted (until 9pm). Entertainment (quiz 8pm Tue; DJs 9pm Thur-Sat, 5pm Sun). Function room (70 capacity). Wireless internet.* **Map p246 T4.**

Vibe Bar
Old Truman Brewery, 91-95 Brick Lane, E1 6QL (7377 2899, www.vibebar.co.uk). Liverpool Street tube/rail or Shoreditch High Street rail. **Open** 11am-11.30pm Mon-Thur, Sun; 11am-1am Fri, Sat. **Food served** 11am-3pm Mon-Thur; 11am-7pm Fri, Sat; 11am-5pm Sun. **Admission** £4 after 8pm Fri, Sat. **Brick Lane**
This ever-popular, long-established, four-room spot in the Truman Brewery bar complex is an all-day hangout which then eases into its role as a DJ and live music bar, with an admission charge at weekends. The large courtyard comes into its own in summer, although better beer options might encourage more people to stay later rather than dash to any number of other options near here. Still, a significant European contingent among the studenty crowd add verve and colour to proceedings, while the graffitied walls inject a bit of squat chic. Food-wise, there's oak-smoked barbecue baby back ribs, deep-fried breaded prawns and, at weekends outside, jerk chicken straight off the grill, all for under a tenner. *Disabled: toilet. Entertainment (bands 8pm Mon-Wed, Sun; DJs 8pm daily). Function room (200 capacity). Tables outdoors (18, courtyard).* **Map p246 S5.**

Also recommended...
CAMP (Good Mixers, *p186*); **Florist** (Good Mixers, *p187*); **George & Dragon** (Good Mixers, *p188*); **Hoxton Square Bar & Kitchen** (Good Mixers, *p188*); **Nightjar** (Cocktails & Spirits, *p35*); **Redchurch** (Good Mixers, *p190*); **Wenlock Arms** (Beer Specialists, *p117*).

Bethnal Green Working Men's Club. *See p212.*

South East

Amersham Arms

388 New Cross Road, SE14 6TY (8469 1499, www.amersham-arms.co.uk). New Cross or New Cross Gate rail. **Open** noon-midnight Mon-Wed, Sun; noon-2am Thur; noon-3am Fri, Sat. **Admission** free-£6.

New Cross

The most interesting live music venue in south-east London brings together the character and prices of an old-school pub with the amenities of a modern music venue: there's an up-to-date sound system, an upstairs arts space, a walled-off garden for smokers and a drinks licence that runs until 3am. Events include Friday's party-hearty Whip It! night ('pretension-free good tunes with recession-crunching cheap entry,' promises the website, which sounds about right) and shows from assorted live acts (everything from electro to ska), but it doesn't take over the entire pub: it's altogether calmer earlier in the week. Food extends to burgers, sandwiches and, on Sundays, roast lunches; the clientele usually includes a healthy number of students escaping from their studies at nearby Goldsmiths College.

Disabled: toilet. Entertainment (bands, comedy and/or DJs times vary Mon, Thur-Sat). Function room (75 capacity). Games (bar billiards, board games). Tables outdoors (10, courtyard). Wireless internet. **Map p253 B2.**

Montague Arms

289 Queens Road, SE15 2PA (7639 4923). Queens Road Peckham rail. **Open** 7.30pm-midnight Mon, Tue; 7pm-midnight Thur-Sat; noon-7pm Sun. **Food served** 12.30-4pm Sun. **Admission** free-£5.

New Cross

The 'Tourist Welcome Coaches Welcome' sign isn't blind optimism: stuck out on a bend of the main road between Peckham and Europe, this idiosyncratic gem once attracted busloads of adventurers bound for Dover. Somewhere in the attics of neat homes across Holland must be snaps of this weird English pub with zebra heads and maritime knick-knacks; perhaps even a group shot with laconic Stan, the timeless landlord, and his evergreen bar ladies. It's not only Eurostar and easyJet that have changed the dynamic of this low-ceilinged anomaly: locals who 20 years ago would have scoffed at the Casiotone entertainment provided by Peter 'Two Moogs' London from the main stage now cherish the place. On Sundays, when medieval-sized hunks of meat are slathered in gravy and served to the compact row of dining tables, you can't move. Regular gigs bring a fresh crowd from Goldsmiths, happier with the plain lagers rather than the three or four ales. The first Friday of the month is alternative night (as if this place weren't already alternative enough): expect wacky bands from Slovenia or anything rhombus-shaped from south-east London. *Entertainment (bands 9pm Thur-Sat).*

New Cross Inn

323 New Cross Road, SE14 6AS (8691 7222, www.newcrossinn.co.uk). New Cross or New Cross Gate rail. **Open** noon-2am Mon-Sat; noon-12.30am Sun. **Admission** free-£5.
New Cross

Without the attraction of regular live music or the guarantee of an easy drink after midnight, this large corner bar close to Goldsmiths would be as it was ten years ago: a workaday Irish pub selling nitrokegs to the low-waged and loan-dependent student. But since New Cross was transformed into 'Rocklands' (no, us neither), indie acts regularly thrash about while pierced types flock to the horseshoe bar or make out on the black sofas. If concentration is required for anything, it's the pool table at the back. The team behind the place has also transformed the nearby Deptford Arms into something similar. *Indie Über Alles!*
Babies & children admitted (before 7pm). Disabled: toilet. Entertainment (bands 9pm daily). Games (pool). Tables outdoors (3, pavement). Wireless internet. **Map p253 A2.**

South

Dogstar

389 Coldharbour Lane, SW9 8LQ (7733 7515, www.antic-ltd.com/dogstar). Brixton tube/rail. **Open** 4-11pm Tue; 4pm-2am Wed, Thur; 4pm-4am Fri; noon-4am Sat; noon-10.30pm Sun. **Admission** £5 after 10pm Fri, Sat. **Brixton**

Party-minded Brixtonites have been gathering at the late-opening, hard-drinking Dogstar since, it feels, the dawn of time. As with the 1960s, if you remember it, you weren't there at all, but we can reassure you that not much has changed: the big long bar with DJ decks to one side; the informal loungey window seating; the pinball machine; the film poster for *Smashing Time* (starring Rita Tushingham); the intimate side space; the back room with a pool table and table football. Beyond is an outdoor plot for smokers. Staff may look like space cadets in dreadlocks, but they're quick, sharp and seen-it-all; ask for a sambuca and it comes to you in an instant. Entertainment is largely DJ-led, a mix of regular nights and one-offs (sometimes thematically tied to what's on that night at the Brixton Academy); beers and wines are standards (Amstel, Grolsch, Corona), but drinking here has always been more about quantity than quality.
Disabled: toilet. Entertainment (bands/DJs 7pm Wed-Sun). Function rooms (200 capacity). Tables outdoors (2, terrace). Wireless internet. **Map p252 E2.**

Plan B

418 Brixton Road, SW9 7AY (7733 0926, www.plan-brixton.co.uk). Brixton tube/rail. **Open** times vary Fri-Sun; check website for details. **Admission** £5-£12.50.
Brixton

It may be small, but this excellent Brixton bar-club punches well above its weight. Refurbished after a fire in 2009, Plan B's flow of hip hop and funk stars resumed with a

East Village. *See p215.*

kicking relaunch weekend that featured DJ sets from Hot Chip and Goldie. It's since continued to go from strength to strength, with the varied programming – you might find A Guy Called Gerald hosting a night of forward-thinking electronica, Don Letts spinning vintage reggae sides or live sets from all manner of acts – bolstered by a powerful Funktion 1 sound system. The venue's in proud possession of a 24-hour drinks licence, which means the action here can go on long into the night.
Disabled: toilet. Entertainment (bands/DJs times vary; Thur-Sun). Function room (180 capacity). Tables outdoors (2, courtyard; 4, pavement). **Map p252 E1.**

White Horse
94 Brixton Hill, SW2 1QN (8678 6666, www.whitehorsebrixton.com). Brixton tube/ rail then 59, 118, 133, 159, 250 bus. **Open** 5pm-midnight Mon-Thur; 4pm-3am Fri; noon-3am Sat; noon-midnight Sun. **Food served** 5-10.30pm Mon-Fri; noon-10.30pm Sat, Sun. **Brixton**
The White Horse attracts an adult, professional but as-yet-unnested clientele happy to enjoy the generous opening hours. It's all slightly clubby yet laid-back: the dangling disco balls are embellished with sunflower petals, there are big candles and flowers on each table, the day's papers rest on the bar counter (tabloids, too – it's a mixed crowd), and there are sofas settled around a TV in one corner. The DJ decks are put to good use several nights a week: funk plays a big role, but you might catch everything from hip hop to house emanating from the speakers. Beers include a couple of ales (Deuchars IPA, seasonal guests); food includes the likes of pan-fried salmon with Asian greens, posh steak sandwiches and, on weekends, breakfasts. Boys, don't trip over the step in the toilets as you take in the bizarre S&M horse mural.
Babies & children admitted (until 9pm). Disabled: toilet. Entertainment (DJs 9pm Thur-Sat, 7pm Sun; jazz 4pm Sun). Games (board games). Tables outdoors (8, courtyard). **Map p252 D3.**

White House
65 Clapham Park Road, SW4 7EH (7498 3388, www.thewhitehouselondon. co.uk). Clapham Common tube. **Open** 8pm-4am Fri, Sat. **Admission** £6 before 11pm Fri, Sat; £8 after 11pm Fri, Sat. **Clapham**
Despite what the outer appearance of the black-coated bouncer might lead you to expect, the youngish crowd at this smart club/DJ bar are an amiable bunch. Within, the White House is a funky, slightly retro spot: a screen plays woozy

images in the front area, while punters mingle on the other side of the bar in a space that could pass for the waiting room in *2001: A Space Odyssey*. A dining area and dancefloor are interwoven; in summer, there's a wow-factor roof terrace with a dancefloor, the venue's best feature. DJs spin house-heavy playlists through a modern sound system: there's music roughly five nights a week. Custom-made cocktails (£6-£7) have oomph and attitude, such as a Manhattan-style daiquiri of Pampero Especial rum, grapefruit juice and Maraschino liqueur; jugs of sangria also get the party going.
Disabled: toilet. Entertainment (DJs 9pm Fri, Sat). Function rooms (up to 250 capacity). Tables outdoors (10, terrace). Wireless internet. **Map p252 B4.**

Windmill
22 Blenheim Gardens, SW2 5BZ (8671 0700, www.windmillbrixton.co.uk). Brixton tube/rail. **Open** 5pm-midnight Mon-Thur; 5pm-1am Fri, Sat; 5-11pm Sun. **Admission** free-£6. **Brixton**
More music venue than pub but a dandy place for a drink nonetheless, the hippy-dippy and completely darling Windmill spreads over a large space down a sidestreet off Brixton Hill. Much of it is playground, covered with festival seating and regularly occupied by muso types smoking roll-ups or dodging the attentions of the rather frantic dog. Inside, beneath a sign with the venue's name in flowery writing, is a dark, often crowded, low-ceilinged room with intimate seating as you enter, a large and completely overworked bar (bohemians, like death and taxes, will always be with us) and, at the far end, a low stage that hosts a constant string of scruffy, good-natured rock and Americana acts. You may not be able to see them, but the bar holds taps of San Miguel, Red Stripe and, perhaps surprisingly, Marston's Pedigree; ask for wine, though, and you'll get it.
Children admitted (until 7pm). Disabled: toilet. Entertainment (bands 8pm daily). Tables outdoors (4, garden; 4, pavement). Wireless internet.

Also recommended...
Effra (Classic Pubs, *p92*); **RVT (Royal Vauxhall Tavern)** (Gay Bars, *p202*).

South West

Bull's Head
373 Lonsdale Road, SW13 9PY (8876 5241, www.thebullshead.com). Barnes Bridge rail. **Open** noon-midnight daily.

Food served noon-3.30pm, 6-10.30pm daily. **Admission** Gigs £5-£12.

Barnes

The writing over the door of this landmark, on the other side of the street from the Thames, says it all: 'Internationally renowned reputation since 1959 for the performance of mainstream and modern jazz. Concerts every evening at 8.30pm, Sundays at noon and 8pm.' Thus the Bull's Head, set beside Nuay's Thai bistro and courtyard tables where horses once slept, brings in punters from far and wide to catch quality jazz. Ronnie Scott, Humphrey Lyttelton and Coleman Hawkins all played here; Don Weller and Stan Tracey still do, as testified by a large concert poster (a rare example of decoration in an otherwise prosaic interior). Gigs take place in the Yamaha Jazz Room, but aficionados equally enjoy milling around the main space before and after, talking jazz with long-time acquaintances, or repairing to the balcony overlooking the river. Beers are the standard Young's varieties. *Entertainment (bands 8.30pm Mon-Sat, 1pm & 8.30pm Sun). Function room (120 capacity). Games (board games). Tables outdoors (10, courtyard). Wireless internet.*

New Cross Inn. See p218.

Half Moon

93 Lower Richmond Road, SW15 1EU (8780 9383, www.halfmoon.co.uk). Putney Bridge tube or Putney rail. **Open** noon-midnight Mon-Sat; noon-11pm Sun. **Food served** 1-8.30pm Mon-Sat; 1-5pm Sun. **Admission** Gigs £2.50-£18. **Putney**

When this seen-'em-all pub and music venue successfully campaigned against proposals to transform it into a gastropub at the end of 2009, its PR war relied heavily on its heritage. Having hosted live music since 1963, the Half Moon named but three groups in its plea (the Rolling Stones, U2 and Kasabian), thus covering five decades in a perfectly concise way. You won't see anyone as famous as that lot here today, but there are still notable shows from old-timers to be found in schedules rich in acoustic music and singer-songwriters. Nudging your way to the bar, you'll find Young's ales, served by staff adept at pouring promptly before and after gig time. Food's a bit of a moot point but there are basic pub meals, weekend breakfasts and Sunday roasts. *Babies & children admitted (until 7pm). Disabled: toilet. Entertainment (bands 8pm daily; jazz 1pm Sun). Function room (220 capacity). Games (board games, pool). Tables outdoors (10, garden). Wireless internet.*

West

Notting Hill Arts Club

21 Notting Hill Gate, W11 3JQ (7460 4459, www.nottinghillartsclub.com). Notting Hill Gate tube. **Open** varies, usually 7pm-2am Tue-Fri; 4pm-2am Sat; 6pm-1am Sun. **Admission** free-£8. **Notting Hill**

The lack of a worthwhile clubbing scene in and around W11 remains a great London mystery, but Notting Hillbillies at least have this venerable basement institution to keep them off the streets after dark. It's not much to look at, and no amount of wall decoration can disguise the fact that the bare-bones design aesthetic is both dated and almost comically anti-intimate. Happily, the programme of events is good enough to distract from the decorative shortcomings, taking in everything from Funk Royale (one of four alternating Friday club nights) to Alan McGee's indie-rocking Death Disco (Wednesdays). Drinks-wise, there are cocktails alongside wine and beer. *Entertainment (bands/DJs times vary Tue-Sun). Wireless internet.* **Map p247 B7.**

Also recommended...

Troubadour (Good Mixers, *p198*).

Indexes

A-Z Index   222
Advertisers' Index   228
Area Index   229

A-Z Index

A

Adam & Eve p128
77A Wells Street, W1T 3QQ
(7636 0717, www.geronimo-
inns.co.uk/theadamandeve).
Gastropubs & Brasseries
Admiral Codrington p60
17 Mossop Street, SW3 2LY
(7581 0005, www.theadmiral
codrington.co.uk). Classic Pubs
Admiral Duncan p200
54 Old Compton Street, W1D
4UB (7437 5300). Gay Bars
**Ain't Nothin' But...
The Blues Bar** p204
20 Kingly Street,
W1B 5PZ (7287 0514,
www.aintnothinbut.co.uk).
Clubs & Music Venues
Albannach p20
66 Trafalgar Square,
WC2N 5DS (7930 0066,
www.albannach.co.uk).
Cocktails & Spirits
Albertine p57
1 Wood Lane, W12 7DP
(8743 9593). Wine Bars
Alibi p184
91 Kingsland High Street,
E8 2PB (7249 2733, www.the
alibilondon.co.uk). Good Mixers
Alma p94
499 Old York Road, SW18 1TF
(8870 2537, www.thealma.
co.uk). Classic Pubs
Alphabet p172
61-63 Beak Street, W1F 9SL
(7439 2190, www.alphabet-
bar.com). Good Mixers
Amersham Arms p217
388 New Cross Road,
SE14 6TY (8469 1499,
www.amersham-arms.co.uk).
Clubs & Music Venues
Amuse Bouche p56
51 Parsons Green Lane,
SW6 4JA (7371 8517,
www.abcb.co.uk). Wine Bars
Anchor & Hope p128
36 The Cut, SE1 8LP
(7928 9898). Gastropubs
& Brasseries
Angel p60
61-62 St Giles High Street,
WC2H 8LE (7240 2876).
Classic Pubs
Anglesea Arms p61
15 Selwood Terrace,
SW7 3QG (7373 7960,
www.capitalpubcompany.com).
Classic Pubs
Anglesea Arms p152
35 Wingate Road,
W6 0UR (8749 1291,
www.capitalpubcompany.com).
Gastropubs & Brasseries
Antelope p148
76 Mitcham Road, SW17
9NG (8672 3888, www.
antic-ltd.com/antelope).
Gastropubs & Brasseries
Anthologist p172
58 Gresham Street, EC2V
7BB (0845 468 0101,
www.theanthologistbar.co.uk).
Good Mixers
Argyll Arms p61
18 Argyll Street, W1F 7TP
(7734 6117). Classic Pubs

Artesian p40
1C Portland Place, W1B 1JA
(7636 1000, www.artesian-
bar.co.uk). Hotel Bars
Artillery Arms p108
102 Bunhill Row, EC1Y 8ND
(7253 4683). Beer Specialists
Asburnham Arms p86
25 Ashburnham Grove,
SE10 8UH (8692 2007,
www.ashburnhamarms.com).
Classic Pubs
Audley p61
41-43 Mount Street, W1K 2RX
(7499 1843). Classic Pubs
Auld Shillelagh p83
105 Stoke Newington Church
Street, N16 0UD (7249 5951,
www.theauldshillelagh.com).
Classic Pubs
Avalon p90
16 Balham Hill, SW12 9EB
(8675 8613, www.theavalon
london.co.uk). Classic Pubs

B

Bald-Faced Stag p138
69 High Road, N2 8AB (8442
1201, www.realpubs.co.uk).
Gastropubs & Brasseries
Balham Bowls Club p192
7-9 Ramsden Road, SW12
8QX (8673 4700, www.antic-
ltd.com). Good Mixers
Baltic p21
74 Blackfriars Road,
SE1 8HA (7928 1111,
www.balticrestaurant.co.uk).
Cocktails & Spirits
Bar Battu p49
48 Gresham Street, EC2V 7AY
(7036 6100, www.barbattu.
com). Wine Bars
Bar Estrela p192
111-115 South Lambeth
Road, SW8 1UZ (7793 1051).
Good Mixers
Bar Kick p185
127 Shoreditch High Street,
E1 6JE (7739 8700,
www.cafekick.co.uk).
Good Mixers
Bar Pepito p49
Varnishers Yard, Regent
Quarter, N1 9FD (7841 7331,
www.camino.co.uk/pepito).
Wine Bars
Bar Polski p172
11 Little Turnstile, WC1V 7DX
(7831 9679). Good Mixers
Barrica p49
62 Goodge Street, W1T
4NE (7436 9448, www.
barrica.co.uk). Wine Bars
Barrio Central p173
6 Poland Street, W1F 8PS
(3230 1002, www.barrio
central.com). Good Mixers
Bathhouse p204
7-8 Bishopsgate Churchyard,
EC2M 3TJ (7920 9207,
www.thebathhousevenue.com).
Clubs & Music Venues
Bear p87
296A Camberwell New
Road, SE5 0RP (7274 7037,
www.thebearfreehouse.co.uk).
Classic Pubs

Beaufort Bar at the Savoy p40
The Savoy, 100 Strand, WC2R
0EW (7836 4343, www.the-
savoy.com). Wine Bars
Bedford p91
77 Bedford Hill, SW12
9HD (8682 8940, www.the
bedford.co.uk). Classic Pubs
Bedford & Strand p50
1A Bedford Street, WC2E 9HH
(7836 3033, www.bedford-
strand.com). Wine Bars
Bell p62
29 Bush Lane, EC4R 0AN
(7929 7772). Classic Pubs
Benugo Bar & Kitchen p173
BFI, South Bank Centre,
Belvedere Road, SE1 8XT
(7401 9000, www.benugo.
com). Good Mixers
**Bethnal Green Working
Men's Club** p212
42-44 Pollard Row,
E2 6NB (7739 7170,
www.workersplaytime.net).
Clubs & Music Venues
Betsey Trotwood p205
56 Farringdon Road,
EC1R 3BL (7253 4285,
www.thebetsey.com).
Clubs & Music Venues
Biddle Bros p184
88 Lower Clapton Road,
E5 0QR (no phone).
Good Mixers
Big Chill Bar p213
off Brick Lane, E1 6QL
(7392 9180, www.bigchill.net).
Clubs & Music Venues
Big Chill House p205
257-259 Pentonville
Road, N1 9NL (7427 2540,
www.bigchill.net). Clubs
& Music Venues
Birkbeck Tavern p114
45 Langthorne Road, E11 4HL
(8539 2584). Beer Specialists
**Bistrotheque Napoleon
Bar** p186
23-27 Wadeson Street,
E2 9DR (8983 7900,
www.bistrotheque.com).
Good Mixers
Black Friar p62
174 Queen Victoria Street,
EC4V 4EG (7236 5474,
www.classicpubs.co.uk).
Classic Pubs
Bleeding Heart Tavern p50
Bleeding Heart Yard, 19
Greville Street, EC1N 8SJ
(7404 0333, www.bleeding
heart.co.uk). Wine Bars
**Bloomsbury Bowling
Lanes** p174
Basement, Tavistock
Hotel, Bedford Way,
WC1H 9EU (7691 2610,
www.bloomsburylanes.com).
Good Mixers
Blue Bar p41
Wilton Place, SW1X 7RL (7235
6000, www.the-berkeley.com).
Hotel Bars
Blue Posts p63
28 Rupert Street, W1D 6DJ
(7437 1415). Classic Pubs
Blues Kitchen p209
111-113 Camden High Street,

NW1 7JN (7387 5277,
www.theblueskitchen.com).
Clubs & Music Venues
Bobbin p91
1-3 Lilleshall Road, SW4 0LN
(7738 8953, www.thebobbin
clapham.com). Classic Pubs
Boisdale p21
13-15 Eccleston Street,
SW1W 9LX (7730 6922,
www.boisdale.co.uk).
Cocktails & Spirits
Boogaloo p209
312 Archway Road,
N6 5AT (8340 2928,
www.theboogaloo.org).
Clubs & Music Venues
Book Club p186
100-106 Leonard Street,
EC2A 4RH (7684 8618,
www.wearetbc.com).
Good Mixers
Boot & Flogger p55
10-20 Redcross Way, SE1 1TA
(7407 1184). Wine Bars
Botanist on the Green p158
3-5 Kew Green, Kew, Surrey,
TW9 3AA (8948 4838,
www.thebotanistkew.com).
Gastropubs & Brasseries
Le Bouchon Bordelais p149
5-9 Battersea Rise,
SW11 1HG (7738 0307,
www.lebouchon.co.uk).
Gastropubs & Brasseries
Boundary Rooftop p163
2-4 Boundary Street,
E2 7DD (7729 1051,
www.theboundary.co.uk).
Rooms with a View
Bourne & Hollingsworth p175
28 Rathbone Place, W1T 1JF
(7636 8228, www.bourne
andhollingsworth.com).
Good Mixers
Bow Wine Vaults p51
10 Bow Churchyard,
EC4M 9DQ (7248 1121,
www.bowwinevaults.com).
Wine Bars
Bradley's Spanish Bar p175
42-44 Hanway Street,
W1T 1UT (7636 0359).
Good Mixers
Brasserie Max p41
10 Monmouth Street,
WC2H 9HB (7806 1000,
www.coventgardenhotel.co.uk).
Hotel Bars
Bread & Roses p192
68 Clapham Manor Street,
SW4 6DZ (7498 1779,
www.breadandrosespub.com).
Good Mixers
Bree Louise p108
69 Cobourg Street, NW1 2HH
(7681 4930, www.thebree
louise.com). Beer Specialists
Bricklayer's Arms p124
32 Waterman Street,
SW15 1DD (8789 0222,
www.bricklayers-arms.co.uk).
Beer Specialists
Bridge House p168
13 Westbourne Terrace
Road, W2 6NG (7266 4326,
www.thebridgehouselittle
venice.co.uk). Rooms with
a View

Brook Green Hotel p97
170 Shepherd's Bush
Road, W6 7PB (7603 2516,
www.brookgreenhotel.co.uk).
Classic Pubs
Brown Dog p151
28 Cross Street,
SW13 0AP (8392 2200,
www.thebrowndog.co.uk).
Gastropubs & Brasseries
Brumus Bar p42
1 Suffolk Place, SW1Y 4BP
(7470 4000, www.firmdale.
com). Hotel Bars
Builders Arms p196
1 Kensington Court Place,
W8 5BJ (7937 6213, www.the
buildersarmskensington.co.uk).
Good Mixers
Bull & Last p138
168 Highgate Road,
NW5 1QS (7267 3641,
www.thebullandlast.co.uk).
Gastropubs & Brasseries
Bull's Head p219
373 Lonsdale Road,
SW13 9PY (8876 5241,
www.thebullshead.com).
Clubs & Music Venues

C

Cadogan Arms p151
298 King's Road, SW3
5UG (7352 6500, www.the
cadoganarmschelsea.com).
Gastropubs & Brasseries
Café 1001 p186
1 Dray Walk, 91 Brick Lane,
E1 6QL (7247 9679, www.cafe
1001.co.uk). Good Mixers
Café des Amis p51
11-14 Hanover Place, WC2E
9JP (7379 3444, www.cafe
desamis.co.uk). Wine Bars
Café Kick p175
43 Exmouth Market, EC1R 4QL
(7837 8077, www.cafe
kick.co.uk). Good Mixers
Café Oto p211
18-22 Ashwin Street, E8 3DL
(7923 1231, www.cafeoto.
co.uk). Clubs & Music Venues
Callooh Callay p34
65 Rivington Street,
EC2A 3AY (7739 4781,
www.calloohcallaybar.com).
Cocktails & Spirits
Camino p175
3 Varnishers Yard, Regents
Quarter, N1 9FD (7841 7331,
www.camino.uk.com).
Good Mixers
El Camion p23
25-27 Brewer Street, W1F 0RR
(7734 7711, www.elcamion.
co.uk). Cocktails & Spirits
CAMP p186
70-74 City Road, EC1Y 2BJ
(7253 2443, www.thecamp
london.com). Good Mixers
Candy Bar p200
4 Carlisle Street, W1D 3BJ
(7287 5041, www.candybar
soho.com). Gay Bars
Canton Arms p147
177 South Lambeth Road,
SW8 1XP (7582 8710).
Gastropubs & Brasseries
Capote y Toros p51
157 Old Brompton Road, SW5
0LJ (7373 0567, www.cambio
detercio.co.uk). Wine Bars
Cargo p213
Kingsland Viaduct,
83 Rivington Street,
EC2A 3AY (7739 3440,
www.cargo-london.com).
Clubs & Music Venues

Carnivale p187
2 White Church Lane, E1
7QR (8616 0776, www.
carnivale.co.uk). Good Mixers
Carpenters Arms p152
91 Black Lion Lane,
W6 9BG (8741 8386).
Gastropubs & Brasseries
Carpenters Arms p116
73 Cheshire Street, E2 6EG
(7739 6342, www.carpenters
armsfreehouse.com).
Beer Specialists
Carpenters Arms pG0
68-70 Whitfield Street,
W1T 4EY (7580 3186).
Classic Pubs
Cask p109
6 Charlwood Street,
SW1V 6EE (7630 7225,
www.caskpubandkitchen.
com). Beer Specialists
Cask & Glass p63
39-41 Palace Street,
SW1E 5HN (7834 7630,
www.shepherd-neame.co.uk).
Classic Pubs
Castle p65
26 Furnival Street, EC4A 1JS
(7405 5470). Classic Pubs
Castle p97
225 Portobello Road,
W11 1LU (7221 7103,
www.castleportobello.co.uk).
Classic Pubs
Cat & Mutton p143
76 Broadway Market,
E8 4QJ (7254 5599).
Gastropubs & Brasseries
Cat's Back p94
86-88 Point Pleasant, SW18
1PP (8877 0818, www.cats
back.co.uk). Classic Pubs
Catch p214
22 Kingsland Road,
E2 8DA (7729 6097,
www.thecatchbar.com).
Clubs & Music Venues
Cellar Gascon p52
59 West Smithfield,
EC1A 9DS (7600 7561,
www.cellargascon.com).
Wine Bars
Cellar Door p175
Aldwych, WC2E 7DN (7240
8848, www.cellardoor.biz).
Good Mixers
Charles Dickens p87
160 Union Street, SE1 0LH
(7401 3744, www.thecharles
dickens.co.uk). Classic Pubs
Charles Lamb p138
16 Elia Street, N1 8DE
(7837 5040, www.the
charleslambpub.com).
Gastropubs & Brasseries
**Charlie Wright's
International Bar** p214
45 Pitfield Street,
N1 6DA (7490 8345).
Clubs & Music Venues
Chelsea Potter p95
119 King's Road, SW3 4PL
(7352 9479). Classic Pubs
Churchill Arms p97
119 Kensington Church
Street, W8 7LN (7727 4242,
www.fuller.co.uk). Classic Pubs
Cinnamon Club p22
Old Westminster Library,
30-32 Great Smith Street,
SW1P 3BU (7222 2555,
www.cinnamonclub.com).
Cocktails & Spirits
Circus p205
27-29 Endell Street,
WC2H 9BA (7420 9300,
www.circus-london.co.uk).
Clubs & Music Venues

Citizen Smith p124
160 Putney High Street,
SW15 1RS (8780 2235,
www.citizensmithbar.co.uk).
Beer Specialists
Cittie of Yorke p65
22 High Holborn, WC1V 6BN
(7242 7670). Classic Pubs
City Barge p169
27 Strand-on-the-Green,
Kew, W4 3PH (8994 2148).
Rooms with a View
Claridge's Bar p42
40 Brook Street, W1K 4HR
(7629 8860, www.claridges.
co.uk). Hotel Bars
Clifton p105
96 Clifton Hill, NW8 0JT (7372
3427, www.cliftonstjohns
wood.com). Classic Pubs
Clissold Arms p139
105 Fortis Green,
N2 9HR (8444 4224,
www.clissoldarms.co.uk).
Gastropubs & Brasseries
Coach & Horses p130
26-28 Ray Street,
EC1R 3DJ (7278 8990, www.
thecoachandhorses.com).
Gastropubs & Brasseries
Coach & Horses p65
29 Greek Street, W1D 5DH
(7437 5920). Classic Pubs
Coburg Bar p42
Carlos Place, W1K 2AL
(7499 7070, www.the-
connaught.co.uk). Hotel Bars
Cock & Hen p95
360 North End Road, SW6
1LY (7385 6021, www.
cockandhenfulham.com).
Classic Pubs
Colton Arms p98
187 Greyhound Road,
W14 9SD (7385 6956).
Classic Pubs
Commercial p88
212 Railton Road, SE24
0JT (7733 8783, www.the
commercialhotelhernehill.
co.uk). Classic Pubs
Commercial Tavern p177
142 Commercial Street,
E1 6NU (7247 1888).
Good Mixers
Compton Arms p78
4 Compton Avenue, N1 2XD
(7359 6883). Classic Pubs
Connaught Bar p43
Carlos Place, W1K 2AL
(7499 7070, www.the-
connaught.co.uk). Hotel Bars
Cork & Bottle p52
44-46 Cranbourn Street,
WC2H 7AN (7734 7807,
www.corkandbottle.net).
Wine Bars
Cottons p22
70 Exmouth Market, EC1R
4QP (7833 3332, www.
cottons-restaurant.co.uk).
Cocktails & Spirits
Cow p153
89 Westbourne Park Road,
W2 5QH (7221 0021,
www.thecowlondon.co.uk).
Gastropubs & Brasseries
Crazy Bear p22
26-28 Whitfield Street,
W1T 2RG (7631 0088,
www.crazybeargroup.co.uk).
Cocktails & Spirits
Cross Keys p65
31 Endell Street, WC2H 9EB
(7836 5185). Classic Pubs
Crown & Goose p183
100 Arlington Road, NW1 7HP
(7485 8008, www.crownand
goose.co.uk). Good Mixers

Crown & Greyhound p88
73 Dulwich Village, SE21 7BJ
(8299 4976, www.thecrown
andgreyhound.co.uk).
Classic Pubs
Crown & Sceptre p67
26-27 Foley Street, W1W 6DS
(7307 9971, www.thecrown
andsceptrew1.co.uk).
Classic Pubs
Crown & Two Chairmen p67
31-32 Dean Street, W1D 3SB
(7487 8192, www.thecrown
andtwochairmenw1.co.uk).
Classic Pubs
Cumberland Arms p98
29 North End Road, W14
8SZ (7371 6806, www.the
cumberlandarmspub.co.uk).
Classic Pubs
Cutty Sark Tavern p164
4-6 Ballast Quay, SE10 9PD
(8858 3146, www.cuttysark
tavern.co.uk). Rooms with
a View

D

Dalston Jazz Bar p184
4 Bradbury Street, N16 8JN
(7254 9728). Good Mixers
Dalston Superstore p211
117 Kingland High Street,
E8 2PB (7254 2273).
Clubs & Music Venues
De Hems p179
11 Macclesfield Street,
W1D 5BW (7437 2494,
www.nicholsonspubs.co.uk).
Good Mixers
Detroit p22
35 Earlham Street, WC2H 9LD
(7240 2662, www.detroit-
bar.com). Cocktails & Spirits
Devonshire p91
39 Balham High Road,
SW12 9AN (8673 1363,
www.dukeofdevonshire
balham.com). Classic Pubs
Dog & Bell p117
116 Prince Street, SE8 3JD
(8692 5664). Beer Specialists
Dog & Duck p67
18 Bateman Street, W1D 3AJ
(7494 0697). Classic Pubs
Dogstar p218
389 Coldharbour Lane,
SW9 8LQ (7733 7515,
www.antic-ltd.com/dogstar).
Clubs & Music Venues
Dollar p23
2 Exmouth Market, EC1R
4PX (7278 0077, www.dollar
grills.com). Cocktails & Spirits
Dove p114
24-28 Broadway Market,
E8 4QJ (7275 7617,
www.belgianbars.com).
Beer Specialists
Dove p169
19 Upper Mall, W6 9TA
(8748 9474). Rooms with
a View
Draft House p122
94 Northcote Road,
SW11 6QW (7924 1814,
www.drafthouse.co.uk).
Beer Specialists
Drapers Arms p139
44 Barnsbury Street,
N1 1ER (7619 0348,
www.thedrapersarms.com).
Gastropubs & Brasseries
Drayton Arms p109
153 Old Brompton Road,
SW5 0LJ (7835 2301,
www.thedraytonarmsnorth
kensington.co.uk).
Beer Specialists

Drayton Court p99
2 The Avenue, W13 8PH
(8997 1019, www.fullers.
co.uk). Classic Pubs
Driver p177
2-4 Wharfdale Road, N1 9RY
(7278 8827, www.driver
london.co.uk). Good Mixers
Dreambagsjaguarshoes p187
34-36 Kingsland Road, E2 8DA
(7729 5830, www.dream
bagsjaguarshoes.com).
Good Mixers
Dublin Castle p209
94 Parkway, NW1 7AN (7485
1773, www.bugbearbookings.
com). Clubs & Music Venues
Duke p68
7 Roger Street, WC1N 2PB
(7242 7230, www.dukepub.
co.uk). Classic Pubs
Duke of Cambridge p141
30 St Peter's Street,
N1 8JT (7359 3066,
www.dukeorganic.co.uk).
Gastropubs & Brasseries
Duke of Sussex p153
75 South Parade,
W4 5LF (8742 8801).
Gastropubs & Brasseries
Duke of Wellington p115
119 Balls Pond Road,
N1 4BL (7275 7640, www.
thedukeofwellingtonn1.com).
Beer Specialists
Duke of Wellington p130
94A Crawford Street,
W1H 2HQ (7723 2790,
www.thedukew1.co.uk).
Gastropubs & Brasseries
Dukes Bar p43
35 St James's Place, SW1A
1NY (7491 4840, www.
campbellgrayhotels.com).
Hotel Bars

E

Eagle p131
159 Farringdon Road,
EC1R 3AL (7837 1353).
Gastropubs & Brasseries
Eagle Ale House p123
104 Chatham Road,
SW11 6HG (7228 2328).
Beer Specialists
Ealing Park Tavern p153
222 South Ealing Road,
W5 4RL (8758 1879,
www.ealingparktavern.com).
Gastropubs & Brasseries
Earl of Lonsdale p99
277-281 Westbourne Grove,
W11 2QA (7727 6335).
Classic Pubs
Earl Spencer p151
260-262 Merton Road,
SW18 5JL (8870 9244,
www.theearlspencer.co.uk).
Gastropubs & Brasseries
East Village p215
89 Great Eastern Street,
EC2A 3HX (7739 5173,
www.eastvillageclub.com).
Clubs & Music Venues
Ebury Wine Bar
& Restaurant p52
139 Ebury Street, SW1W 9QU
(7730 5447, www.eburywine
bar.co.uk). Wine Bars
Edgar Wallace p109
40 Essex Street, WC2R 3JE
(7353 3120, www.edgar
wallacepub.com).
Beer Specialists
Edge p200
11 Soho Square, W1D 3QE
(7439 1313, www.edge
soho.co.uk). Gay Bars

Eel Pie p126
9-11 Church Street,
Twickenham, Middx,
TW1 3NJ (8891 1717).
Beer Specialists
Effra p92
38A Kellet Road, SW2 1EB
(7274 4180). Classic Pubs
El Vino p53
47 Fleet Street, EC4Y
1BJ (7353 6786, www.elvino.
co.uk). Wine Bars
Electricity Showrooms p187
39A Hoxton Square,
N1 6NN (7739 3939, www.
electricityshowrooms.co.uk).
Good Mixers
Elephant & Castle p99
40 Holland Street, W8 4LT
(7937 6382). Classic Pubs
Endurance p177
90 Berwick Street, W1F 0QB
(7437 2944, www.the
temperance.co.uk).
Good Mixers
Euston Tap p110
West Lodge, 190 Euston
Road, NW1 2EF (3137 8837,
www.eustontap.com).
Beer Specialists
Experimental Cocktail
Club p24
13A Gerrard Street, W1D 5PS
(7434 3559, www.chinatown
ecc.com). Cocktails & Spirits

F

Favela Chic p215
91-93 Great Eastern Street,
EC2A 3HZ (7613 4228,
www.favelachic.com).
Clubs & Music Venues
Fellow p177
24 York Way, N1 9AA
(7833 4395, www.thefellow.
co.uk). Good Mixers
Fentiman Arms p92
64 Fentiman Road, SW8 1LA
(7793 9796, www.geronimo-
inns.co.uk/thefentimanarms).
Classic Pubs
5th View p160
5th floor, 203-206 Piccadilly,
W1J 9HA (7851 2468,
www.5thview.co.uk).
Rooms with a View
Filthy MacNasty's p79
68 Amwell Street, EC1R
1UU (8617 3505, www.
filthymacnastys.co.uk).
Classic Pubs
Finborough Wine Café p57
Finborough Road, SW10 9ED
(7373 0745, www.finborough
winecafe.co.uk). Wine Bars
First Floor p196
186 Portobello Road, W11
1LA (7243 0072, www.first
floorportobello.co.uk).
Good Mixers
Flask p79
77 Highgate West Hill, N6 6BU
(8348 7346). Classic Pubs
Flask p105
14 Flask Walk, NW3 1HG
(7435 4580, www.the
flaskhampstead.co.uk).
Classic Pubs
Florence p119
133 Dulwich Road, SE24
0NG (7326 4987, www.
capitalpubcompany.com).
Beer Specialists
Floridita p24
100 Wardour Street,
W1F 0TN (7314 4000,
www.floriditalondon.com).
Cocktails & Spirits

Florist p187
255 Globe Road, E2 0JD
(8981 1100). Good Mixers
Fluid p178
40 Charterhouse Street,
EC1M 6JN (7253 3444,
www.fluidbar.com).
Good Mixers
Folly p178
41 Gracechurch Street,
EC3V 0BT (0845 468 0102,
www.thefollybar.co.uk).
Good Mixers
Fox p144
28 Paul Street, EC2A 4LB
(7729 5708, www.thefox
publichouse.co.uk).
Gastropubs & Brasseries
Fox & Anchor p68
115 Charterhouse Street,
EC1M 6AA (7250 1300,
www.foxandanchor.com).
Classic Pubs
Fox & Grapes p151
9 Camp Road, SW19 4UN
(8946 5599, www.foxand
grapeswimbledon.co.uk).
Gastropubs & Brasseries
Fox & Hounds p96
29 Passmore Street, SW1W
8HR (7730 6367, www.
youngs.co.uk). Classic Pubs
Frank's Café &
Campari Bar p165
10th floor, Peckham multi-
storey carpark, 95A Rye Lane,
SE15 4ST (07580 545 837,
www.frankscafe.org.uk).
Rooms with a View
Freedom Bar p201
66 Wardour Street, W1F 0TA
(7734 0071, www.freedombar
soho.com). Gay Bars
French House p69
49 Dean Street, W1D 5BG
(7437 2799, www.french
housesoho.com). Classic Pubs
Freud p177
198 Shaftesbury Avenue,
WC2H 8JL (7240 9933,
www.freud.eu). Good Mixers

G

Galvin at Windows p43
28th floor, 22 Park Lane,
W1K 1BE (7208 4021,
www.galvinatwindows.com).
Hotel Bars
Garrison p147
99-101 Bermondsey Street,
SE1 3XB (7089 9355,
www.thegarrison.co.uk).
Gastropubs & Brasseries
George & Dragon p18
2 Hackney Road, E2 7NS
(7012 1100). Good Mixers
George & Dragon p99
183 High Street, W3 9DJ
(8992 3712). Classic Pubs
George IV p100
185 Chiswick High Road,
W4 2DR (8994 4624,
www.georgeiv.co.uk).
Classic Pubs
George IV p69
26-28 Portugal Street,
WC2A 2HE (7955 7743).
Classic Pubs
Giant Robot p26
45-47 Clerkenwell Road,
EC1M 5RS (7065 6810,
www.gntrbt.com). Cocktails
& Spirits
Gilgamesh p34
Stables Market, Chalk Farm
Road, NW1 8AH (7482 5757,
www.gilgameshbar.com).
Cocktails & Spirits

Gladstone Arms p191
64 Lant Street, SE1 1QN
(7407 3962). Good Mixers
Golden Eagle p70
59 Marylebone Lane,
W1U 2NY (7935 3228).
Classic Pubs
Golden Heart p85
110 Commercial Street,
E1 6LZ (7247 2158).
Classic Pubs
Golden Lion p70
25 King Street, SW1Y 6QY
(7925 0007). Classic Pubs
Goldhawk p100
122-124 Goldhawk Road,
W12 8HH (8576 6921,
www.thegoldhawkshepherds
bush.co.uk). Classic Pubs
Gordon's p53
47 Villiers Street, WC2N 6NE
(7930 1408, www.gordons
winebar.com). Wine Bars
Gowlett p191
62 Gowlett Road, SE15 4HY
(7635 7048, www.thegowlett.
com). Good Mixers
Gramaphone p206
60-62 Commercial Street,
E1 6LT (7377 5332,
www.thegramaphone.co.uk).
Clubs & Music Venues
Grand Union p169
45 Woodfield Road, W9
2BA (7286 1886). Rooms
with a View
Grapes p163
76 Narrow Street, E14 8BP
(7987 4396). Rooms
with a View
Grazing Goat p131
6 New Quebec Street,
W1H 7RQ (7724 7243,
www.thegrazinggoat.co.uk).
Gastropubs & Brasseries
Green p131
29 Clerkenwell Green,
EC1R 0DU (7490 8010,
www.thegreenec1.co.uk).
Gastropubs & Brasseries
Green & Blue p55
36-38 Lordship Lane,
SE22 8HJ (8693 9250,
www.greenandbluewines.
com). Wine Bars
Green Carnation p201
4-5 Greek Street, W1D 4DB
(8123 4267, www.green
carnationsoho.co.uk).
Gay Bars
Green Man p110
36 Riding House Street,
W1W 7EP (7580 9087,
www.thegreenmanw1.co.uk).
Beer Specialists
Greenwich Union p119
56 Royal Hill, SE10 8RT
(8692 6258, www.greenwich
union.com). Beer Specialists
Guinea p70
30 Bruton Place, W1J 6NL
(7409 1728, www.theguinea.
co.uk). Classic Pubs
Gun p145
27 Coldharbour, E14
9NS (7515 5222,
www.thegundocklands.com).
Gastropubs & Brasseries
Gunmakers p131
13 Eyre Street Hill,
EC1R 5ET (7278 1022,
www.thegunmakers.co.uk).
Gastropubs & Brasseries

H

Haggerston p184
438 Kingsland Road, E8 4AA
(7923 3206). Good Mixers

Hakkasan p26
8 Hanway Place, W1T 1HD
(7907 1888, www.hakkasan.
com). Cocktails & Spirits
Half Moon p88
10 Half Moon Lane,
SE24 9HU (7274 2733,
www.halfmoonpub.co.uk).
Classic Pubs
Half Moon p220
93 Lower Richmond Road,
SW15 1EU (8780 9383,
www.halfmoon.co.uk).
Clubs & Music Venues
Hand & Shears p70
1 Middle Street, EC1A 7JA
(7600 0257). Classic Pubs
Hare & Billet p88
1A Elliot Cottages, Hare
& Billet Road, SE3 0QJ
(8852 2352). Classic Pubs
Harp p110
47 Chandos Place, WC2N
4HS (7836 0291).
Beer Specialists
Harringay Arms p79
153 Crouch Hill, N8 9QH
(8340 4243). Classic Pubs
Harrison p70
28 Harrison Street, WC1H 8JF
(7278 3966, www.harrison
bar.co.uk). Classic Pubs
Harwood Arms p152
Corner of Walham Grove
& Farm Lane, SW6 1QP
(7386 1847, www.harwood
arms.com). Gastropubs
& Brasseries
Havelock Tavern p153
57 Masbro Road, W14
0LS (7603 5374, www.the
havelocktavern.co.uk).
Gastropubs & Brasseries
Hawksmoor p27
157 Commercial Street,
E1 6BJ (7247 7392,
www.thehawksmoor.com).
Cocktails & Spirits
Hemingford Arms p80
158 Hemingford Road, N1
1DF (7607 3303, www.
capitalpubcompany.com/
the-hemingford-arms)
Classic Pubs
Hemingway p188
84 Victoria Park Road,
E9 7JL (8510 0215,
www.thehemingway.co.uk).
Good Mixers
Hermit's Cave p119
28 Camberwell Church
Street, SE5 8QU (7703 3188).
Beer Specialists
Herne Tavern p147
2 Forest Hill Road,
SE22 0RR (8299 9521,
www.theherne.net).
Gastropubs & Brasseries
Hide Bar p37
39-45 Bermondsey Street,
SE1 3XF (7403 6655,
www.thehidebar.com).
Cocktails & Spirits
Hill p157
94 Haverstock Hill,
NW3 2BD (7267 0033,
www.thehillbar.com).
Gastropubs & Brasseries
Hillgate p154
24 Hillgate Street,
W8 7SR (7727 8566).
Gastropubs & Brasseries
Holly Bush p106
22 Holly Mount, NW3 6SG
(7435 2892). Classic Pubs
Honey Pot p133
20 Homer Street,
W1H 4NA (7724 9685).
Gastropubs & Brasseries

Horse & Groom p215
28 Curtain Road,
EC2A 3NZ (7503 9421,
www.thehorseandgroom.net).
Clubs & Music Venues
Horseshoe p157
28 Heath Street,
NW3 6TE (7431 7206).
Gastropubs & Brasseries
Hoxton Square Bar
& Kitchen p188
2-4 Hoxton Square, N1 6NU
(7613 0709, www.hoxton
squarebar.com). Good Mixers
Hunter 486 p44
50 Great Cumberland Place,
W1H 7FD (7724 0486,
www.thearchlondon.com).
Hotel Bars

I
Idlewild p196
55 Shirland Road, W9 2JD
(7266 9198, www.ruby.uk.
com/idlewild). Good Mixers
Ink Rooms p192
14 Lavender Hill, SW11
5RW (7228 5300, www.ink
rooms.co.uk). Good Mixers
Island Queen p80
87 Noel Road, N1 8HD
(7354 8741, www.theisland
queenislington.co.uk).
Classic Pubs

J
Jerusalem Tavern p111
55 Britton Street, EC1M
5UQ (7490 4281, www.
stpetersbrewery.co.uk).
Beer Specialists
Jetlag p27
125 Cleveland Street ,
W1T 6QB (3370 5838,
www.jetlagbar.com).
Cocktails & Spirits
Jolly Butchers p115
204 Stoke Newington High
Street, N16 7HU (7241 2185).
Beer Specialists
Julie's Wine Bar p58
135 Portland Road,
W11 4LW (7727 7985,
www.juliesrestaurant.com).
Wine Bars
Junction Room p184
578 Kingsland Road, E8 4AH
(7241 5755, http://junction
room.co.uk). Good Mixers
Junction Tavern p141
101 Fortess Road,
NW5 1AG (7485 9400,
www.junctiontavern.co.uk).
Gastropubs & Brasseries

K
Kanaloa p179
18 Lime Office Court, Hill
House, Shoe Lane, EC4A
3BQ (7842 0620,
www.kanaloaclub.com).
Good Mixers
Katzenjammers p119
24 Southwark Street, SE1
1TY (3417 0196, www.
katzenjammers.co.uk).
Beer Specialists
Kensington Wine Rooms p58
127-129 Kensington Church
Street, W8 7LP (7727 8142,
www.greatwinesbytheglass.
com). Wine Bars
Kenton p188
38 Kenton Road, E9 7AB
(8533 5041, www.kenton
pub.co.uk). Good Mixers

King & Queen p71
1 Foley Street, W1W 6DL
(7636 5619). Classic Pubs
King Charles I p111
55-57 Northdown Street,
N1 9BL (7837 7758).
Beer Specialists
King Edward VII p85
47 Broadway, E15 4BQ
(8534 2313, www.kingeddie.
co.uk). Classic Pubs
Kings Arms p71
25 Roupell Street, SE1 8TB
(7207 0784). Classic Pubs

L
Ladbroke Arms p101
54 Ladbroke Road, W11
3NW (7727 6648, www.
capitalpubcompany.com).
Classic Pubs
Lamb p71
94 Lamb's Conduit Street,
WC1N 3LZ (7405 0713,
www.thelamblondon.co.uk).
Classic Pubs
Lamb & Flag p72
33 Rose Street, WC2E 9EB
(7497 9504). Classic Pubs
Lansdowne p141
90 Gloucester Avenue, NW1
8HX (7483 0409, www.the
lansdownepub.co.uk).
Gastropubs & Brasseries
Leather Bottle p96
538 Garratt Lane, SW17
0NY (8946 2309, www.
leatherbottlepub.co.uk).
Classic Pubs
Lexington p206
96-98 Pentonville Road, N1
9JB (7837 5371, www.the
lexington.co.uk). Clubs &
Music Venues
Library p44
1 Lanesborough Place,
Hyde Park Corner, SW1X 7TA
(7259 5599, www.
lanesborough.com).
Hotel Bars
Lobby Bar p45
One Aldwych, WC2B 4RH
(7300 1070, www.campbell
grayhotels.com). Hotel Bars
Lock Tavern p209
35 Chalk Farm Road,
NW1 8AJ (7482 7163,
www.lock-tavern.co.uk).
Clubs & Music Venues
Lockside Lounge p163
75-89 West Yard, Camden
Lock Place, NW1 8AF
(7284 0007, www.
locksidelounge.com).
Rooms with a View
Lodge Tavern p196
53 The Mall, W5 3TA
(8567 0173, www.thelodge
tavern.co.uk). Good Mixers
Londesborough p144
36 Barbauld Road, N16
0SS (7254 5865, www.the
londesborough.com).
Gastropubs & Brasseries
London Cocktail Club p27
61 Goodge Street, W1T 1TL
(7580 1960, www.london
cocktailclub.co.uk).
Cocktails & Spirits
Lonsdale p37
44-48 Lonsdale Road,
W11 2DE (7727 4080,
www.thelonsdale.co.uk).
Cocktails & Spirits
Look Mum No Hands! p189
49 Old Street , EC1V 9HX
(7253 1025, www.lookmum
nohands.com). Good Mixers

Lord Clyde p81
340-342 Essex Road, N1 3PB
(7288 9850, www.thelord
clyde.com). Classic Pubs
Lord Clyde p90
27 Clennam Street, SE1 1ER
(7407 3397, www.lord
clyde.com). Classic Pubs
Lord John Russell p111
91-93 Marchmont Street,
WC1N 1AL (7388 0500).
Beer Specialists
Lost Angel p193
339 Battersea Park Road,
SW11 4LF (7622 2112,
www.lostangel.co.uk).
Good Mixers
Lost Society p193
697 Wandsworth Road,
SW8 3JF (7652 6526,
www.lostsociety.co.uk).
Good Mixers
Lounge p195
56-58 Atlantic Road,
SW9 8PZ (7733 5229,
www.loungebrixton.co.uk).
Good Mixers
Loungelover p35
1 Whitby Street, E1 6JU
(7012 1234, www.loungelover.
co.uk). Cocktails & Spirits
Lowlander p111
36 Drury Lane, WC2B
5RR (7379 7446,
www.lowlander.com).
Beer Specialists

M
Mahiki p27
1 Dover Street, W1S 4LD
(7493 9529, www.mahiki.
com). Cocktails & Spirits
Mall Tavern p154
71-73 Palace Gardens Terrace,
W8 4RU (7229 3374,
www.themalltavern.com).
Gastropubs & Brasseries
Mandarin Bar p45
66 Knightsbridge, SW1X 7LA
(7235 2000, www.mandarin
oriental.com). Hotel Bars
Manor Arms p150
13 Mitcham Lane, SW16 6LQ
(3195 6888, www.manorarms.
com). Gastropubs & Brasseries
Mark's Bar p28
66-70 Brewer Street, W1F 9UP
(7292 3518, www.hixsoho.
co.uk). Cocktails & Spirits
Market Place p179
11-13 Market Place,
W1W 8AH (7079 2020,
www.marketplace-london.com).
Good Mixers
Market Porter p120
9 Stoney Street,
SE1 9AA (7407 2495,
www.markettaverns.co.uk).
Beer Specialists
Marquess Tavern p139
32 Canonbury Street, N1
2TB (7354 2975, www.the
marquesstavern.co.uk).
Gastropubs & Brasseries
Mason & Taylor p116
51-55 Bethnal Green Road,
E1 6LA (7749 9670,
www.masonandtaylor.co.uk).
Beer Specialists
Mawson Arms p101
110 Chiswick Lane South,
W4 2QA (8994 2936,
www.fullers.co.uk).
Classic Pubs
Mayflower p165
117 Rotherhithe Street,
SE16 4NF (7237 4088).
Rooms with a View

Medcalf p179
38-40 Exmouth Market,
EC1R 4QE (7833 3533,
www.medcalfbar.co.uk).
Good Mixers
Metropolitan p154
60 Great Western Road,
W11 1AB (7229 9254,
www.themetropolitan
w11.co.uk). Gastropubs
& Brasseries
Milk & Honey p28
61 Poland Street, W1F 7NU
(7065 6841, www.mlkhny.
com). Cocktails & Spirits
Miss Q's p197
180-184 Earl's Court Road,
SW5 9QG (7370 5358,
www.missqs.com).
Good Mixers
Mitre p155
40 Holland Park Avenue,
W11 3QY (7727 6332,
www.themitrew11.co.uk).
Gastropubs & Brasseries
Mitre p102
24 Craven Terrace, W2
3QH (7262 5240, www.
mitrelancastergate.com).
Classic Pubs
Montague Arms p217
289 Queens Road,
SE15 2PA (7639 4923).
Clubs & Music Venues
Montgomery Place p37
31 Kensington Park Road,
W11 2EU (7792 3921,
www.montgomeryplace.co.uk).
Cocktails & Spirits
Morgan Arms p145
43 Morgan Street, E3 5AA
(8980 6389, www.capital
pubcompany.com).
Gastropubs & Brasseries
Museum Tavern p72
49 Great Russell Street,
WC1B 3BA (7242 8987).
Classic Pubs
Mustard Bar & Lounge p180
2 Old Change Court,
Peter's Hill, EC4M 8EN
(7236 5318, www.mustard
bar.com). Good Mixers

N

Nags Head p83
9 Orford Road, E17 9LP
(8520 9709, www.thenags
heade17.com). Classic Pubs
Nags Head p73
53 Kinnerton Street,
SW1X 8ED (7235 1135).
Classic Pubs
Narrow p146
44 Narrow Street, E14 8DQ
(7592 7950, www.gordon
ramsay.com/thenarrow).
Gastropubs & Brasseries
Negozio Classica p58
283 Westbourne Grove,
W11 2QA (7034 0005,
www.negozioclassica.co.uk).
Wine Bars
New Cross Inn p218
323 New Cross Road,
SE14 6AS (8692 1866,
www.newcrossinn.co.uk).
Clubs & Music Venues
Newman Arms p73
23 Rathbone Street, W1T 1NG
(7636 1127, www.newman
arms.co.uk). Classic Pubs
Newton Arms p73
33 Newton Street, WC2B 5EL
(7242 8797). Classic Pubs
Nightingale p83
51 Nightingale Lane, E11 2EY
(8530 4540). Classic Pubs

Nightingale p94
97 Nightingale Lane,
SW12 8NX (8673 1637).
Classic Pubs
Nightjar p35
129 City Road, EC1V 1JB
(7253 4101, www.bar
nightjar.com). Cocktails &
Spirits
Nordic p180
25 Newman Street, W1T 1PN
(7631 3174, www.nordic
bar.com). Good Mixers
Norfolk Arms p133
28 Leigh Street, WC1H
9EP (7388 3937,
www.norfolkarms.co.uk).
Gastropubs & Brasseries
Normanby p195
231 Putney Bridge Road,
SW15 2PU (8874 1555,
www.thenormanby.co.uk).
Good Mixers
North London Tavern p157
375 Kilburn High Road,
NW6 7QB (7625 6634,
www.northlondontavern.co.uk).
Gastropubs & Brasseries
North Nineteen p113
194-196 Sussex Way,
N19 4HZ (7281 2786,
www.northnineteen.co.uk).
Beer Specialists
Northgate p142
113 Southgate Road,
N1 3JS (7359 7392).
Gastropubs & Brasseries
Notting Hill Arts Club p220
21 Notting Hill Gate,
W11 3JQ (7460 4459,
www.nottinghillartsclub.com).
Clubs & Music Venues

O

Off Broadway p185
63-65 Broadway Market, E8
4PH (7241 2786, www.off
broadway.org.uk). Good Mixers
Old Blue Last p215
38 Great Eastern Street,
EC2A 3ES (7739 7033,
www.theoldbluelast.com).
Clubs & Music Venues
Old Brewery p120
Pepys Building, Old Royal
Naval College, SE10 9LM
(3327 1280, www.old
brewerygreenwich.com).
Beer Specialists
Old Coffee House p73
49 Beak Street, W1F 9SF
(7437 2197). Classic Pubs
Old Fountain p117
3 Baldwin Street, EC1V 9NU
(7253 2970). Beer Specialists
Old Pack Horse p102
434 Chiswick High Road,
W4 5TF (8994 2872, www.
fullers.co.uk). Classic Pubs
Old Queen's Head p211
44 Essex Road, N1 8LN
(7354 9993, www.theold
queenshead.com). Clubs
& Music Venues
Old Red Lion p81
418 St John Street, EC1V
4NJ (7837 7816, www.old
redliontheatre.co.uk).
Classic Pubs
Old Ship p102
25 Upper Mall, W6 9TD
(8748 2593, www.oldship
w6.com). Classic Pubs
Old White Bear p158
1 Well Road, NW3 1LJ
(7794 7719, www.the
oldwhitebear.co.uk).
Gastropubs & Brasseries

1 Lombard Street p20
1 Lombard Street, EC3V 9AA
(7929 6611, www.1lombard
street.com). Cocktails & Spirits
190 Queensgate p40
190 Queensgate, SW7 5EX
(7584 6601, www.gore
hotel.com). Hotel Bars
Only Running Footman p133
5 Charles Street, W1J 5DF
(7499 2988, www.the
runningfootman.biz).
Gastropubs & Brasseries
Opera Tavern p134
23 Catherine Street, WC2B
5JS (7836 3680, www.
operatavern.co.uk).
Gastropubs & Brasseries
**Orange Public House
& Hotel** p134
37-39 Pimlico Road,
SW1W 8NE (7881 9844,
www.theorange.co.uk).
Gastropubs & Brasseries
Owl & Pussycat p189
34 Redchurch Street, E2 7DP
(3487 0088, www.owland
pussycatshoreditch.com).
Good Mixers
Oxford p142
256 Kentish Town Road,
Kentish Town, NW5 2AA
(7485 3521, www.the
oxfordnw5.co.uk).
Gastropubs & Brasseries
Oxo Tower Bar p160
Oxo Tower Wharf, Barge
House Street, SE1 9PH
(7803 3888, www.harvey
nichols.com/oxo-tower-london).
Rooms with a View

P

Pakenham Arms p74
1 Pakenham Street,
WC1X 0LA (7837 6933,
www.pakenhamarms.com).
Classic Pubs
Palm Tree p85
127 Grove Road, E3 5BH
(8980 2918). Classic Pubs
Pantechnicon p134
10 Motcomb Street,
SW1X 8LA (7730 6074,
www.thepantechnicon.com).
Gastropubs & Brasseries
**Paradise by Way of
Kensal Green** p198
19 Kilburn Lane, W10 4AE
(8969 0098, www.the
paradise.co.uk). Good Mixers
Pear Tree p96
14 Margravine Road, W6 8HJ
(7381 1787, www.thepeartree
fulham.com). Classic Pubs
Pearl Bar & Restaurant p45
252 High Holborn, WC1V
7EN (7829 7000, www.pearl-
restaurant.com). Hotel Bars
Peasant p134
240 St John Street,
EC1V 4PH (7336 7726,
www.thepeasant.co.uk).
Gastropubs & Brasseries
Pembury Tavern p115
90 Amhurst Road, E8 1JH
(8986 8597, www.individual
pubs.co.uk/pembury).
Beer Specialists
Phoenix Artist Club p180
1 Phoenix Street, WC2H 8BU
(7836 1077, www.phoenix
artistclub.com). Good Mixers
Pig's Ear p152
35 Old Church Street,
SW3 5BS (7352 2908,
www.thepigsear.info).
Gastropubs & Brasseries

Pineapple p183
51 Leverton Street, NW5 2NX
(7284 4631). Good Mixers
Plan B p218
418 Brixton Road,
SW9 7AY (7733 0926,
www.plan-brixton.co.uk).
Clubs & Music Venues
Plumbers Arms p74
14 Lower Belgrave Street,
SW1W 0LN (7730 4067).
Classic Pubs
Polo Bar p45
New Bond Street, W1S
2YF (7629 7755,
www.westburymayfair.co.uk).
Hotel Bars
Porterhouse p111
21-22 Maiden Lane, WC2E
7NA (7836 9931, www.
porterhousebrewco.com).
Beer Specialists
Portobello Star p38
171 Portobello Road,
W11 2DY (7229 8016,
www.portobellostarbar.co.uk).
Cocktails & Spirits
Positively 4th Street p180
119 Hampstead Road,
NW1 3EE (7388 5380,
www.positively4thstreet.
co.uk). Good Mixers
Prague p189
6 Kingsland Road, E2
8DA (7739 9110,
www.barprague.com).
Good Mixers
Pride of Spitalfields p86
3 Heneage Street, E1 5LJ
(7247 8933). Classic Pubs
Prince p144
59 Kynaston Road,
N16 0EB (7923 4766,
www.theprincepub.com).
Gastropubs & Brasseries
**Prince Alfred & Formosa
Dining Rooms** p102
5A Formosa Street,
W9 1EE (7286 3287,
www.theprincealfred.co.uk).
Classic Pubs
Prince Arthur p144
95 Forest Road, E8 3BH
(7249 9996, www.theprince
arthurlondonfields.com).
Gastropubs & Brasseries
Prince Bonaparte p102
80 Chepstow Road,
W2 5BE (7313 9491,
www.theprincebonaparte
w2.co.uk). Classic Pubs
Prince George p84
40 Parkholme Road,
E8 3AG (7254 6060).
Classic Pubs
Prince of Wales p94
48 Cleaver Square,
SE11 4EA (7735 9916,
www.shepherdneame.co.uk).
Classic Pubs
Princess Louise p74
208-209 High Holborn,
WC1V 7BW (7405 8816).
Classic Pubs
Princess of Shoreditch p146
Paul Street, EC2A 4NE
(7729 9270, www.the
princessofshoreditch.com).
Gastropubs & Brasseries
Princess of Wales p90
1A Montpelier Row,
SE3 0RL (8852 5784, www.
princessofwalespub.co.uk).
Classic Pubs
Princess Victoria p155
217 Uxbridge Road,
W12 9DH (8749 5886,
www.princessvictoria.co.uk).
Gastropubs & Brasseries

Priory Arms p123
83 Lansdowne Way,
SW8 2PB (7622 1884,
www.theprioryarms.co.uk).
Beer Specialists
Prospect of Whitby p164
57 Wapping Wall,
E1W 3SH (7481 1095).
Rooms with a View
Proud p211
Horse Hospital, Stables
Market, NW1 8AH (7482
3867, www.proudcamden.
com) Clubs & Music Venues
Punchbowl p74
41 Farm Street, W1J
5RP (7493 6841, www.
punchbowllondon.com).
Classic Pubs
Purl p28
50 Blandford Street, W1U
7HX (7935 0835, www.
purl-london.com). Cocktails
& Spirits
Putney Station p57
94-98 Upper Richmond Road,
SW15 2SP (8780 0242,
www.brinkleys.com). Wine Bars

Q

Queen of Hoxton p216
1 Curtain Road, EC2A 3JX
(7422 0958, www.the
queenofhoxton.co.uk).
Clubs & Music Venues
**Queen's Head
& Artichoke** p135
30-32 Albany Street,
NW1 4EA (7916 6206,
www.theartichoke.net).
Gastropubs & Brasseries
Queens p142
49 Regent's Park Road,
NW1 8XD (7586 0408,
www.youngs.co.uk).
Gastropubs & Brasseries
Queen's Head p112
66 Acton Street, WC1X 9NB
(7713 5772, www.queens
headlondon.com).
Beer Specialists
Queens Larder p74
1 Queen Square, WC1N 3AR
(7837 5627, www.queens
larder.co.uk). Classic Pubs
QV Bar p28
26-29 Dean Street, W1D 3LL
(7437 9585, www.quovadis
soho.co.uk). Cocktails & Spirits

R

Rake p120
14 Winchester Walk,
SE1 9AG (7407 0557).
Beer Specialists
Red Lion p190
41 Hoxton Street, N1 6NH
(7729 7920). Good Mixers
Red Lion p75
48 Parliament Street,
SW1A 2NH (7930 5826).
Classic Pubs
Red Lion p75
23 Crown Passage, off Pall
Mall, SW1Y 6PP (7930 4141).
Classic Pubs
Redchurch p190
107 Redchurch Street, E2 7DL
(7729 8333, www.thered
church.co.uk). Good Mixers
Retro Bar p201
2 George Court, WC2N 6HH
(7839 8760). Gay Bars
Rivoli at The Ritz p46
150 Piccadilly, W1J 9BR
(7493 8181, www.theritz
london.com). Hotel Bars

Rocket p155
11-13 Churchfield Road,
W3 6BD (8993 6123,
www.therocketw3.co.uk).
Gastropubs & Brasseries
Roebuck p126
15 Pond Street, NW3 2PN
(7435 7354, www.roebuck
hampstead.com). Beer
Specialists
Roebuck p106
130 Richmond Hill, Richmond,
Surrey, Richmond, Surrey,
TW10 6RN (0940 2329).
Classic Pubs
Rose & Crown p76
47 Columbo Street, SE1 8DP
(7928 4285). Classic Pubs
Rosendale p148
65 Rosendale Road,
SE21 8EZ (8761 9008,
www.therosendale.co.uk).
Gastropubs & Brasseries
Royal Albert p191
460 New Cross Road,
SE14 6TJ (8692 3737, www.
antic-ltd.com). Good Mixers
Royal Exchange p104
26 Sale Place, W2 1PU
(7723 3781). Classic Pubs
Royal Oak p147
73 Columbia Road,
E2 7RG (7729 2220,
www.royaloaklondon.com).
Gastropubs & Brasseries
Royal Oak p120
44 Tabard Street, SE1 4JU
(7357 7173). Beer Specialists
Royal Vauxhall Tavern p202
372 Kennington Lane, SE11
5HY (7820 1222, www.the
royalvauxhalltavern.co.uk).
Gay Bars
Ruby & Sequoia p197
6-8 All Saints Road, W11 1HH
(7243 6363, www.ruby.uk.
com/sequoia). Good Mixers
Ruby Lounge p30
33 Caledonian Road, N1 9BU
(7837 9558, www.ruby.uk.
com). Cocktails & Spirits
Rupert Street p202
50 Rupert Street, W1D 6DR
(7494 3059). Gay Bars

S

Saf p38
Whole Foods Market,
W8 5SE (7368 4500,
www.wholefoodsmarket.com).
Cocktails & Spirits
St John p135
26 St John Street,
EC1M 4AY (7251 0848,
www.stjohnrestaurant.com).
Gastropubs & Brasseries
**St Pancras Grand
Champagne Bar** p54
Pancras Road, NW1 2QP
(7870 9900, www.searcys.
co.uk/st-pancras-grand).
Wine Bars
Salisbury p76
90 St Martin's Lane,
WC2N 4AP (7836 5863).
Classic Pubs
Salisbury Hotel p81
1 Grand Parade, Green
Lanes, N4 1JX (8800 9617).
Classic Pubs
**Salt Whisky Bar &
Dining Room** p30
82 Seymour Street, W2 2JE
(7402 1155, www.saltbar.
com). Cocktails & Spirits
Sam's Brasserie & Bar p155
11 Barley Mow Passage,
W4 4PH (8987 0055,

www.samsbrasserie.co.uk).
Gastropubs & Brasseries
Scolt Head p84
107A Culford Road, N1 4HT
(7254 3965, www.the
scolthead.com). Classic Pubs
Seven Stars p136
53 Carey Street,
WC2A 2JB (7242 8521).
Gastropubs & Brasseries
1707 p48
Lower ground floor, 181
Piccadilly, W1J 9FA
(7734 8040, www.fortnum
andmason.com). Wine Bars
Shakespeares Head p82
1 Arlington Way, EC1R 1XA
(7837 2581). Classic Pubs
Ship & Shovell p112
1-3 Craven Passage,
WC2N 5PH (7839 1311).
Beer Specialists
Shochu Lounge p30
Basement, Roka, 37 Charlotte
Street, W1T 1RR (7580 9666,
www.shochulounge.com).
Cocktails & Spirits
Simmons p181
32 Caledonian Road,
N1 9DT (7278 5851).
Good Mixers
Sir Richard Steele p106
97 Haverstock Hill, NW3 4RL
(7483 1261, www.sirrichard
steele.com). Classic Pubs
69 Colebrooke Row p32
69 Colebrooke Row,
N1 8AA (07540 528593,
www.69colebrookerow.com).
Cocktails & Spirits
Skylon p161
Royal Festival Hall,
Belvedere Road, South Bank,
SE1 8XX (7654 7800,
www.danddlondon.com).
Rooms with a View
Skylounge p161
Mint Hotel, 7 Pepys Street,
EC3N 4AF (7709 1043,
www.minthotel.com).
Rooms with a View
Slaughtered Lamb p181
34-35 Great Sutton Street,
EC1V 0DX (7253 1516,
www.theslaughteredlamb
pub.co.uk). Good Mixers
Social p181
5 Little Portland Street, W1W
7JD (7636 4992, www.
thesocial.com). Good Mixers
**Somers Town
Coffee House** p136
60 Chalton Street, NW1
1HS (7691 9136, www.
somerstowncoffeehouse.com).
Gastropubs & Brasseries
Southampton Arms p113
139 Highgate Road, NW5
1LE (07958 780073, www.
thesouthamptonarms.co.uk).
Beer Specialists
Southwark Tavern p121
22 Southwark Street, SE1
1TU (7403 0257, www.the
southwarktavern.co.uk).
Beer Specialists
Spaniards Inn p106
Spaniards Road, NW3 7JJ
(8731 8406, http://the
spaniardshampstead.co.uk).
Classic Pubs
Speaker p76
46 Great Peter Street, SW1P
2HA (7222 1749, www.
pleisure.com). Classic Pubs
Star p82
47 Chester Road, N19 5DF
(7263 9067, www.thestar-
n19.co.uk). Classic Pubs

Star of Bethnal Green p216
359 Bethnal Green Road,
E2 6LG (7729 0167, www.
starofbethnalgreen.com).
Clubs & Music Venues
Star Tavern p76
6 Belgrave Mews West, SW1X
8HT (7235 3019, www.
fullers.co.uk). Classic Pubs
Stonemasons Arms p126
54 Cambridge Grove, W6 0LA
(8748 1397). Beer Specialists
**Suburban Bar &
Lounge** p195
27 Hartfield Road, SW19 3SG
(8543 9788, www.suburban
bar.com). Good Mixers
Sultan p124
78 Norman Road, SW19 1BT
(8542 4532). Beer Specialists
Sun & 13 Cantons p182
21 Great Pulteney Street,
W1F 9NG (7734 0934,
www.fullers.co.uk).
Good Mixers
Sun Inn p167
7 Church Road, SW13 9HE
(8876 5256, www.thesun
innbarnes.co.uk). Rooms
with a View
Swan p156
Evershed Walk, 119 Acton
Lane, W4 5HH (8994 8262,
www.theswanchiswick.co.uk).
Gastropubs & Brasseries
**Swimmer at the
Grafton Arms** p82
13 Eburne Road, N7 6AR
(7281 4632). Classic Pubs

T

Temperance p136
74-76 York Street, W1H
1QN (7262 1513, www.
thetemperance.co.uk).
Gastropubs & Brasseries
Ten Bells p86
84 Commercial Street,
E1 6LY (7366 1721,
www.tenbells.com).
Classic Pubs
Terroirs p54
5 William IV Street,
WC2N 4DW (7036 0660,
www.terroirswinebar.com).
Wine Bars
Thatched House p156
113 Dalling Road,
W6 0ET (8748 6174,
www.thatchedhouse.com).
Gastropubs & Brasseries
Thomas Cubitt p137
44 Elizabeth Street,
SW1W 9PA (7730 6060,
www.thethomascubitt.co.uk).
Gastropubs & Brasseries
**Three Kings of
Clerkenwell** p77
7 Clerkenwell Close,
EC1R 0DY (7253 0483).
Classic Pubs
333 p212
333 Old Street, EC1V
9LE (7739 5949, www.
333mother.com). Clubs
& Music Venues
Tiroler Hut p198
27 Westbourne Grove,
W2 4UA (7727 3981,
www.tirolerhut.co.uk).
Good Mixers
Tooting Tram & Social p195
46-48 Mitcham Road, SW17
9NA (8767 0278, www.antic-
ltd.com). Good Mixers
Toucan p77
19 Carlisle Street, W1D 3BY
(7437 4123). Classic Pubs

Town of Ramsgate p163
62 Wapping High Street,
E1W 2PN (7481 8000).
Rooms with a View
Trader Vic's p46
22 Park Lane, W1K 4BE
(7208 4113, www.trader
vics.com). Hotel Bars
Trafalgar Tavern p167
Park Row, SE10 9NW (8858
2909, www.trafalgartavern.
co.uk). Rooms with a View
Trailer Happiness p198
177 Portobello Road,
W11 2DY (7065 6821,
www.trailerhappiness.com).
Good Mixers
Troubadour p198
263-267 Old Brompton
Road, SW5 9JA (7370 1434,
www.troubadour.co.uk).
Good Mixers
Tufnell Park Tavern p183
162 Tufnell Park Road,
N7 0EE (7281 6113,
www.tufnellparktavern.com).
Good Mixers
**28°-50° Wine Workshop
& Kitchen** p48
140 Fetter Lane, EC4A 1BT
(7242 8877, www.2850.
co.uk). Wine Bars
25 Canonbury Lane p32
25 Canonbury Lane,
N1 2AS (7226 0955,
www.25canonburylane.com).
Cocktails & Spirits
Two Floors p182
3 Kingly Street, W1B
5PD (7439 1007, www.bar
works.co.uk). Good Mixers

V

Vertigo 42 p163
Tower 42, 25 Old Broad
Street, EC2N 1HQ (7877
7842, www.vertigo42.co.uk).
Rooms with a View
Vibe Bar p216
Old Truman Brewery,
91-95 Brick Lane, E1
6QL (7377 2899, www.
vibebar.co.uk). Clubs &
Music Venues
Victoria p104
10A Strathern Place,
W2 2NH (7724 1191,
www.fullers.co.uk).
Classic Pubs

Victoria Inn p121
72-79 Choumert Road,
SE15 4AR (7639 5052).
Beer Specialists
Vinoteca p54
15 Seymour Place,
W1H 5BD (7724 7288,
www.vinoteca.co.uk).
Wine Bars
Vivat Bacchus p56
4 Hays Lane, SE1 2HB
(7234 0891, www.vivat
bacchus.co.uk). Wine Bars
Volupté p207
7-9 Norwich Street,
EC4A 1EJ (7831 1622,
www.volupte-lounge.com).
Clubs & Music Venues

W

Warrington p156
93 Warrington Crescent,
W9 1EH (7592 7960,
www.gordonramsay.com/
thewarrington). Gastropubs
& Brasseries
Waterfront p167
Baltimore House, Juniper
Drive, SW18 1TS (7228 4297,
www.waterfrontlondon.co.uk).
Rooms with a View
Waterway p170
54 Formosa Street, W9 2JU
(7266 3557, www.thewater
way.co.uk). Rooms with a View
Wells p158
30 Well Walk, NW3 1BX
(7794 3785, www.the
wellshampstead.co.uk).
Gastropubs & Brasseries
Wenlock & Essex p183
18-26 Essex Road,
N1 8LN (7704 0871,
www.wenlockandessex.com).
Good Mixers
Wenlock Arms p117
26 Wenlock Road, N1
7TA (7608 3406,
www.wenlock-arms.co.uk).
Beer Specialists
Westbourne House p38
65 Westbourne Grove,
W2 4UJ (7229 2233,
www.westbournehouse.net).
Cocktails & Spirits
Wheatsheaf p121
24 Southwark Street,
SE1 1TY (7407 9934).
Beer Specialists

White Cross p170
Water Lane, Richmond,
Richmond, Surrey, TW9
1TH (8940 6844).
Rooms with a View
White Horse p219
94 Brixton Hill, SW2 1QN
(8678 6666, www.white
horsebrixton.com).
Clubs & Music Venues
White Horse p124
1-3 Parsons Green,
SW6 4UL (7736 2115,
www.whitehorsesw6.com).
Beer Specialists
White House p219
65 Clapham Park Road,
SW4 7EH (7498 3388,
www.thewhitehouselondon.
co.uk). Clubs & Music Venues
White Swan p170
Riverside, Twickenham,
Twickenham, Middx, TW1
3DN (8744 2951, http://
whiteswantwickenham.com).
Rooms with a View
**White Swan Pub &
Dining Room** p137
108 Fetter Lane, EC4A 1ES
(7242 9696, www.the
whiteswanlondon.com).
Gastropubs & Brasseries
William IV p115
816 High Road, E10
6AE (8556 2460).
Beer Specialists
Wilmington Arms p207
69 Rosebery Avenue, EC1R
4RL (7837 1384, www.the
wilmingtonarms.co.uk).
Clubs & Music Venues
Windmill p219
22 Blenheim Gardens, SW2
5BZ (8671 0700, www.
windmillbrixton.co.uk).
Clubs & Music Venues
Windsor Castle p77
27-29 Crawford Place,
W1H 4LJ (7723 4371).
Classic Pubs
Windsor Castle p105
114 Campden Hill Road, W8
7AR (7243 8797, www.the
windsorcastlekensington.
co.uk). Classic Pubs
Wine Wharf p56
Stoney Street, Borough
Market, SE1 9AD (7940 8335,
www.winewharf.com).
Wine Bars

Wonder Bar p55
400 Oxford Street, W1A
1AB (7318 2476, www.
selfridges.com). Wine Bars
Woolpack p191
98 Bermondsey Street, SE1
3UB (7357 9269, www.wool
packbar.com). Good Mixers
**Worship Street
Whistling Shop** p35
63 Worship Street, EC2A
2DU (7247 0015,
ww.whistlingshop.com).
Cocktails & Spirits

Y

Ye Olde Cheshire Cheese p77
145 Fleet Street, EC4A 2BU
(7353 6170). Classic Pubs
Ye Olde Mitre p112
1 Ely Court, Ely Place, at the
side of 8 Hatton Gardens,
EC1N 6SJ (7405 4751).
Beer Specialists
Ye Olde Rose & Crown p85
53 Hoe Street, E17 4SA
(8509 3880, www.roseand
crowntheatrepub.webeden.
co.uk). Classic Pubs
Ye White Hart p168
The Terrace, Riverside,
SW13 0NR (8876 5177).
Rooms with a View

Z

**Zeitgeist at The Jolly
Gardeners** p123
49-51 Black Prince Road,
SE11 6AB (7840 0426,
www.zeitgeist-london.com).
Beer Specialists
Zerodegrees p122
29-31 Montpelier Vale,
SE3 0TJ (8852 5619,
www.zerodegrees.co.uk).
Beer Specialists
Zetter Townhouse p46
49-50 St John's Square,
EC1V 4JJ (7324 4545,
www.thezettertownhouse.com).
Hotel Bars
Zuma p29
5 Raphael Street, SW7
1DL (7584 1010, www.
zumarestaurant.co.uk).
Cocktails & Spirits

Advertisers' Index

Please refer to relevant sections for addresses and/or telephone numbers

Early & Covers

Kopparberg	2
The Defectors Weld	6
The Fellow	6
The Lock Tavern	6
The Owl & Pussycat	6
The Blues Kitchen	8
MasterCard	11
The Shoreditch	15
Cargo	15
Garlic & Shots	17
Moo Coffee & Wine Bar	17
Spread Eagle	17
MasterCard	OBC

Cocktails & Spirits

Lost Society	25
Eat17	33
Tacuba	33

Classic Pubs

Quinn's	64

Beer Specialists

Ink Rooms	113

Gastropubs & Brasseries

The Delhi Brasserie	132
The Jam Tree	132
Porcini	132

Good Mixers

Lola Rojo	176
Madsen	176
Yalla Yalla	176

Clubs & Music Venues

Charlie Wright's	208
The Electric Ballroom	208
Troubadour	208
Jazz after Dark	210
The Tiroler Hut Restaurant	210

Area Index

Acton

George & Dragon   p99
183 High Street, W3 9DJ
(8992 3712). Classic Pubs
Rocket   p155
11-13 Churchfield Road,
W3 6BD (8993 6123).
Gastropubs & Brasseries

Aldwych

Edgar Wallace   p109
40 Essex Street, WC2R 3JE
(7353 3120). Beer Specialists
George IV   p69
26-28 Portugal Street,
WC2A 2HE (7955 7743).
Classic Pubs
Lobby Bar   p45
One Aldwych, WC2B 4RH
(7300 1070). Hotel Bars

Archway

**Swimmer at the
Grafton Arms**   p82
13 Eburne Road, N7 6AR
(7281 4632). Classic Pubs

Balham

Avalon   p90
16 Balham Hill, SW12 9EB
(8675 8613). Classic Pubs
Balham Bowls Club   p192
7-9 Ramsden Road, SW12 8QX
(8673 4700). Good Mixers
Bedford   p91
77 Bedford Hill, SW12 9HD
(8682 8940). Classic Pubs
Devonshire   p91
39 Balham High Road,
W12 9AN (8673 1363).
Classic Pubs

Bankside

Charles Dickens   p87
160 Union Street, SE1 0LH
(7401 3744). Classic Pubs
Katzenjammers   p119
24 Southwark Street,
SE1 1TY (3417 0196).
Beer Specialists

Barnes

Brown Dog   p150
28 Cross Street, SW13 0AP
(8392 2200). Gastropubs
& Brasseries
Bull's Head   p219
373 Lonsdale Road,
SW13 9PY (8876 5241).
Clubs & Music Venues
Sun Inn   p167
7 Church Road, SW13 9HE
(8876 5256). Rooms with
a View
Ye White Hart   p168
The Terrace, SW13 0NR
(8876 5177). Rooms with
a View

Barons Court

Colton Arms   p98
187 Greyhound Road, W14
9SD (7385 6956). Classic Pubs

Battersea

Le Bouchon Bordelais   p149
5-9 Battersea Rise, SW11 1HG
(7730 0307). Gastropubs
& Brasseries
Draft House   p122
94 Northcote Road, SW11 6QW
(7924 1814). Beer Specialists
Eagle Ale House   p123
104 Chatham Road, SW11 6HG
(7228 2328). Beer Specialists
Ink Rooms   p192
14 Lavender Hill, SW11 5RW
(7228 5300). Good Mixers
Lost Angel   p193
339 Battersea Park Road, SW11
4LF (7622 2112). Good Mixers
Lost Society   p193
697 Wandsworth Road, SW8
3JF (7652 6526). Good Mixers
Nightingale   p94
97 Nightingale Lane, SW12
8NX (8673 1637). Classic Pubs

Bayswater

Lonsdale   p37
44-48 Lonsdale Road, W11 2DE
(7727 4080). Cocktails & Spirits
Mitre   p102
24 Craven Terrace, W2 3QH
(7262 5240). Classic Pubs
Montgomery Place   p37
31 Kensington Park Road,
W11 2EU (7792 3921).
Cocktails & Spirits
Royal Exchange   p104
26 Sale Place, W2 1PU
(7723 3781). Classic Pubs
Victoria   p104
10A Strathern Place, W2 2NH
(7724 1191). Classic Pubs
Westbourne House   p38
65 Westbourne Grove, W2 4UJ
(7229 2233). Cocktails & Spirits

Belgravia

Library   p44
1 Lanesborough Place, SW1X
7TA (7259 5599). Hotel Bars
Nags Head   p73
53 Kinnerton Street,
SW1X 8ED (7235 1135).
Classic Pubs
Pantechnicon   p134
10 Motcomb Street,
SW1X 8LA (7730 6074).
Gastropubs & Brasseries
Star Tavern   p76
6 Belgrave Mews West, SW1X
8HT (7235 3019). Classic Pubs

Belsize Park

Hill   p157
94 Haverstock Hill, NW3
2BD (7267 0033).
Gastropubs & Brasseries
Sir Richard Steele   p106
97 Haverstock Hill, NW3 4RL
(7483 1261). Classic Pubs

Bermondsey

Garrison   p147
99-101 Bermondsey Street,
SE1 3XB (7089 9355).
Gastropubs & Brasseries

Hide Bar

Hide Bar   p37
39-45 Bermondsey Street,
SE1 3XF (7403 6655).
Cocktails & Spirits
Mayflower   p165
117 Rotherhithe Street,
SE16 4NF (7237 4088).
Rooms with a View
Woolpack   p191
98 Bermondsey Street, SE1
3UB (7357 9269). Good Mixers

Bethnal Green

**Bethnal Green Working
Men's Club**   p212
42-44 Pollard Row, E2 6NB
(7739 7170). Clubs & Music
Venues
**Bistrotheque Napoleon
Bar**   p186
23-27 Wadeson Street, E2 9DR
(8983 7900). Good Mixers
Florist   p187
255 Globe Road, E2 0JD
(8981 1100). Good Mixers
Star of Bethnal Green   p216
359 Bethnal Green Road,
E2 6LG (7729 0167).
Clubs & Music Venues

Blackheath

Hare & Billet   p88
1A Elliot Cottages, Hare &
Billet Road, SE3 0QJ
(8852 2352). Classic Pubs
Princess of Wales   p89
1A Montpelier Row, SE3 0RL
(8852 5784). Classic Pubs
Zerodegrees   p122
29-31 Montpelier Vale,
SE3 0TJ (8852 5619).
Beer Specialists

Bloomsbury

Angel   p60
61-62 St Giles High Street,
WC2H 8LE (7240 2876).
Classic Pubs
**Bloomsbury Bowling
Lanes**   p174
Basement, Tavistock Hotel,
Bedford Way, WC1H 9EU
(7691 2610). Good Mixers
Duke   p65
7 Roger Street, WC1N 2PD
(7242 7230). Classic Pubs
Lamb   p71
94 Lamb's Conduit Street,
WC1N 3LZ (7405 0713).
Classic Pubs
Lord John Russell   p111
91-93 Marchmont Street,
WC1N 1AL (7388 0500).
Beer Specialists
Museum Tavern   p72
49 Great Russell Street,
WC1B 3BA (7242 8987).
Classic Pubs
Queens Larder   p74
1 Queen Square, WC1N 3AR
(7837 5627). Classic Pubs

Borough

Boot & Flogger   p55
10-20 Redcross Way, SE1 1TA
(7407 1184). Wine Bars

Gladstone Arms

Gladstone Arms   p191
64 Lant Street, SE1 1QN
(7407 3962). Good Mixers
Lord Clyde   p90
27 Clennam Street, SE1 1ER
(7407 3397). Classic Pubs
Market Porter   p120
9 Stoney Street, SE1 9AA
(7407 2495). Beer Specialists
Rake   p120
14 Winchester Walk,
SE1 9AG (7407 0557).
Beer Specialists
Royal Oak   p120
44 Tabard Street, SE1 4JU
(7357 7173). Beer Specialists
Southwark Tavern   p121
22 Southwark Street, SE1 1TU
(7403 0257). Beer Specialists
Wheatsheaf   p121
24 Southwark Street, SE1 1TY
(7407 9934). Beer Specialists
Wine Wharf   p56
Stoney Street, SE1 9AD
(7940 8335). Wine Bars

Bow

Morgan Arms   p145
43 Morgan Street, E3 5AA
(8980 6389). Gastropubs
& Brasseries

Brick Lane

Big Chill Bar   p213
Dray Walk, E1 6QL (7392
9180). Clubs & Music Venues
Café 1001   p186
1 Dray Walk, E1 6QL
(7247 9679). Good Mixers
Carpenters Arms   p116
73 Cheshire Street,
E2 6EG (7739 6342).
Beer Specialists
Pride of Spitalfields   p86
3 Heneage Street, E1 5LJ
(7247 8933). Classic Pubs
Redchurch   p190
107 Redchurch Street, E2 7DL
(7729 8333). Good Mixers
Vibe Bar   p216
91-95 Brick Lane, E1 6QL
(7377 2899). Clubs &
Music Venues

Brixton

Dogstar   p218
389 Coldharbour Lane,
SW9 8LQ (7733 7515).
Clubs & Music Venues
Effra   p92
38A Kellet Road, SW2 1EB
(7274 4180). Classic Pubs
Lounge   p195
56-58 Atlantic Road, SW9 8PZ
(7733 5229). Good Mixers
Plan B   p218
418 Brixton Road, SW9 7AY
(7733 0926). Clubs &
Music Venues
White Horse   p219
94 Brixton Hill, SW2 1QN
(8678 6666). Clubs &
Music Venues
Windmill   p219
22 Blenheim Gardens,
SW2 5BZ (8671 0700).
Clubs & Music Venues

Camberwell

Bear p87
296A Camberwell New Road,
SE5 ORP (7274 7037).
Classic Pubs
Hermits Cave p119
28 Camberwell Church Street,
SE5 8QU (7703 3188).
Beer Specialists

Camden

Blues Kitchen p209
111-113 Camden High Street,
NW1 7JN (7387 5277).
Clubs & Music Venues
Crown & Goose p183
100 Arlington Road, NW1 7HP
(7485 8008). Good Mixers
Dublin Castle p209
94 Parkway, NW1 7AN (7485
1773). Clubs & Music Venues
Gilgamesh p34
Stables Market, Chalk Farm
Road, NW1 8AH (7482 5757).
Cocktails & Spirits
Lock Tavern p209
35 Chalk Farm Road,
NW1 8AJ (7482 7163).
Clubs & Music Venues
Lockside Lounge p163
75-89 West Yard, Camden
Lock Place, NW1 8AF (7284
0007). Rooms with a View
Proud p211
Stables Market, NW1 8AH (7482
3867). Clubs & Music Venues

Chalk Farm

Lansdowne p141
90 Gloucester Avenue,
NW1 8HX (7483 0409).
Gastropubs & Brasseries

Chancery Lane

Ye Olde Mitre p112
1 Ely Court, EC1N 6SJ
(7405 4751). Beer Specialists

Chelsea

Cadogan Arms p151
298 King's Road, SW3 5UG
(7352 6500). Gastropubs
& Brasseries
Chelsea Potter p95
119 King's Road, SW3 4PL
(7352 9479). Classic Pubs
Fox & Hounds p96
29 Passmore Street, SW1W
8HR (7730 6367). Classic Pubs
Pig's Ear p152
35 Old Church Street,
SW3 5BS (7352 2908).
Gastropubs & Brasseries

Chinatown

Blue Posts p63
28 Rupert Street, W1D 6DJ
(7437 1415). Classic Pubs
De Hems p179
11 Macclesfield Street, W1D
5BW (7437 2494). Good Mixers
**Experimental Cocktail
Club** p24
13A Gerrard Street,
W1D 5PS (7434 3559).
Cocktails & Spirits

Chiswick

City Barge p169
27 Strand-on-the-Green,
Kew, W4 3PH (8994 2148).
Rooms with a View

Duke of Sussex p153
75 South Parade, W4 5LF
(8742 8801). Gastropubs
& Brasseries
George IV p100
185 Chiswick High Road, W4
2DR (8994 4624). Classic Pubs
Mawson Arms p101
110 Chiswick Lane South, W4
2QA (8994 2936). Classic Pubs
Old Pack Horse p102
434 Chiswick High Road, W4
5TF (8994 2872). Classic Pubs
Sam's Brasserie & Bar p155
11 Barley Mow Passage,
W4 4PH (8987 0555).
Gastropubs & Brasseries
Swan p156
Evershed Walk, 119 Acton
Lane, W4 5HH (8994 8262).
Gastropubs & Brasseries

City

Anthologist p172
58 Gresham Street, EC2V
7BB (0845 468 0101).
Good Mixers
Artillery Arms p108
102 Bunhill Row, EC1Y 8ND
(7253 4683). Beer Specialists
Bathhouse p204
7-8 Bishopsgate Churchyard,
EC2M 3TJ (7920 9207).
Clubs & Music Venues
Bell p62
29 Bush Lane, EC4R 0AN
(7929 7772). Classic Pubs
Black Friar p62
174 Queen Victoria Street,
EC4V 4EG (7236 5474).
Classic Pubs
Bow Wine Vaults p51
10 Bow Churchyard, EC4M
9DQ (7248 1121). Wine Bars
Castle p65
26 Furnival Street, EC4A 1JS
(7405 5470). Classic Pubs
Cittie of Yorke p65
22 High Holborn, WC1V 6BN
(7242 7670). Classic Pubs
Commercial Tavern p177
142 Commercial Street,
E1 6NU (7247 1888).
Good Mixers
Folly p178
41 Gracechurch Street,
EC3V 0BT (0845 468 0102).
Good Mixers
Gramaphone p206
60-62 Commercial Street,
E1 6LT (7377 5332).
Clubs & Music Venues
Hawksmoor p27
157 Commercial Street,
E1 6BJ (7247 7392).
Cocktails & Spirits
Kanaloa p179
18 Lime Office Court, Hill
House, Shoe Lane, EC4A 3BQ
(7842 0620). Good Mixers
Mustard Bar & Lounge p180
2 Old Change Court, EC4M 8EN
(7236 5318). Good Mixers
1 Lombard Street p20
1 Lombard Street, EC3V 9AA
(7929 6611). Cocktails & Spirits
Seven Stars p136
53 Carey Street, WC2A 2JB
(7242 8521). Gastropubs &
Brasseries
Skylounge p161
Mint Hotel, 7 Pepys Street,
EC3N 4AF (7709 1043).
Rooms with a View
**28°-50° Wine Workshop
& Kitchen** p48
140 Fetter Lane, EC4A 1BT
(7242 8877). Wine Bars

Vertigo 42 p163
25 Old Broad Street, EC2N 1HQ
(7877 7842). Rooms with a View
El Vino p53
47 Fleet Street, EC4Y 1BJ
(7353 6786). Wine Bars
Volupté p207
7-9 Norwich Street, EC4A
1EJ (7831 1622). Clubs &
Music Venues
White Swan p137
108 Fetter Lane, EC4A 1ES
(7242 9696). Gastropubs
& Brasseries
Ye Olde Cheshire Cheese p77
145 Fleet Street, EC4A 2BU
(7353 6170). Classic Pubs

Clapham

Bobbin p91
1-3 Lilleshall Road, SW4 0LN
(7738 8953). Classic Pubs
Bread & Roses p192
68 Clapham Manor Street, SW4
6DZ (7498 1779). Good Mixers
White House p219
65 Clapham Park Road,
SW4 7EH (7498 3388).
Clubs & Music Venues

Clapton

Biddle Bros p184
88 Lower Clapton Road, E5
0QR (no phone). Good Mixers

Clerkenwell

Betsey Trotwood p205
56 Farringdon Road,
EC1R 3BL (7253 4285).
Clubs & Music Venues
Bleeding Heart Tavern p50
Bleeding Heart Yard, EC1N 8SJ
(7404 0333). Wine Bars
Café Kick p175
43 Exmouth Market, EC1R 4QL
(7837 8077). Good Mixers
Cellar Gascon p52
59 West Smithfield, EC1A 9DS
(7600 7561). Wine Bars
Coach & Horses p130
26-28 Ray Street,
EC1R 3DJ (7278 8990).
Gastropubs & Brasseries
Cottons p22
70 Exmouth Market, EC1R 4QP
(7833 3332). Cocktails & Spirits
Dollar p23
2 Exmouth Market,
EC1R 4PX (7278 0077).
Cocktails & Spirits
Eagle p131
159 Farringdon Road,
EC1R 3AL (7837 1353).
Gastropubs & Brasseries
Fluid p178
40 Charterhouse Street, EC1M
6JN (7253 3444). Good Mixers
Fox & Anchor p68
115 Charterhouse Street,
EC1M 6AA (7250 1300).
Classic Pubs
Giant Robot p26
45-47 Clerkenwell Road,
EC1M 5RS (7065 6810).
Cocktails & Spirits
Green p131
29 Clerkenwell Green,
EC1R 0DU (7490 8010).
Gastropubs & Brasseries
Gunmakers p131
13 Eyre Street Hill,
EC1R 5ET (7278 1022).
Gastropubs & Brasseries
Hand & Shears p70
1 Middle Street, EC1A 7JA
(7600 0257). Classic Pubs

Jerusalem Tavern p111
55 Britton Street, EC1M 5UQ
(7490 4281). Beer Specialists
Medcalf p179
38-40 Exmouth Market, EC1R
4QE (7833 3533). Good Mixers
Pakenham Arms p74
1 Pakenham Street, WC1X 0LA
(7837 6933). Classic Pubs
Peasant p134
240 St John Street,
EC1V 4PH (7336 7726).
Gastropubs & Brasseries
St John p135
26 St John Street,
EC1M 4AY (7251 0848).
Gastropubs & Brasseries
Slaughtered Lamb p181
34-35 Great Sutton Street, EC1V
0DX (7253 1516). Good Mixers
**Three Kings of
Clerkenwell** p77
7 Clerkenwell Close, EC1R 0DY
(7253 0483). Classic Pubs
Wilmington Arms p207
69 Rosebery Avenue,
EC1R 4RL (7837 1384).
Clubs & Music Venues
Zetter Townhouse p46
49-50 St John's Square, EC1V
4JJ (7324 4545). Hotel Bars

Colliers Wood

Sultan p124
78 Norman Road, SW19 1BT
(8542 4532). Beer Specialists

Covent Garden

Bedford & Strand p50
1A Bedford Street, WC2E 9HH
(7836 3033). Wine Bars
Brasserie Max p41
10 Monmouth Street, WC2H
9HB (7806 1000). Hotel Bars
Café des Amis p51
11-14 Hanover Place, WC2E
9JP (7379 3444). Wine Bars
Cellar Door p175
Aldwych, WC2E 7DN
(7240 8848). Good Mixers
Circus p205
27-29 Endell Street,
WC2H 9BA (7420 9300).
Clubs & Music Venues
Cross Keys p65
31 Endell Street, WC2H 9EB
(7836 5185). Classic Pubs
Detroit p22
35 Earlham Street,
WC2H 9LD (7240 2662).
Cocktails & Spirits
Freud p178
198 Shaftesbury Avenue, WC2H
8JL (7240 9933). Good Mixers
Lamb & Flag p72
33 Rose Street, WC2E 9EB
(7497 9504). Classic Pubs
Lowlander p111
36 Drury Lane, WC2B
5RR (7379 7446).
Beer Specialists
Newton Arms p73
33 Newton Street, WC2B 5EL
(7242 8797). Classic Pubs
Opera Tavern p134
23 Catherine Street,
WC2B 5JS (7836 3680).
Gastropubs & Brasseries
Porterhouse p111
21-22 Maiden Lane, WC2E 7NA
(7836 9931). Beer Specialists

Crouch End

Harringay Arms p79
153 Crouch Hill, N8 9QH
(8340 4243). Classic Pubs

Dalston

Alibi p184
91 Kingsland High Street,
E8 2PB (7249 2733).
Good Mixers
Café Oto p211
18-22 Ashwin Street,
E8 3DL (7923 1231).
Clubs & Music Venues
Dalston Jazz Bar p184
4 Bradbury Street, N16 8JN
(7254 9728). Good Mixers
Dalston Superstore p211
117 Kingsland High Street,
E8 2PB (7254 2273).
Clubs & Music Venues
Duke of Wellington p115
119 Balls Pond Road, N1 4BL
(7275 7640). Beer Specialists
Haggerston p184
438 Kingsland Road, E8 4AA
(7923 3206). Good Mixers
Junction Room p184
578 Kingsland Road, E8 4AH
(7241 5755). Good Mixers
Prince George p84
40 Parkholme Road, E8 3AG
(7254 6060). Classic Pubs
Scolt Head p84
107A Culford Road, N1 4HT
(7254 3965). Classic Pubs

Deptford

Dog & Bell p117
116 Prince Street, SE8 3JD
(8692 5664). Beer Specialists
Royal Albert p191
460 New Cross Road, SE14
6TJ (8692 3737). Good Mixers

Docklands

Gun p145
27 Coldharbour, E14 9NS
(7515 5222). Gastropubs
& Brasseries

Dulwich

Crown & Greyhound p88
73 Dulwich Village, SE21 7BJ
(8299 4976). Classic Pubs
Green & Blue p55
36-38 Lordship Lane, SE22
8HJ (8693 9250). Wine Bars
Rosendale p148
65 Rosendale Road,
SE21 8EZ (8761 9008).
Gastropubs & Brasseries

Ealing

Drayton Court p99
2 The Avenue, W13 8PH
(8997 1019). Classic Pubs
Ealing Park Tavern p153
222 South Ealing Road,
W5 4RL (8758 1879).
Gastropubs & Brasseries
Lodge Tavern p196
53 The Mall, W5 3TA
(8567 0173). Good Mixers

Earl's Court

Finborough Wine Café p57
Finborough Road, SW10 9ED
(7373 0745). www.finborough
winecafe.co.uk). Wine Bars
Miss Q's p197
180-184 Earl's Court Road,
SW5 9QG (7370 5358).
Good Mixers
Troubadour p198
263 Old Brompton Road,
SW5 9JA (7370 1434).
Good Mixers

East Dulwich

Herne Tavern p147
2 Forest Hill Road,
SE22 0RR (8299 9521).
Gastropubs & Brasseries

East Finchley

Bald-Faced Stag p138
69 High Road, N2 8AB (8442
1201). Gastropubs & Brasseries

Euston

Bree Louise p108
69 Cobourg Street, NW1 2HH
(7681 4930). Beer Specialists
Euston Tap p110
West Lodge, 190 Euston
Road, NW1 2EF (3137 8837).
Beer Specialists
Positively 4th Street p180
119 Hampstead Road, NW1
3EE (7388 5380). Good Mixers
Somers Town
  Coffee House p136
60 Chalton Street,
NW1 1HS (7691 9136).
Gastropubs & Brasseries

Fitzrovia

Adam & Eve p128
77A Wells Street,
W1T 3QQ (7636 0717).
Gastropubs & Brasseries
Barrica p49
62 Goodge Street, W1T 4NE
(7436 9448). Wine Bars
Bourne & Hollingsworth p175
28 Rathbone Place, W1T 1JF
(7636 8228). Good Mixers
Bradley's Spanish Bar p175
42-44 Hanway Street, W1T
1UT (7636 0359). Good Mixers
Carpenters Arms p63
68-70 Whitfield Street, W1T
4EY (7580 3186). Classic Pubs
Crazy Bear p22
26-28 Whitfield Street,
W1T 2RG (7631 0088).
Cocktails & Spirits
Crown & Sceptre p67
26-27 Foley Street, W1W 6DS
(7307 9971). Classic Pubs
Green Man p110
36 Riding House Street,
W1W 7EP (7580 9087).
Beer Specialists
Hakkasan p26
8 Hanway Place, W1T 1HD
(7907 1888). Cocktails & Spirits
Jetlag p27
125 Cleveland Street,
W1T 6QB (3370 5838).
Cocktails & Spirits
King & Queen p71
1 Foley Street, W1W 6DL
(7636 5619). Classic Pubs
London Cocktail Club p27
61 Goodge Street,
W1T 1TL (7580 1960).
Cocktails & Spirits
Market Place p179
11-13 Market Place, W1W 8AH
(7079 2020). Good Mixers
Newman Arms p73
23 Rathbone Street, W1T 1NG
(7636 1127). Classic Pubs
Nordic p180
25 Newman Street, W1T 1PN
(7631 3174). Good Mixers
Shochu Lounge p30
37 Charlotte Street, W1T 1RR
(7580 9666). Cocktails & Spirits
Social p181
5 Little Portland Street, W1W
7JD (7636 4992). Good Mixers

Fulham

Cock & Hen p95
360 North End Road, SW6 1LY
(7385 6021). Classic Pubs
Harwood Arms p152
Corner of Walham Grove
& Farm Lane, SW6 1QP
(7386 1847). Gastropubs
& Brasseries
Pear Tree p96
14 Margravine Road, W6 8HJ
(7381 1787). Classic Pubs
Suburban Bar & Lounge p195
27 Hartfield Road, SW19 3SG
(8543 9788). Good Mixers

Greenwich

Ashburnham Arms p86
25 Ashburnham Grove, SE10
8UH (8692 2007). Classic Pubs
Cutty Sark Tavern p164
4-6 Ballast Quay, SE10 9PD
(8858 3146). Rooms with a View
Greenwich Union p119
56 Royal Hill, SE10 8RT (8692
6258). Beer Specialists
Old Brewery p120
Pepys Building, Old Royal
Naval College, SE10 9LM
(3327 1280). Beer Specialists
Trafalgar Tavern p167
Park Row, SE10 9NW (8858
2909). Rooms with a View

Hackney

Cat & Mutton p143
76 Broadway Market,
E8 4QJ (7254 5599).
Gastropubs & Brasseries
Dove p114
24 Broadway Market, E8 4QJ
(7275 7617). Beer Specialists
Hemingway p188
84 Victoria Park Road, E9
7JL (8510 0215, www.the
hemingway.co.uk). Good Mixers
Kenton p188
38 Kenton Road, E9 7AB
(8533 5041). Good Mixers
Off Broadway p185
63-65 Broadway Market, E8
4PH (7241 2786). Good Mixers
Pembury Tavern p115
90 Amhurst Road, E8 1JH
(8986 8597). Beer Specialists
Prince Arthur p144
95 Forest Road, E8 3BH
(7249 9996). Gastropubs
& Brasseries

Hammersmith

Brook Green Hotel p97
170 Shepherd's Bush Road, W6
7PB (7603 2516). Classic Pubs
Carpenter's Arms p150
91 Black Lion Lane,
W6 9BG (8741 8386).
Gastropubs & Brasseries
Cumberland Arms p97
29 North End Road, W14 8SZ
(7371 6806). Classic Pubs
Dove p169
19 Upper Mall, W6 9TA
(8748 9474). Rooms with
a View
Old Ship p102
25 Upper Mall, W6 9TD
(8748 2593). Classic Pubs
Stonemasons Arms p126
54 Cambridge Grove, W6 0LA
(8748 1397). Beer Specialists
Thatched House p156
113 Dalling Road,
W6 0ET (8748 6174).
Gastropubs & Brasseries

Hampstead

Flask p105
14 Flask Walk, NW3 1HG
(7435 4580). Classic Pubs
Holly Bush p106
22 Holly Mount, NW3 6SG
(7435 2892). Classic Pubs
Horseshoe p157
28 Heath Street, NW3 6TE
(7431 7206). Gastropubs
& Brasseries
Old White Bear p158
1 Well Road, NW3 1LJ (7794
7719). Gastropubs & Brasseries
Roebuck p126
15 Pond Street, NW3 2PN
(7435 7354). Beer Specialists
Spaniards Inn p106
Spaniards Road, NW3 7JJ
(8731 8406). Classic Pubs
Wells p158
30 Well Walk, NW3 1BX (7794
3785). Gastropubs & Brasseries

Harringay

Salisbury Hotel p81
1 Grand Parade, Green Lanes, N4
1JX (8800 9617). Classic Pubs

Herne Hill

Commercial p88
212 Railton Road, SE24 0JT
(7733 8783). Classic Pubs
Florence p119
133 Dulwich Road, SE24 0NG
(7326 4987). Beer Specialists
Half Moon p88
10 Half Moon Lane, SE24 9HU
(7274 2733). Classic Pubs

Highgate

Boogaloo p209
312 Archway Road, N6 5AT
(8340 2928). Clubs &
Music Venues
Flask p79
77 Highgate West Hill, N6 6BU
(8348 7346). Classic Pubs

Holborn

Bar Polski p172
11 Little Turnstile, WC1V 7DX
(7831 9679). Good Mixers
Pearl Bar & Restaurant p45
252 High Holborn, WC1V 7EN
(7829 7000). Hotel Bars
Princess Louise p74
208-209 High Holborn, WC1V
7BW (7405 8816). Classic Pubs

Holland Park

Julie's Wine Bar p58
135 Portland Road, W11 4LW
(7727 7985). Wine Bars
Ladbroke Arms p101
54 Ladbroke Road, W11 3NW
(7727 6648). Classic Pubs
Mitre p155
40 Holland Park Avenue, W11
3QY (7727 6332). Gastropubs

Hornsey

North Nineteen p113
194-196 Sussex Way, N19 4HZ
(7281 2786). Beer Specialists

Islington

Charles Lamb p138
16 Elia Street, N1 8DE
(7837 5040). Gastropubs
& Brasseries

Compton Arms p78
4 Compton Avenue, N1 2XD
(7359 6883). Classic Pubs
Drapers Arms p139
44 Barnsbury Street,
N1 1ER (7619 0348).
Gastropubs & Brasseries
Duke of Cambridge p141
30 St Peter's Street,
N1 8JT (7359 3066).
Gastropubs & Brasseries
Filthy MacNasty's p79
68 Amwell Street, EC1R 1UU
(8617 3505). Classic Pubs
Hemingford Arms p80
158 Hemingford Road, N1 1DF
(7607 3303). Classic Pubs
Island Queen p80
87 Noel Road, N1 8HD
(7354 8741). Classic Pubs
Lord Clyde p81
340-342 Essex Road, N1 3PB
(7288 9850). Classic Pubs
Marquess Tavern p141
32 Canonbury Street,
N1 2TB (7354 2975).
Gastropubs & Brasseries
Northgate p142
113 Southgate Road,
N1 3JS (7359 7392).
Gastropubs & Brasseries
Old Queen's Head p211
44 Essex Road, N1 8LN
(7354 9993). Clubs &
Music Venues
Old Red Lion p81
418 St John Street,
EC1V 4NJ (7837 7816).
Classic Pubs
Shakespeares Head p82
1 Arlington Way, EC1R 1XA
(7837 2581). Classic Pubs
69 Colebrooke Row p32
69 Colebrooke Row,
N1 8AA (07540 528593).
Cocktails & Spirits
25 Canonbury Lane p32
25 Canonbury Lane, N1 2AS
(7226 0955). Cocktails & Spirits

Kennington

Fentiman Arms p92
64 Fentiman Road, SW8 1LA
(7793 9796). Classic Pubs
Prince of Wales p94
48 Cleaver Square, SE11 4EA
(7735 9916). Classic Pubs

Kensal Green

**Paradise by Way of
Kensal Green** p198
19 Kilburn Lane, W10 4AE
(8969 0098). Good Mixers

Kensington

Builders Arms p196
1 Kensington Court Place, W8
5BJ (7937 6213). Good Mixers
Churchill Arms p97
119 Kensington Church
Street, W8 7LN (7727 4242).
Classic Pubs
Elephant & Castle p99
40 Holland Street, W8 4LT
(7937 6382). Classic Pubs
Kensington Wine Rooms p58
127-129 Kensington Church
Street, W8 7LP (7727 8142).
Wine Bars
Saf p38
Whole Foods Market,
W8 5SE (7368 4500).
Cocktails & Spirits
Wenlock & Essex p183
18-26 Essex Road, N1 8LN
(7704 0871). Good Mixers

Windsor Castle p105
114 Campden Hill Road, W8
7AR (7243 8797). Classic Pubs

Kentish Town

Bull & Last p138
168 Highgate Road,
NW5 1QS (7267 3641).
Gastropubs & Brasseries
Junction Tavern p141
101 Fortess Road,
NW5 1AG (7485 9400).
Gastropubs & Brasseries
Oxford p142
256 Kentish Town Road,
NW5 2AA (7485 3521).
Gastropubs & Brasseries
Pineapple p178
51 Leverton Street, NW5 2NX
(7284 4631). Good Mixers
Southampton Arms p113
139 Highgate Road,
NW5 1LE (07958 780073).
Beer Specialists

Kew, Surrey

Botanist on the Green p158
3-5 Kew Green, TW9 3AA
(8948 4838). Gastropubs
& Brasseries

Kilburn

North London Tavern p157
375 Kilburn High Road,
NW6 7QB (7625 6634).
Gastropubs & Brasseries

King's Cross

Bar Battu p49
48 Gresham Street, EC2V 7AY
(7036 6100). Wine Bars
Bar Pepito p49
Varnishers Yard, N1 9FD
(7841 7331). Wine Bars
Big Chill House p205
257-259 Pentonville Road,
N1 9NL (7427 2540).
Clubs & Music Venues
Camino p175
3 Varnishers Yard, N1 9FD
(7841 7331). Good Mixers
Driver p177
2-4 Wharfdale Road, N1 9RY
(7278 8827). Good Mixers
Fellow p177
24 York Way, N1 9AA
(7833 4395). Good Mixers
Harrison p70
28 Harrison Street, WC1H 8JF
(7278 3966). Classic Pubs
King Charles I p111
55-57 Northdown Street,
N1 9BL (7837 7758).
Beer Specialists
Lexington p206
96-98 Pentonville Road,
N1 9JB (7837 5371).
Clubs & Music Venues
Norfolk Arms p133
28 Leigh Street,
WC1H 9EP (7388 3937).
Gastropubs & Brasseries
Queen's Head p112
66 Acton Street, WC1X 9NB
(7713 5772). Beer Specialists
Ruby Lounge p30
33 Caledonian Road, N1 9BU
(7837 9558). Cocktails & Spirits
**St Pancras Grand
Champagne Bar** p54
Pancras Road, NW1 2QP
(7870 9900). Wine Bars
Simmons p181
32 Caledonian Road, N1 9DT
(7278 5851). Good Mixers

Knightsbridge

Blue Bar p41
Wilton Place, SW1X 7RL
(7235 6000). Hotel Bars
Mandarin Bar p45
66 Knightsbridge, SW1X 7LA
(7235 2000). Hotel Bars
Zuma p31
5 Raphael Street, SW7 1DL
(7584 1010). Cocktails & Spirits

Leicester Square

Cork & Bottle p52
44-46 Cranbourn Street,
WC2H 7AN (7734 7807).
Wine Bars
Salisbury p76
90 St Martin's Lane,
WC2N 4AP (7836 5863).
Classic Pubs

Leyton

Birkbeck Tavern p114
45 Langthorne Road, E11 4HL
(8539 2584). Beer Specialists
William IV p115
816 High Road, E10 6AE
(8556 2460). Beer Specialists

Limehouse

Grapes p163
76 Narrow Street,
E14 8BP (7987 4396).
Rooms with a View
Narrow p146
44 Narrow Street,
E14 8DQ (7592 7950).
Gastropubs & Brasseries

London Bridge

Vivat Bacchus p56
4 Hays Lane, SE1 2HB
(7234 0891). Wine Bars

Maida Vale

Bridge House p168
13 Westbourne Terrace
Road, W2 6NG (7266 4326).
Rooms with a View
Idlewild p196
55 Shirland Road, W9 2JD
(7266 9198). Good Mixers
**Prince Alfred & Formosa
Dining Rooms** p102
5A Formosa Street, W9 1EE
(7286 3287). Classic Pubs
Warrington p156
93 Warrington Crescent,
W9 1EH (7592 7960).
Gastropubs & Brasseries
Waterway p170
54 Formosa Street, W9 2JU
(7266 3557). Rooms with a View

Marble Arch

Hunter 486 p44
50 Great Cumberland Place,
W1H 7FD (7724 0486).
Hotel Bars

Marylebone

Artesian p40
1C Portland Place, W1B 1JA
(7636 1000). Hotel Bars
Duke of Wellington p130
94A Crawford Street,
W1H 2HQ (7723 2790).
Gastropubs & Brasseries
Golden Eagle p70
59 Marylebone Lane, W1U
2NY (7935 3228). Classic Pubs

Grazing Goat p131
6 New Quebec Street,
W1H 7RQ (7724 7243).
Gastropubs & Brasseries
Honey Pot p133
20 Homer Street,
W1H 4NA (7724 9685).
Gastropubs & Brasseries
Purl p28
50 Blandford Street,
W1U 7HX (7935 0835).
Cocktails & Spirits
**Queen's Head &
Artichoke** p135
30-32 Albany Street,
NW1 4EA (7916 6206).
Gastropubs & Brasseries
**Salt Whisky Bar
& Dining Room** p30
82 Seymour Street,
W2 2JE (7402 1155).
Cocktails & Spirits
Temperance p136
74-76 York Street,
W1H 1QN (7262 1513).
Gastropubs & Brasseries
Vinoteca p54
15 Seymour Place,
W1H 5BD (7724 7288,
www.vinoteca.co.uk).
Wine Bars
Windsor Castle p77
27-29 Crawford Place, W1H
4LJ (7723 4371). Classic Pubs
Wonder Bar p55
400 Oxford Street, W1A 1AB
(7318 2476). Wine Bars

Mayfair

Audley p61
41-43 Mount Street, W1K 2RX
(7499 1843). Classic Pubs
Claridge's Bar p42
49 Brook Street, W1K 4HR
(7629 8860). Hotel Bars
Coburg Bar p42
Carlos Place, W1K 2AL
(7499 7070). Hotel Bars
Connaught Bar p43
Carlos Place, W1K 2AL
(7499 7070). Hotel Bars
Galvin at Windows p43
28th floor, 22 Park Lane,
W1K 1BE (7208 4021).
Hotel Bars
Guinea p70
30 Bruton Place, W1J 6NL
(7409 1728). Classic Pubs
Mahiki p27
1 Dover Street,
W1S 4LD (7493 9529).
Cocktails & Spirits
Only Running Footman p133
5 Charles Street,
W1J 5DF (7499 2988).
Gastropubs & Brasseries
Polo Bar p45
New Bond Street, W1S 2YF
(7629 7755). Hotel Bars
Punchbowl p74
41 Farm Street, W1J 5RP
(7493 6841). Classic Pubs
Trader Vic's p46
22 Park Lane, W1K 4BE
(7208 4113). Hotel Bars

Mile End

Palm Tree p85
127 Grove Road, E3 5BH
(8980 2918). Classic Pubs

Muswell Hill

Clissold Arms p139
105 Fortis Green,
N2 9HR (8444 4224).
Gastropubs & Brasseries

New Cross

Amersham Arms p217
388 New Cross Road,
SE14 6TY (8469 1499). Clubs
& Music Venues
Montague Arms p217
289 Queens Road,
SE15 2PA (7639 4923).
Clubs & Music Venues
New Cross Inn p218
323 New Cross Road,
SE14 6AS (8692 1866).
Clubs & Music Venues

Notting Hill

Castle p97
225 Portobello Road, W11 1LU
(7221 7103). Classic Pubs
Earl of Lonsdale p99
277-281 Westbourne Grove,
W11 2QA (7727 6335).
Classic Pubs
First Floor p196
186 Portobello Road, W11 1LA
(7243 0072). Good Mixers
Hillgate p154
24 Hillgate Street,
W8 7SR (7727 8566).
Gastropubs & Brasseries
Mall Tavern p154
71-73 Palace Gardens Terrace,
W8 4RU (7229 3374).
Gastropubs & Brasseries
Notting Hill Arts Club p220
21 Notting Hill Gate,
W11 3JQ (7460 4459).
Clubs & Music Venues
Portobello Star p38
171 Portobello Road, W11 2DY
(7229 8016). Cocktails & Spirits
Ruby & Sequoia p197
6-8 All Saints Road, W11 1HH
(7243 6363). Good Mixers
Trailer Happiness p198
177 Portobello Road, W11
2DY (7065 6821). Good Mixers

Parsons Green

Amuse Bouche p56
51 Parsons Green Lane, SW6
4JA (7371 8517). Wine Bars
White Horse p124
1-3 Parsons Green, SW6 4UL
(7736 2115). Beer Specialists

Peckham

**Frank's Café &
Campari Bar** p165
10th floor, Peckham multi-
storey carpark, 95A Rye Lane,
SE15 4ST (07580 545 837).
Rooms with a View
Gowlett p191
62 Gowlett Road, SE15 4HY
(7635 7048). Good Mixers
Victoria Inn p121
72-79 Choumert Road,
SE15 4AR (7639 5052).
Beer Specialists

Piccadilly

1707 p48
181 Piccadilly, W1J 9FA
(7734 8040). Wine Bars
5th View p160
5th floor, 203-206 Piccadilly,
W1J 9HA (7851 2468).
Rooms with a View
Brumus Bar p42
1 Suffolk Place, SW1Y 4BP
(7470 4000). Hotel Bars
Rivoli at the Ritz p46
150 Piccadilly, W1J 9BR
(7493 8181). Hotel Bars

Pimlico

Cask p109
6 Charlwood Street, SW1V 6EE
(7630 7225). Beer Specialists

Primrose Hill

Queens p142
49 Regent's Park Road,
NW1 8XD (7586 0408).
Gastropubs & Brasseries

Putney

Bricklayer's Arms p124
32 Waterman Street,
SW15 1DD (8789 0222).
Beer Specialists
Citizen Smith p124
160 Putney High Street,
SW15 1RS (8780 2235).
Beer Specialists
Half Moon p220
93 Lower Richmond Road,
SW15 1EU (8780 9383).
Clubs & Music Venues
Normanby p195
231 Putney Bridge Road,
SW15 2PU (8874 155).
Good Mixers
Putney Station p57
94-98 Upper Richmond Road,
SW15 2SP (8780 0242).
Wine Bars

Richmond, Surrey

Roebuck p106
130 Richmond Hill, TW10 6RN
(8948 2329). Classic Pubs
White Cross p170
Water Lane, TW9 1TH (8940
6844). Rooms with a View

St James's

Dukes Bar p43
35 St James's Place, SW1A
1NY (7491 4840). Hotel Bars
Golden Lion p70
25 King Street, SW1Y 6QY
(7925 0007). Classic Pubs
Rod Lion p75
23 Crown Passage, SW1Y 6PP
(7930 4141). Classic Pubs

St John's Wood

Clifton p105
96 Clifton Hill, NW8 0JT
(7372 3427). Classic Pubs

Shepherd's Bush

Albertine p57
1 Wood Lane, W12 7DP
(8743 9593). Wine Bars
Anglesea Arms p152
35 Wingate Road, W6 0UR
(8749 1291). Gastropubs
& Brasseries
Goldhawk p100
122-124 Goldhawk Road, W12
8HH (8576 6921). Classic Pubs
Princess Victoria p155
217 Uxbridge Road,
W12 9DH (8749 5886).
Gastropubs & Brasseries

Shoreditch

333 p212
333 Old Street, EC1V 9LE
(7739 5949). Clubs &
Music Venues
Bar Kick p185
127 Shoreditch High Street, E1
6JE (7739 8700). Good Mixers

Book Club p186
100-106 Leonard Street, EC2A
4RH (7684 8618). Good Mixers
Boundary Rooftop p163
2-4 Boundary Street,
E2 7DD (7729 1051).
Rooms with a View
Callooh Callay p34
65 Rivington Street, EC2A 3AY
(7739 4781). Cocktails & Spirits
CAMP p186
70-74 City Road, EC1Y 2BJ
(7253 2443). Good Mixers
Cargo p213
83 Rivington Street,
EC2A 3AY (7739 3440). Clubs
& Music Venues
Catch p214
22 Kingsland Road,
E2 8DA (7729 6097). Clubs &
Music Venues
**Charlie Wright's
International Bar** p214
45 Pitfield Street,
N1 6DA (7490 8345).
Clubs & Music Venues
Dreambagsjaguarshoes p187
34-36 Kingsland Road, E2 8DA
(7729 5830). Good Mixers
East Village p215
89 Great Eastern Street,
EC2A 3HX (7739 5173).
Clubs & Music Venues
Electricity Showrooms p187
39A Hoxton Square, N1 6NN
(7739 3939). Good Mixers
Favela Chic p215
91-93 Great Eastern Street,
EC2A 3HZ (7613 4228).
Clubs & Music Venues
Fox p144
28 Paul Street, EC2A 4LB
(7729 5708). Gastropubs
& Brasseries
George & Dragon p188
2 Hackney Road, E2 7NS
(7012 1100). Good Mixers
Horse & Groom p215
28 Curtain Road,
EC2A 3NZ (7503 9421).
Clubs & Music Venues
Hoxton Square Bar p188
2-4 Hoxton Square, N1 6NU
(7613 0709). Good Mixers
Look Mum No Hands! p189
49 Old Street , EC1V 9HX
(7253 1025). Good Mixers
Loungelover p35
1 Whitby Street, E1 6JU (7012
1234). Cocktails & Spirits
Mason & Taylor p116
51-55 Bethnal Green Road,
E1 6LA (7749 9670).
Beer Specialists
Nightjar p35
129 City Road, EC1V 1JB
(7253 4101). Cocktails &
Spirits
Old Blue Last p215
38 Great Eastern Street,
EC2A 3ES (7739 7033).
Clubs & Music Venues
Old Fountain p117
3 Baldwin Street, EC1V 9NU
(7253 2970). Beer Specialists
Owl & Pussycat p189
34 Redchurch Street, E2 7DP
(3487 0088). Good Mixers
Prague p189
6 Kingsland Road, E2 8DA
(7739 9110). Good Mixers
Princess of Shoreditch p146
Paul Street, EC2A 4NE
(7729 9270). Gastropubs
& Brasseries
Queen of Hoxton p216
1 Curtain Road,
EC2A 3JX (7422 0958).
Clubs & Music Venues

Red Lion p190
41 Hoxton Street, N1 6NH
(7729 7920). Good Mixers
Royal Oak p147
73 Columbia Road,
E2 7RG (7729 2220).
Gastropubs & Brasseries
Wenlock Arms p117
26 Wenlock Road, N1 7TA
(7608 3406). Beer Specialists
**Worship Street
Whistling Shop** p35
63 Worship Street,
EC2A 2DU (7247 0015).
Cocktails & Spirits

Soho

Admiral Duncan p200
54 Old Compton Street, W1D
4UB (7437 5300). Gay Bars
**Ain't Nothin' But...
The Blues Bar** p204
20 Kingly Street,
W1B 5PZ (7287 0514).
Clubs & Music Venues
Alphabet p172
61-63 Beak Street, W1F 9SL
(7439 2190). Good Mixers
Argyll Arms p61
18 Argyll Street, W1F 7TP
(7734 6117). Classic Pubs
Barrio Central p173
6 Poland Street, W1F 8PS
(3230 1002). Good Mixers
El Camion p23
25-27 Brewer Street,
W1F 0RR (7734 7711,
www.elcamion.co.uk).
Cocktails & Spirits
Candy Bar p200
4 Carlisle Street, W1D 3BJ
(7287 5041). Gay Bars
Coach & Horses p65
29 Greek Street, W1D 5DH
(7437 5920). Classic Pubs
Crown & Two Chairmen p67
31-32 Dean Street, W1D 3SB
(7487 8192). Classic Pubs
Dog & Duck p65
18 Bateman Street, W1D 3AJ
(7494 0697). Classic Pubs
Edge p200
11 Soho Square, W1D 3QE
(7439 1313). Gay Bars
Endurance p177
90 Berwick Street, W1F 0QB
(7437 2944). Good Mixers
Floridita p24
100 Wardour Street,
W1F 0TN (7314 4000).
Cocktails & Spirits
Freedom Bar p201
66 Wardour Street, W1F 0TA
(7734 0071). Gay Bars
French House p69
49 Dean Street, W1D 5BG
(7437 2799). Classic Pubs
Green Carnation p201
4-5 Greek Street, W1D 4DB
(8123 4267). Gay Bars
Mark's Bar p28
66-70 Brewer Street,
W1F 9UP (7292 3518).
Cocktails & Spirits
Milk & Honey p28
61 Poland Street,
W1F 7NU (7065 6841).
Cocktails & Spirits
Old Coffee House p73
49 Beak Street, W1F 9SF
(7437 2197). Classic Pubs
Phoenix Artist Club p180
1 Phoenix Street, WC2H 8BU
(7836 1077). Good Mixers
QV Bar p28
26-29 Dean Street,
W1D 3LL (7437 9585).
Cocktails & Spirits

Rupert Street p201
50 Rupert Street, W1D 6DR
(7494 3059). Gay Bars
Sun & 13 Cantons p182
21 Great Pulteney Street,
W1F 9NG (7734 0934).
Good Mixers
Toucan p77
19 Carlisle Street, W1D 3BY
(7437 4123). Classic Pubs
Two Floors p182
3 Kingly Street, W1B 5PD
(7439 1007). Good Mixers

South Kensington

190 Queensgate p40
190 Queensgate, SW7 5EX
(7584 6601). Hotel Bars
Admiral Codrington p60
17 Mossop Street, SW3 2LY
(7581 0005). Classic Pubs
Anglesea Arms p61
15 Selwood Terrace, SW7 3QG
(7373 7960). Classic Pubs
Capote y Toros p51
157 Old Brompton Road, SW5
0LJ (7373 0567). Wine Bars
Drayton Arms p109
153 Old Brompton Road,
SW5 0LJ (7835 2301).
Beer Specialists

Spitalfields

Golden Heart p85
110 Commercial Street,
E1 6LZ (7247 2158).
Classic Pubs
Ten Bells p86
84 Commercial Street, E1 6LY
(7366 1721). Classic Pubs

Stockwell

Bar Estrela p192
111-115 South Lambeth
Road, SW8 1UZ (7793 1051).
Good Mixers
Canton Arms p147
177 South Lambeth Road,
SW8 1XP (7582 8710).
Gastropubs & Brasseries
Priory Arms p123
83 Lansdowne Way,
SW8 2PB (7622 1884).
Beer Specialists

Stoke Newington

Auld Shillelagh p83
105 Stoke Newington Church
Street, N16 0UD (7249 5951).
Classic Pubs
Jolly Butchers p115
204 Stoke Newington High
Street, N16 7HU (7241 2185).
Beer Specialists
Londesborough p144
36 Barbauld Road,
N16 0SS (7254 5865).
Gastropubs & Brasseries
Prince p144
59 Kynaston Road,
N16 0EB (7923 4766).
Gastropubs & Brasseries

Strand

Beaufort Bar at the Savoy p40
The Savoy, 100 Strand,
WC2R 0EW (7836 4343,
www.the-savoy.com). Wine Bars
Gordon's p53
47 Villiers Street, WC2N 6NE
(7930 1408). Wine Bars
Retro Bar p201
2 George Court, WC2N 6HH
(7839 8760). Gay Bars

Ship & Shovell p112
1-3 Craven Passage,
WC2N 5PH (7839 1311).
Beer Specialists
Terroirs p54
5 William IV Street, WC2N
4DW (7036 0660). Wine Bars

Stratford

King Edward VII p85
47 Broadway, E15 4BQ
(8534 2313). Classic Pubs

Streatham

Manor Arms p150
13 Mitcham Lane,
SW16 6LQ (3195 6888,
www.manorarms.com).
Gastropubs & Brasseries

Tooting

Antelope p148
76 Mitcham Road,
SW17 9NG (8672 3888).
Gastropubs & Brasseries
Tooting Tram & Social p195
46-48 Mitcham Road, SW17
9NA (8767 0278). Good Mixers

Trafalgar Square

Albannach p20
66 Trafalgar Square,
WC2N 5DS (7930 0066).
Cocktails & Spirits
Harp p110
47 Chandos Place, WC2N 4HS
(7836 0291). Beer Specialists

Tufnell Park

Star p82
47 Chester Road, N19 5DF
(7263 9067). Classic Pubs
Tufnell Park Tavern p183
162 Tufnell Park Road, N7 0EE
(7281 6113). Good Mixers

Twickenham, Middx

Eel Pie p126
9-11 Church Street,
TW1 3NJ (8891 1717). Beer
Specialists
White Swan p170
Riverside, TW1 3DN (8744
2951). Rooms with a View

Vauxhall

Royal Vauxhall Tavern p202
372 Kennington Lane, SE11
5HY (7820 1222). Gay Bars
**Zeitgeist at the Jolly
Gardeners** p123
49-51 Black Prince Road,
SE11 6AB (7840 0426).
Beer Specialists

Victoria

Boisdale p21
13-15 Eccleston Street,
SW1W 9LX (7730 6922).
Cocktails & Spirits
Cask & Glass p63
39-41 Palace Street, SW1E
5HN (7834 7630). Classic Pubs
Ebury Wine Bar p52
139 Ebury Street, SW1W 9QU
(7730 5447). Wine Bars
**Orange Public House
& Hotel** p134
37-39 Pimlico Road,
SW1W 8NE (7881 9844).
Gastropubs & Brasseries

Plumbers Arms p74
14 Lower Belgrave Street,
SW1W 0LN (7730 4067).
Classic Pubs
Thomas Cubitt p137
44 Elizabeth Street,
SW1W 9PA (7730 6060).
Gastropubs & Brasseries

Walthamstow

Nags Head p83
9 Orford Road, E17 9LP
(8520 9709). Classic Pubs
Ye Olde Rose & Crown p85
53 Hoe Street, E17 4SA
(8509 3880). Classic Pubs

Wandsworth

Alma p94
499 Old York Road, SW18 1TF
(8870 2537). Classic Pubs
Cat's Back p94
86-88 Point Pleasant, SW18
1PP (8877 0818). Classic Pubs
Waterfront p167
Baltimore House, Juniper Drive,
SW18 1TS (7228 4297).
Rooms with a View

Wanstead

Nightingale p83
51 Nightingale Lane, E11 2EY
(8530 4540). Classic Pubs

Wapping

Prospect of Whitby p164
57 Wapping Wall,
E1W 3SH (7481 1095).
Rooms with a View
Town of Ramsgate p164
62 Wapping High Street,
E1W 2PN (7481 8000).
Rooms with a View

Waterloo

Anchor & Hope p128
36 The Cut, SE1 8LP
(7928 9898). Gastropubs
& Brasseries
Baltic p21
74 Blackfriars Road,
SE1 8HA (7928 1111).
Cocktails & Spirits
Benugo Bar & Kitchen p173
BFI, South Bank Centre,
Belvedere Road, SE1 8XT
(7401 9000). Good Mixers
Kings Arms p71
25 Roupell Street, SE1 8TB
(7207 0784). Classic Pubs
Oxo Tower Bar p160
Oxo Tower Wharf, Barge House
Street, SE1 9PH (7803 3888).
Rooms with a View
Rose & Crown p76
47 Columbo Street, SE1 8DP
(7928 4285). Classic Pubs
Skylon p161
Royal Festival Hall,
Belvedere Road, South Bank,
SE1 8XX (7654 7800).
Rooms with a View

Westbourne Grove

Cow p153
89 Westbourne Park Road,
W2 5QH (7221 0021).
Gastropubs & Brasseries
Metropolitan p154
60 Great Western Road,
W11 1AB (7229 9254).
Gastropubs & Brasseries

Negozio Classica p58
283 Westbourne Grove,
W11 2QA (7034 0005).
Wine Bars
Prince Bonaparte p102
80 Chepstow Road, W2 5BE
(7313 9491). Classic Pubs
Tiroler Hut p198
27 Westbourne Grove, W2 4UA
(7727 3981). Good Mixers

Westbourne Park

Grand Union p169
45 Woodfield Road, W9 2BA
(7286 1886). Rooms with a View

West Kensington

Havelock Tavern p153
57 Masbro Road,
W14 0LS (7603 5374).
Gastropubs & Brasseries

Westminster

Cinnamon Club p22
Old Westminster Library,
30-32 Great Smith Street,
SW1P 3BU (7222 2555).
Cocktails & Spirits
Red Lion p75
48 Parliament Street,
SW1A 2NH (7930 5826).
Classic Pubs
Speaker p76
46 Great Peter Street,
SW1P 2HA (7222 1749).
Classic Pubs

Whitechapel

Carnivale p187
2 White Church Lane, E1 7QR
(8616 0776). Good Mixers

Wimbledon

Earl Spencer p151
260-262 Merton Road,
SW18 5JL (8870 9244).
Gastropubs & Brasseries
Fox & Grapes p151
9 Camp Road,
SW19 4UN (8946 5599).
Gastropubs & Brasseries

Maps

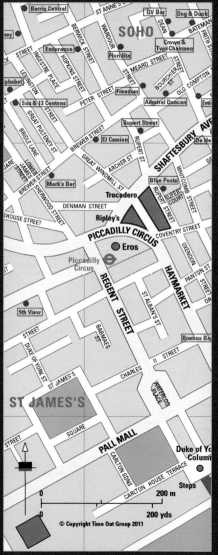

London Overview   236

Marylebone & Mayfair   238

Fitzrovia, Soho, Bloomsbury
  & Covent Garden   240

Holborn, Clerkenwell
  & the City   242

Shoreditch & the City   244

Bethnal Green & Brick Lane   246

Notting Hill   247

Chelsea   248

Victoria, Pimlico &
  Westminster   249

Waterloo & Borough   250

Battersea & Wandsworth   251

Clapham & Brixton   252

New Cross, Deptford &
  Greenwich   253

Camden & Kentish Town   254

Islington   255

London Transport   256

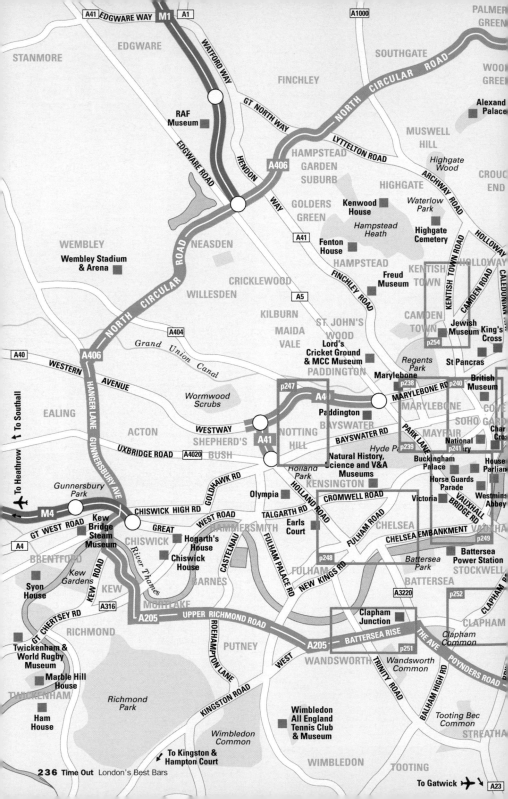

A41 EDGWARE WAY M1 A1

EDGWARE WAY

WATFORD WAY

A1000

PALMER GREEN

STANMORE

EDGWARE

FINCHLEY

SOUTHGATE

WOOD GREEN

GT NORTH WAY

NORTH CIRCULAR ROAD

RAF Museum

HENDON WAY

A406

LYTTELTON ROAD

HAMPSTEAD GARDEN SUBURB

MUSWELL HILL

Alexandra Palace

Highgate Wood

ARCHWAY ROAD

CROUCH END

EDGWARE ROAD

HIGHGATE

GOLDERS GREEN

Kenwood House

Waterlow Park

Highgate Cemetery

HOLLOWAY ROAD

WEMBLEY

NEASDEN

A41

Hampstead Heath

NORTH CIRCULAR ROAD

Wembley Stadium & Arena

CRICKLEWOOD

WILLESDEN

Fenton House

HAMPSTEAD

Freud Museum

KENTISH TOWN

CAMDEN ROAD

HOLLOWAY

CALEDONIAN RD

KILBURN

A5

FINCHLEY ROAD

KENTISH TOWN ROAD

A404

MAIDA VALE

ST. JOHN'S WOOD

CAMDEN TOWN

Grand Union Canal

Lord's Cricket Ground & MCC Museum

Jewish Museum

King's Cross

A40

WESTERN

A406

HANGER LANE

AVENUE

PADDINGTON

p254

St Pancras

Regents Park

Marylebone

To Southall

EALING

Wormwood Scrubs

p247

A40

MARYLEBONE RD

p238

British Museum

p240

To Heathrow

ACTON

WESTWAY

Paddington

BAYSWATER

MARYLEBONE

COVENT GARDEN

GUNNERSBURY AVE

A41

NOTTING HILL

BAYSWATER RD

PARK LANE

MAYFAIR

SOHO

Charing Cross

SHEPHERD'S BUSH

UXBRIDGE ROAD

A4020

Holland Park

Hyde Park

p239

National Gallery

p241

Gunnersbury Park

GOLDHAWK RD

Natural History, Science and V&A Museums

Buckingham Palace

Houses of Parliament

M4

CHISWICK HIGH RD

WEST ROAD

Olympia

HOLLAND ROAD

Horse Guards Parade

GT WEST ROAD

Kew Bridge Steam Museum

GREAT

CROMWELL ROAD

Victoria

VAUXHALL BRIDGE RD

Westminster Abbey

A4

CHISWICK

Hogarth's House

TALGARTH RD

Earls Court

FULHAM ROAD

CHELSEA

VAUXHALL

BRENTFORD

River Thames

Chiswick House

CASTELNAU

FULHAM PALACE RD

CHELSEA EMBANKMENT

p249

Kew Road

KEW

BARNES

FULHAM

Battersea Power Station

Syon House

Kew Gardens

A316

MORTLAKE

NEW KINGS RD

Battersea Park

STOCKWELL

RICHMOND

A205

UPPER RICHMOND ROAD

A3220

BATTERSEA

p252

GT CHERTSEY RD

A205

BATTERSEA RISE

CLAPHAM

Twickenham & World Rugby Museum

ROEHAMPTON LANE

PUTNEY

WEST

WANDSWORTH

p251

Clapham Junction

THE AVE

Clapham Common

POYNDERS ROAD

Marble Hill House

TRINITY ROAD

Wandsworth Common

BALHAM HIGH RD

TWICKENHAM

Richmond Park

KINGSTON ROAD

Ham House

Wimbledon Common

Wimbledon All England Tennis Club & Museum

Tooting Bec Common

STREATHAM

To Kingston & Hampton Court

WIMBLEDON

TOOTING

To Gatwick ✈ A23

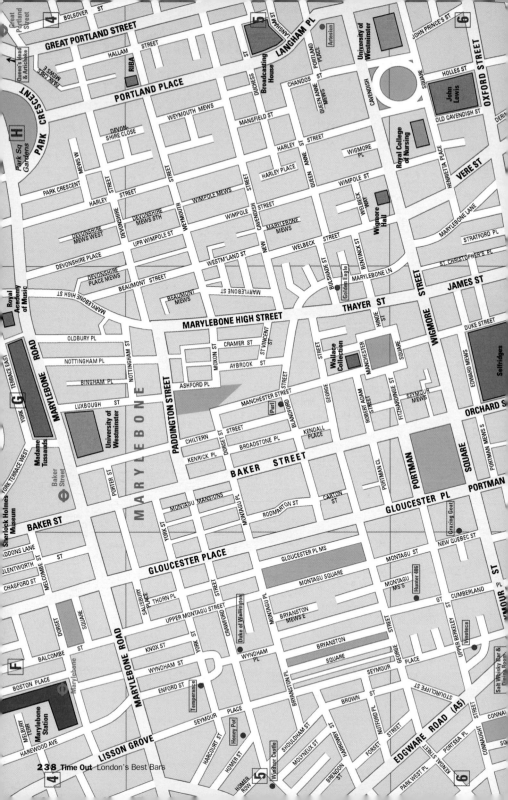

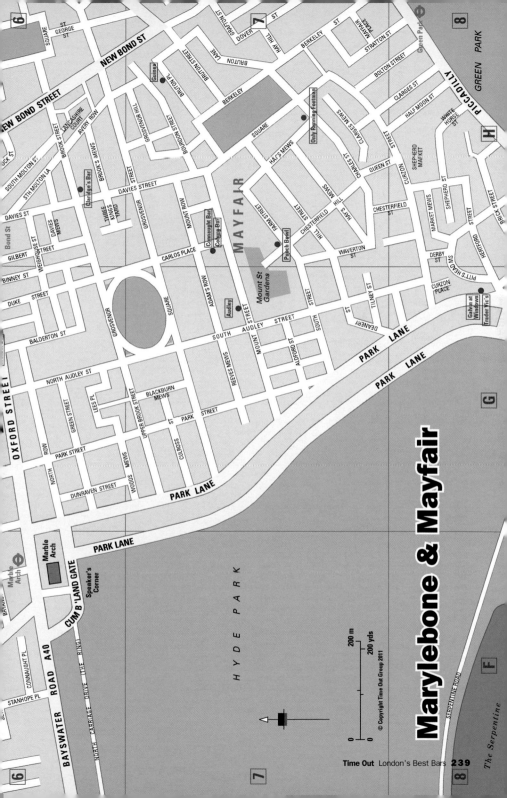

Marylebone & Mayfair

MARBLE ARCH

Marble Arch

OXFORD STREET

NEW BOND STREET
NEW BOND ST

MAYFAIR

GREEN PARK

PICCADILLY

HYDE PARK

PARK LANE

The Serpentine

SERPENTINE ROAD

Speaker's Corner

CUMB'LAND GATE

NORTH CARRIAGE DRIVE (THE RING)

BAYSWATER ROAD A40

CONNAUGHT PL

STANHOPE PL

Mount St Gardens

200 m
200 yds

© Copyright Time Out Group 2011

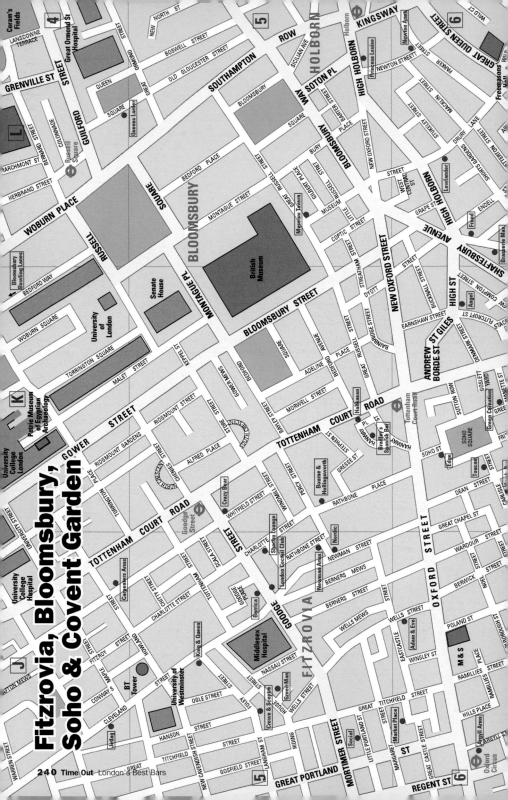

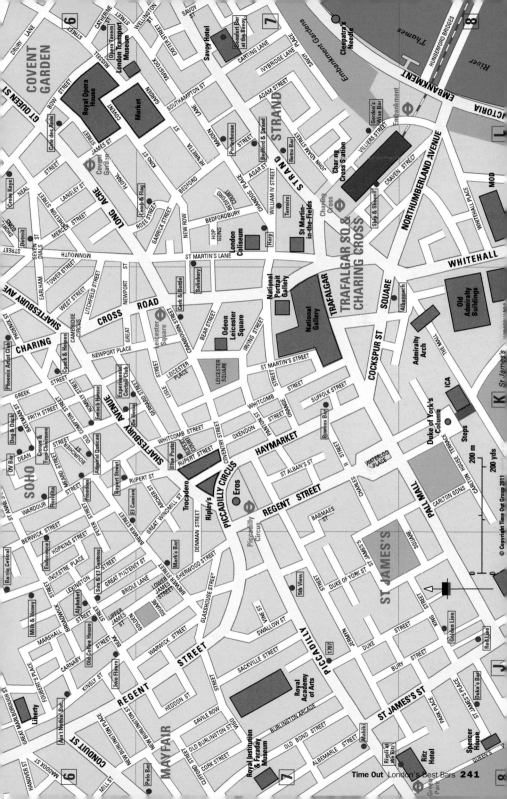

© Copyright Time Out Group 2011

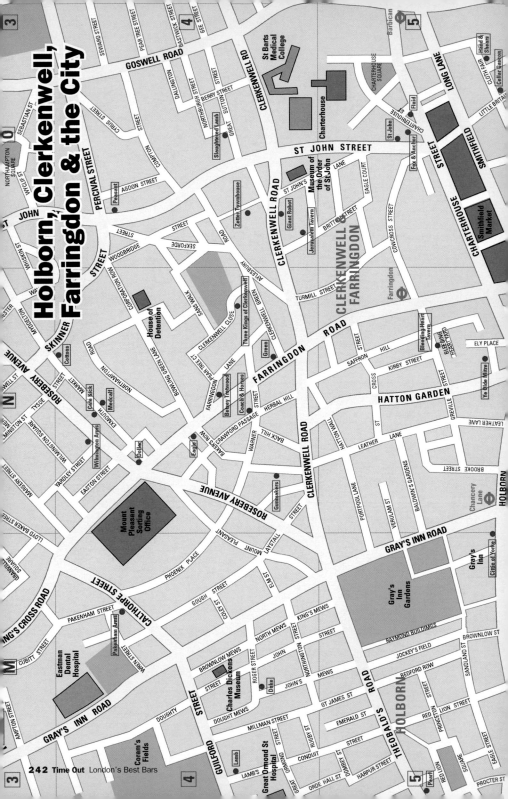

Holborn, Clerkenwell, Farringdon & the City

3 **4** GEE STREET **5** Barbican

SEWARD STREET
PEAR TREE STREET
BASTWICK STREET
GOSWELL ROAD
ST Barts Medical College
CHARTERHOUSE SQUARE
Hand & Shears
CLOTH FAIR
LITTLE BRITAIN
Cellar Gascon

0
SEBASTIAN ST
WYCLIF ST
NORTHAMPTON SQUARE
CYRUS STREET
COMPTON STREET
DALLINGTON STREET
NORTHBURGH STREET
BERRY STREET
GREAT SUTTON STREET
Slaughtered Lamb
Charterhouse
CHARTERHOUSE ST
Fluid
CHARTERHOUSE
SMITHFIELD

JOHN
WHISKIN ST
PERCIVAL STREET
AGDON STREET
Pesanti
CLERKENWELL RD
Zetter Townhouse
St John
Fox & Anchor
Smithfield Market

ST JOHN STREET
ST JOHN'S LANE
Museum of the Order of St John
EAGLE COURT
BRITTON STREET
CHARTERHOUSE

N
ROSEBERY AVENUE
SKINNER STREET
WOODBRIDGE STREET
SEKFORDE STREET
Giant Robot
Jerusalem Tavern
CLERKENWELL ROAD
TURMILL STREET
Farringdon
COWCROSS STREET

Cottons
Café Kick
Medcalf
Wilmington Arms
Dollar
NORTHAMPTON ROAD
BOWLING GREEN LANE
House of Detention
SANS WALK
CLERKENWELL CLOSE
Three Kings of Clerkenwell
Green
CLERKENWELL GREEN
FARRINGDON ROAD
SAFFRON HILL
KIRBY STREET
HATTON GARDEN
ELY PLACE
Ye Olde Mitre

WELL STREET
AMWELL ST
MYDDELTON SQ
EXMOUTH MARKET
YARDLEY STREET
EASTON STREET
PEAR TREE CT
FARRINGDON LANE
Betsey Trotwood
Coach & Horses
HERBAL HILL
Eagle
BAKER'S ROW
CRAWFORD PASSAGE
WARNER STREET
BACK HILL
HATTON WALL
LEATHER STREET
LANE
GREVILLE ST
LEATHER LANE
BROOKE STREET

M
MARGERY STREET
WILMINGTON SQUARE
LLOYD BAKER STREET
MOUNT PLEASANT
Mount Pleasant Sorting Office
ROSEBERY AVENUE
Gunmakers
LACKSTALL
PORTPOOL LANE
VERULAM ST
BALDWIN'S GARDENS
Chancery Lane
HOLBORN

KING'S CROSS ROAD
BAGNIGGE WELLS
GRANVILLE SQUARE
PHOENIX PLACE
GOUGH STREET
COLEY ST
ELMS ST
GRAY'S INN ROAD
Gray's Inn Gardens
RAYMOND BUILDINGS
Gray's Inn
Cittie of Yorke

CUBITT STREET
PAKENHAM STREET
WREN STREET
Pakenham Arms
Eastman Dental Hospital
CALTHORPE STREET
NORTH MEWS
JOHN STREET
KING'S MEWS
NORTHINGTON STREET
MEWS
JOCKEY'S FIELD
SANDLAND ST
BROWNLOW ST

AMPTON STREET
GRAY'S INN ROAD
BROWNLOW MEWS
STREET
DOUGHTY STREET
Charles Dickens Museum
DOUGHT MEWS
ROGER STREET
Duke
JOHN'S
GT JAMES ST
EMERALD ST
THEOBALD'S ROAD
BEDFORD ROW
RED LION STREET
PRINCETON STREET
EAGLE STREET
HOLBORN

3 GUILFORD STREET
Lamb
Great Ormond St Hospital
Coram's Fields
LAMB'S CONDUIT STREET
GREAT ORMOND STREET
MILLMAN STREET
RUGBY ST
DOMBEY ST
ORDE HALL ST
HARPUR STREET
CONDUIT STREET
RED LION SQUARE
PROCTER ST
Pearl
4 **5**

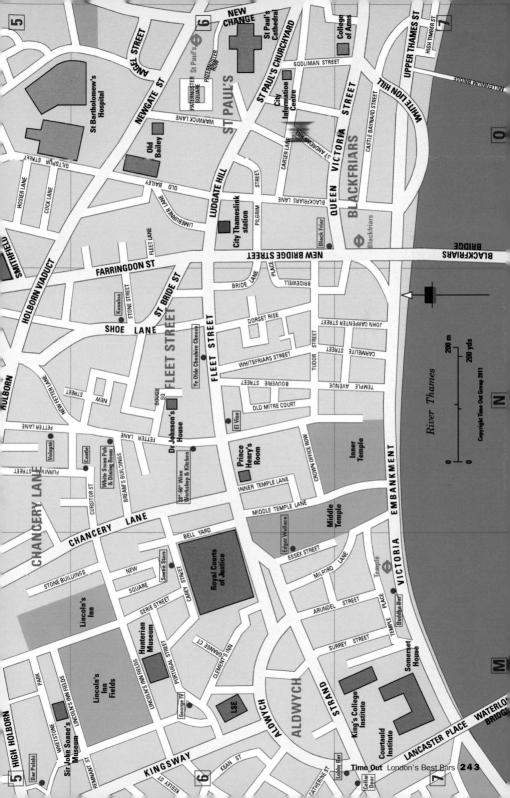

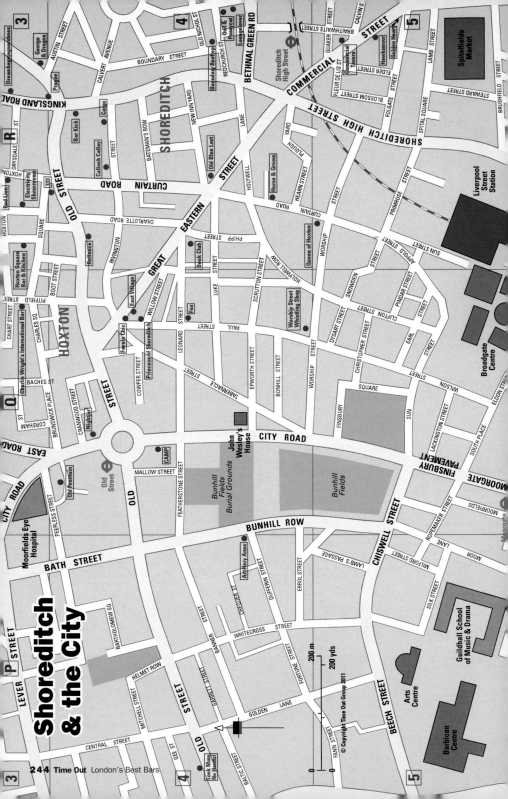

Shoredtich & the City

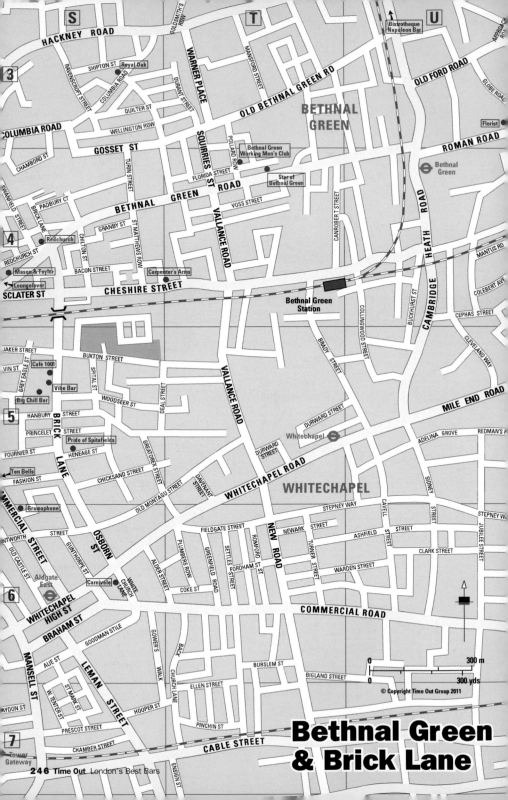

Bethnal Green & Brick Lane

S   **T**   **U**

Bistrotheque
Napoleon Bar

HACKNEY ROAD

SHIPTON ST   Royal Oak

COLUMBIA ROAD

RAVENSCROFT STREET

3

WARNER PLACE

DURANT STREET

QUILTER ST

MANSFORD STREET

OLD BETHNAL GREEN RD

OLD FORD ROAD

GLOBE ROAD

ASHBRIDGE ST

**BETHNAL
GREEN**

Florist

COLUMBIA ROAD

CHAMBORD ST

WELLINGTON ROW

TURIN STREET

GOSSET ST

SQUIRRIES ST

FLORIDA STREET

POLLARD ROW

Bethnal Green
Working Men's Club

ROMAN ROAD

SWANFIELD STREET

PADBURY CT

BETHNAL GREEN ROAD

VALLANCE ROAD

VOSS STREET

Star of
Bethnal Green

CANROBERT STREET

Bethnal
Green

HEATH ROAD

BRICK LANE

GRANBY ST

ST MATTHEW'S ROW

4

Redchurch

REDCHURCH ST

CHILTON ST

BACON STREET

Mason & Taylor

Loungelover

Carpenter's Arms

BUCKHURST ST

CAMBRIDGE

COLEBERT AVE

MANTUS RD

SCLATER ST

CHESHIRE STREET

Bethnal Green
Station

COLLINGWOOD STREET

CEPHAS STREET

CLEVELAND WAY

JAKER STREET

BUXTON STREET

Café 1001

GREY EAGLE ST

VIN ST

SPITAL ST

DEAL STREET

Vibe Bar

WOODSEER ST

VALLANCE ROAD

BRADY STREET

MILE END ROAD

Big Chill Bar

HANBURY STREET

BRICK LANE

PRINCELET STREET

Pride of Spitalfields

HENEAGE ST

DURNARD STREET

DURWARD STREET

Whitechapel

ADELINA GROVE

REDMAN'S

5

FOURNIER ST

GREATOREX STREET

CHICKSAND STREET

OLD MONTAGU STREET

DAVENANT STREET

WHITECHAPEL ROAD

WHITECHAPEL

SIDNEY STREET

STEPNEY WAY

STEPNEY W

Ten Bells

FASHION ST

Gramaphone

COMMERCIAL STREET

STREET

OSBORN ST

GUNTHORPE ST

ALDER STREET

FIELDGATE STREET

PLUMBERS ROW

GREENFIELD ROAD

SETTLES STREET

FORDHAM ST

NEWARK STREET

ROMFORD STREET

NEW ROAD

TURNER STREET

WARDEN STREET

ASHFIELD STREET

CAVELL STREET

STREET

CLARK STREET

JUBILEE STREET

WENTWORTH

OLD CASTLE ST

Carnivale

WHITE CHURCH LANE

COKE ST

BURSLEM ST

COMMERCIAL ROAD

Aldgate
East

6

WHITECHAPEL HIGH ST

BRAHAM ST

GOODMAN STILE

GOWER'S WALK

BACK CHURCH LANE

ELLEN STREET

BIGLAND STREET

300 m

MANSELL ST

AUE ST

W. TENTER ST

ST MARK'S ST

LEMAN STREET

HOOPER ST

PINCHIN ST

300 yds

© Copyright Time Out Group 2011

RAYDON ST

PRESCOT STREET

CHAMBER STREET

CABLE STREET

ENSIGN ST

7

Tower
Gateway

Bethnal Green
& Brick Lane

Notting Hill

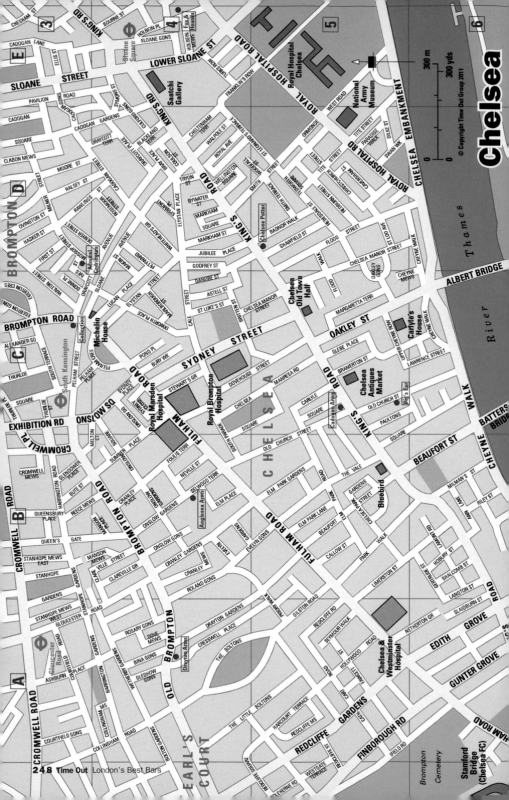

Chelsea

© Copyright Time Out Group 2011

300 m
300 yds

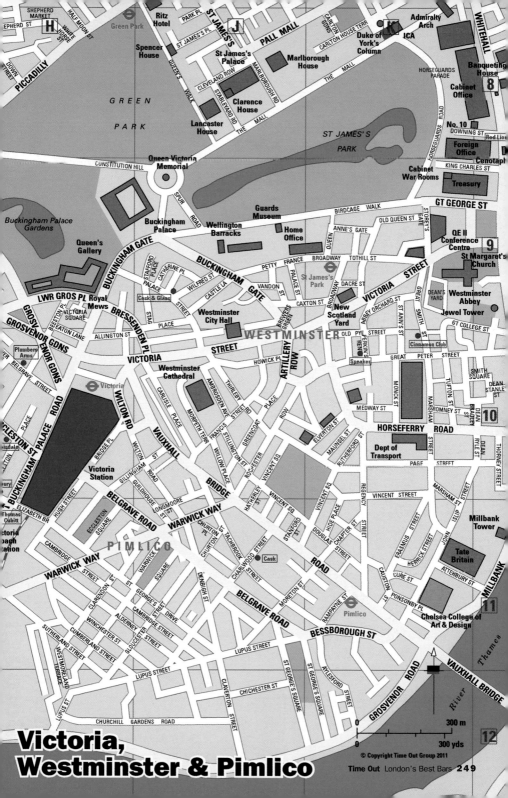

Victoria, Westminster & Pimlico

© Copyright Time Out Group 2011

Waterloo & Borough

River Thames

8
Q
7 Old Billingsgate Market (site of) Custom House
London Bridge City Pier
London Bridge Hospital
Fishmonger's Hall
Hay's Galleria
8 BERMONDSEY STREET
Hide Bar
9
LAMB WALK
MORROCCO STREET
LEATHERMARKET
10
ROTHESAY ST
WALD'S RENT DECIMA STREET
LONG LANE

Winston Churchill's Britain at War Experience
London Bridge Station
London Dungeon
RAILWAY APP
LONDON BRIDGE ST
ST. THOMAS STREET
MAZE POND
Guy's Hospital

DUKE'S HILL
Borough Market
Southwark Tavern
Southwark Cathedral
Rake
Old Operating Theatre
George Inn
Wheatsheaf
Market Porter
Wine Wharf
STONEY ST
CLINK ST
PARK STREET
Clink Exhibition
Vinopolis, City of Wine
Bramah Museum
Rose Theatre
SOUTHWARK STREET
SOUTHWARK BRIDGE ROAD
NEW GLOBE WALK
Shakespeare's Globe
Tate Modern
BANKSIDE
Bankside Pier
Bankside Gallery

WESTON STREET
SNOWSFIELDS
GUY ST
KIPLING ST
PORLOCK ST
CROSBY ROW
NEWCOMEN STREET
St George the Martyr
BOROUGH HIGH STREET
LONG LANE
TABARD ST
NEBRASKA ST
Royal Oak
Gladstone Arms
BOROUGH HIGH STREET
MARSHALSEA RD
Lord Clyde
AYRES ST
REDCROSS WAY
LITTLE DORRIT COURT
Borough
UNION ST
SOUTHWARK ST

GREAT DOVER STREET
HARPER ROAD
BATH TERRACE
TRINITY STREET
CHURCH STREET
SWAN STREET
COLE STREET
GT SUFFOLK ST
STONES END ST
LANT STREET
PILGRIMAGE ST
TABARD STREET
TENNIS ST
MERMAID CT
NEWINGTON CAUSEWAY
TIVERTON ST
ROCKINGHAM
Elephant

London Fire Brigade Museum
Book & Flogger
PEPPER ST
EWER ST
Charles Dickens
LAVINGTON ST
GT SUFFOLK ST
COPPERFIELD ST
LOMAN ST
POCOCK STREET
RISBOR ST
SAWYER ST
STURGE ST
SUFFOLK STREET
GLASS HILL STREET
RUSHWORTH
WEBBER STREET
SILEX ST
LANCASTER ST
LIBRARY ST
SOUTHWARK BRIDGE ROAD
BOROUGH ROAD
South Bank University
London College
KEYWORTH STREET
DOYLE ST
ROTARY ST
LONDON ROAD
GARDEN ROW
ST GEORGE'S ROAD
ST GEORGE'S CIRCUS
GREAT SUFFOLK STREET
SURREY ROW
KING JAMES ST
GREAT GUILDFORD STREET
ZOAR ST
SUMNER STREET
SOUTHWARK STREET
HOLLAND ST
HOPTON ST
BURRELL ST
CHANCEL ST
GAMBIA ST
BEAR LANE
SCORES ST
UNION STREET
Southwark
BLACKFRIARS ROAD
Rose & Crown
COLOMBO
Anchor & Hope
Baltic
MEYMOTT STREET
JOAN ST
HATFIELDS
OXO Tower Wharf
Gabriel's Wharf
BFI Southbank
National Theatre
Bargehouse
Bargo Bar & Kitchen
Skylon
UPPER GROUND
BROADWALL
DUCHY
COIN ST
STAMFORD STREET
PARIS GARDENS
HATFIELDS
RENNIE ST
WATERLOO EAST STATION
GREET ST
WOOTTON STREET
THEED ST
ROUPELL STREET
WHITTLESEY ST
SANDELL ST
King & Arms
THE CUT
Young Vic Theatre
Old Vic Theatre
WATERLOO ROAD
BRAD STREET
CORNWALL RD
BFI IMAX Cinema
EXTON ST
MEPHAM ST
Lambeth North
WATERLOO ROAD
YORK ROAD
Waterloo Station
LEAKE STREET
BAYLIS ROAD
WEBBER STREET
MORLEY STREET
CORAL ST
PEARMAN ST
FRAZIER ST
GERRIDGE ST
GRAY ST
UPFORD ST
VALENTINE PL
CHAPLIN CL
BARONS PL
MITRE RD
LAMBETH
WESTMINSTER BRIDGE ROAD
LAMBETH ROAD
OAKEY LANE
BURDETT ST
LWR MARSH
LOWER MARSH
CENTAUR ST
CARLISLE LANE
FRAZIER ST
UPPER MARSH
MCINNHAM TERRACE
COSSER ST
VIRGIL ST
OAKEY LANE

300 m
300 yds
© Copyright Time Out Group 2011

250 Time Out London's Best Bars

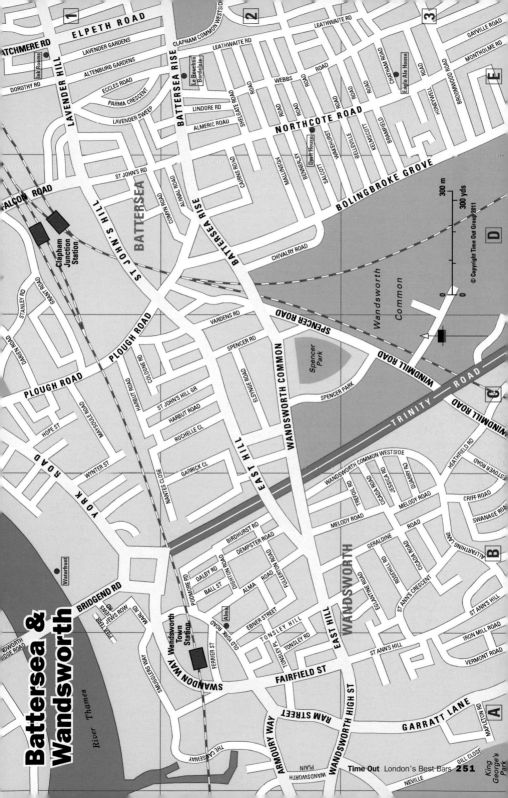

Battersea & Wandsworth

1　**2**　**3**

ELPETH ROAD

TCHMERE RD

Ink Rooms

LAVENDER HILL

Lavender Gardens

Altenburg Gardens

DOROTHY RD

Eccles Road

Parma Crescent

Lavender Sweep

St John's Rd

FALCON ROAD

Clapham Junction Station

ST JOHN'S HILL

BATTERSEA

BATTERSEA RISE

LINDORE RD

ALMERIC ROAD

SHELGATE ROAD

Comyn Road

Aliwal Road

CAIRNS ROAD

Battersea Rise

Le Bouchon Bordelais

LEATHWAITE RD

CLAPHAM COMMON WESTSIDE

WEBBS

ROAD

MALLINSON

BENNERLEY

ROAD

ROAD

ROAD

NORTHCOTE ROAD

Draft House

WAKEHURST

SALCOTT

BELLEVILLE

KELMSCOTT

BRAMFIELD

ROAD

ROAD

WAKEHURST ROAD

LEATHWAITE RD

CHATHAM ROAD

Eagle Ale House

ROAD

HONEYWELL

GAYVILLE ROAD

MONTHOLME RD

BROOMWOOD ROAD

E

BOLINGBROKE GROVE

BATTERSEA RISE

CHIVALRY ROAD

Wandsworth Common

300 m

300 yds

© Copyright Time Out Group 2011

D

STANLEY RD

GRANT ROAD

DARIEN ROAD

PLOUGH ROAD

YORK ROAD

PLOUGH ROAD

HOPE ST

WYNTER ST

MAYSOULE ROAD

NANTES CLOSE

COLOGNE RD

HARBUT ROAD

St John's Hill Gr

HARBUT ROAD

ROCHELLE CL

GARRICK CL

VARDENS RD

SPENCER RD

ELSYNGE ROAD

Spencer Park

WANDSWORTH COMMON

SPENCER ROAD

Spencer Park

WINDMILL ROAD

TRINITY ROAD

WINDMILL ROAD

C

Waterfront

BRIDGEND RD

PER JEWS ROW

WARD RD

TEL

OLD YORK ROAD

SWANDON WAY

SMUGGLERS' WAY

DSWORTH BRIDGE ROAD

THE CAUSEWAY

FERRIER ST

Wandsworth Town Station

PODMORE RD

DALBY RD

BALL ST

BIRDHURST RD

DEMPSTER ROAD

DIGHTON ROAD

ROAD

ALMA

FULLERTON ROAD

Alma

EBNER STREET

TONSLEY PL

TONSLEY HILL

TONSLEY RD

EAST HILL

EAST HILL

FAIRFIELD ST

ARMOURY WAY

RAM STREET

WANDSWORTH PLAIN

WANDSWORTH HIGH ST

GARRATT LANE

WANDSWORTH COMMON WESTSIDE

TREFOIL RD

CICADA ROAD

JESSICA RD

QUARRY RD

MELODY ROAD

ROAD

MELODY ROAD

GERALDINE

EGLANTINE ROAD

ROSENA RD

TILEHURST RD

St ANN'S CRESCENT

St ANN'S HILL

WANDSWORTH

HEATHFIELD RD

ALLFARTHING LANE

CICADA ROAD

St ANN'S HILL

IRON MILL ROAD

VERMONT ROAD

ESTOVER ROAD

CRIFF ROAD

SWANAGE ROAD

B

MAPLETON RD

GILL CLOSE

NEVILLE

King George's Park

River Thames

A

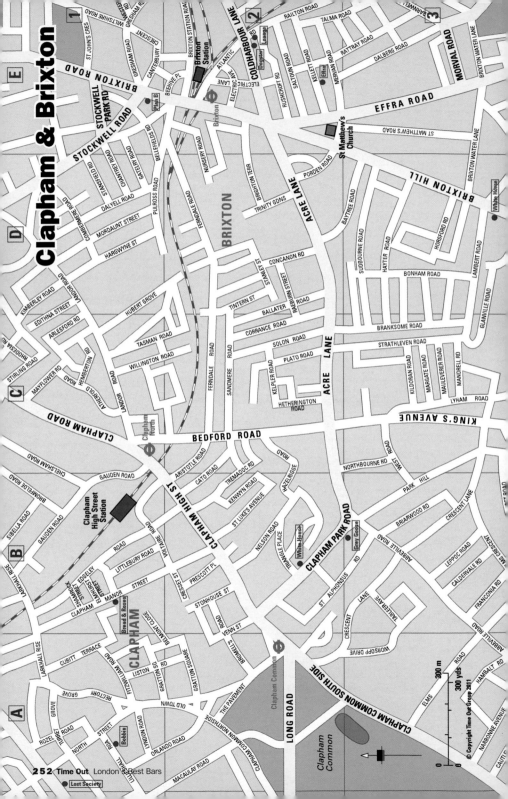

Clapham & Brixton

© Copyright Time Out Group 2011

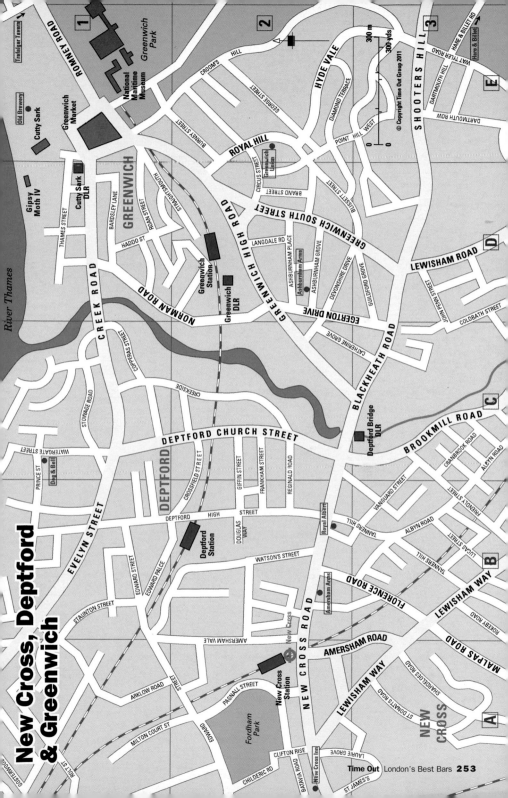

New Cross, Deptford & Greenwich

River Thames

Trafalgar Tavern

Old Brewery

Cutty Sark

Greenwich Market

Gipsy Moth IV

Cutty Sark DLR

ROMNEY ROAD

Greenwich Park

National Maritime Museum

GREENWICH

Thames Street

Bardsley Lane

Roan Street

Haddo St

STRAIGHTSMOUTH

BURNEY STREET

GEORGE STREET

CROOM'S HILL

HYDE VALE

SHOOTERS HILL

Diamond Terrace

POINT HILL WEST

HARE & BILLET RD

WAT TYLER ROAD

Harts Rd

DARTMOUTH HILL

DARTMOUTH ROW

300 m

300 yds

© Copyright Time Out Group 2011

ROYAL HILL

CIRCUS STREET

Greenwich Union

BRAND STREET

BLISSETT STREET

GREENWICH HIGH ROAD

GREENWICH SOUTH STREET

Langdale Rd

Ashburnham Place

Ashburnham Arms

Ashburnham Grove

Devonshire Drive

Guilford Grove

Catherine Grove

EGERTON DRIVE

BLACKHEATH ROAD

LEWISHAM ROAD

John Penn Street

Coldbath Street

Greenwich Station

Greenwich DLR

CREEK ROAD

NORMAN ROAD

COPPERAS STREET

CREEKSIDE

STOWAGE ROAD

WATERGATE STREET

PRINCE ST

Dog & Bell

DEPTFORD CHURCH STREET

DEPTFORD

Crossfield Street

Giffin Street

Frankham Street

Reginald Road

Deptford Bridge DLR

BROOKMILL ROAD

CRANBROOK ROAD

ALBYN ROAD

EVELYN STREET

Edward Street

EDWARD PALCE

DEPTFORD HIGH STREET

Douglas Way

Watson's Street

Deptford Station

Royal Albert

TANNERS HILL

VANGUARD STREET

FRIENDLY STREET

LUCAS STREET

Albyn Road

STAUNTON STREET

AMERSHAM VALE

Amersham Arms

FLORENCE ROAD

TANNERS HILL

LEWISHAM WAY

LEWISHAM WAY

ROKEBY ROAD

MALPAS ROAD

NEW CROSS ROAD

AMERSHAM ROAD

New Cross

New Cross Station

NEW CROSS ROAD

SHARDELOES ROAD

ST DONATT'S ROAD

NEW CROSS

GUSTERWOOD ST

Fordham Park

PAGNALL STREET

ARKLOW ROAD

MILTON COURT ST

EDWARD

CLIFTON RISE

CHILDERIC RD

BATAVIA ROAD

New Cross Inn

LAURIE GROVE

ST JAMES'S

Camden Town
& Kentish Town

© Copyright Time Out Group 2011

200 m

200 yds

G

H

J

24

25

26

1

Junction Tavern

Pineapple

Kentish Town

Kentish Town

Oxford

KENTISH TOWN

CHALK FARM

Chalk Farm

Lock Tavern

Bartly

Proud

Gilgamesh

Stables Market

Lansdowne

Lockside Lounge

CAMDEN TOWN

Camden Road

Camden Town

Queens

PRIMROSE HILL

Dublin Castle

Blues Kitchen

Crown & Goose

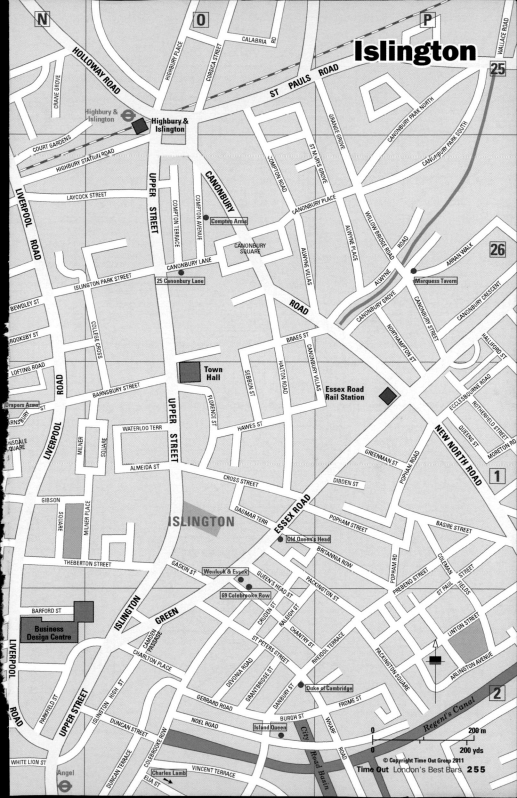

Islington

N O P

25
26
1
2

ST PAULS ROAD

HOLLOWAY ROAD

Highbury & Islington

Highbury & Islington

COURT GARDENS

HIGHBURY STATION ROAD

LAYCOCK STREET

UPPER STREET

CANONBURY

COMPTON AVENUE

COMPTON TERRACE

Compton Arms

CANONBURY LANE

CANONBURY SQUARE

25 Canonbury Lane

ISLINGTON PARK STREET

CRANE GROVE

LIVERPOOL ROAD

HIGHBURY PLACE

CORSICA STREET

CALABRIA RD

JOMPTON ROAD

ST MARY'S GROVE

GRANGE GROVE

CANONBURY PLACE

CANONBURY PARK NORTH

CANONBURY PARK SOUTH

WALLACE ROAD

ALWYNE VILLAS

ALWYNE PLACE

WILLOW BRIDGE ROAD

ALWYNE

ROAD

ARRAN WALK

Marquess Tavern

CANONBURY CRESCENT

BEWDLEY ST

ROOKSBY ST

LOFTING ROAD

LIVERPOOL ROAD

COLLEGE CROSS

BARNSBURY STREET

BARNSBURY

NSDALE SQUARE

Drapers Arms

MILNER

SQUARE

WATERLOO TERR

UPPER STREET

ALMEIDA ST

FLORENCE ST

HAWES ST

SEBBON ST

HATTON ROAD

BRAES ST

CANONBURY VILLAS

CANONBURY GROVE

NORTHAMPTON ST

CANONBURY STREET

HALLIFORD ST

ECCLESBOURNE ROAD

ROTHERFIELD STREET

QUEENS ST

MORETON RD

NEW NORTH ROAD

Town Hall

Essex Road Rail Station

GREENMAN ST

DIBDEN ST

POPHAM ROAD

POPHAM STREET

BASIRE STREET

COLEMAN STREET

QUEENS ST

GIBSON

SQUARE

MILNER PLACE

THEBERTON STREET

ISLINGTON

CROSS STREET

DAGMAR TERR

ESSEX ROAD

Old Queen's Head

BRITANNIA ROW

PACKINGTON ST

POPHAM RD

PREBEND STREET

ST PAUL FIELDS

GASKIN ST

Wenlock & Essex

QUEEN'S HEAD ST

69 Colebrooke Row

ISLINGTON GREEN

CAMDEN PASSAGE

BARFORD ST

Business Design Centre

CHARLTON PLACE

LIVERPOOL ROAD

PARFIELD ST

UPPER STREET

ISLINGTON HIGH ST

DUNCAN STREET

WHITE LION ST

Angel

CRUDEN ST

RALEIGH ST

CHANTRY ST

RHEIDOL TERRACE

ST PETERS STREET

DEVONIA ROAD

GRANTBRIDGE ST

DANBURY ST

Duke of Cambridge

FROME ST

WHARF

PACKINGTON SQUARE

LINTON STREET

ARLINGTON AVENUE

GERRARD ROAD

NOEL ROAD

BURGH ST

Island Queen

City

Road Basin

ROAD

Charles Lamb

VINCENT TERRACE

ELIA ST

COLEBROOKE ROW

DUNCAN TERRACE

Regent's Canal

0   200 m
0   200 yds

© Copyright Time Out Group 2011

London Transport

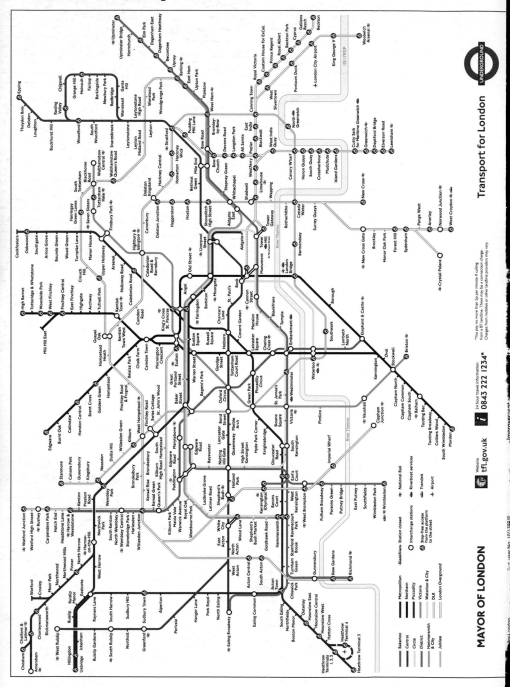